W9-ABM-537

RUFUS CHOATE
THE LAW AND CIVIC VIRTUE

RUFUS CHOATE

THE LAW AND CIVIC VIRTUE

JEAN V. MATTHEWS

Temple University Press   Philadelphia

Temple University Press, Philadelphia 19122
© 1980 by Temple University. All rights reserved
Published 1980
Printed in the United States of America

Library of Congress Cataloging in Publication Data
Matthews, Jean V   1937–
  Rufus Choate, the law and civic virtue.
  Bibliography: p.
  Includes index.
    1. Choate, Rufus, 1799–1859   2. United
States—Politics and government—1815–1861.
3. Legislators—United States—Biography.
4. Lawyers—United States—Biography.   5. United
States. Congress—Bibliography.   I. Title.
E340.C4M37   328.73′092′4 [B]   80–10190
ISBN 0–87722–178–2

Publication of this book has been assisted by a
grant from the Publication Program of the
National Endowment for the Humanities.
Daguerreotype portrait of Rufus Choate by
Southworth and Hawes. Reproduced by permission
of The Metropolitan Museum of Art, Gift of I.N.
Phelps Stokes, Edward S. Hawes, Alice Mary
Hawes, Marion Augusta Hawes, 1937.

CONTENTS

To my husband and my mother

ACKNOWLEDGMENTS

I am indebted to the following libraries for permission to quote from manuscripts and other material in their collections: the American Antiquarian Society, Worcester, Mass.; the Beinecke Rare Book and Manuscript Library, Yale University; the Library of the Boston Athenaeum; the Boston Public Library; the Dartmouth College Library; the Essex Institue, Salem, Mass.; the Houghton Library, Harvard University; the Huntington Library, San Marino, Calif.; Princeton University Library; the University of Vermont Library, Burlington, Vt.; and the Yale University Library.

I wish to thank the staffs of these various libraries, particularly the librarians at the University of Vermont, the Huntington Library, and Yale University who provided me with microfilm and xerox copies. I owe special thanks to Nathan Reingold and the editorial staff of the Joseph Henry papers who allowed me to use the microfilm of documents relating to the Smithsonian Institute which they have assembled.

I owe particular thanks to Professor Donald Fleming of Harvard University for suggesting the topic and for the inspiration and example of his teaching and of his own work in intellectual history. My husband, Fred H. Matthews of York University, has throughout given support, encouragement, and unfailingly intelligent advice.

RUFUS CHOATE
THE LAW AND CIVIC VIRTUE

ONE

FINDING A CAREER

*W*HEN RUFUS CHOATE DIED in 1859, Boston hung its flags at half mast and sounded minute guns in mourning. His death was followed by the appearance of not only the standard New England *Life and Works* but also numerous published recollections and reminiscences by people who had felt the extraordinary impact of his personality. In 1900, when New York University decided to erect a Hall of Fame, Choate only narrowly missed being elected in the legal category and he beat Lemuel Shaw, Henry Wheaton and Roger Taney by a wide margin. As late as 1930, the *Commonwealth History of Massachusetts* noted him as "the Massachusetts lawyer who still attracts more interest than any other, with the exception of Webster." Two years earlier, Claude M. Fuess had brought out a popularly written biography, *Rufus Choate: The Wizard of the Law,* describing him as "a unique and romantic phenomenon" in American history, like a meteor flashing across the sky, "leaving a marvelous afterglow."[1]

Yet Choate has almost disappeared from the consciousness of modern historians. He was only peripherally involved in those areas in which historians tend to be interested. He served the Whig party usefully in both houses of Congress, but took no sustained part in the course of political events. He took the role of abstract thought with great seriousness, and grappled with the problems of loyalty, obligation, and community in the modern state and with the role of culture in the modern world. But he left no formal treatise—his ideas are scattered, as they were communicated, in various speeches and orations. His contemporary reputation rested primarily on transitory sources of fame: he was one of the greatest advocates and orators in ante-bellum America. But Choate's fame was that of the celebrity, the "star"; his excited rhetoric bowled over juries and he won cases. He was not involved to any major extent in the kind of cases that are landmarks in legal development and interest the legal historian. As for oratory, this is a mode of communication which the modern feels unable to take entirely seriously or even to cope with.

Choate flits in and out of discussions of American thought in the ante-bellum period, supplying an arresting phrase to sum up some aspect of Whig thought or the drive towards a national culture, but otherwise not thought worthy of much extended notice. Clinton Rossiter, in his *Conservatism in America,* gives Choate passing mention as one of a list of people who "would get a chapter, or at least a couple of pages, in a definitive, multi-volumed history of American conservatism," though the label of "the archetype of the conservative Whig" is not very revealing. Louis Hartz' assertion that, had the United States been burdened with a feudal past, Choate would have come down to posterity as a "crusading liberal" hero rather than a conservative villain is interesting but unprovable. In any case, it seems to assume there is a solidity in a body of political ideas independent of the circumstances in which they were formed.[2]

The more than "a couple of pages" that follow attempt to elicit from Choate's recorded speeches a fairly consistent philosophy of the relationship between man and the state that, while it has received less serious attention than either Jacksonian democracy or transcendental individualism, represents a widespread set of attitudes and ideas. Choate belonged to the generation who inherited the new republic and busily began transforming it with industry, railroads, the incorporation of vast new territory: the first generation perhaps to realize what a complex fate indeed it was to be an American. He was among the intellectuals who tried to reconcile the forces of the new America with the inheritance of a republican tradition stretching back from the founding fathers, through the English republicans of the seventeenth century, through Machiavelli to Cicero and Aristotle. Choate respected this tradition and managed to infuse it with the modern romantic conservatism of Burke and of Coleridge. In doing so he touched upon what has become one of the major preoccupations of modern political and social thought—the conditions of social cohesion and order.

This is a biography as well as a discussion of ideas. In Choate's case, personality and philosophy are linked in odd ways. On the one hand there is the contrast between the exotic flamboyance of the public persona, the gorgeous and sometimes almost hysterical rhetoric, and the insistence in politics upon order, common sense, compromise, harmony. On a deeper level, Choate seems to have known that he needed this orderly framework to contain a personality for which dissolution was a real possibility. Contemporaries found Choate fascinating but elusive. The historian has few personal records or revelations to provide more insight. As a reviewer of the authorized *Life* noted, "few men of his eminence have ever lived so long and written so few letters."[3] As a result, Choate is usually seen refracted through the eyes of those who knew him. Yet, in spite of the elusiveness of the subject, the attempt to see his ideas as part of his life is a useful corrective to the disembodiedness that is the occupational hazard of intellectual history.

Rufus Choate grew up among the farmers and seamen of Essex County, where the Choate family had maintained a solid, if not brilliant, place since the first Choate, John, had arrived at Winthrop's Ipswich plantation around 1645. John Choate acquired and passed on to his third son, Thomas, three hundred acres of Hog's Island, a high eminence of land in the southeastern section of the old township of Ipswich, separated from the mainland by marshes and in winter sometimes cut off completely. In this isolated and rather desolate spot a self-contained community of Choates grew up, gaining a respectable living as yeoman farmers or putting to sea as ships' masters, but never becoming part of the merchant aristocracy of the seaboard. Here, in the plain two-story farmhouse built by his grandfather, Rufus was born on October 1, 1799, the fourth of six children.[4] To mark the event, the pious household interrupted its daily reading of the Bible ("in at Genesis and out at Revelations every two years") to read, as at the birth of every new child into the family, the first chapter of Genesis: "In the beginning God created the Heavens and the earth and all that in them is."[5]

Choate's mother, Miriam Foster, has been described as "quick in perception, of strong sense and ready wit," and his father, David, was known as a man of superior intellect and judgment. Before settling down on the family farm, he had been a teacher for a while and had then joined Lafayette's infantry during the Revolution, but had seen no action. After the Revolution his family could not afford to send him to college, so he acquired his education on his own—through an addiction to books and, like many young men of his time and place, a long sea voyage that took him to Spain and Cuba. In the process, he accumulated a small library of the standard classics. Thus Rufus grew up in one of those households, peculiar perhaps to New England and Scotland, in which days were spent breaking hard soil and evenings reading Shakespeare and Milton, in which the language of the Bible and the Westminster catechism were integral elements of the daily round.

In this bookish family, Rufus developed an overpowering appetite for the written word. In his own later expression, he threw himself on books like "a famished host on miraculous bread." By the time he was six he had read *Pilgrim's Progress* and devoured the Bible, especially the historical parts, although, bothered by their moral ambiguity, he was constantly demanding of his father if the characters were "good." Six months after his birth the family had moved their winter residence to the mainland, where David Choate built a house in the fishing village of Chebacco that in 1819 became the town of Essex. The village contained a small library of standard works, including Plutarch, Rollin's *Ancient History* and Hutchinson's *History of Massachusetts,* and these too Rufus consumed.[6]

It was an isolated life; except for his younger brother, Washington, the young Choate had few companions. The whole area was dominated by the sea, and no imaginative child could fail to be touched by it. With Choate it remained a lifelong passion: images of the sea and metaphors and illustrations from seafaring continually crop up in his speeches. Yet it was not so much the sea as a force of nature that captivated him, as it was the sea as the bearer of ships, the busy thoroughfare of exotic commerce, the field of glorious battles. In his boyhood he saw British frigates in Ipswich Bay. He attended the funeral in Salem of the two officers killed in the *Chesapeake* and was thrown into ecstasies by the account of Story's funeral oration. His favorite game was to play at sea battles, and he always remained an enthusiast of naval history. Many years later Richard Henry Dana, Jr., found Choate better informed than himself on the details of American naval action in the War of 1812. Choate told him that "he had never got over the effect upon his imagination of the sight of sailors and officers who had seen fight, who had been in action."[7]

The young Choate was lively, charming, and eager to please; he was also a strong boy who took his turn cheerfully at farm chores and was known for being "springy" about his work. His real life, however, was in his imagination, already well stocked with ambitions, examples, and a dazzle of words from his precocious reading; it was clear that he was too brilliant to be a farmer and must somehow be sent to college. His father died when he was nine years old. Finding the money for Rufus's education thus devolved on his older brother, David, who managed to scrape up enough cash for the purpose by teaching at district schools. His formal education until then had been spotty. He studied a few months each winter at the district school or with the local clergyman, but he also got some instruction at home from the area doctor who boarded with his family. First this was Reuben D. Mussey, who went on to become a distinguished professor of surgery at Dartmouth, and then Thomas Sewall, who began the ten-year-old boy on the study of Latin and eventually married his eldest sister, Mary. It was largely due to Sewall that Choate was sent to Dartmouth College rather than to Harvard. The pious and orthodox Sewall feared not only the sensual temptations of Boston, but the intellectual temptations of Unitarian Harvard. Dartmouth was safer as well as cheaper.[8]

After spending seven months cramming at a small, struggling academy in Hampton, New Hampshire, Choate entered Dartmouth in the fall of 1815.[9] The college at Hanover was certainly a small one, with only three professors, two tutors, and one hundred and forty or so undergraduates. Still, it was second only to Harvard in numbers at this point, had libraries with some eight thousand volumes, students from all over New England, and at least one distinguished graduate in Daniel Webster (class of 1801).[10]

The Dartmouth curriculum was the standard one of the New England colleges. The first three years were pretty solidly Latin, Greek and mathematics. In the junior and senior years the student was introduced to the basic shaping influences of the orthodox

New England mind: "Locke on Human Understanding, Edwards on the Will," Dugald Stewart representing Scottish common sense, Paley's *Natural Theology,* and the critical principles of Kames and Alison. Throughout there was emphasis on "Composition and Speaking"; translations were made verbally before the rest of the class; students were required to "declaim before the officers in chapel" every Wednesday, and, in senior year, participate "in a forensic disputation" before the whole college.

As an education, the Dartmouth curriculum was undoubtedly narrow and rigid, and some students found that it gave them very little. Still, with its emphasis on language and a command of the spoken word, it provided a good training for the three professions that claimed the overwhelming majority of graduates: the law, the ministry and teaching.[11] Moreover, to bright students with retentive memories, the regular curriculum left a good deal of time for intellectual exploration in wider fields.

In middle age, Choate looked back on his college days as "exquisitely happy . . . a brief, sweet dream." His letters home during his first year, however, reveal him as less enchanted than bored, homesick and hard up: "Suffice it to say that life here is the same dull round, from day to day the prayer bell rings at night and it rings in the morning . . . no variety nor no unfortunate disturbance to destroy the sluggish uniformity of the day. . . . Send some money."[12]

Variety and disturbance were soon provided, however, in the turmoil of the *Dartmouth College* case, which, though distracting and inconvenient, offered a dash of excitement and the stimulus of participating in great events to offset the tedium of small-town life and a narrow curriculum. Just before Choate's arrival the trustees of the college had dismissed the venerable and autocratic John Wheelock, the founder's son, and had installed in his place as president a young, more pliant, Congregational clergyman, Francis Brown. Wheelock, who felt he had an inherited property right in his position, turned for aid to the state of New Hampshire. The internal squabble broadened into a conflict between the Federalist, Congregationalist trustees of the college, and the Democratic legislature and the liberal and rationalist governor, William Plumer. By December 1816, the legislature had passed an act impounding the buildings and income of the college and creating in its stead a university under state control. Just before the opening of the spring term of 1817, the new university authorities seized the college buildings, but the faculty and trustees refused to submit and sued for the return of the college seal and charter. The result was two rival institutions, one in possession of the buildings and the other of most of the students. "The partisans of Plumer," Choate wrote home to his brother,

> before the commencement of the term, took possession of the College buildings and library and "opened the campaign" I believe on Monday by uniting in prayer, literally with but a single student in the chapel! President Brown and friends immediately engaged a large and convenient hall as a chapel, & entered it the same morning with every scholar in the town, but the one above-mentioned.[13]

The new "university" had taken over the college library, but the college possessed two literary-social fraternities, both of which maintained libraries as large and in some ways more up to date than the official one. When the state supreme court gave its decision in favor of the university in November 1817, its officers determined to take over these libraries too and sent out a raiding party of two professors and five students to take possession. Choate had been made librarian of one of the societies and had already taken the precaution of removing a good many of the books to his own quarters. Now, with other members of the fraternities, he rallied to the defense of the libraries and a minor riot ensued, leaving a door broken, but no heads. Choate and eight others were arrested, but the case was dismissed when brought to trial. The libraries remained in college hands and public opinion on the whole seems to have sided with the students.[14] "You may easily suppose," Choate told his family,

> that it is impossible to sit down coolly and composedly to books, when you are alarmed every minute by a report, "that the library is in danger" or "that a mob is about collecting" . . . even when such reports are entitled to no credit whatever it takes some time to hear them, and also some more to point out their absurdity so that much time on the whole is absolutely wasted.[15]

By his sophomore year Choate had become very happy at Dartmouth, for he had found that he could excel; in addition, he had found a group of talented friends as genuinely drawn to the intellectual life as he was. James Marsh, the future transcendentalist philosopher and president of the University of Vermont, was a junior when Choate arrived; he remained at Dartmouth until 1820 as a tutor. Marsh's cousin, the polymath and pioneer ecologist, George Perkins Marsh, arrived a year later, and George Bush, one of the earliest American disciples of Swedenborg, was a classmate. These scholarly young men gravitated towards one another and formed an intellectual clique, studying the classics beyond the requirements of the curriculum, clubbing their resources to buy books beyond the resources of the library and meeting regularly for the discussion of papers.[16] They taught themselves modern languages and were eagerly alive to the new currents of thought from abroad that offered deeper emotions as well as new ideas. Besides Wordsworth, Scott, and Byron, Choate read Madame de Staël who, he later declared, "helped to shape my mind." James Marsh had already become interested in Coleridge, and the new criticism of the Schlegels that appeared in the United States in 1817 and 1818 also formed part of the extracurricular reading and discussion of this serious and intellectually adventurous group.[17]

Choate later recalled them as a "magic circle," fired with an "intense first love of a new and fascinating department of literature . . . where 'none durst walk but us.' "[18] The message that each nation and epoch has its own unique soul and mind that should reveal itself in a characteristic literature was inspiring to a generation newly aware that independence must mean more than political separation from the old world, that while their fathers had achieved political independence, it was up to them to shape a distinctive culture. "Our learned men are the hope and strength of the nation," declared Choate in a college oration. "They stamp the epochs of national life with their own greatness."[19]

His college contemporaries certainly expected *him* to do so. Even with the Marshes as rivals, by the end of his sophomore year Choate seems to have been universally acknowledged as the most brilliant student in the college. He worked hard, read with great rapidity, possessed a retentive memory, and was able to seize the essence of any subject. Moreover, he already exhibited the verbal facility and felicity of expression of a great orator. In class recitations and orations, a colleague remembered, his style was "more completely original than that of any other man in the institution." Even George Marsh said of him, "the rest of us . . . could not be named with him. He was altogether in a different plane."[20]

His eminence among his fellows was personal as well as academic. Although in early middle age his appearance became rather bizarre, as a youth he was by all accounts extremely good looking: tall, slender, with a mass of dark curling hair and dark eyes "with a suggestion of sadness." There was about him an air of the exotic and foreign that provoked the common remark that "you would not think he was from New England." A witty conversationalist, unassuming and friendly towards everyone, he possessed as well an undeniable reserve. To a generation taken by storm by Byron, his "rapt nature" inevitably reminded people of the poet, "whose moody, lifted, absorbed state of mind was noticed from the first always." The intense personal scrutiny inevitable in a small enclosed society, the opportunities for personal display provided by the practice of public recitation and declamation, the preoccupation with "genius," the disposition to see in every freshman of promise the "great man" who would be the presiding genius of their generation, and the longing of young men like James Marsh to escape the "constrained, cautious and freezing reserve" of New England, all created a milieu ready to be captivated by a beautiful, exotic and eloquent youth. His juniors worshipped him, one recalled, and a classmate some forty years later could remember the effect of hearing Choate recite:

> Choate got up, and in those clear musical tones put Livy's Latin into such exquisitely fit and sweet English, as I had not dreamed of, and in comparison with which all the other construing of that morning seemed the roughest of unlicked rabble. I was on one side of the room and he on the other, and I remember as if but yesterday, his fresh, personal beauty, and all the graceful charm of modest, deferential look and tone that accompanied the honeyed words.[21]

In spite of the modest look, Choate was entirely aware of his own superiority. "I am pursueing branches which the class know nothing about," he wrote to his brother,

and with a relish and perserverance (rather *modest* to be
sure) that I am quite certain not one of them possesses.
. . . You may ask what has occurred which makes me talk
and feel thus self complacently? I can only answer, it
arises from comparing my own acquisitions and abilities
to acquire, with those of others whom I know.[22]

He was intensely ambitious; it was important to him to be acknowledged first in the class, as later it would be important that
his son also be first. A fellow student recalled that Choate was very
vexed when, after he had left Dartmouth, the practice of declaring
rank in scholarship was abolished.

He believed in laudable ambition and honorable competition. . . . He held that a great principle of human action
was invaded by neglecting to rank scholarship; that life
is largely made up of struggles for superiority in mental
and physical efforts; that rewards are won by merit, that
the diligent, exact scholar should receive his merited
honors; and that the idle and stupid should not be protected from the exposure of misspent time and opportunity.[23]

But competitive as he was, he gave the impression of being beyond any vulgar rivalry with his fellows—rather, said one contemporary, he seemed to be in competition "with the eminent scholars of history."[24]

Choate entered college without any particular plans for a
profession, but by the end of his sophomore year he was so absorbed in academic life that he was dreaming of making it his
career. "I shall never be fitted for active life," he told David,

and also neither of the professions has any charms.
. . . I shall never be able to submit to the dull and
tiresome routine of a "special pleader's life'; and Medicine has as little in it which interests me. The situation
which I most envy is that of a professor in a College; and
though I dare not hope to enjoy such an one, I am very
certain it is almost the only place which would just suit
my feelings. I have determined (that is if I have money)
to study 3 or 4 years after I leave College if I live, even
if I should after that think seriously of any profession. &

what think you of a plan which has entered my head, of
spending some years at a foreign university?[25]

Yet some time in 1818 he changed his mind completely about the
dull routine of a "special pleader's life" and determined to go into
the law. By early 1819, he was planning to spend a year at the law
school at Cambridge. No doubt the climax to the *Dartmouth College*
case made a great impression on him. Daniel Webster argued the
case for the trustees before the Supreme Court in March 1818 and
made sure that his argument was widely distributed, even among
the students at Hanover.

The glamor of Webster, the strong feeling among conservative New Englanders that this case was vital to the future of
corporate interests, the excitement of students who felt themselves
an embattled little band of scholars defending the halls of learning
against the mob, all conspired to turn the thoughts of an ambitious
youth towards the law as a way of making his mark. Probably his
own growing mastery at Dartmouth persuaded him that he was
indeed fitted for the "active life," and both his classical studies and
the nationalism of the time induced him to conceive of his talents
in a setting of national public life. The example of Daniel Webster
showed how eloquence in one great case could catapult a man into
national prominence.[26] And it was the law as a vehicle to propel
a talented young man to the heights of national life, rather than
as a profession of "special pleading," that attracted him at the
time. "Mr. Choate evinced when in college," recalled a classmate,

a profound passion to become a national man, a great
statesman like Adams and Jefferson, and Webster and
Clay. The country, the government, the great Fathers of
the Republic, the national glory, were words that carried
a charm to his expanding ambitions. I once asked him for
a subject for a Latin oration. 'O,' said he, 'take some
patriotic theme. We are becoming too desperately literary here. We must push our thoughts and sympathies out
into the real, practical world and address ourselves to the
business and bosoms of men. Take our own Republic for
your subject!' . . . I cannot doubt that in College, the
highest ardor of his spirit was for a lofty public and
national life.[27]

Choate once told another classmate that "he was sure there was never a man of talent who was not perfectly aware that he possessed it. 'Every man understands just about what is his own measure. He knows,' said he, 'just where he belongs.' "[28] At this heady opening to his career he was sure that he belonged at the top.

The entire college would seem to have agreed, but in the general chorus of admiration there were a few carping voices. "He seemed to me," wrote one fellow student in a not-for-publication note to his nineteenth-century biographer, "to have a very feeble conscience." All this rather startling remark turned out to mean, however, was that "if his classmates . . . lazy and vicious, wished him to join them in a jovial evening with a wine bottle, I imagine he was not aware of any moving of conscience *whatever* against it. I cannot say that he appeared to do anything because it was *right* or neglect to do anything because it was *wrong.* "[29] Choate did not in fact lead a particularly riotous life in college, but this was essentially because he was abstemious by nature and found excess aesthetically rather than morally displeasing. What bothered many of his friends was that, while apparently orthodox and always respectful of religion, he remained serenely immune to the religious excitement of the period.

Just before Choate entered Dartmouth, the college had been swept by a strong revival in which his friend, James Marsh, had been converted. Roswell Shurtleff, the professor of divinity and the guiding spirit of the revival, had persuaded the saved to resolve "that they would every day talk with some unconverted person respecting the interests of his soul,"—which must have decidedly irritated Choate, who always considered the state of his soul a profoundly private matter.[30] He was under pressure from the home front too. While his parents had never felt themselves able to formally join a church, the younger generation of the family was more easily moved. David, on recovering from a serious illness, wrote that he had decided to "give himself entirely to God" and that their sisters had "both offered themselves to the Church." His brother-in-law Sewall urged the young man to prepare for death and informed him that the family could receive no more joyful news than that "you have become really pious." Sewall, indeed, hoped, in spite of all signs to the contrary, that he would go into the ministry, "an end which would be happy to yourself and glorious to the church."[31] In spite of all this, at a time when a religious crisis was almost a rite of passage for any serious and sensitive young man, Choate remained not only unconverted but unagonized. The former made him a challenge but the latter was hard to forgive.

To his friend George Bush, such an attitude seemed to betoken an ultimate frivolity of mind caused by overweening ambition. When they were both but a few years out of Dartmouth, at the outset of their careers, he wrote to Choate terminating their college friendship, since he had no time for

> a purely literary or even friendly correspondence, unless it is on the grounds of Christian intimacy. . . . The course of your studies, and your acquired habits of thinking have tended directly to generate a liberal and imposing, yet baneful skepticism. . . . If I err not, my friend, there is, deep in the recesses of your spirit, a fearful suspicion or rather assurance that all is not right between your heart and your God—you are conscious of a controversy with the will of heaven. At the same time instead of being thrown into unutterable anguish of soul, as you would be if you knew what was implied in being at variance with the Almighty Jehova . . . there has appeared to be a dark, desperate awaiting of consequences, that has made me shudder. Indeed, I am mistaken if the love of glory has not sometimes wrought within your bosom with a feeling of fate—with an inward . . . conviction that you *must* be great—great in your rise above other men, and if that involved practical hostility against the Lord of the Universe as you fear it does, and he must arm himself for your overthrow, why then, great, great in your fall.[32]

Whatever Choate's personal conflicts, they did not seek a religious expression. People often said of him in later life that he would have been more at home in ancient Athens than in nineteenth-century Massachusetts, and certainly, his attitude towards religion was essentially classical. He revered the household gods of New England, he appreciated the "binding" qualities of organized religion, at times he would meditate with gentle melancholy on the problems of death and immortality, but his temperament was closed to religious fervor. It was an immunity that preserved him from the excesses of evangelical piety and enabled him to enjoy the pleasures of civilized life without repining. But it would also armor him against the great moral movement of his time—the crusade to abolish slavery.

Choate closed his triumphant undergraduate career as valedictorian of his class, in a packed college church, with Daniel Webster, the savior of the college, as the guest of honor. It was a highly dramatic performance. Except for some trouble with his eyes and the bad headaches that were to plague him all his life, his health had been good until his senior year when he developed a serious illness, probably nervous in origin, and was often absent from classes. Dr. Mussey, now established at Dartmouth, took him into his own house to take care of him and the whole college was in suspense as to whether he would actually make the ceremony. He did appear however, pale, gaunt, "with the aspect of one on whom the shadow of the grave had fallen." When he bade goodbye to his classmates with the thought "my hopes are gone with the bloom of my youth," the audience, both town and gown, dissolved in tears.[33]

For the next year Choate remained at Dartmouth as a tutor, recovering his strength, paying off his debt to the college (he owed it $84.14 on graduation), saving funds for a year at Cambridge, and courting Helen Olcott, the sixteen-year-old daughter of Mills Olcott, a trustee of the college, a staunch Federalist, and one of the most prominent entrepreneurs of the region. In the fall of 1820, having reached an understanding with Helen, Choate left to begin his legal studies. His brother-in-law Sewall, now a physician in Washington, had gotten to know Daniel Webster and had written that the great man was interested in Rufus and was willing to take him into his Boston office. Sewall still opposed Choate's Harvard plans. "Were you to go to Cambridge I should have little expectation of your living beyond the end of the first year—to say nothing of the sentiments taught in that institution."[34] But Choate was determined. Probably he was still enough the scholar to want to lay some broad theoretical foundations before taking up the detailed work of a "special pleader's" life.

The year 1820 was a good one for the newly founded Harvard Law School; it attracted twenty-four students, the largest class until the school acquired a new burst of energy under Justice Joseph Story in 1829. Very few of the students stayed the three years necessary to take a Bachelor of Laws degree and Choate remained only a few months. Money was still a problem, particularly in the more fasionable society of Cambridge. "I shall want no money til December," the new law student wrote to his brother, "but then I shall need considerable. My clothes contrast sadly with those of my fellows." The school offered a course of lectures by the university professor, Asahel Stearns, heavily weighted towards the study of real property, and a much more general introduction to the common law and the American constitution by Chief Justice Isaac Parker, the Royall Professor, and practical experience in the form of moot courts. Choate has left no record of the value of the education he received there—probably he drew more intellectual pleasure from the Harvard community and the general college library. "I was accustomed to meet him more frequently than any other person of his standing in the alcoves of the library of the University," recalled Edward Everett, then professor of Greek.[35]

He had lost the opportunity to join Webster's law office, but early in 1821, Choate at last yielded to the pleas of his brother-in-law and went to Washington, where Sewall had secured him a post in the office of William Wirt, the attorney general. Wirt believed that the student who wished to be an "accomplished advocate" must study not only Blackstone, statute law and the law of nations, but also history, *belles lettres* and composition. "Regular days should be set for composition," he told one aspiring lawyer. "You should enflame your emulation by the frequent study of Cicero's *Orator* and of his *Brutus,* above all, and imagine yourself to belong to that splendid galaxy of Roman Orators which he there displays,"[36]—congenial advice to Choate, whose ideas of glory were already cast in a classical mode. Less congenial was Wirt's conception of what constituted eloquence: "the florid and Asiatic style is not the taste of the age. The strong, and even the rugged and abrupt, are far more successful."[37] This was the style of which Webster was a master, but much as he admired Webster, Choate found an exemplar far nearer to his own taste in the flamboyant and excited rhetoric of William Pinkney. He was in court for Pinkney's last case and remembered later that "his diction was splendidly rich, copious, and flowing. Webster followed him, but I could not help thinking he was infinitely dry, barren and jejune."[38]

Wirt was ill during much of Choate's time in Washington and

so there was little personal contact, but the student could continue his legal education merely by attending the Supreme Court, presided over by John Marshall, and his general education by using the Congressional Library, where, Choate wrote to James Marsh, "I sit three days every week . . . and am studying our own ante-revolutionary history, and reading your favorite Gibbon."[39] Choate was not fond of the capital but would probably have remained a full year had it not been for the sudden death in February 1822 of his favorite brother, Washington, then a promising undergraduate at Dartmouth. Shaken and unhappy, he returned to Essex and, after moping at home for a few months, got down to legal studies once more, first in a local Ipswich law office and then under Judge David Cummins in Salem. In September 1823, at the age of twenty-four, he was admitted to practice in the Court of Common Pleas of Essex County, and hung up his shingle in South Danvers, just outside Salem.[40]

The years between leaving Dartmouth and becoming established in practice were not particularly happy ones. Even apart from the blow of his brother's death, he was in that difficult period of life when "promise" must be channelled into some definite direction and thus both tested and limited. From the protected environment of Dartmouth, where his supremacy and popularity had been won, he was cast into new surroundings where it had to be won again. Then too, while he would become devoted to the law, his first experience of detailed, professional studies was a shock after the liberal and free-ranging reading he had become accustomed to at college. He was determined to be first at the Bar, as he had been at Dartmouth, and, realizing that the law would demand most of his time and energy, perhaps saw it at times, like another young law student, Hugh S. Legaré, as a "sort of Ishmael . . . with its hand raised against all sorts of knowledge, that are liberal and refined but happen not to fall immediately within its own dominion."[41]

His decision to become a lawyer meant forsaking other opportunities for fame. With regret and a touch of envy he realized that his companions in that elite college circle would go beyond him in the world of scholarship. "Your letter and my own reflections, since I read it," he wrote to James Marsh, from Washington,

have assured me of what I was suspicious of before,
though I never owned it to myself, and pretended not
to believe it, that I can really walk no longer within
that magic circle where we used to disport ourselves
. . . that ocean of German theology and metaphysics
(not to say criticism),—ah, Marsh, you may swim on
alone in that if you will, and much good may it do you!
I never could swim in it myself at any rate (it was like
being a yard behind a cuttle-fish), and have long since
made up my mind that any smaller fry than a leviathan
stand no sort of chance in its disturbed, muddy, unfath-
omable waters.

But "incomprehensible science" though it was, he had wistfully
to concede that it was one in which Marsh was *"to be remembered."*[42]

As for himself, he wrote two years later from Danvers, he was
without books, "or literary fellowship and excitement" and could
not work up the right state of feeling to write anything.[43] It was
a block that was to continue throughout his life. When James
Marsh, trying to drum up support for what was bound to be a
controversial book, his edition of Coleridge's *Aids to Reflection,*
asked him to write a review, Choate replied that it was not only
pressure of business that prevented him from doing so.

There are obstacles in the way which lie deeper, such as
the difficulty of gathering up the faculties which are now
scattered over the barren technicalities and frivolous
controversies of my profession, and concentrating them
fixedly upon a great moral and philosophical conception,
like this of yours, worthily to write, edit or review such
a book. . . . I could no more raise myself into the mood
for this achievement than I could make a better epic
poem than the Illiad.[44]

Ambitious, proud, yet shy and awkward, conscious of his
superiority, yet unwilling to test it in situations where it might not
be recognized, he avoided contact with people and often managed
to offend men who wished him well. Marsh wrote reproaching
him for not calling on acquaintances when in Boston and said that
he had heard remarks on Choate's selfishness and ambition.
Choate replied, rather irritably, that he knew no one in Boston

except George Ticknor and Webster. "And on T. I have called accordingly. W. cares for nobody, and was thinking of being made Secretary of State, I dare say, at the very time he gave the invitation and by the way, I don't remember on the whole that he ever did give me one." And then he added, rather desperately:

> It was an early and in some considerable degree an incurable misfortune of mine, to be kept out of society, or to be allowed to keep myself out and to neglect every single graceful personal accomplishment necessary to give or hold one an easy and comfortable place in society so long that I am awkward—miserable—and in short never mingle at all among the men and women of sense, elegance and breeding, without having my feelings severely injured and without a secret very serious resolution never to expose myself to such keen mortification as long as I live. So I cannot deny that such a feeling may have sometimes compelled me to shun what would otherwise have been eagerly caught at as affording a fine chance to see something more of the *minded* men of our generation.[45]

In his first months in Danvers, as winter came in, but few clients, he was plunged into despair by what seemed a prosaic and mediocre ending to his golden and splendid youth. Gloomily he wrote to Marsh:

> I don't remember to have ever looked upon the coming in of the first month of winter, with a more prostrating sense of *miserableness,* than presses upon me every moment that I am not hard at study. Cold is itself an intolerable evil, and it comes with such a dreary accompaniment of whistling wind and falling leaf, that "I would not live alway" if these were the terms on which we were to hold out. I really think that the time of life, when the nakedness and desolation of a fast darkening November could be softened and relieved by blending in it fancy, romance, association, and hope, is gone by with me, and I actually tremble to see lifting up from one season of the year after another, from one *character* after another, and from life itself, even a life of study, ambition, and social

intercourse, that fair woven cover, which is spread upon so much blackness, hollowness, and commonplace.[46]

However, South Danvers, though a small village, had the advantage of possessing only one lawyer—Choate; inevitably his practice began to pick up and with it his spirits. By 1825, he felt sufficiently established to marry the patient Helen Olcott. Helen Choate was described by her husband's first biographer as a woman of "uniform self-control, serenity, and repose," qualities which "served sometimes to conceal, except from those who knew her intimately, the quick insight and sound judgment which gave weight and balance to her mind." But, apart from the notice of her marriage, she does not appear again in the biography.[47] She mixed even less than her husband in society and did not accompany him either on his later political tours of duty in Washington or on his travels in Europe. She seems to have given the high-strung Choate a home life which was peaceful and orderly, apparently happy, and certainly devoid of scandal. The placid tenor of their domestic life was punctuated only by the birth and death of children. There were seven in all, four of whom lived to maturity: Helen, born in 1830, who was to survive into the twentieth century and become, like her father, a haunter of the Athenaeum and a Boston "character;" two other daughters, Sarah (1831) and Miriam (1835); and an only son, Rufus (1834), who was to die without heirs in 1866 as a result of illness contracted while serving in the Civil War.[48]

Meanwhile, Choate was becoming a "personage" in Danvers. He joined the local masonic lodge and the militia, made friends with the younger members of the local gentry, particularly Jonathan Shove, a director of the Warren Bank, and became the leading light of the Danvers "Literary Circle," where his criticisms of members' papers "were made with freedom, tempered with such courteous compliments that, while the writers were instructed, none could take offence."[49] His legal business was increasing; in his third year of practice he entered thirty-five cases in the Court of Common Pleas of Essex in the March term of 1827 and was also admitted to the Supreme Court of Essex County.[50]

Moreover, he was becoming known far outside the confines of Danvers. By 1828, it was obviously time to move on and he was encouraged to do so by his former mentor, Judge Cummins.

He was not yet ready for Boston, but Salem offered a wider field of experience and a likely launching pad. The great days of Salem were over: her commerce was being absorbed by Boston and her principal citizens drawn away by the pull of the Hub, but there were still ships from the East Indies on the wharves, and the town still retained that air of consequence bestowed by splendid houses and trading connections with far and exotic quarters of the world.[51] It also maintained a distinguished Bar, including Leverett Saltonstall (1783–1845), and among the younger men, the maverick Robert Rantoul, and Caleb Cushing, whom Choate recognized as "the strongest man I shall meet at the Essex bar." Cushing and Choate quickly became and remained friends; Rantoul was to become both a political opponent and a champion of legal reforms to which Choate was fundamentally opposed, yet such was the overriding professional fraternity of the Bar that, in 1845, all three men could engage in an abortive business venture together.[52]

With his confidence regained after his successes in Danvers, Choate quickly made his mark among this talented company, both as an advocate and as a personality. He still cultivated his Byronic air. A Danvers acquaintance recalled his "profusion of long, curly, jet black hair flowing about his neck, his shirt collar turned over à la Byron," and his habit of continually running "his slender white fingers through his long jetty hair," which, however, "always fell into comely order when his hand was withdrawn."[53] The literary critic, Edwin P. Whipple, as a boy in Salem, was enchanted by the young man who, like himself, "pervaded" the bookstores of the town. Splendid, yet awkward, "he was an Apollo, though as he walked the streets of Salem, he was an Apollo with a *slouch.* ... Yet he was, on the whole, the most beautiful young man I ever saw." With his glancing wit and a demeanor that suggested something "rich and strange," he seemed more like an exotic import from the Indies, than a domestic product.[54]

His persona obviously accounts for much of his impact on the Bar and on the public. The style that would bring him notoriety was already pretty much formed: the excited emotion, the torrent of words, the imaginative flights, the sweat, the capacity to tear "a passion to tatters." It was altogether "a new sort of thunder and lightening."[55] Very often the storm seemed totally out of proportion to the petty case that occasioned it, but, as Whipple observed,

Choate felt a "horror of the commonplace." Finding himself in a situation where inevitably most of his business was extremely commonplace, his only solution was to treat his clients as heroes and the petty crimes and property disputes of Essex County as matters of great moment with romantic overtones. He spoke of "dogs as though they were lions"; the obscure young man and the prostitute in one of his most celebrated later murder trials took on the dignity of Othello and Desdemona; and of the bankruptcy of a dry goods merchant he could say: "so have I heard that the vast possessions of Alexander the conqueror crumbled away in dying dynasties, in the unequal hands of his weak heirs."[56]

His manner hovered dangerously on the edge of the absurd, and not until perhaps the last decade of his career, when his reputation was securely established, did reverent acceptance of the style become automatic. Until then, he was always aware that he must create the taste he was about to feed, and that he must from the beginning destroy, by sheer force of will, any incipient outbreak of laughter. Usually, he managed this by the mere contagion of his imaginative fervor; once he had to resort to "making one of his potent pauses, sweeping the room with his terrible eyes, and exclaiming: 'no one laughs; no one laughs; such is my cause, it carries all.' "[57] And more often than not it did. Members of the Bar who were disposed to ridicule him were borne down by the fact that he won cases. Moreover, however exaggerated his manner, he was obviously not a charlatan.

He was always an extremely conscientious lawyer who thoroughly prepared each case and continued throughout his life to study the law. While juries delighted in his dramatic courtroom performances, judges appreciated his legal knowledge and preparation. Judges did tend to be resistant to the Choate eloquence ("Tisn't so, Mr. Choate," was the frequent gruff remonstrance of Chief Justice Shaw), but they respected the legal knowledge beneath the "flummery." And so complete was his command of the jury, it was said that while he practiced in Salem, no client of his was ever convicted in a criminal case. This was not an entirely enviable reputation to have. "People began to say that he was the scourge of society, that behind his aegis crime could flourish uncontrolled."[58] It was the beginning of that tincture of mistrust mixed with the admiration that would later earn him the slightly dubious sobriquet, "the wizard of the law."

Popular attitudes towards the young Choate were only reflections of the ambivalent and equivocal standing of the legal profession as a whole. Choate's legal career spanned most of the "formative period of American law," the period that witnessed, as Perry Miller has pointed out, the rise of the "legal profession from its chaotic condition of around 1790 to a position of political and intellectual domination." This feat was accomplished in spite of widespread popular suspicion of lawyers as a class and a well-articulated ideological attack on the system of law that they served.[59] With the growth of corporate enterprise and new modes of public transportation, the services of expert and persuasive lawyers were in increasing demand. Moreover, the profession provided not only services but entertainment. In a period when there were few forms of public pleasure, when theaters were rare and, to many, still of dubious propriety, the sheer entertainment value of a good courtroom drama should not be overlooked. The public crowded courthouses to hear a good case, newspapers often devoted considerable space to printing eloquent legal speeches in full, and the great advocates were stars.

At the same time, however, the distrust of lawyers that had been endemic in colonial times was revitalized by the resentments and ideology of Jacksonian democracy. In this view, the lawyer was a Machiavellian figure who got the guilty off on a technicality, duped the honest man for an exorbitant fee, and clouded simple issues of justice by juggling abstruse technicalities. This image arose partly because the law undeniably, and inevitably, was becoming more technically complicated as the economy became more complex and differentiated. But it also seems to have been a response to the public perception that lawyers were fast becoming a numerous, well-integrated, and prosperous class, increasingly restricted in recruitment and possessed of an arcane body of knowledge that vitally affected the interests of the citizen.[60]

Moreover, in Massachusetts, lawyers had been very vigorous and successful both in monopolizing a major portion of the judiciary and in gaining control of entry into the profession. While only the judges of the state supreme court were required by law to be legally trained, by the 1830s more than 40 percent of judges of the county courts, clerks and quasi-judicial officials were lawyers. The county bar associations, supported by the supreme court, reviewed all candidates for entry to the courts and imposed

quite stiff apprenticeship requirements. The discipline of the profession and the cooperation of the courts had enabled the lawyers,
in effect, to nullify a state statute of 1785 that allowed anyone
either to act as his own attorney or to appoint either a lawyer or
a layman to act for him.[61] In these circumstances there were some
grounds for regarding the legal profession as a monopoly that had
converted the law into a game played by lawyers among themselves, shutting out the people and careless of their vital interests.
Alexis de Tocqueville, trying to discuss America in European
terms, saw lawyers as the nearest equivalent to an aristocracy he
could find in the United States, and many plain citizens were not
slow to make the same accusation.[62]

Choate found himself the target of a pointed attack upon the
aristocracy of the Bar when he ran afoul of Frederick Robinson,
a pioneer trade unionist and radical member of the Democratic
party in the Massachusetts legislature.[63] Robinson decided to challenge the de facto monopoly of court pleading by lawyers. Relying
on the statute of 1785, he had himself appointed by a friend as his
attorney to plead a case. Choate, quick to defend the privileges of
the Bar, informed the presiding judge that Robinson was not a
regularly admitted member of the court and demanded to know
by what right he appeared. According to Robinson's account,
Choate waited until the court had been emptied of the public
before demanding Robinson's credentials—since he knew the
people would sympathize with a David challenging "a secret,
powerfully organized fraternity"—and then told Robinson that if
he attempted to practice the law without being regularly admitted
to the Bar, "we'll put you down."[64]

Choate won the immediate battle—Robinson was denied ac-
cess to the court—but in return received a public letter, summing
up the case against the "secret fraternity of the law." The legal
profession, said Robinson, had made itself into "a proud, haughty,
overbearing, fourfold aristocracy," by allying itself with the other
learned professions and with the rich. Educated in colleges, se-
cluded from the world, they learnt when young to look upon
themselves as a "superior order," the future "governors of mankind." Despising the people, they kept self-educated men out of
the profession and obstructed any attempts to rationalize and sim-
plify the law in order to maintain their own monopoly of arcane
knowledge. Robinson was determined to deflate the pretensions

of the profession: "you are still nothing more than the followers of a trade or calling like other men, to get a living, and your trade like other employments, ought to be left open to universal competition."[65]

The idea that the law was just a trade like any other and they mere "tradesmen" was precisely what the leaders of the profession were unwilling to accept. Continually, young lawyers were exhorted to remember "the worth and dignity" of their profession, and not to regard it as "a mere means of subsistence, an affair of petty traffic and barter."[66] There seems to have been a strong sense that the power of the profession depended not so much on converting public opinion as on maintaining a strong morale and an exalted conception of their functions among lawyers themselves. The legal profession met the threat of Jacksonianism by positing itself as at the same time both the tribune of liberty and the guardian of order. Lawyers were "ex officio natural guardians of the law," declared Chancellor James Kent . . . "to stand sentinels over the constitution and liberties of the country."[67]

The lawyers indeed seem to have been making a bid for that role of authoritative guardianship of values and semi-priestly leadership that the clergy were slowly losing and that politicians had too little appearance of disinterestedness to claim seriously. They hoped to become that "speaking aristocracy" held vital in New England—now against an increasingly noisy and threatening democracy.[68] Hence the importance of a college education for the aspiring lawyer, since it provided a corporate culture and a liberal and wide-ranging habit of mind. Moreover, a healthy majority of men with a classical education would maintain the law as a *gentlemanly* profession. Choate certainly always held that a university education was indispensable for the professional. In urging a young acquaintance not to leave college in the junior year he insisted

> no diligence in a profession ever can meet the want of that liberality, breadth, comprehension and elegance of mind, taste and aims, which it is the specific function of university education to impart. One may grow dexterous, sharp, clever; but he will be an *artisan* only—narrow, illiberal, undeveloped, *subordinate.* [69]

The exalted view of the law and the role and character of the lawyer propagated by the great men of the profession in the early years of the century was one that Choate clung to throughout his career. But by the 1830s the profession was finding it increasingly difficult to retain a capacity for self-regulation or to maintain exclusive entrance requirements. Partly as a result of pressure by radicals such as Robinson, partly because of the proliferation of legal work, the requirements for admittance to plead before the courts were relaxed and one by one formal bar associations throughout the country collapsed.[70]

There were, however, "alternative methods for maintaining discipline and esprit de corps," even without institutional restraints.[71] As Tocqueville had pointed out, lawyers "naturally constitute a *body,*" for "the analogy of their studies and the uniformity of their methods connect their minds."[72] In addition, the remarkable growth in the number of professional legal journals after 1830 provided a means of keeping the profession in touch with legal developments and homogenizing legal thinking. The journals, together with the obituaries and funeral orations on great lawyers, served as a means of keeping before the profession the type of professional character that the aspiring lawyer was supposed to emulate.[73]

Increasingly after 1835, however, the self-image of the profession projected in these organs tended to be much more modest. They portrayed the lawyer as a man of often humble origins who achieved success through dogged industry rather than brilliance. He deserved the same respect as any other honest craftsman who performed a useful service. He did not aspire to any particular role of leadership in the state and he was not dangerous. If this practical man had a classical education and had read widely, these were now merely ornaments that should not be allowed to interfere with business, rather than essential to his competence to practice law. Even Choate himself, while always holding that a good lawyer needed to set his knowledge of the law upon a wide cultural base, felt twinges of guilt when he strayed too far from studies that directly related to his profession. Writing to an old college friend in 1833, he asked for a course of general reading that would still

> connect itself in some measure with my necessary employments and reading, and help me on—not towards

general knowledge but towards those more specific, defined, and limited attainments and accomplishments *which ought to bound the aims of a man of business.*

On Choate's death in 1859, the *Monthly Law Reporter* acknowledged his "rich classical culture," but insisted that these "other studies were only episodes, or rather recreations, renewing his professional energies."[74]

The new image of the ideal lawyer necessarily meant a rethinking of the lawyer's role in politics. To Chancellor Kent, for example, the practice of law was "and ought to be, a sure road to personal prosperity, and to political eminence and fame." The circumstances of a lawyer's life that naturally brought him into contact with wealthy and influential people and into the public eye made the step from the law to elected office an easy and fairly common one, and lawyers served in state assemblies and in Congress in large numbers.[75] But there was an increasing tendency within the profession to sever what had seemed a natural connection and insist that the "real" lawyer stick to his cases and not be tempted by the false lure of political power. Many now spoke of the practice of law as being somehow "above" the petty and interested maneuverings of the politician.[76] As he grew into the profession, therefore, Choate found himself caught between two basically opposed notions of his role, between an ideal of the lawyer as tribune and leader of the people and the lawyer as a "man of business," a specialized professional in a world of other specialized professionals. Indeed, as the law grew more technical and politics more professional, it became increasingly difficult to be equally competent in both. Daniel Webster managed to hold onto his reputation as a brilliant lawyer and great statesman largely because he got a great deal of legal aid from friends and colleagues.[77] Instinctively, most of those who followed him knew that they must choose. Choate, in spite of his earlier ambitions to be a "national man," chose to be a great lawyer.

He was still sufficiently of an earlier school, however, for this to mean merely that he would sacrifice the possibility of political preeminence for the demands of his profession, not that he would eschew politics and office altogether. As a prominent figure in South Danvers, he was elected twice to the Massachusetts legislature—in 1826 and 1827. It was not a role that he seems to have taken very seriously, and though he spoke well on occasion, he was too busy building up his practice at the Bar to devote much time to the business of the House. As his colleague, Caleb Cushing, noted disapprovingly in his diary:

> Practice of R. Choate when in the House to attend only occasionally, neglecting the ordinary business of the House and only making an elaborate speech now and then. Quare of this. He could thus acquire the reputation of talents, but no stable influence as a business member of the House.[78]

After moving to Salem, Choate served a year in the state senate but refused to be renominated on the expiration of his term in 1830. That October, however, some of his Danvers friends put up his name for congressman at the county National Republican convention. For the previous eight years the district had been represented by Benjamin W. Crowninshield, a member of the dominant merchant family of Salem, who had been Monroe's secretary of the navy. The Republican Crowninshields had begun their careers as outsiders challenging the political, commercial and social supremacy of the Federalist aristocracy of Salem in the 1790s. By 1830, however, they had come to regard the district almost as a "pocket borough." Though they had no ideological quarrel with Crowninshield, many of the younger businessmen of the district resented his proprietary attitude and his political passivity. Crowninshield gave his person and his vote to Congress but he did not find it necessary to speak. Jacksonianism had as yet made little impact on solidly conservative Essex, but as the tariff became more important and more problematical, it seemed desirable to have a man in Congress who could speak persuasively.[79]

A number of other names were put up besides Choate's, and the convention went to eight ballots before settling on Choate as a compromise candidate. A number of Crowninshield supporters apparently voted for Choate because they did not expect him to stand if nominated. They miscalculated, however. Congress was far more appealing to the young lawyer than the Massachusetts General Court, and he realized quite well that this was an opportunity that would not soon present itself again. As he explained to James Marsh:

> The matter of my election I do suppose rather a foolish one on my part,—but the nomination was so made that

I could not avoid it without wilfully shutting myself out
of Congress for life,—since my declining would undoubtedly have brought forward some other new candidate, who if elected would go ten years at least,—long
before which time, if living, I might have removed from
the District.[80]

In fact, he intended to move to Boston as soon as it was
professionally possible. It would obviously aid in establishing himself there if he could bring a reputation and contacts made in
Washington. This was not lost on the disgruntled friends of Crowninshield, who denounced Choate as an ambitious upstart. "Is he
now a candidate merely to make himself a great man for the
purpose of moving to Boston with a little more *éclat?*" asked a
correspondent to the *Salem Register;* Robert Rantoul, a staunch
campaigner for the "establishment" candidate, announced flatly
that Choate was only passing through Salem while "he oated his
horse on the way to Boston."[81] Crowninshield decided to run as
an independent, but without party backing did not do well. In a
four-cornered fight, Choate won handsomely, leading Crowninshield even in Salem. In Danvers, where his friends, led by banker
Shove, canvassed assiduously for him, he took almost the entire
vote.[82] Choate represented new blood and an opportunity for the
outlying towns to challenge the dominance of the Salem "clique."
By electing him, Essex County was able to respond to the political
excitement of the times without being disturbed by any new or
radical political ideas.

Although, as he told Marsh, *"political life—between us—*is not
part of my plan," Choate was determined to be a conscientious
representative;

> The responsibilities of this new place I appreciate fully;
> —*pro parte virili,* I shall try to meet them. I have a whole
> year yet, you know, before me, before I take my seat,—
> quite short time enough for me to mature and enter on
> a course of study and thought adapted to this sphere of
> duty.[83]

He laid out a course of study for himself, ranging from "Voice,
Manner, Exercitationes diurnae," through current politics, the
problems of Essex South, the history of the United States, to "Am.

and Brit. Eloquence—Writing, Practice," and made a précis of what a good New England representative should know on the tariff, internal improvements and public lands. Thus prepared, he took his seat in Congress in December 1831.[84]

Choate found Washington "on the whole familiar and pleasant," but full of influenza and soon to be invaded by cholera, "an awful scourge of national and personal sins." Choate was rather a hypochondriac, which provided his friends and acquaintances with considerable amusement. "Don't tell Choate," said his congressional colleague, George N. Briggs, on hearing of a cholera case in the city, "it will frighten him to death." In fact, Briggs was equally nervous: "Don't tell Briggs," warned Choate, "he will have an attack before night." Fortunately, Choate boarded with his doctor brother-in-law Sewall, who provided the fledgling congressman with daily reassurance that he was healthy, as well as the privacy of a third-story room, "a long table—perhaps the most desirable of luxuries,—with two windows looking out upon the shores of Virginia, the setting sun, and the grave of Washington."[85] He renewed old acquaintances, among them George Bush, who, probably prompted by James Marsh, sent Choate a copy of a book he was working on and thus revived their correspondence.[86]

The Massachusetts delegation was a distinguished one, with Webster in the Senate, and John Quincy Adams, Edward Everett and Nathan Appleton in the House. It was certainly an ideal opportunity to make valuable friends, but Choate was careful not to put too much emotional stock into his new political career. "I cannot tell yet," he confided to his brother,

> whether I shall like this business or not. Many interesting acquaintances I shall certainly form—and shall study many instructive subjects. But I confess I should rather prefer active and steady and growing employment at the Bar, at home in Essex—or in Massachusetts.[87]

Choate's conservative cast of mind and his close relations with the entrepreneurial class in Essex had naturally made him a member of the dominant National Republican party of New England. He admired Daniel Webster, and he hated Andrew Jackson for bringing politics down from the elevated republican principles of the founding fathers to mere rabble-rousing. The new congressman had all the proper political reflexes: "saw the President at meeting today," he reported to David, "a great—gray—gaunt— vulgar looking man—hair stiff and standing up all over his head —with spectacles. I knew him at once by his pictures—and never wish to see any thing but his pictures as long as I live." He supported the tariff, like Webster, because it was important to his friends and patrons.[88] As the *Salem Register* had said in recommending him for office:

> his views on national policy are in accord with the great majority of people of the district and New England at large. He is a decided friend of the American system, and as decided in his condemnation of the proscriptive acts and vacillating policy of the present Bourbon administration.

He could certainly be relied on to support "correct National measures."[89] But he was more than just a "Massachusetts Man": two things he believed in deeply—a strong federal government and the Union.

For the first few months in Congress he lay low, making no speeches and causing the *Salem Observer* to wonder if their representative was "afflicted with lock-jaw."[90] His maiden speech, on April 9, was on the relatively non-partisan topic of increasing the pension to veterans of the Revolutionary armies, but the major topic of the session was the tariff, and his friends were waiting for him to bring his weight to bear on that.[91] When he spoke on June 15, he offered what had become the standard defense of the protective tariff—that it ensured respectable employment and income to free labor, and, far from being a conspiracy of the rich, was in fact a boon to the working man. He ended by trying to calm the fears—deliberately fanned by the enemies of protection—that a reasonable tariff would push South Carolina into nullification and destroy the Union. The history of every free state, he said, was full of the clash of apparently irreconcilable interests, that were, nonetheless, reconciled.

> Let us agree to see in it [this diversity of pursuits and interests] . . . merely that combination and that opposition of interests, that action and that counteraction which in the natural and the political world, from the reciprocal

struggle of discordant powers, draws out the harmony of the universe.[92]

It was a bracing common-sense call to take conflict as part of the natural course of political life and not to be afraid of necessary action for fear that it would shatter an unstable world—a position that would become increasingly difficult for Choate to maintain as he grew older.

Nature cooperated with art to make the speech dramatic. When he was halfway through, a violent thunderstorm broke over the Capitol and Choate, nervous from the occasion and from the thunder, stood pale and trembling beneath the center skylight, his words punctuated by the thunder and lightning. Both the speech and the speaker attracted attention and Choate wrote gleefully to his Danvers friends:

I addressed the damned rascals on Wednesday with whatever of fervor and strength I could possibly bring out—(To you whose friendship will excuse it) I will say, that Lawrence and Brown sent me a note next morning congratulating me on what they call my "eminently successful effort in making a great impression on the house" & urging me to print in pamphlet & requesting to take two thousand copies. Old *Adams* told Webster and Everett—as they tell me—it was the best speech which he had heard in C. etc.[93]

Though he had made a personal success, the prospects for his party in the coming elections were, as he told David, "gloomy, gloomy." Jackson's tremendous victory in November 1832 plunged the National Republicans into despair, Choate included. "The news from the voting states," he wrote to Edward Everett, "blows over us like a great cold storm. I suppose all is lost, and that the map may be rolled up for twelve years to come. Happy if when it is opened again, no State shall be missing."[94]

When Congress resumed it faced the crisis produced by South Carolina's defiant nullification of the tariffs of 1828 and 1832. Andrew Jackson responded with a dramatic proclamation warning the state that it was flirting with treason. Choate, with Webster, rallied to the support of the president's stand, but in private he was skeptical about how real the victory over the nul-

lifiers was. "The Proclamation is well enough," he wrote to
Shove,

> but between ourselves it *means* nothing—S.C. *revolts* &
> offers to return to duty—if we will *either reduce the Tariff*
> *to a Revenue Standard* or call a convention. . . . Very good
> says the President—his cabinet—and the whole party—
> the South we will *down* with the Tariff if that is all—but
> damn your eyes if you nullify! That is the whole sum &
> substance of all this *glorious stand* of the administration—
> Shame on them. Sometimes I could solemnly renounce
> & abjure all attachment to a Union under such a Govern-
> ment so administered—But that is wrong—I will tell you
> however—that the Constitution as you & I construe &
> would administer it—*cannot be executed.* [95]

As Choate had anticipated, the administration began the new year
with a new conciliatory tariff bill designed to placate the South and
embarrass the North. "It will be put to us of the Manufacturers'
party," he wrote "will you sacrifice the Union to preserve the
woolen mills of New England?" He denounced the bill in the
House as making "nullification a triumphant and recognized part
of our already sufficiently complicated system."[96] In spite of his
cynicism about Jackson, however, he was swept along by the
excitement of a great constitutional battle—it was the kind of issue
that elevated politics above petty party skirmishes into the grand
sphere he had imagined as a college student dreaming of becoming "a national man." "See if the nation does not come out of this
trial with new strength and the renovation of its principles of life,"
he wrote to Leverett Saltonstall in Salem. "I think a higher tone
prevails and a healthier atmosphere surrounds us."[97]

Much as Choate loved New England, the nation as such had
always been the basic reality in his imagination. The defeat of
Calhoun, the champion of nullification and extreme states' rights,
stirred him as nothing else had done in his Washington career.
"The session is now one of thrilling interest," he wrote exultantly
to George Bush. "Calhoun is *drunk* with disappointment,—the
image of an ardent, imaginative, intellectual man, who once
thought it as easy to set the stars of glory in the hair on his brow
as to put his hat on—now ruined, dishonored." He would have
destroyed the Union for his own glory. "Wherefore *pereat.*"

Choate swept aside any notion that the federal government might become too powerful. The real danger was that it would not act decisively enough. "One single mistake now; any yielding, anything short of a dead march up to the whole outermost limit of constitutional power and the federal government is contemptible forever."[98]

Meanwhile, back home, the disgruntled Crowninshield had removed himself from Essex South to Boston, and his former supporters were free to transfer their allegiance to Choate, who was renominated unanimously by the party in April 1833 and returned with a larger majority.[99] In the new session Choate gave only one major speech, on Jackson's removal of Federal deposits from the Bank of the United States, in which he dwelt, on Webster's advice, less on the question of constitutional right, than on the suffering among the people, especially the middle and laboring classes, that the subsequent curtailing of credit had brought on.[100]

Webster had originally chosen to fight Jackson's Bank policy not so much on economic as on constitutional grounds and to rally opposition to the Bank veto on the question of "executive usurpation." By 1834, however, it was clear that although traditional political leaders might be enraged by Jackson's high-handed attitude towards Congress, the average voter was not. Clearly, any effective opposition must descend from the high ground and appeal more directly to popular interests. Even while he listened with appreciation to Congressman McDuffie of South Carolina "scalding hot, . . . waging annihilating war upon the growing enormous Executive power," Choate mused in a note to a Salem friend:

> I think, constituted as this people is, and overwhelmingly popular as the president is, sluggish as our countrymen are to rally on a naked matter of principle, that although the gravest part of the great deliberation is the legal, and constitutional part, yet Mr. Webster judged right in putting himself at the head of the measures and the party of relief. The illegal act, having by the *mercy* of Providence been followed by great general suffering, the people would hardly sustain opposition in exposing and denouncing the *act,* unless they hold out also some measure

of relief. No kind of opposition to Jackson as such, mere opposition, can succeed, unless we can recommend it to them by its fitness and obvious chief intent to relieve them.[101]

The opposition to Jackson, composed, as Choate realized quite well, of "irreconcilable forces," needed not only to popularize its approach but also to forge the same kind of tight, efficient organization as the Democrats. "We have no candidate, or organization, no *roll,*" he lamented to John Davis, the National Republican governor of Massachusetts. "It is guerilla, peasantry war, firing from 500 bushes and stone walls—on the best disciplined troops in the world."[102] Being a younger man, Choate did not have the same hesitancy about party politics as some of the older leaders. He was, without embarrassment, a party loyalist and as such disapproved of Webster's brief flirtation with Jackson during the nullification crisis. "To my *certain* knowledge," he reassured a fellow Webster supporter, "there was never for a moment a thought of a possibility of a union between Mr. Webster and Regency and Anti-Bank—*never for a moment.*"[103] He wrote to Webster, himself, in August 1833, trying to forestall the possibility before it happened. In that letter he defended himself rather abjectly against a rumor that he had spoken disrespectfully of the great man at a party dinner, and at the same time delivered a clear warning that the younger National Republicans in Massachusetts would never go along with a Webster-Jackson alliance and that Webster was deceiving himself if he thought he could edge out Van Buren as heir apparent.

> The specific & immediate object was to keep our own rank; & to see that none of our numbers were carried away by the recent flow of good feeling.—Our Jackson men here are Van Buren men.
> In all I said . . . my sole purpose was to keep up the spirits & organization of the party—I went on the ground throughout that the object of the party in power was to secure the succession to V. B.—and that our business was to hang together & prevent it.[104]

Enthusiastically, he immersed himself in the work of consolidating the miscellaneous opposition to Andrew Jackson in

Massachusetts into the more dynamic and cohesive organization that by the spring of 1834 would begin to call itself the Whig party. With equal enthusiasm, he worked to ensure that the new party would rally behind Daniel Webster as its natural leader. Choate had arrived in Congress already convinced that Webster was the greatest man he would meet there and a comparison with Henry Clay only confirmed his opinion. "Webster rates above Clay for solidity, depth and grasp," he informed his father-in-law, though he added that Clay had the edge when it came to "popular, interesting and effective debate."[105] By the summer of 1833, after Clay's failure to react with what he regarded as sufficient force to the Nullification crisis, Choate was prepared to write him off as "a retired statesman . . . a character in history."[106] While Edward Everett, another Webster man, canvassed the wealthy Whigs of Massachusetts for $1,000 in contributions to keep Webster, the champion of "property, order and law," in the running politically, Choate, together with his old friend Caleb Cushing, recruited the *Boston Atlas,* the newest and liveliest of the Whig papers, into the Webster camp. In return for the promise of financial indemnity if necessary, plus "intellectual aid," the general editor, Richard Haughton, was prepared to edge out the talented gadfly Richard Hildreth and make the *Atlas* into the solid organ of the Webster Whigs.[107]

Meanwhile, however, growth of the antimasonic party was endangering Whig strength in the state. Choate was convinced that "mere Jacksonianism" could never win in Massachusetts, "our judgments, our prejudices, our tastes, our recollections, our intelligence and good sense, are all irreconcilably hostile to that profligate humbuggism and scollianism. But antimasonry might ruin us by addressing our foibles."[108] Webster was anxious that Whig masons should agree to either disband or to open their lodges, thus removing the antimasons' *raison d'etre* and allowing its members to be absorbed by the newborn Whig party. "If they can see Masonry yielding to the age and to opinion," as Choate wrote optimistically to Davis, "they will probably break from political anti-masonry and come to the only great cause which honest politicians should think of for a moment." As a mason himself, he organized a strategy meeting of Whig masons and, along with Cushing, spent part of the summer of 1834 riding through eastern Massachusetts trying to persuade masons to give up the order for the good of the party.[109]

In that same summer he felt confident enough to make the great move to Boston and consequently resigned his congressional seat. He had made enough of a mark in his two-and-a-half years in Congress to have laid the foundation for a substantial political career had he possessed either the temperament or the inclination. John Quincy Adams called his speech on the removal of the deposits "the most eloquent speech of the session" and noted in his diary that Choate was "a young man of great power and promise, whose political career has been short but brilliant." But though he was to remain deeply committed to the Whig party, Choate found life in Congress increasingly distasteful. In particular, his highly sensitive nature found it hard to bear the personal abuse and ridicule which party politics inevitably aroused. He was the butt of jokes in a Salem Jacksonian newspaper and, though he made light of it, it obviously stung. "Ballads are written about me," he wrote to his colleague George Briggs, "I am the cause of wit and laughter. Twice a week all the people, before breakfast, read the *Commercial Advertiser* and laugh wagging their heads." More than ever the law seemed the way to advancement: "let us do our duty," he exhorted Briggs, "but *stick* chiefly to our profession of law."[110]

The next six years were devoted primarily to building up his practice and making his name at the Suffolk Bar. He went into partnership with Benjamin F. Crowninshield, the son of his old rival, and set up offices on the second floor of Number 4 Court Street, at the corner of Washington. The building housed a number of distinguished or soon-to-be-distinguished men in legal and public life. On the floor above were Horace Mann, Edward G. Loring, and Luther S. Cushing. Theophilus Parsons and Theophilus and Peleg Chandler had their offices on the same floor as Choate, as did Charles Sumner and his partner George Hillard. Choate had already met Sumner that spring in Washington and they became friends until Sumner's increasing involvement with the anti-slavery cause came between them. The building became rather a social center for the legal and literary talent of the city. Sumner's first biographer, Edward L. Pierce, recounts that Judge Story and his fellow Harvard Professor of Law, Simon Greenleaf, the journalist Park Benjamin, Cornelius Felton, Professor of Greek at Harvard, and even George Bancroft, frequently dropped in. The building also had the reputation of being one of the centers of Whig policy-making and intrigue. One of Choate's first law students remembered a rumor that "all the Governors and Senators of the commonwealth were made in a back parlor in Beacon street, and up stairs in No. 4 Court Street."[111]

In this atmosphere, Choate could hardly disassociate himself completely from politics, and in the early months of 1835, he was still campaigning hard to make Webster the unanimous Whig candidate for the 1836 presidential election. Circular letters signed by Edward Everett, Abbott Lawrence and other prominent Whigs, including Choate, were sent out all over the nation to sound out Whig feeling about Webster. The efforts of the Webster men in Massachusetts got him nominated by the state legislature on a platform of national integrity: "Let us be for the constitution and the man who can best defend it."[112] Now an organization was needed at the home base to "offer the nomination to other states and to correspond and help disabuse of wrong impressions and make the right ones." Choate, Everett and a fellow lawyer, Charles Lorimer, were chosen by the Whig organization as a "committee of correspondence . . . to write, i.e. to do all."[113] They did their best, but they could not make Webster look like a winning candidate to Whigs in the Middle States and the West, and they could not undo the impression that Webster was the candidate of the rich. Webster carried only Massachusetts in 1836 and his defeat cost him the valuable support of the wealthy industrialist, Abbott Lawrence. Other Whig leaders like Everett and Choate remained loyal, but Massachusetts would never be so unitedly behind Webster again. As for Choate, his own efforts made him what he would remain for the rest of his life, a Webster man.[114]

Webster's defeat confirmed Choate in his contempt for the national political scene, and for the next four years he watched political affairs with the gloom fashionable in Whig circles. "I contemplate our politics with 'alternate laughter and tears, alternate scorn and terror,' " he told James Marsh. "The report of good men from Washington seems to be of a pretty decisive *giving way* of all the principles, usages, establishments, checks, balances, that used to be the Constitution." Politics was not, as he had once imagined, a matter of great men and great speeches, but of day-to-day trading by professionals. The vital ties that should exist be-

tween the people and their "natural leaders," a tie that for Choate
was created largely by eloquence, had been severed. It seemed to
him as though, in electing Van Buren, the American people had
handed over their right of self-government to a mediocre business
corporation, to do as well as it could and make what profit it could,
in return for being left alone.

> We are melted down as in a crucible, into one great and
> roaring democracy, and the Demos consists of some
> *150,000* persons who *act,* and of 10 or 12 millions, who
> are *governed,* while they honestly, but unreflectingly, pur-
> sue their own business. Of these 150,000, 100,000, con-
> sisting of officeholders, officeseekers, trading politicians
> and editors, have for 8 years, wielding the personal pop-
> ularity of a shewy soldier, ruled us with a sway as abso-
> lute as it was shameful and usurping. They have so far
> gained the ear of an industrious and engrossed people as
> to have a majority of votes, which is all they want and
> have made their fortunes at the expense of a virtual
> revolution in our institutions, and a vulgarizing of our
> general sentiments, and a lowering of our whole tone of
> public feeling and opinion.[115]

Not only were national politics discouraging but a new issue
was surfacing, which Choate, like many others, realized the system
would not be able to handle: slavery. "We sail amid ten thousand
shoals and half sunken rocks and crooked passages and beyond
them all is that vast lee-shore, the slavery question, on which we
are at last to go to pieces."[116]

Though one might think that the anti-slavery agitation mush-
rooming in New England in the 1830s would have supplied that
vein of principle in American politics whose absence he lamented
so much, Choate always perceived the slavery question as primarily a threat to the Union. Moreover, the Garrisons, the Phillipses,
"the radical women, whom he loathed" did not fit his conception
of what a "statesman" should be.[117] They played the political
game by different rules and on different principles; if Jacksonianism had transformed the structure of politics, the reformers would
transform what politics was supposed to be *about.* So when his
friend, Congressman Caleb Cushing, defended the right of anti-
slavery petitioners in the District of Columbia to be heard, Choate

commended the speech, but agreed with Cushing's father-in-law, the conservative Judge Wilde, that it was "the duty of Northern members to frown upon all attempts at immediate emancipation" and to appreciate the position of the South, "assailed as they are by the frantic abolitionists and standing as it were on the crater of a volcano."[118]

Nonetheless, in that same year he was engaged in a slavery case in the courts—on the anti-slavery side. In August 1836 Chief Justice Shaw gave one of his most important decisions in the case of a six-year-old slave girl, Med, who had been brought to Boston on a visit by her mistress. The Boston Female Anti-Slavery Society and others sued for her freedom on a writ of habeas corpus. Ellis Gray Loring took the case and engaged Choate as junior counsel. The abolitionists wanted to hire Webster, the anti-slavery writer Lydia M. Child told her brother, but, since he was busy, were happy to settle for Choate, "a man only second to him in abilities, and whose heart is strongly favorable to anti-slavery." In a case that offered considerable opportunity to pull out a great many emotional stops, Choate's argument, at least as reported, was restrained: he argued that comity between sister states of the Union did not require that the institution of slavery be given legal effect in Massachusetts, where it had been abolished. "Comity," declared Choate, "is only policy and courtesy—and is never to be indulged, at the expense of what the State, as a State, by its public law, declared to be justice."[119] The chief justice accepted the argument and declared that since slavery depended on the mere local law of the Southern states and human beings were not "everywhere and by all nations, treated and deemed subjects of property," comity could not apply. To accept it would result in a situation "wholly repugnant to our laws, entirely inconsistent with our policy and our fundamental principles. . . ." The case established "a monumental precedent in law." Under it the anti-slavery forces successfully sued for the freedom of a number of slaves who had been brought into Massachusetts. It was one of the most influential cases that Choate would ever be engaged in, but it was the last time that he would act for the anti-slavery cause.[120]

He had many other cases, however. He doggedly fought his way to the forefront of the Boston Bar as he had in Salem, now against more brilliant rivals and more unpleasant ridicule. A Bar used to the solemn weightiness of Webster or Jeremiah Mason found Choate's romantic wildness "an impertinent departure from the long-established rule and routine." He beat down the ridicule, as before, by winning cases. On one occasion, asked why he did not reply to some particularly offensive taunt, he answered: " 'I shall retort by getting the case' "—and did. His charm and the fascination that he always seemed to have for the young won him friends among his juniors at the Bar, and his personal connections with Webster, Everett, Ticknor and Lawrence gave him a backing that the older members could not forever ignore. By 1842, Charles Sumner could write of him: "His position here is very firm. He is the leader of our bar, with an overwhelming super-fluity of business, with a strong taste for books and learned men, with great amiableness of character, with uncommon eloquence, and untiring industry."[121]

Much of Choate's success at the Bar, and his growing reputation outside it, was due to his powers as an orator. An address he gave in his last year in Salem drew widespread attention and even during his first years in Boston he found the time to give an occasional lecture to young men's associations.

The modern sensibility tends to see an antithesis between speech and action and is more likely to agree with Carlyle that "all deep talent is a talent to *do,* and is intrinsically of a silent nature." The young republic's imaginative identification with the classic tradition of Greece and Rome, however, led America to retain the Greek conception of speech and action as being necessarily con-joined and together creating the world of politics. Oratory was the essential art of democracy: there men should be moved not by force, but only by the persuasive action of one mind and will upon another through the faculty that defined man's humanity—speech.[122]

Edward G. Parker, who entered Choate's law office in the late 1840s, later wrote a book on great speakers in which he called the first half of the nineteenth century the Golden Age of American oratory. Certainly it was an age that provided an extraordinarily large number of occasions for public speaking, not only in political debating and electioneering, but in making the "oration" the focal point of every community celebration, from college com-mencements, inaugurations, commemorations, meetings of soci-eties and fraternal organizations to the Fourth of July. All of these public communal rituals centered upon the spoken word, and careers were made and reputations established by the power to speak.[123]

The public oration was both ritual action and public entertainment, and the audience both participants in the rite and critics of the performance. Public speaking was an art form that generated schools of criticism and huge audiences. Twenty thousand people assembled to hear Webster's Bunker Hill oration in 1825, and a lecture by Choate on English poets could draw an audience of four thousand. These audiences had stamina and critical appreciation; they came prepared to be moved, swept away, to submit to the mastery of a dominating and seductive voice. The normally self-controlled George Ticknor, listening to Webster at Plymouth Rock, felt as though his "temples would burst with the gush of blood. . . . I was beside myself."[124]

Orators honed their skills to produce these kinds of effects. Every college curriculum included rhetorical training, and, in spite of increasing emphasis on mere elocution and delivery, colleges strove to maintain the classical role of rhetoric as almost a liberal education in itself. Ideally, eloquence was the ultimate product of a full mind, an expression of a thorough mastery of the subject matter, tempered by a deep knowledge of human nature and wide experience in human affairs. As the election of 1844 approached, Choate jotted down a memorandum to himself that reveals his conception of oratory as a *total* art. A Whig victory was necessary to secure "the true national policy of the country":

> To induce the people to elect such an administration, you must first teach them to prefer, to desire that policy. To do that it must be explained, contrasted, developed, decorated. To do that it is to be deeply studied . . . in all, through all,—an impulsive presentation of truths—such an one as will move to the giving of votes for particular men, representing particular opinions, is the aim. Every one ought to be and to involve, 1st, an honest study of the topic—and so an advance in political knowledge; 2nd, a diligent effort to move the public mind to *action* by its treatment; and so an exercise in *speech* . . . truth for the staple—good taste the form— *persuasion to act*—for the end.[125]

The great orator needed not only a well-stocked mind but a passionate nature, for the communion between speaker and audience should be a deeply emotional one. "The foundation of eloquence, in the mind of the speaker," Chauncey Goodrich, professor of rhetoric at Yale, told his students, "is deep and absorbing emotion." But this had to be met by the audience's own capacity for feeling. "The capital of the orator is in the bank of the highest sentimentalities and the purest enthusiasms," commented Edward Parker. "If these are not stored away in the hearts of the people, so that whenever he speaks he can draw on them, his drafts will be dishonored, and his speech will not rise above a shopkeeper's oratory." In addition, the really effective orator needed a certain personal force, for he was engaged in a struggle for mastery with his audience. Emerson, who was rather a connoisseur of eloquence, chose "character" as the most necessary quality of the great public speaker and much of Webster's power as an orator stemmed from the fact that his contemporaries were willing to acknowledge him as a "great man." He had that quality of "exceeding life" which made every listener gladly consent "to be nothing in his presence."[126] But if it was Webster's persona that lent magic to his words, for others, the magic of the words might bestow force and dignity on the person. What Choate hoped for from the sublime gift of eloquence is revealed in a quotation from the Odyssey that he translated in his journal:

> One man has a figure and personal exterior, mean, contemptible: but God crowns and wreaths about his form with eloquence. Men look on him delighted; he speaks unfaltering, but with a honeyed modesty; he is foremost of the assembly; as he walks through the city they look on him as on a god.[127]

The three greatest American orators, by general consent, were Daniel Webster, Henry Clay and John C. Calhoun. Choate, however, won himself a secure place in the second rank, among men like Edward Everett and Theodore Parker. Though his natural talent for public speaking had been evident in his college days, for the rest of his life Choate worked on his rhetorical skills, just as he continued to study the law. He made it a practice, every day, to read aloud "a page from Burke, or some rich author," not only to improve the flexibility of his voice and expression, but as what he called "a culture of the emotional nature . . . to *feel* all the emotions of indignation, sarcasm, commiseration, etc." Before an audience, Choate could work himself up into such a pitch of passion that his voice would rise to a shriek and the sweat pour from his head; he would sway back and forth on his heels or even whirl himself entirely around. During a stump speech for Harrison in 1840 his gestures were so violent that he split his frock coat right up the back. By the time Choate, along with Webster, had become a marked enemy of the anti-slavery cause, Wendell Phillips likened him to a "monkey in convulsions." On the whole, however, such exhibitions were used sparingly, to terrify a jury or overwhelm an audience. As Emerson noted, he was a "nervous, fluent speaker, with a little too much fire for the occasion, yet with a certain temperance in his fury, and a perfect self-command."[128]

Whatever his occasional emotional excesses, generally Choate followed the maxim of his idol, Cicero, that the orator's effect must be achieved mainly by the choice and arrangement of words. He worked systematically at acquiring and storing up words, phrases, images, to provide that basic necessity for the orator: *copia verborum*— a ready flow, not just of words, but of the exact and most persuasive word. He habitually *read* the dictionary, he told George Perkins Marsh, and he also spent a few minutes each day translating from Latin into English, seeking for every Latin word five or six English synonyms. Much of his English reading too, was to stock his vocabulary, to "avoid sinking into cheap and bald fluency, to give elevation, energy, sonorousness, and refinement," to produce a "diction whose every word is full freighted with suggestion and association, with beauty and power." The English classics were ransacked for nuggets of eloquence: "it is a *mine*—a *magazine,*" he said of *Paradise Regained,* " 'horrent,' blazing with all the weapons of the most exquisite rhetoric." He read pen in hand, and he wrote constantly, for "careful constant writing is the parent of ripe speech."[129]

The result was a remarkably wide vocabulary, which so astonished one admirer that he undertook a comparative word count of Choate's speeches with those of other well-known orators and men of letters. Choate's printed speeches, he found, contained 11,693 unrepeated words; of the comparisons, only Macaulay, who used over 3,000 unrepeated words in a single speech, came close. "For Heaven's sake don't let Choate hear of it," exclaimed

Chief Justice Shaw on learning a new dictionary was out.[130]

Apart from his extraordinary flow of words, Choate's style was chiefly noted for its cumulative quality: the string of adjectives, as when he described the classic Greek mind as "subtle, mysterious, plastic, apprehensive, comprehensive, available"; and the long, labyrinthine, parenthetical sentences (one, in a eulogy of Webster, covers three printed pages), which he always managed to steer to a conclusion without loss of grammar or sense. When his speeches were collected and published after his death, many friendly critics thought that without the vehement personality of the speaker to carry the audience onwards, the long, disjointed sentences would be too bizarre and irregular for the reader to follow or appreciate. In fact, in comparison with other more "correct" orators of the period, for example Edward Everett, Choate reads rather well; the long parentheses amplify rather than disrupt the thought and the cumulative lists whip up the pace.[131]

One critic of Choate's style suggested that the parentheses were the orator's way of drawing his audience into his own mental world, of involving them so completely in his own processes of thought that they could not sustain a critical distance from his conclusions.

> He seemed to use words not exactly to *convey* ideas to his hearers, but rather to assist and guide their minds in the work of constructing the same ideas that were his own. In carrying their minds through this process, he must give them, not merely the idea which had been the result of his own thinking, but its elements, their proportions, their limitations, their bearings on the results. . . . The practical effect was, that the hearer found himself not merely overwhelmed by the multitude of grand things that had been said, but also led, by a safe logical process, to the desired conclusion.[132]

Generally, Choate's technique was less analytical and less logical than this comment implies. But it does touch on an essential feature of this kind of oratory—the effort of the speaker to involve the audience with him in creating a world of meaning. In a typical Choate passage the audience is not asked to analyze an idea but to explore with the speaker its implications and resonances, amplify its associations, and increase their own stock of mental images and connections.

> All that happens in the world of Nature or Man,—every war; every peace; every hour of prosperity; every hour of adversity; every election, every death; every life; every success and every failure,—all change,—all permanence,—the perished leaf; the unutterable glory of stars, —all things speak truth to the thoughtful spirit.[133]

With Burke, who influenced his style a good deal, Choate realized that "it is one thing to make an idea clear, and another to make it *affecting* to the imagination." The popular mind, he felt, could deal with quite "profound" matters, but these must always be presented in "anecdote or sparkling truism, or telling illustration, or stinging epithet, etc.; always in some concrete form, never in logical abstract, syllogistic shape." The modern political scientist, John H. Schaar, discussing the decline both of political language and of authority in the modern state, points out that "the knowledge appropriate to humanly significant leadership" must be expressed in the language of metaphor and illustration. "Teaching in this language is done mainly by story, example, and metaphor—modes of discourse which can probe depths of personal being inaccessible to objective and managerial discourse."[134] Choate always followed the classic practice of storing up "commonplaces" from his reading—*general observations*— maxims, proverbs,—they fix attention, they are argument, authority, illustration, the signs of full minds." These commonplaces were aids to the orator, ready at hand to attach themselves to particular arguments, but much of their power came from precisely their "common" quality; they were already half-familiar to his audience and would conjure up both a chain of associations and an automatic assent through that very familiarity. Choate's speeches are full of half-quotations, evocative snatches, that, at least to an audience that shared some of his erudition, would bring the charm of a familiar universe of discourse.[135]

Language, indeed, like money, is primarily a medium of exchange that enables men to enter into complicated relationships and build up complex, "abstract" communities. "Webster's phrases," said Choate, "run through the land like *coin*," and like all currency their usefulness depended on a general willingness to accept them at face value. Typically, the ante-bellum orator dealt neither in slogans nor ideas, but in "truths": assumptions about the nature and destiny of man, the course of history, the fundamentals of government. These were not objects of analysis but building blocks of community; they reminded the heterogeneous members of a new nation of the common moral assumptions upon which transactions between them took place. Sometimes, of course, the orator minted new coin, like Webster's inspired linking of "liberty and Union," which through constant repetition and amplification in the speeches of others, became at last a "truth."[136]

Choate always thought of himself as essentially a forensic orator, for whom the object was persuasion to act. Though he would sometimes lecture to lyceums he did not attach much value to lecturing. "It leads to nothing and comes to nothing," he told Parker, who surmised that "he wanted some tangible object always before him—an election by the people, a vote by a representative body, a verdict by the jury."[137] Only in the case of a jury trial, however, and sometimes perhaps in Congress, did oratory usually involve the attempt to change minds. Electioneering was largely aimed at generating enough enthusiasm in one's own supporters to get them to the polls, rather than trying to win converts from the other party. Most of the time, orators spoke to those already persuaded of the truth and worth of what they were about to say: Whigs spoke to Whigs, eulogists to those who came to mourn, Fourth of July orators to the patriotic, lyceum lecturers to those already convinced that personal and social improvment lay in learning about the "English Poets" or the "Advances of Modern Science." Some of the most characteristic and interesting examples of American oratory in this period, in fact, and some of Choate's own most popular efforts, were of the non-parliamentary kind, in which the object was not so much to win over, or persuade to action, as to confirm and articulate the rightness of certain enthusiasms and emotions, to validate the moral and political coin.

Every Fourth of July or memorial or patriotic address stocked and restocked the common mind with a store of selected memories and sought to attach them wherever possible, as a mnemonic device, to some concrete symbol: Plymouth Rock, Mount Vernon. As a contemporary critic said of Webster, "he struggled to make Bunker Hill Monument *visible* from every portion of the land." Like the sermon, the Fourth of July address confirmed the

believer and reminded the waverer. It was a communal experience of affirmation, and the object of the orator was essentially to
create a state of consciousness: for one heightened, suspended
moment to make the abstract real. When people recalled hearing
the great orators, they remembered this heightened sense of reality. "I could form no idea of eternity," said one Boston lady,
"until I heard Channing say the words "from everlasting to everlasting,' and then it overwhelmed me." Webster on Plymouth
Rock or Bunker Hill, Choate on nationality or the Union, Everett
on Washington, all aimed at providing that communal shock of
recognition that would enable their audience to say: "this has been
our experience, this is the kind of people we are." In a new and
undefined nation, the orators described what America was,
brought into focus the outlines of identity, pointed out a meaning.
They made the whole American experience comprehensible to a
wide popular audience; they served, in the words of Archibald
MacLeish, to "impose upon the world of chaotic phenomena an
order of understanding, a moral order—to extend the hold of
word on fact."[138]

In a young democracy with a mass electorate, the orator had
a particularly crucial role. It was not so much that he educated the
electorate on specific issues but that he drew this electorate into
the world of politics and defined for it the structure of that world.
By providing the vocabulary and defining the terms of political
discourse, he created a "symbolic framework in terms of which to
formulate, think about, and react to political problems," and thus,
out of an amorphous populace, he helped to create a "public."[139]
It is significant for the development of American thinking in the
Northern and Western states that the greatest and most famous
orators of the period were Whigs. Though they never managed
to capture the White House for any length of time, the Whigs left
their imprint on the national consciousness through the generally
Whiggish orientation of important means of communication, from
the *North American Review* through the school text book, to the
printed collections of famous orations. The speeches of Webster,
Clay, Everett, even Choate, made their way into respectable par-
lours and, more importantly, into schoolhouses across the nation.
It was Webster's Reply to Hayne that schoolboys memorized, not
Jackson's Bank Veto. Just as the nation's judges and lawyers were
creating an essentially conservative fabric of law, the Whig orators

were weaving an essentially conservative consciousness. Although Choate won an acknowledged position for himself as a lawyer, an orator, and a useful, if minor, luminary of the Whig party, he was always to remain something of an outsider. As his eccentricities became domesticated, Boston adopted him as a "character," but he was not "of Boston."[140] The mercantile-industrial-patrician elite that dominated the city was by no means closed to outsiders who were able and willing to assimilate to its code of propriety, conduct and opinion, though it could viciously turn upon the "disorganizers" and deviants within its own ranks. With their strong belief in duty and public responsibility, their cultivation and genuine respect for learning and the life of the mind, above all in their conviction that these must be combined in any worthy governing class, the Boston merchants and Brahmins provided for their city a leadership whose uniqueness has been recognized both by those who grew up under it and by later commentators. But they have usually recognized too that the civilization that this elite embodied and helped to create was based upon an avoidance and suppression of anything that might upset its precarious equilibrium, upon a tacit agreement to "let the abyss alone."[141]

If Choate failed to become fully a part of the Boston elite, it was certainly not because his opinions were unorthodox: as much as any of them, he had "sound views on the tariff, . . . a deference for Southern opinion . . . and a worship of Mr. Webster."[142] He made a respectable living at the Bar and his origins were no humbler than those of Edward Everett or the Lawrences—though he was not allied with any prominent Boston family in that much intermarried society. He was elected to the Massachusetts Historical Society and quickly joined the Athenaeum, the "major cultural institution" of the Brahminate. He was on easy, if not intimate, terms with the leading men of the city and had entrée to the house of George Ticknor (who also was a Dartmouth graduate)—the imprimatur of Boston society. Perhaps it was his lack of social assurance that prevented Choate from ever being fully accepted into the Boston elite. There was always a certain uncouthness to his manner; "he had no grace of action," recalled one of his law students, "in a social set or dress party he was a forlorn looking man." He was known for his sweet temper and exquisite courtesy —yet, in that courtesy as in his oratory, Boston perceived a certain excess: "he treated every man as though he were a gentleman," said a friend, and "every gentleman almost as he would a lady." Cultivated, courteous, yet nervous, physically awkward, a trifle bizarre, he always remained in some ways a hinterland Yankee, never quite assimilated to the metropolis.[143]

If Choate's status in Boston was that of the "celebrity" rather than the totally integrated member of any of the city's elites, it was partly due to his own choice. He lived in Winthrop Place, near Summer Street, a handsome, pleasant area, but not quite as fashionable as Beacon Hill; and he sent his son to Amherst rather than Harvard, though the latter was the primary institution for acculturating and incorporating the young into the upper class. The shy avoidance of "society" that had made his first few years after college difficult continued, and in his leisure hours he much preferred the solitude of his library to company. But, though he loved literature, he loved it in books, not in living authors: he never sought to attach himself to the literary world of Boston and its environs.[144]

Choate's deliberate self-segregation can perhaps best be seen in his selection of a church. The Boston elite was overwhelmingly either Unitarian or Episcopalian and, as a young man in Danvers and Salem, Choate too had often attended Unitarian services. But his own family and his wife's remained Congregationalist, and when he settled in Boston he attached himself to the old Essex Street Congregationalist church. Its pastor, Nehemiah Adams, was a personable and cultivated young man, a good speaker and prolific author. Besides conventional devotional works his oeuvre included a treatise proving the scriptural authority and reasonableness of the doctrine of eternal punishment. Adams, however, was one of that increasing number of orthodox clergy who no longer quite had the courage of their convictions. "Dr. Adams believes in Hell," said Choate's daughter Helen, "but he doesn't believe there is anyone in it." Certain that his sensibilities would not be shocked by either uncharitableness or uncouthness, Choate settled comfortably into the congregation and remained with it for the rest of his life, though he never made a formal profession of faith or joined the church.[145]

Choate's orthodoxy seems to have been simultaneously a deliberate opting out of the society of fashionable Boston, a personal resolution of the problem of religion, and a statement on the role of religion in social life. It is difficult to gauge the extent to which Choate ever became a "believer." After his death his pious friends were a little too anxious to insist that in spite of his lack of formal profession and his determined avoidance of any discussion of religious matters, his faith was fundamentally sound. But the less devout were more skeptical: Choate would have been horrified to know that "Ben Hallett would take the opportunity of his death to eulogize his *religious character,"* commented the journalist William Robinson, "Ought there not to be a statute against such outrages?" Choate's student, Parker, thought he believed only in "Euclid and in what he could see."[146] But he read devotional works sometimes, especially towards the end of his life, and undoubtedly the language of the Bible and the traditional forms of religion had a profound aesthetic resonance for him.

It seems likely that at some point in his Salem years Choate had made a deliberate decision to assent. Some time in 1834–1835 he had come across a little book by the self-taught English polymath Isaac Taylor, called *The Natural History of Enthusiasm,* that he praised to James Marsh as "the best thing" he had seen. Taylor denounced "enthusiasm," extravagance of piety, and especially the belief in direct communications from God, as likely to lead to all kinds of unfortunate social results, but he also offered a rationale for belief that would appeal to someone of Choate's temperament. "We do not now wish to ask a seraph," he wrote, "if such a dogma is held to be true in heaven; what we have to do is to learn from the suffrage of the millions of mankind whether it has a permanent power to command and to retain ascendancy over the human mind."[147] Choate had an instinctive reverence for those ideas and forces that had proved their capacity to move and inspire mankind. In assenting to Christianity he assented to Western civilization; in joining the Congregational church he attached himself to the most authentic tradition of his own part of it—New England. If he could not share a deep religious feeling, he could certainly participate in the rituals of this social bond.[148]

Religion was thus given a conventional place in his life, a safe and separate place from which it would not be allowed to spill over into other, properly secular, areas, including both the world of the intellect and the world of politics. Once he had made this decision he did not want his precarious psychic equilibrium disturbed by any further speculation that could only produce a "laceration of mind." Gently he turned aside George Bush's attempts to interest him in Swedenborg: "I have a timorous disinclination to being shocked, waked or stunned out of the 'trivial fond' prejudice and implicit takings up of a whole life. But it is your privilege to be a seeker for truth. . . . *Sit mea anima cum tuâ.*"[149]

This statement on religion might stand for his political philosophy and loyalties too. The political ideas and assumptions and the loyalty to Webster that he had evolved as a young man in Essex were to be developed and deepened in subsequent years, but never fundamentally questioned. To have done so would have produced a laceration too deep in a mind that, for its own stability, increasingly needed to cling to certain unwavering principles of union and of order.

TWO

AN AMERICAN CONSERVATISM

*D*URING HIS FIRST YEARS in Boston, Choate not only had to make his reputation but also support his growing family. After 1836, he dropped out of active party business to concentrate on building up his law practice, leaving it to others to work out the strategy that would bring the victory of 1840. Once the Whig campaign for General Harrison got under way, however, he threw himself into it with enthusiasm. In that same year his youngest daughter died at the age of three; no doubt political involvement helped to temper his personal grief. He gave several campaign speeches throughout Massachusetts and in Boston, and the *Essex Register* suggested the public might "demand that his services be continued in requisition."[1]

Now in his early forties, Choate was a striking figure: just over six-foot tall, robust though rather gaunt, with a mass of curling hair that remained jet black until his death. But his face was prematurely aged: sallow, haggard and crisscrossed by a maze of deep wrinkles. As was true of Webster, his appearance contributed to his impact upon an audience; in particular, his expressive dark eyes—often "dreamy and rapt," but when roused, piercing and "almost wild"—could mesmerize those within reach.[2] Although Choate did not actively seek political office, he did not effectively discourage the impression that he might be available. His known devotion to Webster, his past services to the party and his growing forensic reputation made it inevitable that his name should come up as a successor to Webster in the Senate when the latter resigned to become Harrison's secretary of state.

Both Abbott Lawrence and John Quincy Adams were also in

the running, but Webster threw his weight behind Choate. No doubt he felt that Choate in the Senate would be much more *his* man than the independent Adams and that, while Choate would fill the seat well, he would hardly rival the reputation of its former incumbent. According to the distinguished lawyer and Whig activist, Theophilus Parsons, it was only with the greatest reluctance that Choate agreed to stand, and then only with the express understanding that he would resign in two or three years. But the other Massachusetts senator, Isaac Bates, told party stalwart John Clifford he "knew Rufus Choate wanted the post and expressed a desire he might get it."[3] Perhaps the excitement of what Choate, like many other Whigs, came to call "the Revolution of 1840," had rekindled his earlier ambitions to be a "national man" and undermined his conviction that congressional politics were not his metier. At any rate, he consented to stand and was elected by the general court to fill the vacant seat.

The choice was by no means universally popular. The abolitionist John Greenleaf Whittier wrote bitterly to Caleb Cushing:

> For myself, I see no reason for the election of Choate. What has he done for the party? What for Massachusetts? He has been acting upon the advice of honest Iago— "put money in thy purse"; and left thyself and others to peril health, property and reputation in the long and stern struggle which preceded the late Revolution. And now, forsooth, the old war-tried veterans are to be set aside, to allow this "carpet-knight" to enjoy the spoils![4]

More important members of the party were also lukewarm. The *Courier* pointed out that there were other Whigs with more experience of public life, such as John Quincy Adams. Adams' son, Charles Francis, not unnaturally, felt that Choate's election was a slight upon his father, although he eventually voted for him, "after much and patient reflection entirely because I did not feel that he was unworthy of the situation as was the case with Bates." From Washington, Robert Winthrop in the House confided to Clifford:

> Between you and I, I have no great confidence in his doing any great things here. He has not confidence enough, nor communicativeness enough. He will make

a brilliant speech once in a while, but he will not attend to everyday matters etc. But we shall see what we shall see.[5]

Before Choate could embark on his senatorial career, the general who had swept the Whigs to the giddy victory of 1840 was dead, and Choate's first duty as incumbent senator was to deliver his eulogy in the crepe-hung Faneuil Hall. There was not a great deal to say about "that firm, wise, kind old man," but Choate took the occasion to plead for party harmony and the softening of factional strife.[6] It was soon to be clear, however, that the death of Harrison would deepen the rift between Webster and Clay and imperil the entire cohesion of the party.

The Washington to which Choate returned in the summer of 1841 still had "the air of some projector's scheme which has failed"; nor did he find the general tone of political life any more elevated than in Jackson's heyday. "Dexter says this city reminds one of Rome," he wrote to Charles Sumner. "I suppose he meant in its spaces, solitudes, quiet, vices, etc. . . . The debauched state of public opinion exceeds belief, *pejor actus.*"[7] Like many congressmen, he did not bring his family to the capital, but since he stayed, as before, in the house of his brother-in-law Sewall, he was not part of the convivial world of the "messes." However, when George P. Marsh entered the House in 1843, they resumed their old intimacy, and through Sumner's introduction he also struck up a correspondence with Francis Lieber, the German emigré political philosopher.[8]

Choate was quite taken with Lieber, whom he described as the "most fertile, indomitable, unsleeping, combative, and propagandizing person of his race." "I am *impelled* and *taught* by your book on Property and Labor," he assured him. But the friendship on both sides had a strongly practical aspect: Choate pumped Lieber for detailed opinions on the right of search on the high seas and the rights of slaveowners over slaves who jumped ship in the West Indies—problems bedevilling the relations between the U.S. and Britain. Lieber, for his part, was always ready to latch on to any likely source of patronage. "Is Choate a man of influence with you?" he wrote to Sumner. "When he comes home you and Hillard must keep him warm for me, for should heaven be pleased to open a path, he may be useful."[9]

When Choate took his seat in the special session of Congress, convened on May 31, he was appointed a member of the committee on foreign relations and naval affairs, a position from which he could back Webster's foreign policy; his maiden speech was a defense of the secretary of state's handling of the McLeod affair. He was also appointed to the select committee on currency and finance, chaired by Henry Clay, and almost immediately found himself caught in the battle for preeminence between Clay and Webster.[10]

The great Whig victory of 1840 was not merely a result of hard-sell campaign tactics. It was due as much to a protest against the hard times following upon the Panic of 1837. The repercussions of an English depression together with the loss of faith in paper money which followed Jackson's Specie Circular of the previous year brought an end to the speculative boom of the mid-1830s. Numerous bank failures produced a serious shortage of currency, businessmen went bankrupt, and in the Eastern industrial cities there was widespread unemployment and wage cuts. Although the Whigs had not issued any party platform in 1840, the basic tenets of their economic policy were well known and the belief that they could do something about the depression was implicit in their campaign. In the special session, the Whigs immediately launched into their recovery program, the essentials of which were a national bank, a higher tariff, distribution of the revenue from the sale of public lands to the states as a means both of stimulating public improvements and maintaining the need for a revenue tariff, and a bankruptcy bill to bring relief to corporations and individual businessmen. All these measures were designed to stimulate industry and commerce and both revitalize and stabilize the economy.[11]

The death of Harrison put this whole program in jeopardy, for the new president, Tyler, was a strict constructionist, unalterably opposed to a strong national bank like the one destroyed by Andrew Jackson. Clay, from his position of leadership in the Senate, was quite prepared to make a stand on the Whig doctrine of congressional supremacy and force a showdown with the president, thus cementing his dominance over the party and laying the foundation for his own nomination in 1844. Webster, on the other hand, was convinced that the party's future, and his own, depended upon avoiding a decisive break between Tyler and the Whigs.[12]

"Our unity as a party—our existence, the whole question of the next presidency—and much more," wrote an anxious Choate from Washington, depended on the willingness of congressional Whigs to meet the president half way. Choate's own strong instinct for compromise, as well as his devotion to Webster, put him with the minority of Whigs who were prepared to defy Clay and settle for a bank bill that would make some concession to the states'rights position. "I wish our Boston press would realize that Harrison is *dead,*" he wrote plaintively to his friend John Davis, the governor of Massachusetts, "and allow a little for perplexities of which they know nothing." Choate completely accepted Webster's analysis that the unity of the party and its ability to accomplish long-standing Whig goals were being endangered less by principles than by Clay's presidential ambitions. "Mr. Clay (this is confidential and conjectural)," he told Davis, "would like to drive Tyler *out of the next term and take it himself.*" So he had persuaded the majority of Whigs to support a bank bill that he knew Tyler would never accept. When the president vetoed the bill, the administration would lose the support of the party and collapse. "The locos who *surround* Tyler daily and flatter him in debate—but whom he repels—will take him up and there you are —with Clay and Tyler in the field—on the mere question of compulsory branching power."[13]

In the Senate the Webster Whigs tried to head off disaster. Rives of Virginia proposed an amendment to Clay's bill, restraining the proposed bank from setting up branches except with the consent of the states concerned. Webster was solidly behind the amendment and, on July 2, Choate spoke in its defense.[14] The speech revealed both Choate's conception of practical politics and his attitude towards constitutional issues. As a nationalist, Choate assigned the widest powers to the federal government, but philosophically as well as practically he did not feel that the logic of a situation was the best guide to the actual living of it. The proper way to handle contested constitutional questions was to skirt around them, rather than meet them head on. While the constitution was sacred, a too precise constitutional doctrine, like a too precise theology, led to schism. Unity, which was to become the emotional heart of Choate's philosophy, was more likely to be secured by turning towards practical measures for economic benefit than by a determination to explore constitutional issues to their core and insist on constitutional principles.

> All things which are lawful are not convenient, are not practical, are not wise, are not safe, are not kind. . . . To exercise a contested power without necessity on a notion of keeping up the tone of government is not much better than tyranny, and very improvident and impolitic tyranny, too.

This sounds very much like Edmund Burke defending the American colonists. Choate's mode of argument on most political questions was always essentially Burkean: to focus attention on the particular discrete problem to be solved, to begin from the particular circumstances in which it was embedded, and to avoid whenever possible any debate on first principles. The circumstances included, in this particular case, the states' rights convictions, or prejudices, of Southern Whigs as well as Southern Democrats. Compromise might leave some fundamental issues unresolved but it would also allow an effective bank to be in operation "to some useful and substantial extent by the first of January," and the economy could begin its process of recovery. Why not then "let the constitutional question whether Congress can make a bank by its own powers or not stand over for argument on the last day of the Greek kalends, when the disputants may have the world all to themselves to wrangle it out in"? A bank that avoided the objectionable features of Biddle's bank would in reality be stronger, since it would possess the basic requirement of every stable institution—public acceptance.

> I desire to see the Bank of the United States become a cherished institution, reposing in the bosom of our law and of our attachments. . . . I do not wish to see it standing like a fortified post on a foreign border—never wholly at peace, always assailed, always belligerent, not falling perhaps, but never safe, the nurse and the prize of an unappeasable hostility.[15]

Choate's speech was a direct challenge to Clay and, coming from a man who was seen as representing both the secretary of state and the financial interests of Massachusetts, it had particular import. In the course of the speech Choate made the blunder of remarking that Clay's bill, unamended, even if it passed Congress, could not become law. Clay immediately pounced upon him and demanded to know, in very peremptory terms, how he knew for a fact this was so. Choate denied he was the mouthpiece of the executive, and asserted, rather lamely, that he based his belief on many "facts and deductions" he did not think it "necessary to explain." The exchange was very heated and, since Clay happened to be seated temporarily a mere seat away, was literally a face to face confrontation. The two were called to order, and the following day Clay apologized.

The incident showed Clay at his most overbearing, but Choate suffered more from it in popular esteem. The *New York Herald* commented that the "Massachusetts gentleman cowered and quailed before the violence of Mr. Clay, when he should have repelled his insolence with equal violence, even at the risk of his life. . . . Mr. Choate must be utterly deficient in energy and spirit or he would never have submitted to the tyrannical insolence of Mr. Clay."[16] His apparent deficiency of nerve undoubtedly weakened Choate's reputation in that essentially Southern city and caused him to be taken less seriously at the outset of his senatorial career. An eyewitness told Hugh McCulloch that "Choate was one of the ablest men in the Senate. If he had knocked Mr. Clay down instead of quailing before him, he would have been a Webster." Choate was temperamentally incapable of knocking anyone down; his imagination may have been captured by men "who had seen fight, who had been in action," but he shrank from visceral confrontations of force, except in court, where the context was ritualized and depersonalized. For all its exaggeration, however, the public contempt, caught an essential political defect in Choate, which his friends also recognized. He lacked the essential attribute of a leader, the ability to project personal force. He was to remain always a secondary figure in the Whig party, a useful and zealous supporter.[17]

As Choate grew older, his devotion to Webster became a rooted and integral part of his personality and philosophy. As senator he would devote himself primarily to defending the foreign policy of the secretary of state, representing his position on economic matters and vindicating his equivocal position in the Tyler cabinet to the increasingly skeptical party leaders of Massachusetts.[18] He was, moreover, committed to the Whig party; in the touchy political situation of the early 1840s his was to be a voice for party unity, desperately trying to prevent the party from splitting over either principles or personalities, urging it towards practical measures and the *juste milieu*. In November 1841, he was haranguing Whig caucus meetings throughout Massachusetts in an effort to rally the demoralized party for the state elections. His correspondence of 1841 and 1842 contains many references to the necessity of persuading Massachusetts Whigs to settle for what they could get in the way of a bank and a tariff. "Is not this better than to rail out Mr. W. and go into a factious, senseless, censorious, assinine, objectless fight?" he demanded of Parsons. And to another Boston correspondent: "Think of separating from our friends—and going to the people on so absurd an issue as a high-toned Bank. Stand by the *existing* order of things—just see that all our friends—*Atlas* and all do that." As he explained pragmatically to John Davis, compromise on the bank "keeps the P from the locos—keeps us together—keeps us *in*. Any other course puts us in opposition—and we disappear."[19]

The right-wing members of his party always seemed to him a liability, ever likely to relapse into high Federalist statements totally inapplicable in the context of expansive democratic America. A great tirade by Mangum of North Carolina in the Senate against the "un-American" doctrine, that called for "repeal of charters, and the destruction of vested rights," rampant among a "mass of population already deeply tainted, and more and more imbibing the poison of agrarian principles," seemed to Choate an example of the "extreme right" of Whiggism, which bordered on the absurd. "I was out of the city," he wrote to Parsons, "but it reads comical." Choate was young enough to accept without question not only the reality of party but also an America in which universal white male suffrage, along with the inevitable democratization of political tone and activity that must accompany it, were facts of life. To continue to be politically relevant, the party would not only have to thoroughly absorb the lesson of 1840 but also model itself into a moderately conservative party firmly committed to pragmatic efforts to achieve material prosperity. "In politics," he wrote to Lieber, "does not the whole nation and do not all things, and all signs, point to and desiderate and cry out for a *juste milieu*, tertium quid—*repose* on some ground half way between locofocism and intense Whig-gery?"[20]

His compromising approach did not always sit well with other Massachusetts Whigs, however, nor did his particular style. "Did you like Choate's speech [on the McLeod affair]?" Win-throp asked Clifford. "His manner was not fancied here and there were many minds as to his success, tho' some admired him greatly. I confess there is a manly statesmanship about Rives' speech on the same subject which better fits my idea of senatorial eloquence." Two months later Clifford was complaining: "However brilliant Choate may be at the Bar, his first impression upon the public mind as a Senator has not realized expectations and some of his constituents are greatly dissatisfied at the ground taken both by him and Bates upon Rives' amendment."[21]

When he felt it necessary, however, Choate was quite capable of taking a strong and unyielding stand on a matter of principle. It was largely due to a brilliant two-hour speech he delivered in executive committee that Edward Everett narrowly won confirma-tion as minister to England after being denounced by James Bu-chanan and others as an abolitionist. "In all my life," Choate wrote to Parsons, "I never felt half the interest in anything whatever." He knew he was defending not only a friend but the Union; a Southern defeat of such a central figure in the Massachusetts Whig establishment as Edward Everett would be a challenge that New England could not ignore. If Everett were defeated over abolition, Choate wrote to Sumner, "the Union goes to pieces like a potter's vessel."[22]

Unfortunately for Choate's public reputation, this was an effort behind closed doors and no record was kept. Although his speeches in the Senate were always well-prepared and highly finished productions worthy of note, he did not participate very often in the ordinary day-to-day debate. This was partly because he was so high strung that after every major public speech he was left prostrate with sick headaches and exhaustion; and partly be-cause much of his time was still devoted to legal work. Several months of the winter of 1843–1844 were taken up with the case concerning the boundary between Rhode Island and Massachu-setts, which he argued aided by Charles Sumner as junior counsel. It was not a case in which he saw much "fertility or *heights,*" but it was complicated and time consuming, and he withdrew from the

Senate for a time in order to prepare his brief. Stung by criticism from Massachusetts that he was not playing an active role in the tariff debates and by persistent rumours that he was about to resign, he begged his friends, Sumner and Parsons, discreetly to let it be known that his silence was not due to dereliction of duty, merely to absorption in other services for the state: "I have labored six months day and night—absorbed on Mass. and R.I.—withdrawing myself utterly from all else. . . . I should like a candid public to think it *possible* that this may have kept me away from the tariff debate. . . .²³ It is true and might be kind."²⁴

As Winthrop had predicted, Choate's shyness and aloofness, his lack of "communicativeness," prevented him from being a very useful committeeman or party manager. And his nervous illnesses were liable to remove him from the scene at key moments. For example, when the congressional Whigs caucussed in July 1841 to decide on a bank policy in face of Tyler's hostility, Choate was too ill to attend. Moreover, he was not sociable, hated late hours and "convivial dissipation," and "could not drink." Though he could summon up tremendous nervous energy for a set-piece oration or an argument in court, he did not have the necessary stamina or insensitivity for "smoke-filled-room" maneuvres or political bonhommie. As Edward Everett put it circumspectly after Choate's death:

> In the daily routine of legislation he did not take an active part. He rather shunned clerical work, and consequently avoided, as much as duty permitted, the labor of the committee-room. . . . [He had] no aptitude whatever for the out-doors management,—the electioneering legerdemain,—for the wearisome correspondence with local great men . . . which are necessary at the present day to great success in a political career.²⁵

Nor was Choate ambitious to be a policy maker for the party. George P. Marsh told Brown that Choate was rather "inclined to leave the determination of the policy of his party to more active and more aspiring statesmen" and that in conversation "he much oftener discussed the arguments by which a given measure proposed by his friends could be successfully defended or assailed, than inquired into its absolute expediency as a point yet to be determined."²⁶ Choate's usefulness to the Whig party lay primarily in his talent as an orator. As a campaign speaker on the hustings he was lively, combative, and witty, and he always delighted partisans. Even Winthrop could not help but admire Choate's "scintillations" in the 1844 election campaign for Clay, in which he "used up poetry and rhetoric enough to have lasted common men a life time." But, he added, "he has a strong thread of sense and logic . . . in his speeches, which I am by no means disposed to undervalue."[27] However infrequent his speeches in the Senate, when he spoke it was to a full house and a full gallery.

Much of Choate's time in the Senate was taken up with foreign affairs, particularly with supporting Webster's efforts to keep the peace with England. He ably defended the secretary of state's treaty with Lord Ashburton settling the Maine boundary dispute as one of the "triumphs of reason and of civilization."[28] To the Massachusetts Whigs, the "instinctive cousinship" that Henry Adams noted between Massachusetts and England, together with the Atlantic network of financial interest, cultural influences and personal friendships, made war with England over such issues as the Maine boundary or the possession of Oregon unthinkable. Outside their own rather insulated world, however, as they discovered, there were many Americans to whom it was not at all unthinkable. Thus even Whigs who deplored Webster's position in Tyler's cabinet rallied to his conciliatory diplomacy.[29]

By the 1840s, the temper of America seemed to many dubious Whigs to be characterized by what John Higham has called "the spirit of boundlessness," an inordinate appetite for territorial, economic or spiritual expansion, an aggressive refusal to accept any kind of limit. Webster in 1838 attributed this reaction to the "licentiousness of feeling and action" released by prosperity,

> as the steed, full of the pasture, will sometimes throw himself against its enclosures, break away from its confinement, and feeling now free from needless restraint, betake himself to the moors and barrens, where want, ere long, brings him to his senses, and starvation and death close his career.

Ten years later an anonymous Whig quoting this description exclaimed "this is Loco-Focosim. . . . Is it true, then that there are no differences in principle between the two parties? Have you and

I been contending for nothing—been fighting shadows for the last twenty years?"[30]

Nowhere was the spirit of boundlessness more evident than in the enthusiasm for westward expansion. Much of the Whig effort, of Massachusetts Whigs in particular, in the 1840s, was devoted to trying to stem the aggressive nationalism that expressed itself in an urge for more territory and a ready belligerence towards other nations that might stand in the way. The Whigs were opposed to war and lukewarm on the question of new territory; both would be likely to upset that delicate harmonious balance they were trying to uphold within the Union and within society. Expansionism released all kinds of energies better kept confined: "all along the Western borders," warned the *American Review*, "in ever straggling villages . . . are great numbers of bold and restless spirits, men gathered out of all the orderly and civilized portions of society as its most turbulent members, and ready for any movement that can minister to their reckless manner of life and love of danger and change."[31] Such men might easily drag the United States into war with Mexico over Texas or with England over the Oregon territories.

Events such as the McLeod affair showed how easily the pugnacity of individual states could embroil the whole nation in diplomatic difficulties, and Choate spoke fervently for the bill aimed at dealing with such cases by extending the jurisdiction of the federal courts. One of the great uses of the national government was that this "vast but restrained and parental" central power served to discipline the expansive and restless urges of the age, holding back border states like Maine and New York from overrunning the international boundary.[32]

The Ashburton treaty had not attempted to settle the conflicting claims to Oregon, but American settlers were already moving into the Willamette valley, and there was a rising demand for a unilateral ending of the joint occupation and an extension of the American claim north to the Alaska panhandle, even if this meant war. Choate, as one of the major Whig spokesmen on foreign policy, urged that the Oregon question must be solved, not unilaterally, but through "a wise and a firm and a good-tempered diplomacy." He denied that American patriotism must include a kind of hereditary hostility towards England and told the Senate that if they would only be content to let matters be, the sheer pressure of American settlement in the area would drive out the Hudson's Bay company. Oregon would fall to the United States "in the natural course of things," as long as the

> exasperated and mad national will, stimulated to un-
> designed and unreasonable action, is not substituted for
> the natural sequence of things; if the whole could re-
> main, as now it is, entrusted to the silent operation of
> those great laws of business and man, which govern in
> the moral world as gravitation among the stars.[33]

Irritating as the clamor over Oregon was, the problem of Texas, as all the Whigs realized, was infinitely more dangerous. If Texas were annexed to the Union, not only would the balance of power between the South and the North be disrupted, but, since it would be annexed as a slave state, the slavery issue would be propelled to the forefront of American politics. As long as he was secretary of state, Webster stalled any move on Texas, but once he resigned, Tyler was free to pursue his own interests and, in April 1844, a treaty of annexation was presented to the Senate. New England Whig opinion was solidly against the treaty—indeed the treaty gave the Massachusetts Whig establishment the opportunity to reaffirm its dominance in the party and put down incipient attempts at schism.[34]

The growth of abolitionist sentiment had spawned a new party—the Liberty party—which, even if it was not a real threat to the Whigs of Massachusetts at the polls, nevertheless complicated the political scene. More importantly, abolitionism was beginning to win over important younger Whigs like Charles Francis Adams and Charles Sumner, who were increasingly restive at the deference of the Whig leadership to Southern opinion. The unity of the Whigs as a national party had always meant playing down the slavery issue to avoid offending Southern Whigs; now the more urgent question of the unity of the party in Massachusetts meant that the Whig establishment had to make clear that they were morally sound on the question of slavery. Abbott Lawrence in particular was anxious that the Whigs as a united party quickly make their position plain on Texas, in order, as he said, to prevent the abolitionists getting in first and giving the question "a wrong turn."[35]

Choate's position on slavery was essentially that of Whig leaders like Lawrence, Webster and Nathan Appleton: he disapproved of it, hoped that in some distant and enlightened future it would disappear, but meanwhile regarded it as a domestic matter of the Southern states with which the North had no right to interfere. All abolitionist agitation of the slavery question was to be deplored because it disrupted the fragile harmony of the Union on which the Whig economic interests and political vision depended. Thus Choate was reluctant to present any petitions to the Senate dealing with the rights of blacks that might offend Southern sensibilities. In the spring of 1842, he was so dilatory about presenting a petition against the imprisonment of free colored seamen in Southern ports that the petitioners eventually withdrew the document they had sent him and submitted it instead to Robert Winthrop in the House.[36] In January of the following year he did submit a similar petition to the Senate without comment— three days after Winthrop had read to the House an exhaustive report on the subject.[37]

This lack of zeal did not go unremarked at home. Early in 1844, Choate and Bates were denounced in the Massachusetts legislature for their "want of spirit" in defending resolutions of the general court on the subject of slavery, presented to the Senate amidst great Southern indignation and vituperation. In the Massachusetts Senate Henry Wilson proposed an amendment to resolutions against the annexation of Texas, requiring the state's senators to "use their most zealous and unremitting exertions" to defeat such a project. The amendment was expressly intended as a rebuke—a reminder, said Wilson, that Massachusetts wished her representatives "to feel, to think, and to act as Massachusetts men, who have been reared under the institutions of the Pilgrim Fathers, should think, feel, and act." Charles Francis Adams declared that the people were dissatisfied with the actions of their senators and that the amendment was a way of saying that "Massachusetts would forgive the past if they would make great exertions for the future." The amendment was adopted by the state senate, but defeated in the House, largely through the efforts of Choate's old friend Leverett Saltonstall, who assured everyone that both senators "felt very keenly the criticisms which had been made in the legislature upon their course."[38]

In the election of 1844 Texas was a major issue. The temporary unity of the party in opposition to Texas offered Choate an opportunity to recoup some of the public esteem he had lost due to the growing anti-slavery sentiment in the state. Campaigning for Clay, he took care to point out that annexation must be opposed because, among other things, it meant extending the area of slavery, "this great evil, this great curse," but, at the same time, he insisted "I would leave to the masters of slaves every guaranty of the Constitution and the Union—the Constitution as it is, the Union as it is,—without which there is no security for you or for them—no, not for a day."[39]

His most heartfelt and eloquent opposition to the annexation, however, was that it would endanger the Union and distort the forming character of the nation. Every time one of the states into which the new territory would probably be divided applied for entry, the fragile balance of the Union would be shaken to its foundations by the controversy.

> Is there a man, out of a mad-house, who does not see that five, three, *one,* such application could not be acted on and either rejected or granted, without shaking this government to its foundation? Is there a man who does not see that if all the malice and all the ingenuity of Hell were appealed to, to devise one fiery and final trial of the strength of our American feeling, of our fraternal love, of our appreciation of the uses of union, of all our bonds of political brotherhood, it could contrive no ordeal half so dreadful as this?[40] Do you not, then, bear in mind, that the very struggle is one of the greatest evils that the union can bear? It must shake the union to its centre.[41]

Even apart from the danger to the Union, the accession of such vast territory, "appended . . . to one side, one region, one interest, of the many which compose the State," must change irrevocably the entire nature and direction of the national identity, "not merely . . . make a small globe into a large one, but . . . alter the whole figure of the body; . . . vary the shape and the range of its orbit; . . . launch it forth on a new highway of the heavens." Those who were tempted by the glory of expansion should remember that "there are limits of a nation's territorial extent, which the laws of nature and of man do not permit them to transcend, beyond which the warm tides of the national heart cannot be propelled, or cannot flow back,—beyond which, unity, identity, nationality, are dissolved and dissipated." The ultimate meaning of Texas was "not a question of national politics, but of national identity."[42]

The treaty was resoundingly defeated in the Senate, but Clay was narrowly defeated in the country and Tyler, taking this as a vote for annexation, urged Congress to move in that direction. In January 1845, the House passed a joint resolution for the admission of Texas. Choate argued for three hours in the Senate that the federal government had no constitutional power to annex a "foreign nation," but he wrote with resignation to Parsons, "Texas will be added or the Union dissolved." Though New Englanders continued to denounce the idea of annexation through the spring and summer of 1845, the conservative Lawrence wing of the leadership decided that the matter had been settled and that further opposition was fruitless. Choate could only counsel that all "northern gentlemen of our opinions" whenever the subject of Texas came up should "repeat the Greek alphabet deliberately once at least to themselves." "Texas is in," he told George Perkins Marsh flatly. "Her representatives will sit next you next winter. We should have shed blood to defeat them. *Nothing* can be done. . . . Morally we are clean of this."[43]

Although Choate was not a policy maker for the party, he was one of the most eloquent and persuasive of the men attempting to formulate a conservative ideology and project a particular Whig vision of the good society. The Whigs had become a party before they had evolved a workable or coherent philosophy. They had come together out of an almost instinctive reaction to the policies and person of Andrew Jackson, and now the task facing Whig propagandists was to articulate the assumptions—about the proper conduct of the polity and the proper direction of the Republic— on which that reaction had been based. As several historians have pointed out, however bitter the party battles of the period, by the 1840s both Whigs and Democrats accepted the general philosophy of liberal capitalism. Within that overall consensus on modernity, however, it was entirely possible, as Major Wilson has shown, for there to be real debate among "liberals" about the particular path society should take.[44]

The revival of a self-conscious conservatism in the United States in the 1950s produced a number of attempts to define conservatism and identify a consistent conservative stream in

American thought. The most useful of these discussions seems to me to be that of Samuel P. Huntington, largely because he does not offer an ideological test of conservatism that would read out of the canon a good many people who have thought of themselves —and have been thought of by their opponents—as conservatives. Huntington defines conservatism as a recurring phenomenon in specific circumstances, a defensive reaction forced to become articulate when cherished established institutions appear to be under attack by other social groups strong enough to make the danger real. It is, by definition, the philosophy of those who feel they have more to lose than to gain by fundamental changes, and while it does not necessarily offer a design of the ideal society, it does rest upon certain assumptions about the nature of man and society, the way in which change should take place, and particularly about "the institutional prerequisites of social order."[45]

In these terms the American Whigs were as conservative as Edmund Burke, even if their defense of institutions centered not on church and king but on a national bank. The backbone of the Whig leadership was composed of men who felt that, with the advent of Jacksonianism, the settled direction of the republic had been wrenched violently askew.[46] They were not opposed to change as such, indeed their own economic program of internal improvement and industrial development would produce the most profound change. But they had thought they saw clearly the contours of the path ahead and they had thought themselves securely in control of the processes of change. They had assumed that the dynamics of economic development could take place within the solid structure of existing institutions and without disturbing established social arrangements and patterns of power and deference; they had assumed that sectional differences could be settled within the firm bond of the Union. In the future they had envisaged, the United States would develop steadily as a stable and socially harmonious liberal republic directed by a propertied, enlightened, and open, upper class, and embark on a course of purposive economic growth under the fostering care of benevolent national and state governments. It would be an integral part of an Atlantic civilization, though its purest and most prosperous part.

The Jacksonian attack on the Bank, the tariff, corporations and "privilege," amidst a precipitous decline in that deference on

which social harmony in an economically unequal society seemed
to depend, called into question all these confident assumptions
about the future. Taking for granted an "end to ideology," they
suddenly found themselves, as Clay said when Jackson removed
the deposits from the Bank, "in the midst of a revolution." In face
of that challenge, the leaders of what became the Whig party
found that they had to reshape their rhetoric, abandon some aspects of the vision and reaffirm others, and above all, educate the
public to the necessity of a solid institutional underpinning for
social order.[47]

Choate brought to this task not only a flexible attitude towards political realities and a complete acceptance of the economic outlook of New England's mercantile and industrial elite
but a passionate patriotism and a long acquaintance with the ideas
of the two major philosophers of English conservatism, Edmund
Burke and Samuel Taylor Coleridge. He had become familiar
with Coleridge's ideas as an undergraduate, through his friend
James Marsh, and he had become a devoted admirer of Burke at
the same time. "No Englishman or countryman of ours has the
least appreciation of Burke," he told Charles Sumner. "The
Whigs never forgave the last eight or ten years of that life of glory,
and the Tories never forgave what preceded; and we poor, un-
idealized Tom Painefied democrats do not understand his marvel-
lous English, universal wisdom, illuminated, omniscient mind,
and are afraid of his principles." Choate absorbed both Burke's
principles and his language and, to an only slightly lesser extent,
those of Coleridge, so that his own political and social ideas
seemed not so much to be borrowed from, but grounded in, their
more developed philosophy, just as his speeches are filled with,
not so much direct quotations, but echoes and reverberations of
their language.[48]

The expansionist fervor of the 1840s brought very sharply
into focus the whole problem of a national character that was in
the process of being formed. Choate deplored the possibility that
the growing nation might become "a great, rapacious, proselytiz-
ing power, madly grasping at the empire of the whole new
world." In a campaign speech in the presidential election of 1848,
he summed up very neatly the Whig concept of the identity and
character that they wished their country to grow into: an increasingly complex, modern, civilized nation, eschewing both the

primitive and the sublime along with imperial expansion. The Whigs, he said, were the true party of progress, but "progress upwards, and not down nor sideways; that progress is *upwards, upwards.* We think it is not wild table land, but high-minded men; not a great barbarous wilderness frontier, but a commodious and polished life and cultivated fields." The vast, fruitful territory that the United States already possessed offered the opportunity to build "the most consummate civilization ever developed upon earth," not a new Eden, but "a holy and beautiful city." All the resources of the nation, the federal government, "corporated capital," labor, individual talent and skill, had their part to play in developing the nation, "to construct harbors, to clear rivers, to tunnel mountains, to bridge valleys, to level hills, to pour out a wide and scientific agriculture . . . and the result shall be a moral grandeur and beauty, worthy of the age in which we live."[49]

In Massachusetts this vision of a consummate civilization was bound up less with "scientific agriculture" than with the growth of industry. Yet while the Whigs as a party were fully committed to fostering industrial development, they were quite aware of the socially disintegrating potential of modern industrial organization. There is a certain beleaguered quality to much Whig thinking in this period: to the west lay the frontier, the great empty spaces luring more and more people to remove themselves beyond the moral and practical restraints of civilization, and to the east, an ultimately even more devastating problem. Across the Atlantic, in the factory towns of Britain, a whole new class of people was being created, not people who were escaping from civilization, but people who appeared never to have been in it. To an industrializing New England, old England was no longer the past; it was the future, a future fraught with political and social peril. The Americans who read the British government blue books and Christian socialist novels, or who visited Manchester, found there a terrifying vision of incipient social anarchy and class warfare. Certainly the existence of such an "underclass" in the United States would not be compatible with the American polity.[50]

The New England pioneers of industrialism, however, thought they could ride the tiger, effect an economic revolution, and still maintain social harmony. In early paternal experiments, such as the Lowell textile mills, they tried to marry social responsibility and economic rationality, to plunge into modern industrial organization while maintaining a traditionally harmonious community based on status rather than class. The attraction of the famous Lowell girls to both native and foreign observers was that they were not a permanent proletariat. As a candid minister of the town observed: "upon any embarrassment of affairs they return to their country homes, and do not sink down here a helpless caste, clamouring for work, starving unless employed, and hence ready for a riot, for destruction of property, and repeating here the scenes enacted in the manufacturing villages of England."[51]

By the 1840s, however, it was clear that Americans had not hit upon any new principle of social and economic organization which would fundamentally differentiate industrialism in the United States from that in Europe. Throughout the forties the position of labor in the northeastern states declined as wages were reduced, but the pace of work speeded up. The glory of the Lowell experiment was fading fast; the mill owners had broken several strikes and reduced wages; by 1845, the Lowell girls were organizing a trade union. Soon they were to be displaced entirely by Irish immigrants who seemed indeed a separate and permanent class.[52] Meanwhile, although the Whig industrialists did not entirely abandon their original idea of government as a positive force in the economy, they did increasingly resist attempts by government to regulate as well as aid industry. Their property might be social, both in the benefits it dispensed and the fostering it deserved, but its management they regarded as a purely private matter. The Whigs as a party never entirely lost the conviction that society had a certain organic unity and that government had the obligation to act for the common good, but they were prepared to exempt more and more of the economy from that obligation.[53]

The result was a deep fissure of inconsistency in the Whig position. In the same year, for example, that the great Whig industrialist Abbott Lawrence defended public provision of a water supply to Boston on the grounds that a "devotion to the public welfare demands of every citizen, of all men of all kinds, to make this provision for the wants of the whole community," the Whig legislature of Massachusetts rejected legislation for the ten-hour day, preferring to wait for a "progressive improvement in art and science" and "a higher appreciation of man's destiny."[54]

Increasingly, in fact, the Whigs were prepared to shift the responsibility for the maintenance of social harmony away from the purposive political action of men to the impersonal and self-regulating machinery of the economy. Sheer economic prosperity would have to do what men were no longer inclined to. The tariff became the kingpin of Whig economic policy at the federal level and the standard defense of a protective tariff was that it protected and advanced the interests of the working classes. This was not mere hyperbole; for the tariff was the bearer not only of the Whigs' economic hopes but of their social fears. The tariff and the high wages that it would allow were to prevent the American worker from sinking into the degradation of his European counterpart.[55]

A prosperous working class made possible one of the main pillars of Whig belief: that in a developing economy the interests of all men were essentially the same. Over and over Whig publicists asserted that the interests of capital and labor were not opposed, or even that it did not make sense to speak of two camps at all; in the United States there was only a vast variety of "working men." "You and I are children of labor at last," Choate told his audience at the dedication of the Peabody Institute, an adult education foundation directed at working men, and Webster insisted that the whole North consisted of "laboring people." This was an assertion, not of a spurious social equality, but of an over-arching metaphysical unity. Men like Webster or Everett or Choate asserted "we are all laborers" as in an earlier age they might have affirmed "we are all Christians"; whatever the differences in economic or social condition, men were still united on the proper end and conduct of life.[56]

A common commitment to the work ethic, however, proved to have less appeal than a candid invitation to the individual worker to advance himself out of the ranks of labor. In 1840, Thurlow Weed had touted the Whig cause as the party of "Enterprise—of Ambition. Its principles are the steps by which Young Men can alone climb the rugged and difficult ascents of human life" that would raise them from "obscurity . . . poverty, toil and privation" to "worldly excitements" and "ultimate success." By the 1850s this emphasis on social mobility, with its inevitable implications of contempt for the losers in what Lincoln called "the race of life," had become the central idea in Whig economic philosophy, an attitude and idea that was then taken up by the new Republican party. Most Whigs used both kinds of argument indiscriminately with little realization of the logical inconsistency between affirming that the position of labor in the new industrial economy was tolerable because prosperous and *therefore* honorable, and affirming that it was tolerable because there were numerous ways out of it for those with initiative. Few seemed to see how far the metaphor of society as an obstacle course or a race track had taken them from society perceived as a commonwealth.[57]

A major part of Whig intellectual effort was put into this task of domesticating industrialism to America, of converting what had appeared a force of social disruption into a force of social harmony.[58] So committed were the Whigs to the acceptance of this new world that, in spite of their strong belief in the organic nature of society, no native version of "Tory radicalism," or social criticism of industrial society, like that of Carlyle or Ruskin or Disraeli ever developed among them—partly no doubt because the material conditions of labor in the United States were so much better than in England, but perhaps also because in America the available fund of idealism and revolt was captured by the cause of antislavery. The essential complacency of mainstream Whig thought, which so alienated men like Emerson, rests on the fact that, by the 1840s, the Whigs had labelled themselves solidly, as a contributor to the *American Review* proudly proclaimed, "the party of the present," with a vision of the future as only a bigger and richer version of that present.[59]

Choate, certainly, could never have become the American Carlyle, since he embraced enthusiastically the economic developments of the age. At the same time, however, his ideas about society and the state remained far more traditional than those of Thurlow Weed. He apparently had some private doubts about protection as an economic policy, but he defended the tariff vigorously because his party believed it necessary to the development and prosperity of American industry. The burgeoning economic growth fostered by that tariff, however, he defended out of a passionate conviction that it would create a richer and more interesting civilization in the United States. When his ex-student, Parker, was preparing a volume of his speeches, he was particularly anxious that those on the tariff be included, and for his contribution to the *Boston Book* of 1850, he chose an extract from one of these speeches in which he had defended "manufacturing and mechanical industry" as indispensable to "the higher forms of a complete civilization."[60]

Choate was a man who felt very keenly the adventure of commerce and the romance of production, who appreciated the heroic nature of the great material expansion upon which his age was embarked. A clumsy man himself, he had a genuine respect and admiration for people who could create with their hands; *homo faber* appeared to him as man in one of his most splendid aspects. The great tragedy, he said, if industry declined due to lack of protection, would be not so much the loss of money as the inevitable loss of skills, when "the splendid triumphs of mind over matter" were cast aside, like "an old bow, which none of this generation knows how to bend." On his death, his minister summed up this aspect of his character:

> He was, in his own sphere, creator, and he loved things not only for themselves but as creating. The ocean must have its ships and commerce to please him; it must report to him how it fills harbors and estuaries, that he may love it supremely. Nothing was more poetical to him than that which he so often speaks of in his addresses,—"the hum of labor." A mechanic was with him Homeric. The ringing of an anvil, the whirring of a planing machine, the factory bells, and wheels, and looms, were all of them to his mind impersonations of beauty.[61]

Choate never adopted the notion of society as merely the arena for competitive individualism, but, like Lincoln, he felt a healthy respect for the material basis of republican freedom. The American Revolution, he told a Whig gathering, was made "to secure to the workmen of America the work of America." "Freedom is nothing unless you have the means to support it. Is it first liberty and then bread; or is it first bread, and then liberty? *It is bread first!*" He warned the Senate that social stability depended on national prosperity. Without adequate protection, however, "you can have no harmony and no stability; and they would not be worth having if you could. . . . Systems inadequate to the demands, the hopes, the glory, of a free, busy and aspiring people, will not be stable. They ought not to be."[62]

"Free, busy and aspiring" was both Choate's assessment of the American character and his ideal of civilization. In an address on "mental culture," that same year, he included a great encomium to the industrial success of England.

British industry, as a whole, is among the most splendid
and extraordinary things in the history of man. . . . When
you look . . . at that vast body of useful and manly art,
—not directed like the industry of France—the industry
of vanity—to making pier-glasses and air-balloons and
gobelin tapestry and mirrors, to arranging processions
and chiselling silver and twisting gold into filagrees,—
but to clothing the people, to the manufacture of
woolen, cotton, and linen cloth, or railroads and chain-
cables and canals and anchors and achromatic telescopes,
and chronometers to keep the time at sea,—when you
think of the vast aggregate mass of their manufacturing
and mechanical production, which no statistics can express, . . . it is really difficult to restrain our admiration
of such a display of energy, labor, and genius, winning
bloodless and innocent triumphs everywhere, giving to
the age we live in the name of the age of the industry
of the people.[63]

But this was not mere economic success alone. "That same race, side by side with the unparalleled growth of its industry, produces Shakespeare, Milton, Bacon, and Newton," the common law, a great navy and an empire. "Such an industry as that of England demanded such an intellect as that of England." To Choate the lesson of England was that the creative energy of nations must be allowed, encouraged, to proliferate in as many directions as possible. Then the circuit of energy would be self-reinforcing and self-fertilizing. A simple agricultural republic might certainly be virtuous, but the "national mind" would never be stimulated to any soaring heights and the United States would remain an incomplete civilization.[64]

Moreover, the denser texture of an urban, industrial civilization offered the individual greater freedom to expand his own particular talents and escape (as Choate himself had done) from the monotony of rural life. Choate offered to the Senate a parable of a family of five sons: "In some communities they would all become hedgers and ditchers; in others, shore fishermen; in others, hired men in fields, or porters or servants in noblemen's families. But see what the diversified employments of civilization may make of them." One, who has a passion for adventure, goes to sea; another has a taste for trade, "there are Wall-street, and Milk-street, and clerkships and agencies at Manilla, and Canton and Rio Janeiro, for him." A third, who prefers "the fixed habits, the hereditary opinions" of his fathers, carries on the family farm. The fourth early shows signs of an inventive talent. "There may be a Fulton, or an Arkwright; there may be wrapped up the germ of an idea which, realized, shall change the industry of nations, and give a new name to a new era. Well, there are the machine shops at Lowell and Providence for him." The fifth has the "flashing eye" and "beaming brow" of genius and will be either a poet or a scholar—for him there are "traditions, and all the food of the soul."

> And so all the boys are provided for. Every fragment of mind is gathered up. Nothing is lost. The hazel rod, with unfailing potency, points out, separates, and gives to sight every grain of gold in the water and in the sand. Every taste, every faculty, every peculiarity of mental power, finds its task, does it, and is made the better for it.[65]

All this is essentially a gloss on Hamilton's *Report on Manufactures*. But as Nehemiah Adams said of him, "his taking of another man's thoughts was as when the sun plagiarizes the waters, and turns them into showers, and rainbows and gorgeous sunsets." Hamilton's tough call for industrialization as a means to national power becomes in Choate a promise of personal self-fulfillment. The division of labor, the villain of so much romantic thinking in the nineteenth century, is here made to serve the principle of individual flowering.[66]

As late as the 1840s, Whigs still felt that they had to rebut the traditional fear that commerce and industry were not entirely compatible with republican freedom, begetting as they did both luxury and subservience. Speaking to the Senate in April 1844, Choate took up the charge made by Calhoun in 1816 that manufacturing reduced its workers to an unhealthy dependency. On the contrary, he declared, if one viewed the question historically, it was clear that "in all ages and in all nations" manufactures had been "the parents and handmaids of popular liberty." In the states of Renaissance Italy, in the small, late-medieval commercial and manufacturing towns of Northern Europe, where "law, order, self-government, popular liberty, art, taste, and all the fair variety of cultivated things, sprang up together," Choate told the Senate, they would find sufficient evidence that an essentially bourgeois commercial and industrial society could organize itself upon the republican principle of popular self-government.[67]

Moreover, he argued that, in fact, the very circumstances of the lives of urban labor made them peculiarly fitted to be citizens of a republic, since their characteristics as a class impelled them to active and intelligent participation in public affairs.

> Brought together in considerable numbers, and forming part of a still larger urban population in immediate contact; reciprocally acting on, and acted on by, numerous other minds; enjoying every day some time of leisure, and driven by the craving for stimulus which the monotony of their employments, their own mental activity, and all the influences about them, are so well calculated to produce—driven to the search of some external objects of interest, they find these in conversation, in discussion, in reading newspapers and books, in all the topics which agitate the crowded community of which they are part; and thus they become curious, flexible, quick, progressive.[68]

When he spoke of "labor" Choate clearly had in mind the skilled artisans in the shops and small-scale industries which were still dominant in the economy of Boston—men who usually voted Whig. Respectable and self-respecting, attuned to self-improvement and upward mobility, they were a class easily incorporated into the conservative's vision of a liberal republic. The *"juste milieu"* that Choate had proposed to Lieber was to be a "Liberty and Labor party." It was not this class of people whom the Whigs feared, but people who might drop through the net entirely and remain sullen and alienated, altogether outside of the *res publica*. It was necessary to the American theory of government, declared the *American Review,* that constant political discussion and even a certain "wholesome excitement" should be kept up. It was only when this continuous drawing of the people into the political process lapsed that voting became not "an expression of opinion, but of passion, feeling, or blind prejudice, or simply the dictation of demagogues." Choate could never have spoken with approval, as Burke did, of the people as "great cattle," immovable and silent, chewing the cud under the shadow of the oak.[69]

Choate's conservatism, unlike Burke's and unlike that of some modern conservatives, indeed, was not based on any nostalgia for a stable rural society dominated by a landed aristocracy.[70] Though his thought was saturated with the philosophy of Burke, that philosophy and that language were combined in his mind with an essentially classical republicanism. Many Whigs delighted to trace American liberty back to Magna Carta, or even, like George Perkins Marsh, back to the ancient "Goths" and the Teutonic forests, but Choate saw American institutions and liberty as stemming from other sources: out of Athens by way of Geneva.[71]

The freedom of America was not a racial inheritance but an intellectual appropriation. In a widely publicized address before the New England society of New York in 1843, he described how the Puritan exiles in Geneva had conceived a "dream of republican liberty." Readers of "Aristotle and Thucydides and Cicero," they already had "the idea of a commonwealth," but in Geneva they saw the problem solved: "Popular government was possible. The ancient prudence and the modern, the noble and free genius of the old Paganism and the Christianity of the Reformation, law and liberty, might be harmoniously blended in living systems." In Geneva, said Choate, in a phrase that gained considerable vogue, "there was a state without king, or nobles; there was a church without a bishop"; there the Puritans found "a people governed by grave magistrates which it had selected, and equal laws which it had framed."[72]

English freedom was essentially feudal; it rested upon inequality and hierarchy; a limited monarchy "overhung and shaded by the imposing architecture of great antagonistic elements of the state."

> Such was not the form of liberty which our fathers brought with them . . . it was republican freedom, as perfect the moment they stepped on the rock as it is to-day. It had not been all born in the woods of Germany; by the Elbe or Eyder; or the plains of Runnymede. It was the child of other climes and days. It sprang to life

in Greece. It gilded next the early and the middle age of Italy. It then reposed in the hallowed breast of the Alps. It descended at length on the iron-bound coast of New England, and set the stars of glory there.[73]

This tradition of republican freedom was based not on popular passivity but on public participation, tempered by self-imposed restraint and self-discipline. It assumed a people willing to follow the leadership of the "best men" in the sense of an aristocracy of character and talent rather than birth. It was founded on loyalty to institutions and assumed that these could be maintained without dependence on a social hierarchy. It depended, above all, on an enlightened public spirit to always put the public good ahead of private interest or passion. Ultimately it was grounded in those qualities of the people that it also fostered: their sobriety, energy, and integrity, their "virtue."

As J. G. A. Pocock has recently shown, this civic humanism was in the mainstream of Western political thinking from the fifteenth through to the eighteenth centuries and in its English Whig incarnation formed the political culture of the American colonies. Every university-educated man, too, would have imbibed the tradition at its classical source in Aristotle.[74] One of the more radical developments of the American Revolution, however, as Gordon Wood has demonstrated, was the gradual departure from this major stream of Western political thought. The framers of the federal constitution thought they had devised a system of government which would insure the republican goods of liberty and justice, while bypassing the need for republican virtue; the mere balancing of interests would achieve a rough approximation of the common good.[75]

By the early nineteenth century, however, men of conservative disposition were no longer confident that a mere science of government, mere institutions, or a politics of conflicting interests were sufficient to maintain a just and stable society—or indeed, even to maintain an organized society in being at all. "What are formal compacts, what is self-government, what are majorities of wills, taken as foundations of civil order?" demanded Horace Bushnell, summing up a nagging conservative anxiety, "What stronger bond in these to hold a community, than in those recent compacts made to share the gold of our Western Ophir—all dissolved as by a breath of air, the moment the adventurers touch the shore?"[76] The security of civil order must rest on some deeper foundation. To a certain extent this foundation could be supplied by material prosperity; plenty was the peculiar "virtue" of the American continent that made democracy compatible with republican institutions and the sanctity of property. Yet prosperity also brought the spectre of enervation and decadence, or that arrogant impatience of restraint that Webster had compared to "the steed full of the pasture." Increasingly, Whigs turned back to the idea that only the character of the people, certain essential traits, either natural or acquired, could provide a secure foundation for a stable republic. Throughout the ante-bellum period much anxious Whig thought was devoted to discovering some modern equivalent to "Virtue."[77]

Yet there were considerable difficulties in preserving this quality in the nineteenth century. For one thing, in its Anglo-American incarnation the tradition had equated virtue with the possession of freehold land, a possession which guaranteed the autonomy of the individual and kept him free from client-like dependence on other people or the government. In the modern world, this kind of autonomy was increasingly less possible. In spite of Choate's efforts to find the urban working man particularly suited for citizenship, the fact remained that neither he, nor the business community which employed him, could be virtuous in this traditional sense. Further, in an age in which economic development and diversification both increasingly differentiated the ideas and interests of the individual from those of others and offered him unprecedented opportunities to maximize his own personal satisfactions, the temptation to prefer private to public good, or merely to retire into a private world and renounce any obligation or responsibility for the larger whole, was overwhelming. But once the wider community came to be seen either as an irrelevance or an intolerable restraint upon personal freedom, then the republic in its traditional sense, it seemed to Choate and men like him, was no longer possible: it must succumb either to anarchy or Caesarism. The American people had already shown a deplorable lack of virtue in deserting "the wise and the good" in favor of Andrew Jackson and Martin Van Buren. Indeed, to the overheated Whig imagination, the Democratic mode of politics as founded by Andrew Jackson had already subverted the complicated participation of all men according to their different qualities into the simple government of what Choate liked to call "a flushed majority and a Presidential Veto."[78]

The traditional fear about loss of virtue among the people was compounded by the particular anxieties of the nineteenth century. One of the most striking aspects of much nineteenth-century Western thinking, both on the Left and the Right, is its poignant sense of loss: loss experienced as separation—from God, from the self, in particular from the community of fellow men—so that the Golden Age inevitably took the form of *Gemeinschaft.* Once the traditional order of the West had been broken down by the impact of the industrial and French revolutions, men were made aware of society as problematic. Once the analytical intellect was turned upon the social ties binding man to man they were revealed as frighteningly insubstantial. The eighteenth century could cheerfully reduce the state to a contract made by independent individuals acting out of enlightened self-interest because they still moved, in fact, in societies in which traditional pieties, deference and notions of civility operated to preserve a day-to-day acceptance of social norms. Men of the nineteenth century no longer felt themselves in that secure position. They were acutely aware of living in an age of disassociation and disaffiliation, of being poised always on the edge of dissolution. "The social sentiments are weak," wrote Emerson, "the sentiment of patriotism is weak; veneration is low. . . . The association of the time is accidental and momentary and hypocritical, the detachment intrinsic and progressive."[79]

Loss of virtue, in the sense of the vital spirit in the people which maintains a free society in being, thus took on a double aspect. On the one hand, it was seen in traditional terms as the particular corruption that takes place when one contributing part of the republic oversteps its proper boundaries and aggregates excessive power to itself at the expense of justice. In the case of democratic America the main danger came from the people, who seemed less and less disposed to follow the lead of the wise and the good and instead constituted themselves a "flushed majority." On the other hand, it was perceived as a loss of connection that left the individual incapable of feeling that his fate was communal —that there *was* a common good. For Choate and his fellow conservatives, then, the restoration of virtue was a twofold process. It meant persuading the people to refrain from using the full power of a numerical majority, to voluntarily assume the yoke of self-restraint; it also meant somehow repairing the severed synapses, awakening in the hearts of individuals a perception of themselves as part of a whole, and rebinding the emancipated individual into the collective.[80]

Across the Atlantic, John Stuart Mill, deploring the "moral anarchy and unsettledness, which we have witnessed and are witnessing," credited the conservative thinkers of the "Germano-Coleridgian school" with being the first to concern themselves with discovering the "essential principles of all permanent forms of social existence." What the nineteenth century learnt from German social philosophers such as Herder, as well as from Coleridge and Burke, was the importance of affective factors in the creation and maintenance of society; that, quite apart from the utility of the state and the protection it gave to individuals, people were bound into society and to each other by a complex web of memory, affection, identification, shared symbols and patterns of meaning and sympathy, and that these, though difficult to express, were the essential ligaments of nations.[81] Mill listed as the three principal conditions of free but stable polities: first, "a system of *education,* beginning with infancy and continued through life, of which . . . one main and incessant ingredient was *restraining discipline;* second, the existence of "the feeling of allegiance, or loyalty . . . its essence is always the same, viz. that there be in the constitution of the State *something* which is settled, something permanent, and not to be called in question"; third, "a strong and active principle of cohesion . . . a principle of sympathy, not of hostility; of union, not of separation . . . a feeling of common interest." What is notable here is that Mill hinges the health of the state upon essentially subjective qualities. What the seventeenth and eighteenth centuries had worked out as a sociology of virtue, the nineteenth century transformed into a *psychology* of virtue. In an increasingly industrial and urban world of great social mobility and also great social and economic inequality, virtue apparently could no longer be grounded in objective and stable socio-economic conditions. It could only rest in habits and dispositions of mind, on the proper emotional attachments, on "feeling right." In the very widest sense of that word, therefore, the maintenance of virtue became a problem of education.[82]

When the Whigs tried to express the quality of mind that, in the circumstances of modern America, must form the heart of virtue, the word that emerged most frequently was "reverence." An education for virtue now seemed to depend above all on inculcating in the American people a spirit of reverence towards their institutions and the state in general. This was the necessary counterpart to deference towards "natural" superiors and leaders; both reverence and deference were a willing, and neither servile nor irrational, submission to authority. The temper of the times, however, from transcendental individualism, and radical abolitionism, to sheer mob violence, seemed increasingly disposed to ignore or contemptuously reject the normal institutional forms for public action.[83]

To the conservative, the formal structure of society is of fundamental importance; it is in the stability of its institutional forms that the continuity of society subsists, for they are the vehicle by which patterns of behavior are transmitted from generation to generation. Through them the forces of change are assimilated and domesticated, allowing society to retain its identity while undergoing sometimes quite drastic transformation. It is through participation in these institutional forms that the individual is tied in to the wider society. "Simply to 'go through the forms,' " as Allen Guttmann points out, "is to acknowledge, however reluctantly, one's place in a social system, one's role in the institutional drama." Conservatives doubted that shattering the embodying institution freed the spirit. "Form is throughout the Universe the necessary condition of every spiritual manifestation," said the Whig educator, C. S. Henry.

> The moral life of a nation is displayed and seen and felt only in its forms. . . . When the people cease to reverence the institutions and persons which embody and represent the ideas of Justice, Law and Public Order, it is but a short step to cease to reverence the ideas themselves. With the decay of reverence for the forms, dies out also the reverence for the substance.

In this crisis of legitimacy, Whig orators geared themselves to reinstate among their errant countryman the established norms of human society.[84]

This was not an easy task; "the youth of our country and the stern genius of utility, by whose iron sceptre we are swayed," complained Choate's friend, George Hillard, on the Fourth of July, were hardly favorable to "unbought, spontaneous reverence." Yet the cold calculation of mere utility seemed an impossibly fragile foundation on which to base national institutions. In one of his most important speeches, delivered to the law school at Cambridge soon after leaving the Senate, Choate diagnosed what seemed to him the fatal disease of modern societies. There seemed to be growing in the general mind "a singularly inadequate idea of the State as an unchangeable, indestructible and, speaking after the manner of men, an immortal thing.

> The tendency appears to be, to regard the whole concern
> as an association altogether at will, and at the will of
> everybody. Its boundary lines, its constituent numbers,
> its physical, social, and constitutional identity, its polity,
> its law, its continuance for ages, its dissolution, all these
> seem to be held in the nature of so many open questions
> ... it might almost seem to be growing to be our national
> humor to hold ourselves free at every instant, to be and
> do just what we please, go where we please, stay as long
> as we please and no longer; and that the State itself were
> held to be no more than an encampment of tents on the
> great prairie, pitched at sun-down, and struck to the
> sharp crack of the rifle next morning.

It was one of their highest duties, Choate told the fledgling lawyers, to "keep the true idea of the State alive and germinant in the American mind," "to keep alive the sacred sentiments of obedience and reverence and justice."[85]

The kind of *pietas* that Choate had in mind demanded that the individual regard the state as greater than himself but not antagonistic to his hopes and interests, awe-inspiring but not terrifying, outside himself but not alien. The most appropriate imagery to express this idea of the state seemed to be found in the language of architecture. The eighteenth century had spoken of the state in terms of machinery, but the exemplary machine to men of that period had been the clock, a model of precision and regularity; to the nineteenth century, whose image of machinery was the steam engine, the machine meant primarily power. It was now the enemies of the state who used the language of mechanism: "let your life be a counter-friction to stop the machine," advised Thoreau. Nor was the pastoral imagery of the cultivated garden appropriate for a party committed to factories and railroads. The imagery of building, however, suggested vividly the ideas of permanence and stability with grandeur, but, unlike organic metaphors, did not include the inevitable implications of decline and death. Institutions, like buildings, were the work of men, but they existed beyond them to accommodate succeeding generations.[86]

Instead of the migrant camp, Choate offered the image of the state as a stately home—a "structure, stately and eternal, in which the generations may come, one after another, to the great gift of this social life." It was their relationship to this structure which prevented the generations of men from being mere "successive flights of summer flies, without relations to the past or duties to the future," and made them feel instead that all, "all the dead, the living, the unborn—were one moral person,—one for action, one for suffering, one for responsibility,—that the engagements of one age may bind the conscience of another; the glory or the shame of a day may brighten or stain the current of a thousand years of continuous national being." They constituted in themselves a "House."[87]

The metaphor was perhaps not an entirely happy one for a nation that, as a contributor to the *American Review* complained, pulled down its houses as fast as it built them, but it did convey Choate's intention that the individual must learn to feel towards the state that instinctive affection and respect one feels towards an ancestral home. As James Boulton has pointed out in his discussion of Burke's language, the imagery is not a mere ornament to the argument; it is in itself the argument, the image contains within it a whole philosophy of the relationship between the individual and the state. What Choate was helping to create, in his function as democratic orator, was a public symbolic structure within which individuals could think about their political relationships with one another, an indication of the way in which the state should be apprehended, a "unit of feeling."[88]

"The disposition to be conservative," as Michael Oakeshott has remarked, "asserts itself where there is much to be enjoyed." Choate cannot be described as a happy man, but he had a considerable capacity for pleasure, particularly the kind of pleasure offered by a rich and settled civilization. He wished to communicate to his listeners this sense of present enjoyment as the emotional basis from which they should think about politics; to the idea of the state as a home he explicitly linked "all the warm, precious, and multifarious interests of the social life," "all that attracts us to life, all that is charming in the perfected and adorned social nature." He wished the individual to feel that the institutions of his country were there as an arena for the exercise of his talents, or at least a benevolent protection of them. Twenty-five years earlier in his valedictory address at Dartmouth he had rejoiced that "we have a country whose institutions will guard our infirmity, and reward our strength, and allow our characters to expand beneath them, in all the fulness of perfection that belongs to the condition of humanity." Now he reiterated the idea that the state was essentially one great educational institution, existing not so much to compel man as to humanize him, what Herder called *"Bildung."* They must remember, he told the lawyers, that the immortal state "was designed by the Infinite Wisdom, to enable the generation who framed it, and all the generations, to perfect their social, moral, and religious nature; to do and to be good; to pursue happiness; to be fitted, by the various discipline of the social life, by obedience, by worship, for the life to come."[89]

For Choate, the loss of this filial affection produced an internal corruption more deadly than any external calamity. What had ultimately destroyed the democracies of ancient Greece was not Philip of Macedon but "that diseased universal opinion, those tumultuous and fraudulent practical politics . . . which dethroned the reason of the State, . . . and set up instead, for rule, the passion, ferocity, and caprice, and cupidity, and fraud of a *flushed majority* cheated and guided by sycophants and demagogues." The fate of the American republic depended ultimately upon the emotions and attitudes that the American people brought to their role as citizens, for "a nation, a national existence, a national history, is nothing but a production, nothing but an exponent, of a national mind . . . and so the dying of a nation begins in the heart."[90]

So the heart must be schooled; not only in reverence but in what Mill called one of the necessary principles of social stability, a principle "of sympathy . . . of union . . . of common interest." In the modern world this meant a feeling of national identity, a loyalty to a community much wider than the immediate community of the individual's experience and one that, in an increasingly mobile world, would continue to give support and meaning when local and traditional ties were abandoned or disintegrated. That astute student of nationalism, Francis Lieber, recognized the function of nationalism in both providing the modern individual with a communal identification and in rescuing him from being submerged in the mass. "It is the general *anxiety* of man to be an individual," he wrote, "and to individualize everything around him. . . . We must single out one country . . . to call ours. The sound, 'My country,' is so delicious—'my home,' 'my garden'—because we feel rescued from vague generality, stabilitated; we see our *humanity* reflected."[91] A consciousness of national identification, therefore, was part of *Bildung,* part of the transformation of man into citizen.

In the United States, however, men were continually reminded of the weakness of national sentiments when challenged by sectional interests. Choate always thought of American nationality as something that had to be consciously and continuously *willed* into existence, but he knew, as a student of Jonathan Edwards, that the will is passionate and responds primarily to the reason of the heart and the heart, as Hawthorne said, is "the great conservative." The conscious will to national unity and identity must be bolstered by a net of sentiments and associations that would eventually constitute a great well of social instinct from which the will could draw its strength and motive.[92]

The oration that first brought Choate widespread notice as a public speaker was an address in Salem in 1833 in which he called for American Walter Scotts to immortalize the Revolutionary and pre-Revolutionary history of America in a series of historical romances. The nullification crisis through which the nation had just passed seemed to show how lightly the yoke of union was borne, how shallow were the roots of national unity. To deepen those roots Choate offered his conception of a great body of romantic literature about the American past. Such a literature "might do *something* to perpetuate the Union itself"; it "would be a common property of all the States,—a treasure of common ancestral recollections,—more noble and richer than our thousand million acres of public land; and, unlike that land, it would be indivisible. It would be as the opening of a great fountain for the healing of the nations. . . . Reminded of our fathers, we should remember that we are brethren."[93]

Still, nationalism is not necessarily a conservative force. The editor of the *Democratic Review*, for example, also believed in "nationality," and in a famous editorial offered a particular version of national identity linked to the expansive and the sublime.

> The expansive future is our arena. We are entering on its untrodden space with the truth of God in our minds, beneficient objects in our hearts, and with a clear conscience unsullied by the past. We are the nation of human progress and who will, what can, set limits on our onward march? . . . the far-reaching, the boundless future will be the era of American greatness.[94]

To Whigs like Choate, who did not respond emotionally to the appeal of "untrodden space," who valued "limits" and distrusted "boundlessness," who even perhaps realized the destructive potential of that "clear conscience," this was not the kind of national feeling they wished to foster. To Choate, fraternity must be tied, not to an orgiastic commitment to an expansive and open-ended future, but to a filial relationship to the past: thus nationality and reverence would reinforce each other.

One of the results of the blending of Burkean conservatism with classical republicanism was a transformation in the value given to time. By conceiving of the state as a partnership of generations in the progressive development of civilization, Burke had transmuted time from the dangerous element which threatened corruption to *the* necessary dimension in which the state must have its being. What Coleridge called the "Idea" of the state unfolded itself in time, seen as both unified and progressive. A temporal continuity was now seen as necessary to the health of the state. This temporal continuity embodied itself in institutions that should be both strong and flexible, but it must also be present as a psychological factor in the minds of the present generation. Institutions could not really survive without the emotional assent of the people and this in turn depended upon a vivid awareness in present minds of past ancestors and future progeny. "And yet is the past nothing," Choate told an audience at the New England Society of New York,

> even our past, but as you, quickened by its examples, instructed by its experience, warned by its voices, as-

sisted by its accumulated instrumentality, shall repro-
duce it in the life of today. . . . 'The sleeping and the dead
are but as pictures.' Yet, gazing on these, long and in-
tently and often, we may pass into the likeness of the
departed,—may emulate their labors, and partake of
their immortality.[95]

American conservatives, however, were convinced that this
essential consciousness was disappearing. They, like Tocqueville,
were obsessed with the idea that "the track of generations" was
being effaced, that "those who went before are soon forgotten; of
those who will come after, no one has any idea . . . not only does
democracy make every man forget his ancestors, but it hides his
descendants and separates his contemporaries from him; it throws
him back forever upon himself alone and threatens in the end to
confine him entirely within the solitude of his own heart." Tran-
scendentalists like Emerson might find this alienation from all but
the Infinite invigorating, but to men of less robust temperament,
it meant the dissolution of one of the most necessary yet easily
borne restraints upon man—his consciousness of being emeshed
in a network of generations. To the conservative, then, one of the
most essential tasks in America was to reconnect these severed
links and bring a hallowed past vividly to the mind of the present.[96]

Lieber recommended the study of history because "it makes
us conscious that we belong to a great union of beings, existing
for important purposes." Choate lauded the value of history in the
same political terms:

> History teaches us to appreciate and cherish this good
> land, these free forms of government, this pure worship
> of the conscience, these schools of popular learning, by
> reminding us through how much tribulation, not our
> own, but others, these best gifts of God to man have
> been secured to us. It corrects the cold selfishness which
> would regard ourselves, our day, and our generation, as
> a separate and insulated portion of man and time; and,
> awakening our sympathies for those who have gone be-
> fore, it makes us mindful, also, of those who are to
> follow, and thus binds us to our fathers and to our poster-
> ity by a lengthening and golden cord. It helps us to

realize the serene and august presence and paramount claims of our country, and swells the deep and full flood of American feeling.[97]

But the past was no longer naturally present as a living reality in contemporary minds—it had to be created. And Americans, more particularly New Englanders, enthusiastically went about the task of stocking the national mind with suitable memories. As George Calcott has pointed out, in the ante-bellum period an "extraordinary portion of the nation's creative energy went into writing history, but equally important was the sudden prominence of history in the schools, the rise of historical societies, the movement for preservation of historical sites and documents, the fashion for genealogy, and the prominence of historical themes in architecture, painting, sculpture, the theatre, fiction, poetry and oratory. America was finding its identity in history." And America was also finding its legitimacy, for the historical writing and compiling of the age was designed to show how the present had necessarily developed from the past and thus took on the character less of a critical inquiry than a sacred and affirmative myth.[98]

A sacred past which must be available to the sense and emotions of the whole people needed not only its books but its iconography, and Americans busily set about supplying visible memorials of the great men and moments of the country's history—to begin to create what Henry James called a "visitable past." Choate's generation, who had been educated on the critical theories of Lord Kames and Archibald Alison, knew that the American landscape lacked those *human* associations of heroism, pathos, terror, that moved the memory and the imagination and thus made it worthy of emotional response. "I am *rebuked* at finding that the great treatises on Will and Sin were not written at West Stockbridge, after all," wrote Choate whimsically to his youngest daughter, after returning from an expedition to see Jonathan Edwards' house. "How still and studious looked West Stockbridge —and now what a poor, little, half-starved saw-mill of a situation it is!" Choate might make light of it, but the fact remained that not only was the American landscape unpicturesque, more importantly it was *unpolitical*. The moral emotions induced by the sublime in nature were quite unspecific; the Whigs wanted palpable explicit mementos of social and political virtue. "O! let us build monuments to the past," exclaimed Job Durfee, the Chief Justice of Rhode Island. "Thus shall the past be made to stand out in monumental history, that may be seen by the eye and touched by the hand. Thus shall it be made to subsist to the senses."[99]

It was in an appeal to the senses that Choate saw the value of the historical romance. The "grave narrative . . . of Marshall, Pitkin, Holmes and Ramsay," had recorded the essential features of early American history for the educated mind, but, said Choate at Salem, "I should love to see it assume a form in which it should speak directly to the heart and affections and imagination of the whole people." When it came to a popular appreciation of the Puritans in particular, something was "wanting yet to give to their character and fortunes a warm, quick interest, a charm for the feelings and imagination, an abiding-place in the heart and memory and affections." The new Scott would remedy this defect by his picturesque descriptions of the landscape and his moving portrayal of the "toil and privation, of wearisome days and sleepless nights, of serious aims, grave duties, and hope deferred without making the heart sick."

The romantic novelist had a further advantage over the historian: he could be more selective in his choice of subjects. Knowing that not everything is inspirational to be remembered, "he remembers that it is an heroic age to whose contemplation he would turn us back; and as no man is a hero to his servant, so no age is heroic of which the whole truth is recorded." The Scott tradition of *vraisemblance* overlaid a rich, satisfying texture of accurate detail upon a story designed to illustrate those moral verities that sober men regarded as eternal. The American Waverley novels would have to exclude those aspects of the past that might provoke irritation or lead the reader into questioning rather than contemplation. Choate would have excluded from the romance of the Puritans precisely those people and events that have most fascinated modern historians—specifically, "the controversies with Roger Williams and Mrs. Hutchinson."[100]

Essentially, the historical romance would do for the Puritan forefathers what the image of the house did for the state: tie them to the emotions of the present as worthy not merely of awe but also of a certain protective tenderness, making one more emotional bond between the individual and the total society, consisting of past and future as well as present, as he realized his own indebted place in the chain of human suffering and sacrifice. In fact, the emotionalism that was repressed by so many aspects of contemporary New England life could well up in a quite remarkable way in response to the pathos of the past. When Choate gave an address to the New England Society of New York in 1843, "The Age of the Pilgrims: The Heroic Period of Our History," he reduced his entire audience, including Daniel Webster, to tears. According to an eyewitness, after leading his audience through the rise of Puritanism, to the landing of the *Mayflower,* to the many deaths in the first hard winter, Choate paused and

> . . . with a sad, far-off look in his eyes, as if the vision had suddenly risen upon his memory, and with a voice inexpressibly sweet and pathetic, and nearly choked with emotion, he said: "In a late visit to Plymouth I sought the spot where those earlier dead were buried. It was on a bank somewhat elevated, near, fronting, and looking upon the waves—symbol of what life had been to them; ascending inland behind and above the rock—symbol also of that Rock of Ages on which the dying had rested in that final hour."
>
> I have never seen an audience so moved. . . . As Choate approached the climax, Webster's emotion became uncontrollable; the great eyes were filled with tears, the great frame shook; he bowed his head to conceal his face in his hat, and I almost seemed to hear his sob. The audience was flooded with tears, a handkerchief at every face; and sighs and sobs soughed through the house, like wind in the tree-tops. The genius of the orator had transferred us to the spot; and we saw the rocky shore, and with him mourned the early dead.

The past, seen thus through a haze of tears, could hardly be regarded as a "dead hand" to be thrown off, a mere record of vice and folly to be repudiated.[101]

Burke had praised the English capacity of "always acting as if in the presence of canonized forefathers." This was exactly the same pattern that the Whigs wished to inculcate in America. George Washington, of course, was the great admonitory father figure, but in fact, with the Pilgrim Fathers and the Founding Fathers, the United States had a rather large supply of hallowed parental figures, who, if their presence could only be preserved vividly enough in the imagination of their descendants, would presumably prevent the sons from kicking over the traces. The great advantage of the history of the Revolutionary period was that it depicted a time when North and South had worked together towards a common goal and was thus an antidote to sectionalism. From the point of view of the New England Whigs, however, the Puritan founders of New England were even more suitable objects of veneration than the Revolutionary generation. The advantage of the Puritans as *the* "authentic race of founders" was not only that they emphasized the centrality of New England in the identity of the United States but that they seemed to their descendants particularly rugged examples of republican virtue. The attraction of the Puritans was that, having moved beyond the sphere of established, overt authority, they had voluntarily submitted themselves to a sterner, self-imposed discipline. They combined, as Choate told the New England Society, "the loftiest sense of duty" with the "fiercest spirit of liberty."[102]

As national heroes, indeed, the Puritans presented a direct opposite to the frontiersman. Speakers at the New England Society or at Pilgrim Society celebrations never tired of extolling the particular quality that made them such desirable exemplars: "their love of order and their submission to those just restraints whereby society is held together," their exercise of "the severe and restrictive virtues," their "reverence for authority, a stern sense of order, the submission of the one to the many, a horror of insubordination, and faith in elders and magistrates." The distinguished lawyer, William Evarts, summed up the burden of numerous orations when he told the New England Society in 1854 that for the Pilgrim fathers liberty was never an end in itself, but merely a means to *duty*. "Emancipation from existing authority they sought only to subject themselves to a more thorough discipline; loyalty to a ruler they replaced by obedience to law; they threw off the yoke of their king only to pursue the stricter service of their God."[103]

The Puritan foundation of New England was to Choate the true "Heroic Age" of America. An heroic age, he told the New England Society, in the sense of an age "the course of whose history and the traits of whose character, and the extent and permanence of whose influences, are of a kind and power not merely to be recognized in after time as respectable or useful, but of a kind and a power to kindle and feed the moral imagination . . . an age far off, on whose moral landscape the poet's eye may light . . . an age 'doctrinal and exemplary,' . . . to which the discouraged teachers of patriotism and morality to corrupted and expiring States, may resort for examples how to live and how to die." Above all it was an heroic age because the Puritans had accomplished the greatest of human tasks—they had founded a state: "The planting of a colony in a new world, which may grow, and which does grow, to a great nation where there was none before, is intrinsically, and in the judgment of the world, of the largest order of human achievement. Of the chief of men are the *conditores imperiorum.*"[104]

In a lecture he gave in 1849, "Thoughts on the New England Puritans," Choate followed up this train of thought with a wistfulness that betrayed how far short his own career, and the circumstances in which it had developed, fell from his college dreams of being a "national man." He asked his audience at the Mercantile Library Association to compare the day-to-day life of "an educated public man of Massachusetts about the year 1688—a governor; a magistrate; . . . a foremost man" to a modern counterpart. "And see if you are quite sure that a man of equal ability, prominence, and learning is as high or as happy now."

> First, last, midst, of all the elements of interest in the life of such a man was this: that it was in a just and grand sense, a public life. He was a public man. . . . He was, he felt himself to be—and here lay the felicity of his lot, —he was in the very act of building up a new nation where no nation was before. . . . Instead of being born ignominiously into an established order of things, a recognized and stable State, to the duties of mere conservation, and the rewards of mere enjoyment, his function he felt to be that rarer, more heroical, more epic—to plant, to found, to construct a new State upon the waste of earth. He felt himself to be of the *conditores imperiorum.* . . . Public life in Massachusetts that day did not consist in sending or being sent to Congress with a dozen associates, to be voted down in a body of delegates representing half of North America.

He went on to describe how this "foremost man" in the course of a day might negotiate with other independent states on the subject of boundaries; instruct agents to the court in London; take military decisions with respect to the Indians or the French; communicate with learned judges and learned divines on the state of the law and the state of the Church.[105] Colonial Massachusetts, he seems to have felt, would have offered greater opportunities to a man like himself to have taken a truly directing part in the *polis* than the modern nation in which the public realm no longer unified so many aspects of experience.

In his address at Salem, Choate had suggested that an American *Iliad* and *Odyssey* might come out of the artist's contemplation of colonial New England. Yet clearly for him, and many other Whigs, the true American epic would have to be a modern *Aeneid:* a celebration of the founding of the state. Seen in this light even the westward movement could be assimilated to a conservative vision and be perceived, under the surface aberrations, as the successive reestablishments of order. The meaning of America was essentially political: the voluntary establishment, under conditions of freedom, of legitimate authority.[106]

To shift the essential founding of America back from the still-looming revolutionary generation to the Puritans perhaps gave the post-revolutionary sons more psychic breathing space. Moreover, this emphasis on the Puritan colonial past as *the* heroic and formative period of America naturally meant a certain downplaying of the Revolution itself. Indeed, historical interest in the American past, while turning up more facts and information about the Revolution, also tended increasingly to relegate it to the status of one historical event in a chain of development. As Charles Francis Adams said in the *North American Review* "we are now beginning to regard our whole history, from the settlement of the country to the present time, as but one chain of events, each and every link of which is equally important and equally necessary to the consummation of its grand design." The tendency among educated Americans, when they thought about their own past, to convert history, with its chances, struggles, defeats and paths not taken, into *natural* history, with the inevitable unfolding and development of the mature result from the first tiny seed, inevitably deprived individual events of much decisive importance. "The spirit of the colonies demanded freedom from the beginning" as

Bancroft said, and Whigs added, not only demanded, but *had* freedom from the beginning.[107]

An historical interpretation of the revolution that saw it, not as the creation of something new, but as the 'realization' or firmer establishment of an already existing state, had become a standard Whig doctrine by the 1840s. "Massachusetts was very, very nearly as free before the Revolution as it is now," Josiah Quincy, the President of Harvard, told Tocqueville. "We have put the people's name in place of that of the king. For the rest one finds nothing changed among us." "The revolution was a change of forms, but not of substance; the breaking of a tie, but not the creation of a principle," according to the historian Jared Sparks. At the seventy-fifth anniversary of the battle of Bunker Hill, Edward Everett rejoiced that in the *American* revolution there had been "no convulsion in society, no revolution in those institutions which make up the aggregate of social and political existence." In the same year, the critic Edwin P. Whipple, in a Fourth of July oration, gave a thoroughly Burkean interpretation of the revolution: "it was the peculiar felicity of our position, that free institutions were planted here at the original settlement of the country, . . . and accordingly our Revolution began in the defence of rights which were customs, of ideas which were facts, of liberties which were laws."[108]

This kind of historical "placing" of the revolution both justified it and defused it as a vital force in contemporary life; the Revolution was natural, legitimate—and over. Choate regarded it as a kind of puberty rite, a national coming of age: "The Colonial period, as I regard it," he said in an address of 1834, "was the charmed eventful infancy and youth of our national life. The revolutionary and constitutional age, from 1775 to 1789, was the beginning of its manhood." "The Declaration of Independence, the succeeding conduct of the war of Independence, the establishment of our local and general governments," however, were not new beginnings, but merely "effects, fruits, outward manifestations!" In his address to the law school in 1845, he subsumed the revolution into the whole colonial past as a vitally important, but completed, historical period. "The passage of the sea, the occupation and culture of a new world, the conquest of independence, —these were our eras, these our agency, of reform." The liberal achievements of this long era were now solidly embodied in institutions: "our written constitutions," the judiciary "whose loftiest function it is to test the legislation of the day by this standard for all time," "our jurisprudence of liberty."[109]

The Dorr rebellion of 1842, however, in which the radicals, wrapping themselves in "the sacred mantle of 1776," had overthrown the established government of Rhode Island and attempted to set up a more democratic constitution, revealed to startled conservatives that some people still regarded the revolution as a living guide, rather than an historical event. Choate managed to take the affair coolly: "Rhode Island is going through a kind of ridiculous mimicry of revolutionary excitement," he wrote to Everett in England. "The intervention of the President's letter is felt to be reasonable and will be effective. If she was a great state the thing would be serious, or if she were an independent state, very serious. As it is, it is *tea-pottish*, and yet it exemplifies the grand usefulness of the Union."

Many Whigs, however, were badly shaken and hastened to demonstrate that the Dorr rebellion had nothing in common with the events of 1776. There was nothing in the American Revolution, wrote a heated contributor to the *North American Review*, "which harmonizes with the disorganizing and anarchical theory and practice of the Suffrage party in Rhode Island." If Dorr won in Rhode Island, "the constitution of no State in the union is safe."

> A body of individuals may at any time come together, declare that they are "the people," pull down the whole structure of the government, and put one of their own fashioning in its place. The question, is, therefore, whether we really have a permanent habitation, or are only tenants at will of a crazy building, of which the walls may crumble, and the roof topple down on our heads at any moment.[110]

The conservative opposition to Dorr in Rhode Island had shrewdly called themselves the "Law and Order" party. But this did not oppose it to America's revolutionary heritage, for, increasingly, conservative commentators were stressing the law-abiding and orderly quality of the revolution itself. It had been "the most orderly revolution, that the world has ever witnessed," "all was done decently, and deliberately and legally." It had been a rebellion in defense of law and legality. It was a commonplace to contrast the sober practicality of the American patriots with the doctrinaire and ruthless ideologues of the French Revolution. Choate commended the "sober, rational, and practical views and conduct which distinguished even the first fervid years of the Revolutionary age. How little giddiness, rant and foolery do you see there! No riotous and shouting processions, no grand festivals of the goddess of reason,—no impious dream of human perfectibility—no unloosing of the hoarded-up passions of ages from the restraints of law, order, morality, and religion, such as shamed and frightened away the new-born liberty of revolutionary France." So completely, indeed, had American Whigs managed to identify their own revolution with law and disciplined conduct that, referring to the Dorr rebellion, Abbott Lawrence could exclaim, without a trace of irony, "as long as a drop of Revolutionary blood remains in my veins . . . I am ready to peril my life in defence of law and order."[111]

No American could deny the "great, transcendental" right of revolution, but, Choate told the lawyers,

> I do not know that any wise man would desire to have this theory every day, or ever, acted upon up to its whole extent, or to have it eternally pressed, promulgated, panegyrized as the grand peculiarity and chief privilege of our condition. . . . True wisdom would seem to advise the culture of disposition of rest, contentment, conservation.

Not only was revolution to be banished from the forefront of the American consciousness, even the stimulus of its principles as an impetus to political or social reform would be paradoxically a betrayal of its achievements. "We need reform enough, Heaven knows," Choate told the lawyers, "but it is the reformation of our individual selves, the bettering of our personal natures." America needed to develop its arts, its intellect, its culture, but the framework of its polity was sound and should not be tampered with: "Government, substantially as it is; jurisprudence, substantially as it is; the general arrangements of liberty, substantially as they are; the Constitution and the Union, exactly as they are,—this is to be wise, according to the wisdom of America." In the "actual circumstances" of the United States, "the one grand and comprehensive duty of a thoughtful patriotism" was conservatism.[112]

George M. Fredrickson has pointed out that to many Northerners by the middle of the Civil War "if American 'loyalty' meant anything . . . it meant that the American Revolution was over and the revolutionary ideology had no further application to American society." This attitude, in fact, was pretty firmly established among Northern Whigs by the 1840s. The message of numerous Whig Fourth of July orations was that the Revolution the day celebrated had not been particularly revolutionary and that it was a grand historic event inspiring patriotism and devotion rather than a set of living principles directly applicable to current problems.

None of this meant, of course, that the revolution should be forgotten. It was an aspect of the American past particularly worthy of pious recollection. But it should be remembered for the heroism and self-sacrifice of its soldiers; for the wisdom of its leaders who knew that the proper outcome of revolution is the firmer establishment of government; for its place in a process of developing institutional liberty. Above all, the revolution should be regarded as the birth of American nationality. It was in the struggle for independence that men of the different colonies learnt to regard themselves as one people. The men of Concord and Lexington, said Choate at the seventy-fifth anniversary of the battle of Concord, "went into that battle British colonists; the baptism of fire was laid upon their charmed brows, and they rose from their knees American citizens." And he toasted "the sentiment of American nationality" that "woke to life on the 19th of April, 1775, on the banks of the Concord and on the green of Lexington." The revolution had brought forth a new nation—and had died in giving birth. Fidelity to the revolution then must mean loyalty to its offspring: the nation, its institutions, the Union.[113]

As Whigs contemplated the American experience, they did not find its deepest meaning in a struggle for freedom. Freedom had been present from the beginning, freedom was a "given" of the situation. The struggle in America was, first, against a potentially fruitful but harsh and wild landscape—a battle to break Nature to human purposes—and, second, against the wild and anarchic in human nature. The American struggle was for discipline against the natural propensity of man to strain against the bonds of civil liberty—in an environment in which the siren call of natural liberty was particularly strong. It was the glory of America that—so far—the dangerous goddess of liberty had been domesticated and, like a great river, confined within channels where she could be a productive agent of civilization rather than its destroyer. "American liberty," said Whipple, "is no opinionated, will-strong, untamable passion, bursting all bounds of moral restraint, and hungering after anarchy and license, but a creative and beneficient energy, organizing itself in laws, professions, trades, arts, institutions." In 1889, Woodrow Wilson, commenting on the centennial of the French Revolution and Washington's inauguration, used a revealing phrase: "we *manifested* one hundred years ago," he said, "what Europe *lost,* namely self-command, self-possession."[114] He spoke in the tradition of antebellum Whigs like Rufus Choate, for whom also the stern curb of self-restraint and civic discipline was the only lasting and moral basis for freedom.

THREE

THE SCHOLAR IN THE REPUBLIC

BOUT TO SET OFF to Washington, there to close
in two months, forever, my political life," Choate
noted in his journal in December 1844. His term in the Senate
expired in March 1845 and he had no intention of seeking reelec-
tion. Webster, now readmitted to the Whig fold, was ready to take
up "his" seat in the Senate once again. Choate's term in the Senate
had cut into his career at the Bar without elevating him to a real
position of leadership in politics, or adding, unequivocally, to his
reputation. "No one . . . could do anything in politics of consequence," he told Parker some years later, "except by making it
a deliberate experiment, business, and occupation." And he knew
for certain now that he did not have the qualities or the temperament for that. The American who committed himself to politics,
he went on,

> . . . runs all the risks of being thrown over any moment
> by a fickle and demagogue-blinded people. You have to
> mix for ever with people whom you can't shake off;
> while, you have to *labor* with much more serious and
> brain-taxing themes (if you aspire to the rank of states-
> man, not a mere politician) in Congress than at the Bar.
> At the latter, a man has his side given to him; then he
> labors to sustain it. In politics you have to cast and fore-
> cast from a wider and much more difficult range of con-
> siderations, what side the party shall take; as well as then,
> afterwards, go through the toil of supporting it; and, of
> course, no man of decided abilities wants to go into

politics, except in anticipation of marching on through high steps to great posts.

But he added:

> If I myself could be permanently and happily in the Senate . . . I should like that better than anything in the world; but to be just enough in the Senate to be out of the law and not enough in the Senate to be a leader in politics, is a sort of half-and-half business very contemptible.[1]

"Debate oftener than formerly," Choate reminded himself in his journal at the beginning of his last session in the Senate. "Less preparation is really needful, yet seek one great occasion." He did in fact speak more frequently than before, though, in the case of Texas and the joint admission of Florida and Iowa, with little success. But the "one great occasion" was in a cause close to his heart: the provision of national aid and recognition to American scholarship.[2]

Choate's early dreams of a life devoted to learning had been abandoned even before he left college, but he remained passionately attached to literature and the classics and determined to remain a member, if a silent one, of that republic of letters he had known as a student. He made it a practice to read and translate a few lines of Greek and Latin every day, Thucydides and Homer, Tacitus and Cicero in particular. At the Bar and among his friends, he gained a considerable reputation as a classical scholar. "He never made a false quantity," said Richard Henry Dana, Jr., in eulogy, "who ever detected him in a misquotation?" His readiness and felicity in classical quotation indeed was famous. Once, at a dinner in Washington in which Webster was denouncing the waywardness of "Young America," Choate maintained that practically every age could show similar traits in its young, and trumped his mentor with a quotation from the younger Pliny on Roman youth: " 'From their cradles they know all things, they understand all things; they have no regard for any person whatever, high or low, rich or poor, religious or otherwise, and are themselves the only examples which they are disposed to follow.' " The classical languages were for him the "crowning accomplishment of the individual and the nation." "We are but a vulgar people without such learning," he told his philosopher friend, George Bush.[3]

Like many other of the New England gentry, he was a bibliophile, and by the time of his death his library numbered some seven thousand volumes and had encroached on most of the second story of his house at Winthrop Place. His devotion to books, like his illegible handwriting, became part of the legend that New England loved to weave around its luminaries. Afternoons in Boston were spent at the Athenaeum, until the 1850s, when the pressure of both legal work and public affairs crowded out this indulgence; on Saturday afternoons he would habitually go and buy himself a book as a reward for the week's labors. His own library was his refuge from the world, and his books, said Parker, were "the loves of his life." "Men, he was kind to, but I do not think he trusted men much. But his books he believed in, with all his soul."[4]

Choate read incessantly, almost compulsively—while walking, at meals. Several books would be kept going at the same time and his restless mind could never settle to one for more than short periods, though for that brief time he could sink himself totally in what he read. Every spare five minutes had its appropriate snatch of reading planned so that there would never be a hiatus in which his mind would be allowed to drift unoccupied and without bounds. He tried hard to shape his reading into a mental discipline, for "desultory reading" he regarded as a "waste of life." While still a young lawyer in Salem he had begged George Bush to prescribe for him a regular course of study: "the Punic Wars —the origin of the Doric race—Gustavus Vasa—demonology— prophecy—Mohammed—or what you will." For otherwise, "I drift from book and subject to subject, in the torture of irresolution, of balanced, neutralizing, capricious tastes, cravings, loathings," By the 1840s he had learnt to map out his own course and the fragmentary journals which he kept during these years are full of resolutions and plans for some systematic study which would provide order and structure to his mental life.

> How can I hit on some other field or department of knowledge [besides the law] which I may hope to master; in which I can feel that I am making progress; the collateral and contemporaneous study of which may rest,

refresh and *liberalize* me—yet not leave mere transient impressions, phrases, tincture; but a body of digested truths and an improved understanding, and a superiority to others in useful attainment?[5]

He was continually thinking up "projects." He began a formal translation of Thucydides: "my purpose is to study deeply the Greece of the age of Pericles, and all its warnings to the liberty and the anti-unionisms of my own country and time." He never got more than halfway through Book I, however. His intention to study modern history systematically and reduce it to "a few condensed and comprehensive paragraphs the result of hours and of days' study," or to compose a series of discourses on the development of the American constitution remained merely programs in his journal. The journal itself was part of the discipline. It was not a record of his "life and times," but neither was it a confidant. It has throughout a curiously external, warning quality and consists largely of projects and intentions, records of what he had read, translations and précis, only occasionally accompanied by comments. Choate apparently used his journal essentially as a schoolmaster from whom he received tasks and to whom he recited his lessons:

> With Thucydides I shall read Wachsmuth, with historical references and verifications . . . *W.* especially, I am to meditate and master. Dacier's Horace, Ode 1, 11th to 14th lines, translation and notes,—a pocket edition to be always in pocket. . . .
> Walk an hour before breakfast; morning paper; Johnson and Milton before breakfast. Add, if possible, with notes, an Essay of Bacon also, or a paper of the Spectator, or a page of some other paper of Addison.

Above all, the journal was to be a vindication that time had not been wasted: "something to evince that an acquisition has been made, a hint communicated; a step taken in the culture of the immortal, intellectual, and moral nature."[6]

Choate's literary studies provided not only a more liberal discipline than did the law, they also educated and released his emotions. Literature healed the laceration of spirit inflicted by the daily petty warfare of the courts and of Congress and, most of all, provided emotional release for a high-strung, passionate nature that could not, or would not, find any other outlet. "Literature," he told Parker, "is full of enthusiasm; life is not." He preferred works of large and heroic feeling and commanding language— Shakespeare, Milton, Burke, Coleridge, the Bible. Within this inner world he lived at a level of emotional intensity that, when it errupted in an address to a jury, or a political speech, excited Boston, but made it uneasy.[7]

The violent sick headaches that would incapacitate him before or after a major case or speech were probably psychosomatic in origin, and Parker suspected that Choate sometimes wondered if he might not go mad. Both his wide general reading and his more concentrated studies were, among other things, a form of therapy, a defense against the depression that almost overwhelmed him in the early days in Danvers. One senses that when he spoke in an address of "poor, rich Cowper," who "stayed that fainting reason, and turned back those dark billows that threatened to overwhelm him, by his translation of the Iliad and Odyssey," he was also referring to himself. He was surely speaking personally when he described to a Danvers audience the delights of reading, rather than sleep, as the "true balm of hurt minds," and told of the busy lawyer who, coming home "his temples throbbing, his nerves shattered, from a trial of a week" heals himself in the "still region of delightful studies." "Well may he prize that endeared charm, so effectual and safe, without which the brain had long ago been chilled by paralysis, or set on fire by insanity."[8]

The intellectual life, however, was more than opiate; by the 1840s Choate was learning German with one of his daughters, because "all the new and daring thought and speculation is in the German Mind,"—"*in it move the whole new springs of modern thought,* archaeology, ethnology, and all." He was also seriously thinking of writing a book himself. His friends often urged him to write a history of Greece or of the United States that would give his eloquence and erudition permanent form, but he could never quite bring himself to plunge into the unknown sea of authorship. Sometimes this seems like a deliberate self-denying ordinance: though he told Bush that he considered "a good book and a good sermon to be not only well *per se,* but to be worthy, fitting, and adequate achievements of good minds," he habitually spoke of his own studies as "luxuries," pursued in moments that were "stolen," "snatched," "rescued" from business. It was as though, having once deliberately chosen the life of active business in the world, he felt it would be both frivolous and presumptuous of him to make any major public commitment to anything else.[9]

As he grew older, however, it was harder to forget that a lawyer's fame is transient and that, as he told Parker, "a book . . . is the only immortality." "Political life forever is ended," he noted in his journal in 1850.

> Henceforth the law and literature are all. I *know* it must be so, and I yield and I approve. Some memorial I would leave yet, rescued from the grave of a mere professional man, some wise or beautiful or interesting page,—something of utility to America, which I love more every pulse that beats.

A few months before he died, he said that all he cared about, outside the circle of his friends, was "intellectual labor, with its results of *truth,*" that money, society, and fame meant nothing to him. That he was indifferent to money and society had always been true, but the desire for fame, the intense ambition that had so struck his companions in college, remained a powerful, if hidden, emotion right to the end. During his last few months in the Senate, when he knew that his political career was largely finished, his hopes of glory began to crystallize around the idea of writing a history of Ancient Greece. The project was an ambitious one, an attempt to lay bare the secret of the Greek "mind" and to trace political development to national character; then to apply the lessons drawn to America. To the classically educated Whig, the history of Greece seemed to speak directly to modern America, for it showed the decline of a brilliant civilization brought about by the quarrels of sister states and the excesses of a licentious democracy. The enterprise, Choate noted enthusiastically in his journal,

> would be a vast achievement of scholarship and philosophy and statesmanship. To me, *cogitante saepenumero* on what one such labor I may concentrate moments and efforts else sure to be dissipated and unproductive, this seems to be obviously my reserved task. It is large

enough, and various enough to employ all my leisure, stimulate all my faculties, cultivate all my powers and tastes, and it is seasonable and applicable in the actual condition of these States. He who should perform it adequately would be not merely the best Greek scholar of this country; the best read in one brilliant chapter of the history of man; the most accomplished in one vast department of literature, art, philosophy, fact; but he would have added to his means of counselling the people on the things of their peace. He would have learned more of the uses and dangers of liberty, and the uses and dangers of union.[10]

Back in Boston, in March 1845, he was still serious—"I have but to procure a Niebuhr and Müller"—but the great work was now to be secondary to the serious business of life: "all this is to be held in strictest subordination to law and business. It is to be relaxation and recreation strictly, yet is it to improve style, reason, taste, and habits of research." He did not formally abandon the project until the appearance of Grote's *History of Greece* in 1846, but by then it had slipped away from the center of his attention —even though he lived in a city that took literature seriously and accepted the literary life as something proper, manly, and broadly useful to the republic. His problem was partly financial: he had no income except what he made in his profession. His basic difficulty, however, seems to have been a personal ambivalence, an unwillingness to risk his reputation in new territory, or to risk his mind in a field which did not provide the constant external discipline of the courts. "I might seize the time," he said to Parker, "but I can't get *my mind into the frame to compose.* When I come home, even if I have an hour or two to spare, my mind is torn to pieces by the jar of the day, and I cannot do more than get in the mood for composition when I find my time is up."[11]

Still, he could not escape the nagging awareness that he had not fulfilled his earlier promise, nor could he regard life as an aesthetic experience in which self-culture was an end in itself. He was haunted—as were so many of his contemporaries—by the notion of time as an aggregate of separate moments, all equal in value, so that one moment lost or misused could never be recouped by heightened intensity in another, and by the ever oppressive need to justify one's life, no longer to God through faith, but to posterity through production. "Thus far," he chided himself in his journal,

> I have squandered these moments away. They have gone —not in pleasure, nor the pursuit of gain, nor in the trivialities of society—but in desultory reading . . . without method and without results. No doubt taste has been improved, sentiments enlarged, language heightened, and many of the effects of liberal culture, impressed on the spirit. But for all this, who is better? Of all this, who sees the proofs? How selfish and how narrow the couch of these gratifications! How idle the strenuousness of daily labor! How instantly the air will close on this arrowy path! How sad, how contemptible, that no more should be satisfied, on this side and that! . . . I would arrest these moments, accumulate them, transform them into days and years of remembrance![12]

His plan this time was to compose a series of papers—called, significantly, *"Vacations"*—on various topics: Demosthenes, the *Odyssey*, Cicero and Burke, the conservatism of the Bar, "the literature of this century, to the death of Scott or Moore—so grand, rich and passionate." Though some of these topics eventually became the subjects of public speeches and lectures, all that emerged of the proposed volume was a preface, explaining that the papers had been written in the "half-hours before breakfast, or after dinner, Saturdays at evening, intervals between the going out of one client and the coming in of another . . . snatches and interstitial spaces" that were the only vacations of the American lawyer. He offered them to the public so that "others should know that the time which I have withheld from society, from the pursuit of wealth, from pleasure, and latterly from public affairs, has not been idle or misspent; *non otiosa vita; nec desidiosa occupatio.*"[13]

Choate's personal involvement with literature spilled over into a political concern for the relationship between the state and the intellectual life. He shared fully the Whig faith in popular education as a necessary safeguard for property and order in a democratic society. In an address entitled "The Power of a State Developed by Mental Culture," delivered before the Boston Mercantile Library Association in 1844, he urged his audience to maintain the state's financial commitment to the development of public education. "You have a great deal of money. The world never saw such a provision for popular and higher education as you could make in a year in Massachusetts, and not feel it." He referred them to Horace Mann's fifth report to the Board Of Education in which he had demonstrated the "cash value" of education in terms of increased worker efficiency, and added:

> You speak of tariffs to protect your industry. . . . You cannot lay a tariff under the Constitution, and you cannot compel Congress to do so; but you can try to rear a class of working-men who may help you to do something without one. . . . Are you sure that if everybody,—*every mind,* I should say,—which turns a wheel or makes a pin in this great workshop of ours, all full from basement to attic with the various hum of free labor, was educated to the utmost degree compatible with his place in life,— that this alone would not be equal to at least a uniform duty of about twenty-eight per cent ad valorem, all on the home value?

Massachusetts, moreover, would have increasingly to depend upon "mental power" at the highest level, for the weight of numbers and of power was swinging to the West. This address was delivered just a few days after the Whig defeat to the expansionist Polk in the elections of 1844. Polk's triumph seemed to signal the further decline of New England in national influence, unless it could become the intellectual power house of America and the primary directing influence in forming the national "mind." "Suppose," he invited his audience,

> the school-boy boast could be achieved, and you were the Athens of America; suppose the libraries, the schools, the teachers, the scholars, were here, the galleries of art, the subtle thinkers, the weavers of systems, the laurelled brow. . . . Knowledge is power as well as fame. . . . Think of that subtle, all-embracing, plastic, mysterious, irresistible thing called public opinion, the god of this lower world, and consider what a State, or a cluster of States, of marked and acknowledged literary and intellectual lead might do to color and shape that opinion

to their will . . . He who guides public opinion moves the hand that moves the world![14]

Choate's faith in education, however, was not merely prudential and economic. If the state was indeed a great institution for the progressive "humanization" of man, then part of its duty towards him was to provide him with the means to develop every faculty and capacity to the fullest. Any truly enlightened nation should foster not merely elementary schooling but the institutions—libraries, lyceums, universities, institutes, museums, art galleries—that would enable the citizen to enlarge his mind throughout his life. He had felt in his own life the constricting demands of a profession that squeezed out other uses of the mind, that seemed to dwarf the imagination and deaden the feelings. His sympathy with working men, on whom the pressures of daily work were as great and whose opportunities for "mental culture" far fewer than his own, was genuine, and he thoroughly approved the various institutes and associations aimed at the "self-improvement" of mechanics and artisans. When the philanthropist George Peabody donated the money for an institution incorporating a library and courses of lectures, essentially a foundation for adult education, in his home town of Danvers, Choate gave the opening address. "Our lot is labor," he told his audience.

There is no reversal of the doom of man for us. But is that a reason why we should not aspire to the love and attainment of learning, and to the bettering of the mind? . . . Surely we need not add a self-inflicted curse to that which punished the fall. . . . Who has doomed us, or any of us, to labor so exclusive and austere, that only half, the lower half, of our nature can survive it? . . . Do you feel that the mere tasks of daily labor ever employ the whole man? Have you not a conscious nature, other and beside that which tills the earth, drives the plane, squares the stone, creates the fabric of art,—a nature intellectual, spiritual, moral, capacious of science, capacious of truth beyond the sphere of sense, with large discourse of reason, looking before and after, and taking hold on that within the veil?[15]

He urged the people of Danvers to regard themselves as having become *"permanently the members of an institution* . . . an institution of learning . . . henceforth part and parcel, through its corporate existence, of the civil identity and privilege of Danvers" and as much a real school "as the Seminary at Andover, or the Law School at Cambridge." The courses in such institutes need not be narrowly vocational or utilitarian—indeed, quite the reverse, since one of the purposes of these institutions was to bridge the culture gap between upper and lower classes that had come to seem dangerous in a way it had never done before. Essentially, however, at the adult as at the elementary level, it was not so much the specific content as the process of learning, in a systematic and disciplined fashion, and in concert with others, that was important. "There is in all knowledge," Francis Lieber remarked, "even the most indifferent as to moral effect, for instance arithmetic, a softening power, which renders the mind more pliable . . . it forms one more link which connects the individual with the society in which he lives." Education integrated the individual into what the leaders of society defined as the civilized community, attached him to the republic.[16]

Choate had picked up the idea developed by Herder and by Coleridge that what distinguished nations from one another was, essentially, particular ways of thinking, that there existed something which could be called the national "mind." This "mind," which developed through the historical experience of a people and the transmission of its traditions over generations, consisted of not merely intellectual functions but also the sensibilities and the emotions, qualities of character and will. Thus, it not only stored past culture, but determined the direction and energy of national development into the future. National greatness, Choate told his Boston audience, was not

> a spontaneous or necessary development and manifestation according to some mechanical and organic laws;— it is a production of the human mind; it is a creation of the human will. . . . All of it rests at last on enterprise, energy, curiosity, perseverance, fancy, talent,—loftily directed, heroically directed. . . . I approve, therefore, of these expressions: the Roman mind, the Grecian mind, the Oriental mind, the European mind. There is

true philosophy and an accurate history in them. They penetrate to the true criteria which distinguish races,— the mental criteria.

Everything, therefore, that served to discipline and to energize this mind could be considered education and the proper concern of the fostering care of the state. Because it was in some sense an organic whole, in which various parts fed each other, it was important that every aspect of the national mind be equally encouraged to its fullest development. It was necessary that curiosity and culture be widely stimulated and diffused, but it was also vital that those who contributed the "higher" and more specialized function of the mind be given adequate support and encouragement, otherwise it would be truncated and never reach its fullest potential.[17]

As a believer in the unity of the national mind, and as a scholar manqué himself, Choate was always deeply sympathetic to the claims of scholarship for public support and consideration. As soon as he arrived in Washington in 1841 he joined the National Institution (later Institute) for the Promotion of Science, founded the previous year by the politician-naturalist secretary of war, Joel Poinsett. The National Institute was essentially an eighteenth century philosophical society, embracing professionals, literati and gentlemen amateurs, aiming at mutual enlightenment and general elevation of mind. Though the emphasis was on "science," the term retained its undifferentiated eighteenth century sense, and the institute dedicated itself to the cultivation of everything which might be considered useful and/or ornamental, including technology, agriculture, American history, literature and the fine arts. It was to operate largely as an agency of collection and exchange for the growing number of specimens and interesting objects that the acquisitive curiosity of the country was laying up, and also as a propagandist for culture as a leisure pursuit. "It is an error to suppose," Poinsett assured potential members, "that letters cannot be cultivated without neglecting the fulfillment of the obligations we owe to our families and to our country."[18]

As the word "national" in the title indicates, the officers of the institute wanted the official patronage of government, and by September 1842, Choate was serving on a committee to urge Congress to grant it federal funds. To apply pressure, Choate's committee arranged a giant convention of scientific men, scholars and interested parties in Washington in April 1844. The meeting was a brilliant affair, with the cabinet in attendance and an opening address by President Tyler, but Congress showed no inclination to offer more than words in support of science. A joint effort by Choate and George P. Marsh in June, urging Congress to take over title to the institute's collections and make it a paid agent for their care, also met with hostility or indifference.[19]

The attention of the public and the learned community, however, was shifting to a different project for the recognition of scholarship. In 1835, the American government had been offered a bequest from the estate of James Smithson, an English amateur chemist and illegitimate son of the Duke of Northumberland. Smithson left the bulk of his fortune at the death of his heir, more than $500,000, to the government of the United States to establish an institution in Washington for "the increase and diffusion of knowledge among men." After protracted debate, in which John Quincy Adams managed to triumph over constitutional objections by Calhoun and others, Congress decided in 1836 to accept the legacy, but additional years of discussion were needed to agree on the method of carrying out Smithson's deceptively simple instructions. It was not until the session of 1844–1845 that Congress got down seriously to disposing of the Smithson bequest, and thus Choate was given the opportunity to play an important role in the establishment of the Smithsonian Institution.[20]

Since 1841, the Senate had turned over its responsibility for deciding what to do with the Smithsonian bequest to the Library Committee, consisting of Choate, Benjamin Tappan of Ohio, an old Jacksonian, and William C. Preston of South Carolina. Preston, a member of the National Institute, wanted the Smithson legacy to be administered by that body; Tappan, who considered their collections "trash," was violently opposed to turning over a public fund to a private corporation; and Choate was maturing plans of his own. It was impossible for the committee to reach any consensus, so Tappan took the initiative and introduced his own bill in December 1844.[21]

Tappan's bill represented a marked break from earlier proposals in the long debate on the use of the fund, such as a great national university or John Quincy Adams' long-cherished project for a national observatory. Tappan proposed a conglomerate institution, part museum (which would receive all natural history and geological specimens belonging to the U.S.), part technical school, part agricultural experiment station. Lecturers were to be appointed in a variety of subjects and were to concern themselves especially with "the introduction and illustration of subjects connected with the productive and liberal arts of life, improvements in agriculture, in manufactures, in trades, and in domestic economy." The institution was to have a library consisting of works "especially such as relate to the ordinary business of life," and from time to time the managers might issue publications "in popular form on the sciences and on the aid they bring to labor."[22]

The Tappan bill stated clearly for the first time in Congress that the "knowledge" the nation should officially support was that concerned directly with aiding the average man to manipulate the material environment to his advantage. This was a new note: John Quincy Adams, while acknowledging the practical uses of astronomy, had approached it essentially as an aspect of the sublime, as a science that allowed the intrepid mind eventually to "look undazzled at the throne of God." Outside of Congress, however, there was a strong tendency towards more mundane proposals. Memorialists petitioned Congress in favor of agricultural schools, schools for the blind, or women, or, on a more sophisticated level, for a school of "practical science" like the French École Polytéchnique.[23]

As the debate dragged on, moreover, there was a growing disposition to assume that the bequest must be used not for the propagation of "knowledge" in general, but for the "advancement and diffusion of science." This had by no means been taken for granted originally. Indeed, John Quincy Adams had explicitly disclaimed, on Smithson's behalf, any intention to so limit the domain of knowledge. To many people, however, two characteristics of the physical sciences made them infinitely superior to other forms of intellectual activity: they were universal and useful. Unlike literature, science was not culture bound, its language was international and its technological products available for the benefit of men everywhere. As one enthusiast picturesquely stated it, "the Aeneid is the property of Italy—the printing press, the property of the universe."[24]

The national "romance of science" involved its popular association with technology, useful inventions, and a manipulative approach to nature, in which the sublimity involved in understanding the world attached itself even more strongly to changing it. Francis Bacon, as the father of modern experimental science, became one of the culture heroes of ante-bellum America. The democratic and utilitarian implications associated with the study of "things not words" meant that in extreme cases, scientific knowledge tended to be regarded essentially as merchandise: discrete facts or discoveries rendered immediately available and useful and offered to the public to meet the test of the market. William Darlington, the Pennsylvania physician and botanist, proposed that the Smithsonian Institution should become "a great national warehouse of knowledge, where everyone might find something suited to his wants, and to which he could freely resort whenever he became conscious of his necessities."[25] The Tappan bill thus represented a sizable body of popular thought on the character and function of knowledge in a democratic society.

It was a style of thought, however, which would not go unchallenged. American scholars and men of science were becoming both restless and assertive by the 1840s. They envied the European scholar, whose society, whatever its other deficiences, provided him with libraries and laboratories, with university positions devoted to research rather than elementary teaching, with royal patronage, pensions, orders of merit, and respect. In America, on the other hand, as George Perkins Marsh, complained, "there is no appropriate place, no recognized use, for a purely literary class, and the mere scholar feels that *here* and *now* he hath no vocation." If America did not wish to remain a perpetual debtor nation, culturally as well as financially, then she must be prepared to give substantial aid to foster an intellectual elite. "Let the nation make provision for a literary class who may devote their whole lives to science and letters," demanded a Yale professor in 1846, "let their wants be supplied; let them have a place to which they may retire from the busy throng; let them receive encouragement and sympathy from a generous people."[26]

An increasing number of young men, particularly in New England, were being drawn into a literary life, especially into historical research. What such men, particularly the historians, needed, were libraries. Just before his death, Fisher Ames had remarked that Gibbon's *Decline and Fall* could not have been written in the United States because no library existed that could have supplied his sources. This example was taken up again and again to illustrate the peculiar difficulties that the American scholar faced if he was not wealthy enough, like Prescott or Ticknor, to build his own library and seek his sources in Europe. "No one, except he who has had the occasion to pursue a particular branch of study," wrote one mathematician, "can feel the utter dearth of books that exists in this country." Harvard and the Boston Athenaeum had over forty thousand volumes each by the 1840s, but no private library had the resources to accumulate all the possible sources needed to meet "the extensive learning which is required of even the most gifted genius in an age like ours." Only a national library could rise to these requirements, and in particular, serve as the official depository of the sources for American history by collecting the papers of men prominent in American life. Given the growing needs of scholarship, the question was, "How far is our community prepared to supply the savants?"[27]

A beginning at least could be made with the Smithsonian fund. This money, Choate noted in his journal, "ought to be applied to a great library; and a report and a speech in favor of such an appropriation are the least I owe so grand and judicious a destination of a noble gift." When he rose in the Senate to deliver a major speech on the Smithsonian bequest in January 1845, it was to challenge Tappan's "somewhat narrow utilitarianism," and to advance the claims of scholarship and a scholarly class. Between them, Tappan and Choate set the essential terms for the subsequent Congressional debate.

The best possible use for Smithson's money, Choate told the Senate would be to create a "grand and noble public library, one which for variety, extent and wealth, shall be, and be confessed to be, equal to any now in the world." Two-thirds of the annual income of the fund, about $20,000, to be spent on books for some twenty-five years, would build up a representative collection of works on the model of a good modern library like that of the University of Göttingen, and thus remove the major barrier that prevented the American scholar from equalling the European— lack of materials for research. Through books the American could appropriate the essence of European culture, past and present; they were civilization condensed, the portable past, transmitting all the glories of the heritage with none of its inconveniences. The library would be

> a vast treasure of all the facts which make up the history of man and of nature, so far as that history has been written; of all the truths which the enquiries and experiences of all the races and ages have found out; of all the opinions that have been promulgated; of all the emotions, images, sentiments, examples of all the richest and most instructive literatures: the whole past speaking to the present and the future; a silent, yet wise and eloquent teacher; dead, yet speaking—not dead! for Milton has told us that "a good book is not absolutely a dead thing —the precious life-blood rather of a master spirit; a seasoned life of man embalmed and treasured up on purpose to a life beyond life."[28]

Choate was aware of the egalitarian argument that a great library would benefit only an elite, and met it with the metaphor of organic nationalism. By meeting the needs of the scholar, the library would indirectly provide a shot in the arm for the whole of American culture.

> It would raise the standard of our scholarship, improve our style of investigation, and communicate an impulse to our educated and to the general mind. . . .
> Our learned men would grow more learned and more able; our studies deeper and wider; our mind itself exercised and sharpened; the whole culture of the community raised and enriched.

The phrase *"our* mind" demonstrates one of the advantages of a Burkean view of society, in enabling the theorist to skirt the awkward question of who benefits. If the state is indeed "a partnership in all science; a partnership in all art; a partnership in every virtue and in all perfection," then the scholar and the scientist, like the artist and the poet, were only pioneers in that joint enterprise in which all men, as members of the ethical body of the state, were engaged—the advance of civilization.[29]

In the waste spaces of Washington, as, more abstractly, in the sparse texture of American national life, the library would be a palpable declaration of intent, a concrete sign of the nation's conception of its character and destiny, an "exponent of civilization permanent, palpable, conspicuous, useful . . . durable as Liberty, durable as the Union." Since scholars would come from all over the Union to consult the library, Washington would become the intellectual as well as the political capital of the nation, and the political and intellectual worlds would vitalize and strengthen each other. New ties of personal contact and friendship would bind the scholarly community together, and proximity with the world of national politics would give it a deeper sense of the nation. "Someone has said that a great library molds all minds into one republic. It might, in a sense of which he little dreamed, help to keep ours together."[30]

Choate suggested that the remaining third of the income should be devoted to a series of lectures to be delivered for two or three months each year while Congress was in session. The form was a holdover from the Tappan bill, but in Choate's version, the lecturers would be "gentlemen eminent in science and literature," drawn from the civilized world, who would address themselves to Washington's special audience—members of Congress, the administration, diplomats and other men in public life. The lectures would be framed both to enlighten and broaden the mind engaged in practical politics and bring to bear the knowledge and "wisdom" of the scholar upon political action. For the governing classes, "liberal culture" was of the very highest utility.

> Would it not be as instructive to hear a first-rate scholar and thinker demonstrate out of a chapter of Greek or Italian history how dreadful a thing it is for a cluster of young and fervid democracies to dwell side by side, independent and disunited, as it would to hear a chemist maintain that to raise wheat you must have some certain proportion of lime in the soil?[31]

Indeed, if republican virtue now meant essentially the right disposition of mind, then it was essential that the mind of the people, but especially of its elected leaders, be directed aright. This gave the scholar, the writer, the intellectual—all those who in some way influenced the national mind—a much greater political importance than they had ever had before. In a fragmented world it was they who had to articulate coherently and authoritatively the values and attitudes necessary to the maintenance of the republic. It became a commonplace of the Phi Beta Kappa and commencement address that the American scholar was to exercise a sort of lay ministry: elevating and refining the public mind and guiding public opinion. More than the average man, he would have the imaginative capacity to grasp the unity of society over time and thus preserve that awareness of the nation extending beyond the present generation that had come to seem so crucial. He was to be " 'Homo, naturae minister et interpres' in the moral as in the physical world," as Charles Haddock of Dartmouth said, "the proper link between the present and the past."[32]

Yet in the nineteenth century there appeared to be a widening gulf between the wielders of political power and men of culture and intellect. The problem was how to make power recognize the moral authority of culture and how to harness the intellect to the defense and service of the body politic. Coleridge, who influenced Choate's thinking considerably, met the problem with his concept of a "clerisy": a guild of the learned, from the parson and schoolmaster in every parish, to the erudite scholar devoted to the free and serious development of philosophy, maintained by the nation as the third estate of the realm, with the task of preserving and extending its civilization and guiding the mental and moral development of the people. The lectures Choate proposed would be some small provision towards the establishment of an American clerisy by providing an official public forum for scholars; scholars, in turn, would imbue the leaders of the people with a sense of their responsibility for the continuity of civilized existence.[33]

Choate's plan for the Smithsonian was an expression of his intellectual cosmopolitanism and distaste for the idea of America as an Eden of ignorant innocence. He challenged Americans to decide whether they were indeed an organic part of and full heirs to Western civilization, or whether, in some superstitious thanksgiving for their unique political and social felicity, they would deliberately deny themselves the dangers and delights of the higher flights of mind. "I do not think, Mr. President," he concluded his Senate speech,

that I am more inclined than another to covet enviously anything which the older civilization of Europe possesses which we do not. . . . But I acknowledge a pang of envy and grief that there should be one drop or one morsel more of the bread or water of intellectual life tasted by the European than by the American mind. Why should not the soul of this country eat as good food and as much of it as the soul of Europe? . . . Can we not trust ourselves with so much of so good a thing? . . . Are we afraid that the stimulated and fervid faculties of this young nation will be oppressed and overlaid? Because we have liberty which other nations have not, shall we reject the knowledge which they have and which we have not? Or will you not rather say that because we are free, therefore will we add to our freedom that deep learning and that diffused culture which are its grace and its defence?[34]

The *North American Review* later described Choate's speech as having rendered "more memorable the day on which it was delivered than that gallant military achievement of which it is the anniversary," and the listening Calhoun is said to have exclaimed, somewhat ambiguously, "Massachusetts sent us a Webster, but, in the name of heaven, whom have they sent us now?" The Senate was sufficiently impressed to agree to all Choate's proposed amendments and attach most of the income to founding a library. There were a few final skirmishes. Tappan grumbled that there were not so many books worth buying; there was a last ditch attempt to get the management of the Smithsonian fund transferred to the officers of the National Institute, which Choate countered with the charge that it would be "antirepublican and antidemocratic" to surrender a public trust into private hands, with no congressional control. Finally, William Allen, the other Democratic senator from Ohio, who had coined the catchy phrase "54/40 or fight," announced that he intended to vote against the whole project since

the Constitution did not give us charge of the mind and genius of the American people. It was the privilege of a despot, not of a free government to control the mind and direct the genius of the people; . . . Our government is the creature of the public mind, and not the creator. . . . We have no right to presume that the people are so ignorant that we ought to legislate for enlightening them.[35]

Allen was almost alone, however, and the Smithsonian bill, as amended to create a great library, passed the Senate handily. In the House, however, it ran into the opposition of Tappan's friend, the Fourierite social reformer, Robert Dale Owen, and the bill expired. When the question was reopened in the next session, it was with an entirely new bill, fathered now by Owen. By this time both Choate and Tappan had left Congress, but their contest was reenacted in the House on a larger scale and in more explicit terms, with Owen as the champion of "useful knowledge," widely diffused, and Choate's friend from college days, George Perkins Marsh, taking up the banner of high scholarship.[36]

Owen's bill reduced appropriations for a library to "not more than $10,000" and devoted the bulk of the fund to the establishment of a normal school to train teachers, particularly teachers of natural science, for the common schools. Owen's speech in defense of this new bill centered around an attack on Choate, who had obviously misconceived the nature and destiny of America. Because the United States was committed to reducing the artificial inequalities among men, her first duty was to elevate the educational standards of the masses. "I hold this to be a far higher and holier duty than to give additional depth to learned studies, or supply curious authorities to antiquarian research." The "world-subduing science of primary education" was essentially *"republican."* Scholarship, he implied, was a form of *luxury,* a concept that had played a prominent role in Jacksonian mythology.

A "pang of envy and grief" shall we feel? . . . I feel no envy if we republicans are outdone by luxurious Europe in some high-seasoned delicacy of the pampered soul. . . . Men have we; a people, a free people, self respecting, self governing; . . . bravely battling their onward way; treading with liberty at their side, the path of progressive improvement, each step upward and onward—onward to the great goal of public virtue and social equality.[37]

Owen obviously had a great deal of support in the House, but the following day George Perkins Marsh rose to give a rousing defense of Choate's library plan, presenting, as the *New Englander* said unkindly, "before the eyes of some of our western members, what many of them have never seen, the spectacle of a living scholar." Marsh had caught in Owen's bill, as in Tappan's, an imperialistic claim that only experimental and applied science provided worthwhile knowledge. A certain abrasiveness of tone and vocabulary had become apparent during the debate. For the "practical" men, books and libraries were "musty," "antiquarian," "asleep in dust and cobwebs," "to be wondered at more for their extent than for their usefulness," associated with the dead hand of the past and with aristocratic exclusiveness. As for their users, there was some confusion as to whether they were desiccated pedants, pampered epicures, or both. Science, on the other hand, was associated with life, energy, and democracy, with "the great future, with its glorious fruits, ready to burst from a teeming soil, warmed and enlightened by the great sun of science", with the improvement of "the condition of the human race, and particularly of the common people." Although a naturalist as well as a linguist, Marsh had the breadth of view which would later produce his pioneer ecological writings.

> I must be permitted to express my dissent from the doctrine implied by the bill . . . which confines all knowledge, all science, to the numerical and quantitative values of material things. . . . True science is the classification and arrangement of necessary primary truths, according to their relations with each other, and in reference to the logical deductions which may be made from them. Such science, the only absolute knowledge, is the highest and worthiest object of human inquiry, and must be drawn from deeper sources than the crucible and the retort.[38]

What Marsh was trying to hang on to was the traditional concept of science as *Wissenschaft,* "knowledge in a systematic form and connected by some method," a definition that maintained at the highest level the unity of the realm of learning and knowledge. Within this unified sphere there was a hierarchy: "I should hope that at this time and in this place, one might safely venture a plea in behalf of all that higher knowledge which serves to humanize, to refine, to elevate, to make men more deeply wise, better, less thoughtful of material interests, and more regardful of eternal truths." The library that would hold all the materials for this "higher" learning was not a luxury—it was an essential republican institution. The "truths" learned there by "extensive reading and diligent research" would enable the scholar to reemerge to guide the people with wisdom and restraint.

> Our own independence was declared and maintained by scholars. . . . It is this very point—the maintenance of principles discovered and defended by men prepared for that service by severe discipline and laborious study—that so strikingly distinguishes the English rebellion of 1649 and our own Revolution from most other insurrectionary movements, and particularly from the French revolution.

Finally, Marsh, like Choate, reaffirmed that a great library would indicate America's commitment to Western civilization and enable it to take its "proper place among the nations of the earth, not merely as a political society, but as patrons of knowledge and the liberal arts."[39]

The rest of the debate was vigorous, but largely variations upon the themes of the two principals. The House was impatient to settle the issue and eventually passed a conglomerate bill, providing for the erection of a building in the Mall to include a museum and art gallery, and allowing appropriation from the income "not exceeding an average of $25,000 annually for the gradual formation of a library composed of valuable works pertaining to all departments of human knowledge." The disposition of the remainder of the income was left to the discretion of the governing board. Perhaps Congress was swayed in favor of a library by the eloquence of its proponents, perhaps by the observation of the Ohio Democrat, Allen Thurman, that unlike other plans, a library would create "no large body of office holders, no patronage, no favoritism, no partial sectional advantage." At any rate, the Smithsonian Institution, as established in the act, did seem to represent a substantial triumph for the Choate-Marsh axis.[40]

In the decade or so of intermittent debate in Congress and the press over the disposition of Smithson's bequest, politicians, journalists, men of letters and science and other articulate Americans had pondered the responsibility of government towards the life of the mind and especially the problem of what *kinds* of intellectual pursuits America needed—an issue which involved implicit national self-definition. In a democracy, must all knowledge be accessible to the masses? Did "knowledge" implicitly mean "useful knowledge?" If so, how was utility to be determined? The first round of the Smithsonian battle had been fought essentially between those who, like Choate, wished to throw national support behind scholarship as essential to high civilization and a fully developed polity, and those who demanded some clear and widespread "cash value" in social benefit from intellectual activity. The controversy, which lasted well beyond the passing of the act of establishment, served as a rallying point for those whose notion of civilization demanded that the United States recognize the existence and value of an intellectual elite. As subsequent developments were to show, however, within that elite there was an increasing divergence over intellectual priorities.

The implementation of the act was the duty of a board of regents, consisting of the vice president, the chief justice, and the mayor of Washington ex officio, with three members from the Senate, three from the House, and six citizens chosen by joint resolution. Choate was nominated as one of the members at large, together with Richard Rush, who had nursed the bequest through the Court of Chancery ten years before, and Alexander Dallas Bache, the superintendent of the U.S. Coast Survey. The Speaker of the House, a fellow Democrat from Indiana, used his appointing power to recoup some of Owen's fortunes and appointed him, together with two like-minded congressmen as the representatives of the House—bypassing a furious Marsh.[41]

The board of regents thus began its career with three distinct parties: the library interest represented by Choate, the utilitarian-popular education interest, represented by Owen, and a new force in Alexander Dallas Bache. From his niche in the federal bureaucracy, Bache became one of the great entrepreneurs of American science. Determined to expand the facilities and support for scientific research in America, Bache had seen the Smithsonian bequest as a providential "bounty for research," and, whatever Congress might have intended, he was not about to let it slip through his fingers. The most important step was to secure the appointment of the right man as secretary of the Smithsonian, the officer who would be in day-to-day control of the Institution.[42]

Bache's nominee was an old friend, Joseph Henry, then professor of Natural Philosophy at Princeton. At fifty, Henry was America's most distinguished physicist; he had done important work in electro-magnetism, anticipated Faraday's discovery of self-induction, and laid the theoretical foundations that made Morse's commercial development of the electric telegraph possible. Besides being an active researcher himself, he was deeply concerned with the conditions and prospects for science in the United States and in complete agreement with Bache about the proper use of the Smithsonian bequest. Indeed, as he said later, although the concise terms of the bequest had caused such confusion to the "general public," "to the cultivators of science, to which class Smithson himself belonged, the language employed failed not to convey clear and precise ideas." In particular it conveyed the idea that the "increase" and "diffusion" of knowledge were logically distinct and that the former was more important than the latter.[43]

Since the act did appear to allocate the greater portion of the income to his own plan of a library, Choate had been thinking not of a scientist, but of a librarian for the all important post of secretary. His nominee was Charles Coffin Jewett, the young librarian of Brown University, who had recently published a widely acclaimed catalog of the university library. But the dynamic Bache won Owen over to his point of view and then dispatched him to Boston to persuade Choate. Owen reported back that he had assured Choate that "to produce harmony, we all felt disposed to go as far to meet him as our sense of right would permit. He replied in the same tone."[44]

Choate's caution was understandable; the appointment of Henry would mean the acquisition not only of a man but of a program. As soon as Bache had broached the possibility of the secretaryship to him, Henry had drawn up a comprehensive plan of operations centering around the encouragement and publication of original research. Occasional grants would be made to particular research projects, but the main encouragement offered to the "real working men" of science would be the opportunity to have their work published in prestigious volumes to be called the *Smithsonian Contributions to Knowledge.* With publication and aid to research as the Institution's *raison d'être,* there would obviously be very little income left over for a library. Before Henry's proposals were formally submitted to the board of regents, in December 1846, a disturbed Choate withdrew to his Washington hotel room and drew up a counterblast in defense of the library as required by Congress and the cause of American civilization. Henry had mentioned ethnology as a field particularly deserving of Smithsonian support. Sharply, Choate told the regents that "the most instructive collections of the recorded history, the published thoughts and sentiments, the intellectual and imaginative achievements of all the races and ages of man" constituted "the true and indispensable materials of ethnology." Choate's eloquence persuaded the regents to pass an immediate appropriation of $20,000 for the purchase of books and the setting up of a library, but he lost the crucial question of the secretaryship. Henry was elected on December 4 with seven votes out of twelve. Bache wrote to him exultantly: "Science triumphs in you my dear friend."[45]

And it did. Henry abandoned a successful career in research to take the helm of the Smithsonian, but he saw in it the opportunity to realize the dreams that he and Bache shared for the future of science in America: as Bache told him, "you can be a new institution ready to grow to your stature." Henry had no intention of implementing the appropriation of up to $25,000 for books, but the specific requirements of Congress could not be entirely ignored, and Choate had to be placated somehow. Outside of the courtroom Choate was not a fighter, he was outnumbered on the board of regents, and he was not anxious to engage in personal confrontation. In the event, it was Choate himself who came up with a compromise solution: the annual income of the Institution should be split, half to be spent on the museum and library, half on the research and publication that Henry, with a flair for language that would evoke contemporary sympathies, came to call "the *active* operations." The compromise would go into effect on the completion of a building for the Institution, probably within two or three years. In addition, Jewett, Choate's choice as secretary, was to be appointed assistant secretary in charge of the library.[46]

On December 13, 1847, the regents formally accepted Henry's plan of organization as amended by Choate's compromise, and on this basis a precarious equilibrium among opposing attitudes towards the pursuit of knowledge was maintained for a few years. The battle in Congress had been essentially a contest between the proponents of scholarship and research on the one hand, and the advocates of disseminating "practical" knowledge on the other. Now a new fissure could be seen opening up be-

tween the scientists and the humanists. Choate was not opposed
to the spirit of experimental science as understood by educated
men of the eighteenth and early nineteenth centuries, though in
moments of irritation he tended to equate science as a whole with
natural history, which he felt—as did Henry—to be merely descriptive and so not requiring much intellectual power. His library
contained a number of general works on scientific subjects and he
later felt the proper awe when touring Newton's rooms in Cambridge. For his part, Henry was not philosophically opposed, like
Owen, to the establishment of great libraries, and his views on the
civic role of educated men in leavening society was very similar
to Choate's. But, in a climate of very scarce resources for the
support of higher learning in any form, it was necessary to make
choices and designate clear priorities.[47]

To Choate, all the physical sciences shared the drawback of
being ethically neutral and indifferent to the meanings and purposes of men in history. He was quite willing to accept that modern science must eliminate problems of value and meaning from
its pursuits, but assumed that this self-limitation must demote it in
the scale of human knowledge. While the sciences might provide
pieces of information about the world, only literature, history, and
philosophy could provide man with the psychological grasp that
enabled him to feel at home in it. What men needed to know,
essentially, was "the best that has been thought and written in the
world," not the structure of physical reality but the mental con-
structs by which men have ordered their existence. Words, in this
view, became not the veil between man and reality, the fog that
prevented him from fronting a fact, but, as Coleridge had said,
"living powers, by which things of most importance to mankind
are activated, combined and humanized." In any healthy culture
the sciences could never play such an essential role as "letters,"
since neither the dissection of nature nor its mastery were as
crucial for man as what Matthew Arnold would later define as the
function of literature—"the criticism of life." The philosophy
necessary for civilized men, Choate told a commencement audience at the University of Vermont, was one that took questions
not of fact but of value for its center:

> not unmindful certainly of material nature, of number,
> of quantity, of mechanical force and the Preadamic

Earth, but conversant more with man, with human life; such philosophy as your Marsh loved, adorned and honored; seeking to discern and fix the nature and ground of justice; the office and education of conscience; the grounds of government; the conditions and dangers and blessings of liberty, with all holy, beautiful and useful speculations and institutions whereof the fruit is the highest style of man.[48]

Scientific discovery was likely, in the modern world, to be one of the offspring of an inventive and well-developed "national mind." Science, however, could not itself shape and direct that mind, largely because its concept of knowledge was too narrow. Henry thought of "knowledge," strictly speaking, as a product of the scientific method of experimental verification. Choate, however, thought of the mind in the same way as Coleridge and the romantic poets, not as analytic intellect alone, but as an active unity of intellect, feeling, imagination and will; the mind was neither a *tabula rasa* nor a thinking machine, but an organ of "insatiate desires," for which "knowing," was not categorizing and analyzing, but a sensuous possession. The mental culture which could produce a noble national mind must be a combined "culture of the reason and of the heart."[49]

Choate had hoped that the Smithsonian as a great library might become one of the institutions from which such a culture could be generated, but he had more than met his match in Joseph Henry. Henry was determined to stamp his own conception of its mission so deeply upon the Smithsonian that its pattern would be set for posterity. For this he needed both time and a free hand. In the event, his friends and his enemies cooperated to give it to him. In January 1847, Bache carried a resolution of the regents that stretched the erection of the building over five years or longer, using part of the regular income instead of the accrued interest allotted by Congress. This would mean that Choate's compromise would not in fact go into effect before 1852 at the earliest. Choate, absorbed in his growing law practice, did not attend any more regents' meetings until 1854, leaving the fortunes of the library to the care of Jewett. It was part of the "antique" quality of Choate's character that he invested an excessive faith in formal legislation and the documents that contained it. This faith, together with his impatience and aversion to committee work, was a serious weakness in a politician, since it led him to neglect the fact that institutions are often shaped less by their fundamental laws than by the men who guide them from day to day. Choate's absence from regents' meetings removed him as an immediate threat; there remained Owen, who although he might side with Bache and Henry against the library men, was essentially out of sympathy with Henry's emphasis on pure research. Congress, however, solved that problem by failing to reappoint Owen when his term expired. His replacement, Marsh, acquiesced rather uneasily in the compromise, but he too departed in 1849. With this fortuitous freedom of maneuver, Henry set out to make the Smithsonian the dynamic center of American science.[50]

In the summer of 1850, Choate had the opportuni.y to sample some of that European cultural feast he had ventured to envy in his Smithsonian speech. He had hardly taken a vacation since setting up his practice; now, tired and strained, he took off some ten weeks for a trip to Europe. Helen was, as usual, left behind, and he travelled in the company of a brother-in-law, the well-to-do lawyer Joseph Bell, who had married one of Helen's sisters, and whose son married Choate's eldest daughter. He went well supplied with letters of introduction—from Edward Everett to Henry Hallam and Sir Robert Peel, and from Webster to Lord Ashburton—together with advice on when to arrive at country houses (*"after* lunch and *before* dinner"") and what to talk about. "Talk as much as you please, but *never* of your own country. Follow their lead. . . . You will find no difficulty in being acceptable to English gentlemen and ladies."[51]

They left Boston in late June. Choate was seasick for much of the passage over, but, once arrived in Liverpool, he recovered and immediately set down his proposed daily discipline in his journal.

> Before breakfast I shall walk at least an hour *observantly,* and on returning jot down any thing worth it.
> . . . I am next to read every day a passage in the Bible.
> . . . Then, I must carefully look at the papers, for the purpose of thoroughly mastering the actual English and European public and daily life. . . . Then I must get, say half an hour a day, for Greek and Latin and elegant

English. . . . This lest taste should sleep and die, for which no compensations shall pay!

For all the rest, I mean to give it heartily, variously, to what travel can teach,—men—opinions—places,— with great effort to be up to my real powers of acquiring and imparting. This journey shall not leave me where it finds me. Better, stronger, knowing more.

Liverpool struck him as "a larger but *worse* New York—*trade, trade, toujours*—and an immensity of that—and nothing else," but he was enchanted by the music in the Anglican church he attended on Sunday, "the best church service music I ever heard." Throughout his trip, indeed, he revelled in the music: "last eve, I heard Sontag and Lablache in La Tempeta and saw the faded Pasta,"—"the most magnificent theatre, audience, music, I ever heard or saw."[52]

He had arrived in England to find that Peel had just died, but he was entertained by Lord Ashburton, Lord Lonsdale, Macaulay, and the Prussian minister, Bunsen, and was rather overwhelmed by the late hours of metropolitan society. Macaulay, he later recalled as "the finest talker I ever saw or knew of in any country," but if anything of interest was said at these soirées, he made no note of it either in the surviving letters home or in his journals. The journal entries are impressions of what he saw on his travels rather than of his encounters with people. In London, he made the usual round of sights, including the British Museum, with its "transcendent Library . . . the catalogue alone fills two hundred or three hundred volumes." He also indulged his professional interests and visited the law courts, which did not particularly impress him. He heard part of the Old Bailey trial of Robert Pate, an unstable young man who had struck Queen Victoria. Choate commented:

Pate would have been acquitted in Massachusetts. . . . The prisoner's counsel, in my judgement, gave up his case by conceding; . . . I thought and believed he might have saved him. . . . The whole trial smacked of a judiciary, whose members, bench and bar, expect promotion from the Crown. Their doctrine of insanity is scandalous. Their treatment of medical evidence, and of the informations of that science, scandalous.

He was shocked to see the barristers occasionally hesitate for a word: "All narrated dryly; not one has in the least impressed me by point, force, language, power; still less, eloquence or dignity. The wig is deadly." The debate in the House of Commons, too, failed to live up to his expectations of parliamentary eloquence. Webster, he told Parker later, could never "have got off the great Hayne speech in England. It's too eloquent . . . They stand right up in Parliament, with their hands in their pockets, and *hum and ha.*"[53]

In the middle of July, Choate and Bell moved on to the continent, where they were to travel through France, Belgium and Switzerland. Paris delighted him—including the Chamber of Deputies and the law courts. "The dress and manners," of the latter, he noted, "far better than the English bar. The silk gown or cloak is graceful and fit, and might well have been (it is too late now) among the costumes of our bar." He passed up Brussels in favor of a ride to Waterloo "a spot memorable and awful above all I shall see or have seen . . . the *last* of the battles!" Then they travelled along the Rhine ("would form a grand subject of a lecture," he noted) into Switzerland. Catholic Switzerland around Lucerne confirmed all his Protestant prejudices: the countryside was covered with crucifixes and weeds. However, "once in Berne, all changes. Man does his duty. Excellent stone bridges; good fences; fewer weeds. . . ." The city of Geneva, "the city of thought, liberty, power, influence," and its lake, he contemplated with deep emotion, as "the scene in which the character and fortunes of Puritanism were shaped and made possible—the *true* birthplace of the civil and religious order of the northern New World."

Like all thoughtful nineteenth-century Americans in Europe, Choate had to attempt to evaluate what had been gained and lost in the transition from the Old World to the New. What did his instinctive aesthetic response to the charm of Europe mean in terms of his commitment to American ideals? In his hotel room at Basel, overlooking the Rhine, Choate mused on the problem in his journal. "The higher charm" of Europe, he decided was due only to the visible memorials of the last eight hundred or so years. The essence of the ancient world was in books "and may be appropriated by us, as well as by her." But, he added,

the gathering of that eight hundred years, however, collected and held here,—libraries, art, famous places, educational spectacles of architecture, picture, statue, gar-
dening, fountains,—are rich, rich, and some of them we
can never have nor use. . . . What . . . can never be
transferred? Picture, statue, building, grounds; beyond
and above, *a spirit of the place;* whatsoever and all which
come from living in and visiting memorable places.

But these were the idle sighs of the "mere scholar"; to put the
matter in perspective it was clear that "the *vast mass* is happier and
better in America, is worth more, rises higher, is freer; its standard
of culture and life higher." Even the scholarly mind, in fact,
should be able to live as happily in America as in Europe, "it must
modify its aims and sources somewhat, live out of itself, seek to
do good, educate others. It may acquire less, teach more; suck into
its veins less nutriment, less essence, less perception of beauty, less
relish of it (this I doubt), but diffuse it more." Institutions such
as the great Smithsonian library would enable America to appropriate as much as possible of all that was worthwhile in the past,
leaving Europe as a giant museum for all the remains that could
not be pocketed. Here the American could visit with relish and
then return gratefully to his own country where the past, because
unstained by the crimes of Europe, could be revered without
ambivalence, and was always locked in a fruitful dialectic with the
forces of progress. "In which hemisphere," Choate formulated
the question, "would an imaginative and speculative mind most
enjoy itself?"

In America, land of hope, liberty,—Utopia sobered,
realized, to be fitted according to an idea, with occasional visits to this picture gallery and museum, occasional studies here of the objects we can't have; or here,
under an inflexible realization, inequalities of condition,
rank, force, property, *tribute* to the Past,—the Past!!!55

For though the past had a great hold on Choate, it was the past
as part of a continuous process of time that was valuable to him,
not the past frozen and preserved as a monolithic bar to all change.
    A leisurely return journey took the travellers through Coppet
where they stopped to visit the home of Mme. de Staël, then to

Paris again and from thence back to England.[54] They spent a few more days in England before returning home in mid-September, and Choate took this opportunity to visit the universities at Oxford and Cambridge. Oxford repelled him:

> The exterior of the Colleges, . . . was not old only—that was well—but all old, only old, grim, and with a worn and neglected look, as if the theory were to keep forever before the eye the old, old time and art and product, unwarmed, unacidulated, unlivened by the circulation of a drop of later life. [He was] oppressed at every step with—I know not what—of the retrograding or stationary and narrow and ungenial in opinion, in policy, in all things.

Cambridge, on the other hand, the home of Newton, the nurse of Puritanism, seemed to embody in stone Choate's idea of conservatism.

> The architecture is striking. The old is kept in repair; the new harmonizes, and is intrinsically beautiful, so that here seems a reconciliation of past, present, and of the promise of the future. Conservation and progress—the old, beautified affectionately and gracefully linked to the present— . . . the new recalling the old, filial, reverential, yet looking forward—running, running a race of hope.

He made the final entry to his journal in Cambridge, summing up his impression of the university. His appreciation of Cambridge might stand for his ideal of what a great institution was, the kind that America needed, and that the Smithsonian might begin to be.

> Here is a profusion of wealth, accumulated and appropriated for ages, to a single and grand end,—the advancement of knowledge and the imparting of knowledge. It is embodied to the eye in a city of buildings, much of it beautiful, all of it picturesque and impressive, and in grounds shaded, quiet, fittest seats of learning and genius. Something there is of pictures; great libraries are here. Learned men,—who are only the living generation of a succession which, unbroken, goes back for centu-

ries, and comprehends a vast proportion of the mind of the nation in all its periods,—in increasing numbers, tenant these walls, and are penetrated by these influences. A union of the old, the recent, the present, the prediction of the future, imaged in the buildings, in the grounds, by every thing, is manifested,—giving assurance and a manifestation of that marked, profound English policy, which in all things acquires but keeps,—and binds the ages and the generations by an unbroken and electric tie.[56]

Meanwhile in Washington the secretary of the Smithsonian had rather different notions. Choate's conception of an institution required the outward and visible signs as palpable symbols of function. Joseph Henry, on the other hand, would have been quite happy to operate the Smithsonian out of rented rooms, so opposed was he to spending any of the limited funds on "gratification of a *sensuous* kind." Determined that the true mission of the Smithsonian was to facilitate original scientific research, Henry was convinced that this task must not be hampered by the dead weight of "things"—books, collections, curiosities—clogging the machinery of "active operations," especially since he felt that the natural tendency of institutions was towards a "statical state." He would have liked to unload both the library and the collections on Congress. Failing that, they could only be made innocuous by being strictly subordinated to a hierarchical plan, in which the material elements directly served the theoretical.[57]

In making original research and publication, which were nowhere mentioned in the act of Congress, the major activity of the Smithsonian, Henry was undertaking a rather breathtaking *coup d'institution.* "Is it an ascertained fact," Charles Hodge of Princeton had written to him when he first took up the secretaryship, "that either Congress or public sentiment will sanction the proceedings of the Regents in organizing the Institution on a plan so different from that obviously contemplated when the bill creating it passed Congress?" In fact, Congress was happy to have the whole matter off its hands, and did not interfere. Henry had also received expressions of approval of his scheme of organization not only from scientists, but from scholars such as Francis Wayland, Edward Everett and Jared Sparks. He had even reached an uneasy accommodation with Jewett on the question of the library. The two men agreed that the library should at first be largely scientific and that it should also become a center of bibliographic information and guidance for American libraries. Accordingly, Jewett worked out a scheme for producing a great Union catalog of all American public and college libraries. Thus the Smithsonian library would perform much the same function for the literary world as the "active operations" did for the scientific: facilitate the work of researchers, and rationalize and coordinate the work of libraries throughout the country.[58]

As time passed, however, Jewett grew increasingly discontented. Though he was enthusiastic about his own "active operations," it was incongruous to think of this library, that by 1850 contained only about nine thousand items, as the dynamic heart of a national library system. In vain he tried to persuade the regents that, in a library, comprehensiveness and sheer quantity can make a qualitative difference.

> It should be particularly observed that any article, however apparently worthless, acquires value and importance as an integral part of a complete collection. A collection of all the productions of the American press would if perfect and entire, teach lessons which could not be gleaned from its parts. . . . There ought, . . . to be in every country one complete collection of everything published—one library where everything printed should be garnered up, treated as of some importance.

The Smithsonian could not pretend to anything like this completeness. Despite the provisions of the law, the Institution did not in fact receive more than one-quarter of the books it was entitled to under the copyright section of the act, and every year Henry and the majority of the regents voted smaller appropriations for the purchase of books; in 1853, the library was allocated $874. As Jewett pointed out bitterly in his report for 1848, this penuriousness had lost the Institution the bargains made available by the revolutions in Europe. Henry, too, became restive as the building neared completion and the time for the Choate compromise, in which half of the income would have to be allocated to the library and museum, would come into force. He tried to win over Jewett, promising his entire cooperation with the bibliographic work if the librarian would accept a shoe-string budget for acquisitions. In a highly emotional scene, Jewett refused, and from 1853 almost all communication between the two men was conducted in writing. The conflict over the future of the Institution was complicated by a personal clash of temperament and conflict of status. Henry, who saw himself as the captain of a frail vessel in perilous seas, demanded absolute loyalty from his assistants. But Jewett regarded himself as having been appointed not only by Henry, but by the board of regents, and so responsible to them as representative of the great coequal "interest" of traditional learning.[59]

In March 1853, Henry broached to the board the idea of abrogating the compromise. A special committee was appointed to consider the matter, to which Jewett submitted an emotional report that attacked Henry personally. The committee took a year to report; meanwhile Jewett and his friends in Boston and Washington began a newspaper and magazine campaign against the way the Smithsonian was being managed. From Boston, Choate wrote plaintively to Jewett:

> Situated so far off, I cannot comprehend the reasons on which the compromise is sought to be disturbed. It was the result of years of disagreeing opinions, and of reflections on all modes of administering the fund. . . . The necessity of reconciling opinions by concessions was seen to be coercive. It was yielded to, and the matter was put, as it was thought, at rest. . . .
>
> For myself, I should deplore any change in the distribution of the fund. I appreciate the claims of science on the Institution; and the contributions which, in the form of discovery and investigation, under its able Secretary, it is making to good knowledge. But I insist that it owes a great library to the Capital of the New World; something to be seen,—preserved,—and to grow,—into which shall be slowly, but surely and judiciously, gathered the best thoughts of all the civilizations. God forbid that we should not have reach, steadiness, and honor enough to adhere to this as one great object of the fund.

Not only was Choate adamant that the compromise should not be disturbed, he was convinced now that the secretary's power must be tightly curbed. In an attempt to bring some official pressure to bear upon the regents, he wrote to the attorney general, his old friend, Caleb Cushing, delicately asking him to use his own authoritative position to urge the claims of the library upon the board. In Washington, tactics were more direct: Mayor John W. Maury, a member of the special committee, reported that a friend of Jewett's told him he would not be reelected if he did not vote the right way.[60]

Against this background, the regents' committee to inquire into the fate of the compromise reported on May 20, 1854, at a meeting at which Choate, as Henry put it, "after an absence of six years . . . made his appearance to support the assumptions of his favorite." The report, drawn up by James Pearce of Maryland, entirely supported Henry's position, arguing that the sum of $25,000 per annum that the act allocated for the purchase of books was obviously to be taken as a limiting, not a substantive appropriation. It concluded by recommending the abrogation of the Choate compromise and suggesting that future distribution of the income should be left to the discretion of the regents on the recommendation of the secretary. Of the seven committee members, only Representative James Meacham of Vermont, who had succeeded Marsh, dissented. He put in a minority report.[61]

The board adjourned without discussion to mull over the Pearce and Meacham reports; meanwhile, the public campaign mounted, actively aided by Jewett. When the *Boston Daily Advertiser* published an article in defense of the library, Jewett had his brother John, the publisher of *Uncle Tom's Cabin,* issue it in pamphlet form and urged his friends to distribute it. "It is very necessary," he wrote to George Livermore, sending him a batch, "that any connection of myself with it should not be made known or be traceable." This furtiveness played into Henry's hands. At a meeting of July 8, at which neither Choate nor Meacham was present, the regents upheld the right of the secretary to remove his assistants. Two days later, Henry dismissed Jewett. The librarian had warned Henry during one of their confrontations that any attempt to get rid of him would "shake the institution to its foundations." The dismissal did indeed spark a public battle in the press that not only covered the question at issue—the library versus the "active operations"—but also reanimated the old arguments in favor of practical utility and brought into the open a groundswell of sullen indignation against the elitist tendencies of the Institution.[62]

Many of the popular defenders of science turned out to be just as opposed to mere formulas as to mere words. The *New York Tribune* summed up several years of utilitarian sniping when it accused the Smithsonian of having become an effete, aristocratic and un-American institution, "a lying-in hospital for a little knot of scientific valetudinarians." The *Smithsonian Contributions to Knowledge* made very little positive impact on the popular mind. As Meacham pointed out, the Institution "makes no demonstration before the public. It looks like an affair of the closet, and such in truth it is. The public are ever asking what is done here." As Choate had shrewdly pointed out in his speech in the Senate, one practical political advantage of an imposing library was that it was "visible property." "There is something to point to if you should be asked to account for it unexpectedly." In its present state, however, the Smithsonian appeared to many people, like the "Taxpayer," in the Washington Evening Star, *"an inscrutable abstraction."*[63]

Henry disliked idle curiosity and discouraged random inspection by the public. Nor was he anxious to open the affairs of the Smithsonian to prying by the press. When the regents met on January 12, 1855, to consider the Pearce Report, the pro-Henry majority on the board voted against allowing representatives of the press to attend. This naturally provoked journalistic remarks about the "close corporation proceedings" of the board. "Do the public require any better evidence," asked the *New York Daily Times,* "that there is something rotten in Denmark?" The absence of reporters meant that there is no record of Choate's speech before the board in defense of Jewett, the compromise and the library. Stephen A. Douglass, now a regent and a defender of the library, remarked that "it seemed impertinence for anybody else after it to say a word." Bache reported more prosaically: "Mr. Choate was in brilliant form but changed no votes."[64]

By a vote of eight to six, the board agreed to abrogate the compromise and to leave the distribution of the income to the discretion of the regents. The next day, Choate sent to Congress a letter of resignation as regent. He claimed that the discretionary powers given to the board by the act to facilitate efficient administration, had been "transformed into means of practically disappointing" the will of Congress, and "of building up an institution substantially unlike that which it intended; which supersedes and displaces it, and in effect, repeals the law." To Jewett he wrote privately,

> I sympathize with you in so far as my indignation does not swallow up all minor feeling. Be firm, be calm. I advise *not* to *sue* til after the session. *I am earnest in this.* Prepare a statement of the whole case, law and fact—be ready for "press." But move our friends in Congress.[65]

In the Senate, the reaction to Choate's action was mixed but visible; Regents-Senators Pearce and Mason of Virginia were outraged that their integrity was being impugned—"a mere rhetorician should never aspire to the judgment seat," commented Mason. Others were irritated that the problem of the Smithsonian should rise to plague Congress again. Choate's letter was merely laid on the table, but the management of the Institution was referred to the Committee on the Judiciary. In the House, a select committee of five was appointed, headed by Charles W. Upham, who represented Choate's old district of Essex South.[66]

Meanwhile, the affair, fanned anew by Choate's letter of resignation, continued to be canvassed in the press, to the disgust of Henry and his supporters. Chief Justice Taney, an ex-officio member of the board and a Henry supporter, felt that the verbal literary people would be bound to win any open public battle. "If we get into the newspapers," he wrote to Richard Rush, "we must meet a judge perfectly organized . . . in its opinion and . . . in its institutions. . . . We could not reply and thus after a little while they would have all their own way." He exaggerated the resources of the Choate faction, however, even in New England, the heart of the library interest. The oracle of New England culture, the *North American Review,* came out with a quite temperate article condemning the course of the regents as contrary to the intent of Congress; the *Christian Examiner* demanded archly, "what can it profit us . . . to be able to predict the goings and comings of the most respectable planet; if we cannot rely upon the course of respectable men appointed to responsible stations." But *Putnam's* published an almost lyrical defense, drawn partly from Henry's *Annual Reports,* of the "high and holy mission" of the Smithsonian to aid the advance of science. Of the daily press in Boston, only the *Daily Advertiser* took a firm stand against the regents; the *Post* and *Atlas* strongly defended Henry.[67]

Meanwhile, Upham, the chairman of the House committee, was bombarded with letters and memorials from distinguished scientists and learned societies in defense of Henry's policy. He sympathized with the library faction, however, and wrote to Choate asking for a formal statement to the committee on the legality of the regents' actions. A very good case could have been made that Henry's management of the Institution was in fact in violation of the intent of the act. Choate's frantic legal busyness, however, prevented him from drafting a full statement that might possibly have persuaded the committee. By February 19, he was writing apologetically to Upham: "my engagements are so utterly out of proportion to my health, that I am prostrated and imbecile for all effort but the mill-horse walk of my daily tasks." He pointed out, however, that the issue had to be fought using the parliamentary history of the act to show that the intentions of Congress had been violated. "I entreat you to do two things," he concluded excitedly, "1. Vindicate the sense of the law. 2. Vindicate art, taste, learning, genius, mind, history, ethnology, morals, against sciologists, chemists and catchers of extinct skunks."[68]

Upham did his best, but the Senate committee reported in favor of the regents, and Upham found that he could not even carry his own colleagues on the select committee, let alone the House. The investigation ended in something of a fiasco, with Upham issuing a report of his own, two other members signing a report in support of the regents, and the remaining two declining to sign either. Upham's report pointed out that a great national library had a special claim on the attentions of Congress, because it would enable the collection in one place of all the materials pertaining to the nation's history. "The annals of all other countries, running back into the past," he wrote,

> are soon shrouded in fable or lost in total darkness; but ours during their whole duration, are within the range of unclouded history. The great social, moral, and political experiment here going on to test the last hope of humanity is capable of being described in clear and certain records.

The House, however, was unmoved and refused to take any action on the Upham report and so the whole controversy petered out. The newspapers lost interest almost as quickly, and only a few periodicals were still reviewing the controversy by mid-1855. Benjamin Peirce in the *American Journal of Science and Arts* concluded that the present policy of the Institution was "heartily approved by the whole scientific interest of this country and appears to be favorably regarded by a large share of our best scholars and literary men."[69]

This was broadly true. Men of letters still felt an interest in and responsibility towards the advancement of science. Moreover, in a culture deeply hostile to intellectual elitism of any kind, scientists and scholars realized that it was necessary to stick together.[70] Yet when Benjamin Gould maintained that the dispute over the library was really only the deliberate mischief-making of interested individuals who had tried "first to create a discord regarding the Institution between the purely scientific and purely literary men in the nation; and, when this was found impossible, to create an impression in the public mind that such discord existed," he was being slightly disingenuous. Choate and the other supporters of the library did feel put upon and edged out by the scientists of the Smithsonian. "The scientific men are down upon us as if their craft were in danger," Meacham expostulated to Congress, and concluded that the Smithsonian question had "become one of physical science versus everything else." The library men had perceived a certain aggressiveness among the devotees of science towards other forms of knowledge. "A particular meaning has been crowded upon the word 'knowledge,'" complained Upham in his report to Congress, "not its ordinary meaning in common usage, but a narrow, technical, and special meaning. This has been done by confounding it with 'science.' . . . 'Knowledge' is all-comprehensive—embracing science, art, literature, politics, business, the whole world of nature and culture, the entire realm of facts and reality, all ages and all that they have contained."[71]

The actors in the drama resumed their lives without too much damage. Jewett, who had suffered the greatest personal humiliation, was appointed librarian of the new Boston Public Library, and thus ended his career as head of a great institution dedicated to supplying the wants of the scholar as well as the general reader. The triumphant Henry succeeded eventually in unloading the greater part of the Smithsonian library onto the Library of Congress and in making the Institution what Choate had hoped the library would be, a center of intellectual life in Washington. As for Choate, "I am chagrined more than I can indeed express," he wrote to Jewett, "at the past and the future." He had suffered a bitter disappointment and a rather humiliating personal defeat; being out-maneuvered by Henry was an index of his weakness and lack of tenacity as a politican. He had played an important role, however, in the founding of a great institution dedicated to the disinterested pursuit of knowledge. As such, it embodied one of the more admirable traits of Western culture. Still, it was not the great memory bank of the stored recollections of man's consciousness that Choate had seen as the essential commitment to civilization: the public avowal that nothing of worth should be lost. The scientists who clustered around the Smithsonian might give valuable technical advice to the federal government during the Civil War, but they were not a clerisy nor *"minister et interpres"* since their attention was necessarily diverted from the world of human values and ambitions towards the world of nature.[72]

Because the disposition of the Smithsonian bequest had been the responsibility of the national government, the use to which it was put had to be seen as a political statement. Choate did not see libraries as mere distillations of the past, but, on the contrary, as launching pads into the future, enabling scholars "to place themselves along the line of demarcation between what is known and what is unknown and make this the base of operations for extending the conquests of science, enlarging the boundaries of human knowledge." But because a library was an institution centered upon language, it was essentially an instrument for the transmission of tradition. To Choate, the presence of a great library on the Mall would have been a symbol of America, not as a new Eden, but as the most vigorous heir of all the ages.[73]

FOUR

THE LAW AND THE STATE

CHOATE CONTINUED TO BE involved in politics and to be a political figure for the rest of his life, but he held no more political offices after leaving the Senate in 1845. "To my profession, *totis viribus,*" he vowed to his journal, "I am now dedicated." His years in the Senate, while conferring a certain prestige, had interrupted his legal career, and he felt that heroic efforts must be made to make up for lost time and consolidate his position among the first at the Boston Bar, as well as overwhelm by sheer success those who were still inclined to sneer. "A little attention to things, and persons, and reputations about me," he noted in the journal,

> teaches me that uncommon professional exertions are necessary to recover business to live, and a trial or two teaches me that I can very zealously, and very thoroughly, and *con amore,* study and discuss any case. How well I can do so, compared with others, I shall not express an opinion on paper—but if I live, all blockheads which are shaken at certain mental peculiarities, shall know and feel a reasoner, a lawyer, and a man of business.

He made good his resolution and, by the 1850s, when he was engaged on the average in about seventy cases a year, he was certainly, after Daniel Webster, the most famous lawyer in New England and the generally acknowledged leader of the Massachusetts Bar.[1]

In 1849 he amicably terminated his fifteen-year-old partnership with B. F. Crowninshield and formed a new one with his nephew and son-in-law Joseph M. Bell. The new arrangements meant greater efficiency and regularity in the business of the office and also in the collection of fees. Choate was always extremely careless and forgetful about money, and his former partner was apparently no more astute, so his early successes had not brought the material security that might have been expected. Bell was a better businessman; he kept records, made sure that fees were collected and set them at a level commensurate with Choate's eminence and with those received by lawyers of comparable renown. In the eleven years from 1849 to 1859, the average annual income of his office was about $18,000. He could now ask fees of $1,500 to $2,000 in important cases and, on four occasions, he received a fee of $2,500 and, once, a retainer of $1,500. These were respectable sums but by no means excessive for an established lawyer.[2]

Choate himself continued to be oblivious to money, spending and giving freely when he had it, indifferent when he lacked it. Though he remained quite aloof from the numerous movements for reform current in Boston, he would unhesitantly and gracefully dispense personal charity. A student who spent a year in his office remembered the "poor ministers, politicians, missionary agents by scores, solicitors of book subscriptions, poor inventors, and poor scholars" who would importune him and "instantly, without thought or inquiry except the briefest, he would either give the money or subscribe his name to the subscription paper, ten, twenty, thirty dollars thus disappearing at each request, the gift always accompanied with a profound bow to the applicants." Outside the courtroom, indeed, he could be remarkably naive. His daughter Miriam remembered one occasion on which a man presented himself at their home as the chief justice of Arkansas and said he was temporarily without money and far from home, but felt he could take the liberty of applying to Choate, whom he claimed to have met in Washington. Choate immediately proffered a loan, though he afterwards confessed in bewilderment to his wife, "Helen, I was mortified that I had quite forgotten him." Like all friends of Webster, of course, he was often called upon to lend money to the defender of property and the constitution. He usually paid up with good grace, though on at least one occasion, when he was hard up himself, he was reduced to making a covert getaway from his office when he knew that Webster was on his way, intent on borrowing. Aided by a confederate, however, Webster ran him to earth and he was forced to pay. "There was a great joke," according to Parker, "wandering round State street for a long time, in the shape of a promissory note payable *on demand,* drawn by Webster and endorsed by Choate. It was shaved again and again at the most fluctuating rates."[3]

Choate impressed himself on his fellow members of the Bar not only because of his success and his learning but also because he possessed a certain unique charm that everyone with whom he came into contact seems to have felt. It was a mixture of sweetness of temper, wit, and personal elusiveness. He was seldom in company, seldom sought out others, yet in the fleeting moments as he moved between court, office, and home, or in the chance encounters in the early morning on Boston common, he would bestow one of his glancing, witty remarks and the recipient would receive not only a lasting impression but a story to carry him through several social encounters of his own. Choate stories indeed became part of the currency of Boston legal and political circles. Wit is one of the hardest qualities to convey when detached from the tone of voice, the nuance of expression and the total context. In the numerous reminiscences that try to retell Choate's sallies, the shaft of wit tends to be smothered by the laborious reconstruction of the circumstances. What comes through, however, is Choate's verbal readiness ("it's a flagrant likeness," he said of the self-portrait of a rather plain artist), his strong sense of the ludicrous, and above all, his playful mind. The latter was a quality more likely to be found in Concord than in Boston—but in Concord it was associated with dangerous, disorganizing ideas. Choate's playfulness, like his emotional excess and his "radical sensibility," was allied with the most sound and conservative ideas and thus could be accepted with genuine delight by Boston society, once they got over the initial shock. They could assimilate Choate as a licensed eccentric, a Boston "character."[4]

Though always affable, charming, kind, he remained an essentially solitary person. "He has no hearty sympathies with his kind," Hillard commented harshly to Francis Lieber, "he dwells in an ideal world; he has no friend; he needs no one's society, sympathy and companionship. I don't think there is a man on earth whose society he seeks." Only with his children, when they were young, could he sometimes set aside his reserve. He appears to have been a delightful father—funny and indulgent; in his brief descents from his library, ready to give himself up wholly to amusing the young people. He would even participate in wild games of tag—but his daughter Miriam remembered "although he was so frolicsome and bubbling up with fun when with us alone, he would change wholly if any 'outsider' by any chance were with us. If one of our playmates came in during our game of *tag,* he at once stopped the game, took his green bag and was off." His detachment in adult society appeared in odd ways in his conversation, which could be brilliant, but as Parker remarked, had something "isolated" about it, "as it were soliloquizing. It was all out of his head. He begins instanter to pour forth intellectualities, and he pours on, and on, ceaselessly." The remarks flowed from the preoccupations of Choate's inner world rather than from any vital connection with the person to whom he was actually speaking. To the young and romantic, however, this abstracted quality was part of Choate's mysterious charm. William Wetmore Story recalled to Brown that, as a young man, he was captivated, not merely by the great advocate's fame and ability,

> but beyond all this for what it is difficult to explain—for a certain somewhat of mysterious and poetic which always seemed to me to haunt him, and which lay below all his outward show of character. There was something in his silent eyes and in his often abstracted and involved bearing—in the gloom and worn expression of his face at rest which seemed to hide an inner life, given to far aspirations and longings, fed by secret springs outside the public and ordinary life he seemed to lead. This may have been all visionary—I know nothing—but I cannot in speaking of him refrain from giving expression to this singular influence which he always exerted on one— what he had missed—what he wanted I cannot say—nor can I say that he missed and wanted anything definite, except as we all miss and want somewhat that which is denied us—indefinite, unexplained, but not the less vaguely desired. Still, it always seemed to me in the little I saw of him nearly, that there was to him another life behind and beneath this that we know, "of purer ether"

of "diviner air," perhaps of disappointment around which a mystery hovered.

This air of mystery, together with his haggard looks, may explain one of the widely believed rumors about him—that he was an opium addict, and that a hotel room where he had slept or the courtroom where he had argued would smell strongly of the drug. This was a charge which his friends all vehemently denied. He himself was very sensitive on the point, for he knew, said a student, "that what credit was given to the stimulant would be taken from his genius."[5]

He had an exalted conception of the legal profession as almost an order of chivalry in the service of the state; his courtesy, which was applied to everyone, became particularly exquisite in his dealings with fellow members of the Bar. He had too, a filial reverence for the Bench even though judges, Chief Justice Shaw in particular, often gave him a hard time in court. He swallowed his irritation, however, not only because he had to, but because he saw in the figure of the judge the great defense of "life, liberty and property." "I always approach Judge Shaw," he remarked dryly, "as a savage approaches his fetish, knowing that he is ugly, but feeling that he is great." The courtesy extended downwards to his juniors. He was a particularly popular senior counsel, deferential towards his juniors' opinions, always ready to give them credit in court for their ideas ("My brother reminds me . . ."), and equally prompt to take responsibility for their mistakes. The students in his outer office might get little practical preparation for day-to-day legal business (Parker remarks that he hardly saw "a writ, or a copy of the Revised Statutes" until Bell entered the office), but they had the knowledge that Choate regarded them as fellow votaries of a vast and noble science that they must be prepared to serve with enlarged minds rather than crabbed technique. Parker was set to reading Roman Civil Law, Justinian's *Institutes* and German historical commentators. Choate advised another young student, who even in college was anxious to get down to legal work, against devoting any part of college life to professional studies, but if he was bent on a "foretaste" of the law, suggested he read Hallam, Hume and Gibbon, Montesquieu and Beccaria.[6]

When Bell first joined the office, Choate would arrive punctually at nine and, after spending the morning interviewing clients in his cluttered inner room, or writing at his old-fashioned stand-up desk, would disappear to the Athenaeum for the afternoon. But soon the sheer amount of business he was engaged in made that indulgence impossible, and the whole day, except when in court, would be spent at the office. Outside of his library he had few relaxations, except for the theatre, which he loved. His brisk pre-breakfast walks over Boston Common were his only exercise and, apart from the trip to Europe, he took no vacations of more than a day or two outside the city. Not that he craved any: his whole orientation to life was urban and, in a period when it was an almost essential mark of sensibility, his lack of response to nature was proverbial. A single day spent relaxing amid the beauties of nature was about all he could stand. When one of his married daughters invited him to spend a week at the seashore he exclaimed: "A week! Why in forty-eight hours the only question left would be, 'where is the highest rock and the deepest water?' " His industry was legendary, but while he was never idle, he presented, as one observer told Brown, "a curious combination of the methodical and the desultory—of extreme dilatoriness and persistent activity." In routine business he was very unmethodical, and while he had great powers of concentration, the periods of concentration on any one topic tended to be short, and he would postpone important tasks until the last minute. Once a case was actually upon him, however, he would sink himself entirely in it, think of nothing else and be tireless in researching every conceivably relevant legal point. Most of his business came on retainers in cases already begun by other counsel and, in his later years, according to Parker, he rarely knew much about the case until he actually got into court. But he seemed to grasp the whole case as he listened to the opening presentations of his junior and the opposing counsel. He took copious notes, in his famous wild and illegible handwriting, on all the evidence offered, which he would pore over and ponder in the evening as he shaped his final address to the jury.[7]

It was the pride of the American legal profession that, unlike their brethren in England, they were not narrow specialists; the same man acted in and outside the court and in a great variety of cases. This enabled the lawyer to take a broad and scientific view of the law, to understand its basic principles, instead of becoming bogged down in details. Choate was engaged in a very broad spectrum of legal practice, including, what was already becoming somewhat unusual for a man of his eminence by the 1850s, a large number of criminal cases—though the case had to be a good one and "the retainer $100." He had as little contact as possible with clients in criminal cases; in his most celebrated murder trial he did not meet the defendant until he was in the dock, when he went up to him and asked: "Well, Sir, are you ready to make a strong push for life with me to-day?" But in whatever kind of case, his devotion to his client was absolute; for the length of the trial he seemed almost to absorb himself *in* his client. "Choate is rarely Choate," said one observer, "and he don't know himself, when he gets up in the morning, *who he is to be;* but he takes up his papers, looks in the glass, and says to himself, 'Am I Mr. A or Mr. B to-day?' and not until he has scrutinized his brief does he know how to baptize himself for that day; then *he is* that person whom he undertakes to be."

Theophilus Parsons, who knew him well, said that Choate had a naturally *forensic* mind, the kind that, when presented with a problem, sees only what will aid its own side and exerts all its resources to *win.* But losing a case seemed not to trouble him unduly; he would sweep it out of his mind as completely as he had previously absorbed himself in it. Once when he had lost a case before a legislative hearing, Webster found him calmly exploring the stacks of the Athenaeum and wondered at his lack of concern. "Oh," said Choate, "when I have once argued a case, and it is settled, I am done with it. . . . I should go mad if I allowed it to abide in my thoughts."[8]

Unlike Webster, Choate was engaged in few cases that can be considered landmarks of legal history. The public interest in his cases was less because of the legal principles involved than because of the often sensational nature of the cases and the notoriety of the advocate. Choate's presence imparted a certain glamor to even the most banal cases. Whenever he argued a cause, the courtroom was packed with spectators; for one particularly sensational divorce case the streets leading to the courthouse were jammed with people early in the morning, all hoping to get in to see the great man. Choate touched the imagination as few other lawyers could. There were others as learned as he, said one contemporary, and some as skilled in managing a trial, but "they were not men of whom anecdotes are told; men who say things worth reporting and remembering, poetical things. . . . There are single tones and phrases and words of his which haunt the memory."9

Though Choate could argue as eloquently and pathetically before a single judge as before a packed court in a jury trial, his public reputation rested chiefly on his ability to manipulate a jury. So notorious indeed was this talent that in his later years jurors often began the trial determined not to give in to Choate, though more often than not they capitulated in the end. As soon as he entered the courtroom, and had deliberately, and with great dramatic effect, divested himself of the numerous coats and capes that he wore against the cold, Choate began to study the jury. If he picked out any individual among the twelve whom he thought likely to be particularly resistant, he would address the full force of his argument to him, so that a trial sometimes seemed a personal dual of wills. Whipple remembered a trial for fraud in which Choate dragged out his closing speech for four hours, though the substance of his case had been disposed of in the first hour, because he could see that the foreman of the jury was not completely convinced and Choate was determined to break down the man's resistance. But though his addresses to the jury were often long, he believed that it was the opening remarks that were decisive. "A speaker makes his impression, if he ever makes it," he told Parker, "in the *first hour,* sometimes in the first fifteen minutes." After that, the attention of even the most dutiful jury could be expected to wander. So they needed a good deal of repetition from the advocate and plenty of variety to recapture their attention. Choate liked to alternate his most flowery language with a popular slang phrase or "homely" expression, and he was fond of the ludicrous analogy that would break the tension and bring a laugh from the spectators. But playing to the audience in the courtroom was also part of his assault on the jury. Every laugh or expression of emotion he could conjure up from the crowd was one more influence on the twelve men in the jury box.10

Choate spoke with great velocity, and accompanied the rush of words with convulsive gestures, sometimes extending a trembling arm, or shaking himself all over, or, as emphasis for a particularly impassioned point, rising on his heels and coming down with a force that could make the whole courtroom reverberate. With his startling black eyes, loud voice, and violent gestures, he could terrify any timid juror whom he decided to pick on. George Perkins Marsh recalled him suddenly pointing at a hostile juror and shouting, "I will make this point plain—I will make it plain even to *you,* sir." The wretched man quailed. Usually, however, he preferred to impose his will on the jury through a friendly, confidential approach and, through an appeal to the imagination, suspend their disbelief while he created for the length of the trial a universe of discourse in which the terms were entirely his. "Gently and insensibly," recalled one observer, "he would entice the jury into . . . a rarified and glittering region of his own . . . where the magician could make for them new laws, new reasons, new facts, new motives." And when in this absorbed state he had "jumped" the jury over any awkward contrary evidence, he would restore them to earth. The torrential eloquence would be replaced by a common-sense, matter of fact tone, the flowery metaphors by a homely phrase, and the jury would believe that "what he had showed them above was part of the normal routine of life." When younger members of the Bar thought to achieve his success by adopting his style, the results could be disastrous. Choate himself got away with his excessès, largely, it seems, because he appeared not to be acting but to be entirely rapt in his own argument, almost possessed by it. The shrewdest of his opponents had learned by the late forties that the best way to deal with the Choate vehemence was not to ridicule it but to deflate it. Webster was particularly good at this. Whenever he found himself arguing against Choate, he would take pains to present himself at his most weighty, down-to-earth, and plain-spoken. An Amherst student, who saw Choate and Webster argue against each other in a celebrated case involving a disputed will, summed up the difference between them: "Choate's speech filled me with an impression of *brilliancy,* but Webster's seemed to weigh down the mind with the idea of immense *power."*[11]

In the conduct of a trial Choate relied very heavily on the testimony of witnesses and was expert in drawing out his own and cutting down his opponents'. Nonetheless, his shrinking from personal confrontation made cross-examination difficult for him. "I remark a disinclination to cross-examine," he noted in his journal, "which I *must at once check."* "Never cross-examine any more than is absolutely necessary," he told Parker. "If you don't break your witness, he breaks you." He had a real talent, however, for discovering the weak points of witnesses and aiming his few questions directly at them. One fellow lawyer, indeed, felt that he was quite unscrupulous in taking advantage of witnesses and in stretching the meaning of what they had said.[12] He could certainly be quite ruthless in destroying the character of a hostile witness and did not hesitate to use *ad hominem* arguments with little regard to the relation between the witness' character and the evidence presented. The aim was to dispose of the evidence by destroying the credibility of the individual. In an insurance case, for example, he could not budge the testimony of one witness even after a day-long cross-examination, but he did bring out the man's general "bad character" and reputation and dwelt at length on this in his closing remarks to the jury. "Do you suppose, gentlemen, that in this vast violation of all the sentiments and virtues that bind men together in civil society, *veracity* alone would survive in the chaos of such a character?" Choate won the case and Whipple commented: "the rogue may or may not have testified truly as to the point under discussion, but truth could not be reasonably expected from a person who was self-convicted of almost every wickedness but perjury."[13]

The personalities of the people involved assumed great importance in Choate's conduct of a case. Where possible he aimed to impress upon the jury the general worthiness and uprightness of his clients and their witnesses and the dubious character of the people involved on the other side. Where this was not possible he would shrewdly concede much to the opposition's case, but draw the line at the crucial issue. Thus, in a capital case, the defendant had undoubtedly led a profligate life, certainly deserved censure, *but* had not committed murder. In a divorce case he might admit that the wife had been imprudent, flighty, but the evidence did not warrant a conviction for adultery ("they were playful . . . not guilty. . . . They only wished to *soften the asperities of hay making"*). This was a tactic which conceded much to the jury's prejudices and then encouraged them to see themselves as fair-minded men of the world by bringing in a not-guilty verdict. Indeed, Choate was especially effective in these defenses of the "half-guilty," who under his magic became figures of tragic and poetic interest.[14]

Choate believed in copiousness of evidence just as he believed in copiousness of words. Not only would he endeavor to overwhelm the jury with a plethora of favorable witnesses but he would also marshal as much evidence as possible on points of law. He was never afraid to read to the jury favorable rulings on similar cases, or passages from law books explicating a legal rule, or long extracts from lay authorities—such as Sir Thomas Browne on melancholia—to bolster his case. Above all, he relied on the fact that the burden of proof must lay with the prosecution. A favorite approach was to deal with the opposition's case by presenting to the jury a plausible case of what *might* have happened, which would fit the evidence and yet show his client to be innocent. In Choate's impassioned narrative, however, the possible scenario tended to take on the color of fact. In one extraordinary instance, when one of his own witnesses had been damaged by being revealed as the mother of an illegitimate child, he recouped her— and his own—position with the jury by the imaginative explanation that the young man to whom "she had pledged her untried affections, to whom she was to be wedded on the next Lord's day" had been "suddenly struck dead at her feet by a stroke of lightening out of the heavens!"[15]

He used this method of defense by alternative hypothesis with great effect in what was probably his most famous trial, though one that did his reputation little good. In 1846, Albert J. Tirrell, a young man of good family, was accused of the murder of his mistress in a brothel where they had been living together. Their room had caught fire and, when it was put out, the body of the woman was found with her throat cut. Tirrell, meanwhile, early that morning had appeared in an agitated state at a livery stable, hired a vehicle to take him to his family home in Weymouth and from there had escaped to New Orleans, where he was later arrested and returned to Boston. The press gave considerable coverage to the story, and, as the trial began, there was much public feeling against Tirrell, who was assumed to be guilty. Choate, who had been engaged for the defense, attacked the character of the government witnesses, most of whom were associated with the brothel, and based his case on the fact that the evidence against Tirrell was purely circumstantial—there were no witnesses to the actual crime and there was no motive.[16]

Choate then offered the jury *two* plausible hypotheses, both, he suggested, as compatible with the evidence as the government's case. The most likely was that the victim, Maria Bickford, had committed suicide: "waking sadly, with her hold upon the prisoner about giving way, . . . what proof is there that she did not rise from her bed, set fire to the house, and in the phrenzy of the moment, with giant strength, let out the stream of life. . . . Suicide is the natural death of the prostitute." Alternatively, since the prisoner was known from his youth to have been a sleep-walker, if he *had* committed the deed, he must have done it while asleep, under the influence of a nightmare, and so was not responsible. Choate reminded the jury that, in a case of this nature, the accused could not hope for clemency from the governor, so a guilty verdict would mean death. He drove the point home by reading them an article from the *North American Review* against capital punishment.[17]

The jury acquitted Tirrell and most of the legal profession seems to have felt that this was a just verdict on the evidence. Among much of the public, however, there was considerable outrage and a revival of the distrust that Choate had evoked as a young lawyer in Salem. His somewhat dubious reputation was brought home to him in a very disconcerting manner in the course of a trial some years later when he was defending a ship's captain accused of embezzling specie from his ship stranded off the coast of Sumatra. He was cross-examining an opposition witness, a conspirator with the captain, who had turned state's evidence. The man insisted he had been persuaded into the crime by Choate's client, who had assured him that if anything went wrong "there was a man in Boston named Choate and he'd get us off if they caught us *with the money in our boots.*" Choate for once was nonplussed.[18] This slight tinge of mistrust hung around Choate for the rest of his life. Parker said that at Boston dinner tables he had heard him called a "grand engine of social oppression," and quoted an obituary that denounced his "superfluous zeal" in defending Tirrell. Even Choate's admirers, said the newspaper, could not forget that occasionally

> the lightnings of his genius were brandished with little regard to consequences, and that it was comparatively a matter of indifference to the great actor of the scene whether they purified the moral atmosphere by vindicating the cause of truth and justice, or struck down the fair fabrics of public virtue and public integrity.

To the pantheon of great lawyers, declared Wendell Phillips bitterly, Massachusetts offered up as her representative, Choate, "who made it safe to murder; and of whose health thieves asked before they began to steal."[19]

Yet among his professional colleagues Choate's reputation was much more solid—solid enough at least for him to be offered several honors. In 1844, Yale University gave him an honorary doctor of laws degree and some four years later he was informally offered a professorship at Harvard Law School. Harvard was apparently so anxious to secure his services that it was willing to arrange his teaching duties in a way that would allow him to appear before the Supreme Court during its entire term. It was assumed he would receive a retainer in a large number of the cases going up from New England and probably other states as well. The advantages to both the school and to Choate seemed considerable: Choate would have the advantage of more leisure, a great law library and a group of eager assistants to prepare cases of greater weight and more likely to lead to a lasting reputation than most of those he normally dealt with; the school would have the services of a man vitally engaged in the actual working out of the law at the highest level. The scheme would, however, have required Choate to move to Cambridge and to entirely renounce jury trials. Also, "there was another consideration . . . which was, that, the breaking off from the former scenes of his labors and triumphs, so necessary to his success in the plan proposed, would be more effectually accomplished by his establishing at once a new residence, and contracting new habits." In short, Harvard required that the flamboyant advocate become thoroughly genteel. Choate turned down the offer. He also declined an offer of a seat on the Supreme Court of Massachusetts. When Benjamin F. Curtis resigned from the Supreme Court of the U.S., after the Dred Scott decision, Choate's name was canvassed as his replacement, but he quickly made it clear that he was not interested.[20]

His refusals seem to have stemmed from both his lack of money and his usual reluctance to venture into new and untried fields. As a young man in Salem, he had remarked to a friend that the office of a Supreme Court judge was a post "of highest honor, usefulness and opportunity for a learned lawyer in the last twenty years of life" and appeared to see it as a possibility for himself. But when the opportunity arose he remarked: "I am too poor. I must remain as I am, live or die." And he added: "I know my power and reputation in my profession, and I love it, but I do not know what the change would bring upon me, or whether I should like it. I cannot leave my profession." Perhaps he realized, as Theophilus Parsons said, that he had a forensic, rather than a judicial, mind. Perhaps in some ways he needed the rough, even sordid, warfare of the ordinary courtroom. As an undergraduate he had maintained, "every man knows just about where he belongs"; by the time he was fifty his ambitions had narrowed considerably from those earlier dreams of being "a national man"; he felt now that he "belonged" in a courtroom, wrestling with a jury.[21]

He did, however, accept one official position. In 1853 he was appointed attorney general of Massachusetts, but he resigned after a single year in office. He had apparently accepted the post as a way out of criminal practice, but he disliked the routine of the office and found himself uneasy in the role of prosecutor. He seemed to hold his eloquence in check lest he be responsible for the conviction of an innocent man.[22] Much of his time as attorney general was taken up with defending the "Maine" liquor law of 1852, which provided for virtual prohibition in the state. Some eight years earlier he had argued, along with Webster, before the Supreme Court that such licensing laws were attempts by the state to regulate commerce and thus an infringement of the rights of Congress. The Supreme Court, however, upheld the opposing view that regulation of the sale of liquor was a proper use of the police power. Now, as attorney general, he found himself defending the power of the state government to destroy property under the police power to protect public health and morality. In an important case before Chief Justice Shaw, on the Maine law, *Fisher v. McGirr,* Choate's defense of the police power was accepted, but he could not make palatable the enforcement procedures of the act, which, according to Shaw, deprived the citizen of due process and made him liable to unreasonable search and seizure. Shaw declared the act unconstitutional.[23]

As the offers of a professorship and a seat on the bench indicate, Choate was a solidly grounded lawyer as well as a flashy advocate. Indeed, all his life he was a student of the law and, in middle age, he devised a particularly formal and painstaking way of studying it. In the summer of 1843, as he prepared to ease himself out of politics and back into the law, he began a practice that continued for the rest of his life: taking the most recent volume of Massachusetts Reports and "making a full brief of an argument on every question in every case, examining all the authorities, finding others, and carefully composing an argument as well reasoned, as well expressed, as if I were going tomorrow to submit it to a bench of the first of jurists." This was a formidable task, especially as he noted that he must try to become thoroughly familiar, too, with the latest English and federal cases, as well as those of New York, Maine, and New Hampshire. But there was considerable psychological satisfaction for someone of Choate's temperament in this formal and disciplined study—it gave him mental security and self-confidence. "A charm of the study of law," he noted in his journal, "is the sensation of advance, of certainty, of 'having apprehended,' or being in a progression towards a complete apprehension, *of a distinct department and body of knowledge.*" The new cases were to be studied *scientifically,* thus both training the mind and leading to a grasp of the law as a whole as an organized and rational body of knowledge. "I seem to myself to think it is within my competence," he confided to the journal, "to be master of the law, as an administrative science." And then he added: "But let me always ask at the end of an investigation, can this law be reformed? How? Why? Why not? *Cui bono* the attempt?" While he may have asked himself such questions, however, they had no public outcome. Choate was a master technician of the law and a devoted defender of its political funtions, but he never became a legal reformer.[24]

Nevertheless, like all lawyers of any eminence in this "formative period" of the American law, he participated in the process by which the legal profession adapted the "taught tradition" of the common law to the exigencies of an economically expansive, technologically innovative and politically democratic nation. In a process outside the formal political realm, resources were allocated and the economy steered in certain directions through the fostering of the law. In accommodating the law to a developing economy the problem was essentially one of flexibility: to preserve the essential feature of the common law, the defense of existing property rights, without allowing it to block the formation of new property; to build the law into a "minimum framework of reasonably predictable consequences" within which men could act innovatively and boldly, without allowing it to become a constricting "dead hand." In Massachusetts at least, a reverence for the received traditions of the law, with its emphasis on private rights, was combined with a lively awareness of the public interest. By the 1840s, however, this public interest tended increasingly to be identified with dynamic economic development. While old-line conservatives of the type of Chief Justice Story or Chancellor Kent might see the law primarily as a bulwark to defend property against the jacobinical tendencies of the populace, more moderate Whigs like Choate, or Chief Justice Shaw, saw that what was at issue was adjustment between various kinds of property rights, in which the law should look most kindly on the most productive.[25]

There is no record of what Choate initially felt about the Supreme Court's decision of 1837 in the Charles River Bridge case, in which it had held, against the arguments of Webster, that in the absence of any specific grant of exclusive privileges to a corporation, the public interest must be held to be superior to vested private rights. By the mid-forties, however, he was prepared to hail it as "well worth all the time, labor, and money which it cost, for the sake of the great principles it determined." This landmark decision and its effects, particularly on railroad development, illustrate very well the dilemmas the law faced in its role of adjudicator of economic revolution. On the one hand the way had to be opened for new enterprise, on the other, in a country short of capital, there had to be a certain guarantee of security to encourage men to risk their money. The 1840s were a decade of vastly accelerated railroad building in New England; communities were clamoring for the railroads without which they would become stagnant backwaters cut off from metropolitan markets, and there was a good deal of popular feeling against "monopoly." On the other hand, two directly competing lines could not survive economically. The "public interest" demanded both that railroads proliferate and that they be "sound."[26] In an important case, Choate, appearing for the Boston and Lowell, demanded an injunction against two other roads, which were using each other's lines to make a direct competing connection between those two cities, on the grounds that an explicit contract between the state and the corporation had been violated. Shaw upheld Choate's case. The Boston and Lowell had taken the precaution of having written into its charter an express promise that the legislature would not allow the creation of any competing lines for thirty years. The legislature, Shaw affirmed, had the right to create monopolies in the public interest, and in this case, such a grant had been necessary to induce men in difficult times to venture their capital.[27]

On the other hand, as the Charles River Bridge decision had made plain, it was not desirable that corporations be protected from all competition in all circumstances. In the case of railroads, the moderate view became that while "competing parallel roads," very close together should not be allowed, new roads which opened up new territory, brought new towns into the network, and were only indirectly competitive, were healthy. Appearing before a legislative committee on behalf of petitioners for a new line, Choate affirmed:

> I am a conservative of the strictest type, and maintain conservatism in all its forms; and therefore I have gone very far to maintain the doctrine that this legislature no longer charters competing roads. But by the same token, we only render that doctrine perfectly absurd, when we undertake to push it to the protection of this Providence railroad against our road going in another direction. To complain of competition in every case where there is no competition, is only taking from every railroad all that it derives from the conservative, practical policy of the legislature. To maintain the doctrine of the competition of railroads, it must be retained within its proper limits.[28]

"Proper limits" is at the heart of conservative philosophy. Choate and Whigs like him realized that the security of vested property rights depended very largely upon their not being pushed to an extreme position that would block the hopes and ambitions of an energetic people and especially of that citizen to whom Choate was particularly partial, "the middling man—living by his wits, with his fortune to make." "I was born and bred a conservative," he informed the legislature, in behalf of another railroad petition,

> But let me remark, that next to him who openly attacks and seeks to overthrow that great principle, as I regard it, of our political and social safety [vested property

rights], he is its bitterest enemy who would wish to strain it beyond its proper limit and sphere . . . of all sacred things on earth, the most sacred is the *reality of vested rights*—of all offensive and pernicious cant, the most offensive and the most pernicious is the *cant of vested rights*. It is dangerous; it disgusts sound minds; it alienates the regard of the judicious; it debauches the legislative mind; it unfits us to see and acknowledge them where they really do exist.[29]

An expanding, go-ahead town (in this case, Danvers), "full of energy, of capital—the capital of middling men," must not be allowed to feel that the government would disregard the "rights of twenty-five thousand inhabitants, having occasion to send and receive 30,000 tons of merchandise per annum, from the apprehension of a contingent effect on existing rail-road stock. Sir, the days of that administration which sustains such a policy are numbered."[30]

Much the same kind of issues were involved in the working out of a new branch of law that Choate was beginning to make something of a specialty in the last ten years of his life—patent law. As the pace of technological innovation speeded up, so did the number of patents issued and the number of cases appearing before the courts for adjudication. Here too the problem was one of protecting the rights of the original inventor in a climate of opinion inclined to regard the patent as a species of "monopoly," while at the same time not making the protection so all-embracing that it discouraged attempts at improvement.[31] As late as 1848 Choate thought it necessary to defend the idea of the patent to a jury as a means of

> calling away genius from the land of dreams to practical results; . . . the patent law holds that he who has conceived an idea, shall hold it . . . put it into a machine, describe it in a specification, put it into the treasury of the land, showing that invention is a part of the riches of the land. It is in this way that men can profit by the genius of others.[32]

The patent was a form of property which encouraged productivity and progress.

In such a new field of law, judges and lawyers in the courts had to work out, case by case, how far the protection of a patent extended and what exactly could be said to constitute infringement. Lawyers for defendants in patent cases were inclined not only to deny that their client's invention was an infringement but to attack the validity of the original patent on the grounds that the plaintiff was not the first inventor. In two of the numerous suits brought by Samuel F. B. Morse for infringement of his telegraph patent, Choate as counsel for the defendants used both tactics and collected an impressive array of expert testimony attacking Morse's originality. He won both cases in the circuit court, though the Supreme Court later vindicated Morse's patent.[33] But, in the very important case of *Goodyear* v. *Day,* before the Supreme Court in 1852, in which Choate appeared opposite Webster, he found that trying to impugn the plaintiff's patent only played into his opponent's hands. The high point of Webster's peroration came when he announced that it was not enough to show that aspects of Goodyear's process had been used before, he challenged Choate to produce an actual man who had invented vulcanized rubber earlier than his client. Choate spoke very affectingly for five hours, but he lost the case; later he told Parker that the way to handle the case for the defendant in a patent dispute was "to insist on the non-infringement, and not to rely too much on the non-novelty of the plaintiff's invention"— the now commonly accepted position. Choate also lost an important point of law in this case. He had insisted that the court could not grant an injunction without first submitting the facts as to infringement to a trial by jury. Webster managed to convince the court that it had the authority to decide the case itself on grounds of equity. This established the possibility of removing an extremely technical class of cases from the purview of the jury who, many lawyers felt, were unable to grasp the details and were likely to be swayed by prejudice.[34]

The encouragement of productive enterprise involved not only the question of how far business should be protected against various forms of competition but also how far it must submit to regulation by the state and how far it was liable to claims of individuals it might have injured. In a case in 1839, involving the power of the state to regulate banking, Choate appeared for a bank against which an injunction had been issued and argued that the regulatory legislation was invalid since the bank's charter was

a grant of power "to do business, not while the corporation pro-
ceeds legally or with safety to the public, but so long as the grant
remains in force." He lost the case, and Chief Justice Shaw delivered a great justification of the power and duty of the legislature
to regulate chartered businesses like banks in the public interest.[35]

Choate did not always appear for corporations; in a damages
suit that aroused much interest, *Shaw* v. *Boston and Worcester Railroad* in 1857, he was counsel for the plaintiff, a woman crippled
when a train crashed into her horse and buggy at a railroad cross-
ing. Both parties alleged negligence by the other: Choate claimed
that the train did not give sufficient notice of its approach, the
railroad that the plaintiff's husband, who had been driving, and
was killed in the accident, had been drinking. Choate did not so
much disprove this allegation as ridicule it out of court:

> This witness swears he stood by the dying man in his last
> moments. . . . Was it to administer those assiduities
> which are ordinarily preferred at the bedside of dying
> men? Was it to extend to him the consolations of that
> religion which for eighteen hundred years has com-
> forted the world? No, gentlemen, no! He leans over the
> departing sufferer; he bends his face nearer and nearer
> to him—and what does he do! (in a voice of thunder)
> what does he do?—*Smells gin and brandy!*[36]

The jury found for the plaintiff and awarded damages of $15,000.
In his closing argument Choate had offered a graceful, if ironic,
compliment to the opposing corporation. The "honorable and
high-minded" directors had no doubt felt the necessity of a judgment at law before dispensing the funds of their corporation, "but
I have no doubt, gentlemen, if you establish the liability, every
one of them would lay his hand on his heart and say, 'Give her
all that she asks, and God bless her!'" The directors were not
impressed with this testimonial to their finer feelings and took the
case to two appeals, both of which Choate won, both of which
resulted in higher damages, the last $22,500, the highest amount
ever awarded in this kind of case up to that time.[37]

This was in some ways a pyrrhic victory. The case is remembered less because, in this particular instance, the individual won
against the railroad, than because Shaw took the occasion to affirm
the principle that in this kind of case the burden of proof must rest

with the plaintiff to show that he had used all reasonable care and that the "defendant railroad did not use such precaution and care as men of ordinary skill, prudence, and experience would have used." Like his more famous decision in *Farwell* v. *Boston and Worcester Railroad,* in which he established the "fellow-servant" rule effectively preventing employees from claiming damages for many kinds of accidents suffered on the job, this seemed to sacrifice the unfortunate individual to the interests of the corporation. Shaw, however, seems to have felt that, if capital was to be preserved for productive purposes, limitation of liability to the public or to employees was as necessary as limitation of liability to creditors. From this point of view, the interests of the individual, as individual, were subordinate to the interests of the individual as member of a public that would benefit from that general economic expansion of which the railroad was the symbol.[38]

For the conservative in the law, as in politics, sound policy depended upon knowing what was fundamental principle that must be defended without wavering and what were matters of expediency and technique to be adapted as efficiently as possible to the demands of a new era. In an argument before the legislature on a petition to split off the increasingly industrialized portion of Worcester County and create a new county with its seat at Fitchburg, Choate stated what seemed to him the proper balance of change and conservatism in America. It is a statement that might also summarize the position of the numerous legal practitioners who were busily adapting the principles of the common law to the new needs of a modern economy.

> Sir, is it not quite true, that the general law of American and Massachusetts civil life is growth? Is it not undoubtedly true that the general law is a ready and prompt and perpetual adaptation of the instrumentalities, the devices, and contrivances, and means from day to day, to the varying circumstances of the hour?

The fundamental institutions of the country and the constitution were conserved with reverence, as transmitted, "but the old ploughs, and scyths and muskets of our fathers; the old modes of agriculture . . . where are these?" The uniqueness of America lay precisely in its ability to combine veneration for fundamental principles and established institutions with "a ready adaptation of mere instrumental means and contrivances to essential ends." "This it is," he told the legislature, "that has made us exactly what we are."[39]

In fact, the proposed division of Worcester County was not just a matter of "mere contrivances and instrumentalities" for the more efficient transaction of daily business. There were also important political interests involved, concerning the ability of the agricultural interests of the state to maintain themselves in face of the power of its commercial and industrial interests, and particularly the power of Boston. Choate tried to dismiss opposition to the split as "nothing but that old stereotyped, old fogey, phraseology, by which a certain class of minds resists every change of everything, everywhere." But from his opponent's point of view a large Worcester was necessary as "representative of the great country interests of the state, and as an essential barrier against that centralizing tendency of the mass of metropolitan influnces, that, year by year, are building up Boston at the expense of every and all other sections of Massachusetts." It was a question of maintaining the "independence, if not the supremacy of the country against the all-subduing, all subverting influence of the city."[40] In the wider context of modernizing America it would not prove so easy to separate out the minor details and tools and material contrivances while preserving inviolate, as in some watertight compartment, the inherited polity. Efficient "contrivances" such as the corporation did not merely facilitate industrial expansion, they created new sources and concentrations of power. In some ways, Jacksonian paranoia was a better guide to the drift of events than brisk Whig common sense.

Of all Choate's cases, the one that interested him the most, less from its legal than from its political importance, was the *Methodist Church* case, fought in the U.S. Circuit Court in 1851. The growing anti-slavery feeling among Northern Methodists and the accompanying defensive belligerence among Southern members culminated in 1844 in a Southern determination to secede from a church that balked at accepting slavery as an "American rather than merely a Southern 'household reality.'" The General Conference adopted a plan of separation and the following year, 1845, Southern Methodists met in Louisville, Kentucky, to organize themselves into the Methodist Episcopal Church South. Meanwhile, sober second thoughts, particularly among Western Methodists, led to a revulsion against the idea that the church had let itself be dismembered so easily. The General Conference of 1848 repudiated the plan of separation; Southerners might secede from the church, but there would be no agreed-on division. This made no difference to the existence of the new independent church in the South but it did mean that the Southern church now had to sue at law for a share of the pension fund from the profits of the Methodist publishing houses in New York and Cincinnati.[41]

Choate was engaged as senior counsel by the Northern church and was immediately excited by the case: "This is the greatest case I ever studied," he told his junior. The division among Methodists had almost immediately been followed by a split among Baptists over the same cause—slavery. The political implications of these severances were clear and ominous: they showed how fragile some national institutions were as bonds of Union. To Choate, the case presented itself essentially as a question of Union, and though he admitted to the court, "it is after all a question of mere property," his argument was full of deliberate parallels between disunion in the church and disunion in the nation.[42]

On behalf of his clients, Choate refused to admit that any legal separation had taken place or that the undoubted *de facto* division was due, as the plaintiff's counsel had pleaded, to any "inevitable moral necessity." To allow public men to "trace the consequences of their own acts, and the work of their own hands, to the finger of Providence" was extremely dangerous. The church, like the Union, was the work of the will and reason of men, and it was this same human will and reason that would either preserve or dissolve them. The split was not inevitable; the church could have been held together

> if fifty of these gentlemen—twenty-five, ten, five—had remembered that they were patriots as well as Methodists . . . if they had remembered that this Church was originally created in 1784 for the nation, for America . . . if they could only have remembered that, in addition to all that was demanded of it as a Church, it was one of those beautiful instrumentalities—how rare and indispensable!—by which the larger union outside, which embosoms it, was to be kept together.[43]

He emphasized the conciliatory actions of the bishops in reproving all "local agitation" over slavery; the Southern churches had no valid reason for disaffection. The General Conference certainly had no valid authority to break up the church any more than the federal government would have the right to dissolve the Union, for the church like the Union had been created by a special constituent convention, representing "the general and collective will." For a day and a half, Choate spoke with great eloquence and passion ("the rain fell from his bushy locks"), but he lost the case. The day after the verdict, his client's agent urged him to appeal and gave him a fee of $2,000. "Well," said Choate, "I declare these religious people fight harder and pay better than any clients I ever knew."[44]

The failure of a major church to surmount the divisive issue of slavery, however, was not something he could as easily dismiss from his mind as the circumstances of his other cases. On the political front too, it seemed that the two great national parties would founder on the same issue. Choate had always regarded the political party as a "nationalizing" institution; it divided men ideologically, but transcended sectional lines, which in America were more dangerous. "The very madness of party strife," he said in the election campaign of 1848, had so far helped to cement the Union.

> *Idem sentire de republica,* a community of opinions makes the masses of the people, however widely scattered, next-door neighbours and friends; and thus the volcanic fires have blazed, but have prevented the earthquake. Our railroads, our telegraphic wires themselves, conduct along the strong galvanic stream of consentaneous opinions and view. Time and space have been annihilated. Every man's national politics make him at home everywhere; and thus the sharpest, the noisiest, and the most dangerous moments of political discussion, have been the safest for the country.[45]

By the summer of 1848, however, a new party had appeared, made up of dissidents from the Democrats and the Whigs, which would not fit Choate's description—the Free Soil party. Organized to prevent any extension of slavery, the new entity was a purely Northern party, and to Choate profoundly disturbing. The tension between "conscience" and "cotton" in Massachusetts Whiggery had been growing stronger ever since the annexation of Texas—but the catalyst for the final split was the nomination of General Taylor, the hero of Buena Vista, as the Whig presidential candidate at the Whig Convention in the summer of 1848. The Massachusetts delegation was pledged to Webster, but it was clear from the beginning of the convention that he stood no chance. When the final ballot gave the majority to Taylor, a slaveholder, and a man of no known political opinions, the two Massachusetts' "conscience" delegates left the hall in disgust. In early August, in Buffalo, dissident Whigs joined with anti-slavery Democrats to form the new organization.[46]

The leaders of the Whig party and the major Whig journals of the state, however, fell into line behind the nomination with surprising ease. Indeed, Abbott Lawrence, whose feud with Webster had never really been reconciled, had supported Taylor's candidacy from the beginning. To men like Lawrence, the looming prospect of disunion was not only a question of emotion but of basic economic interest. The coming election was crucial, for while a Democratic victory might throw open the Western lands to unrestricted slavery, too good a showing of conscience Whigs might destroy all hope of continuing friendship and cooperation with Southern Whigs. Only a conservative Whig victory, it seemed, offered the hope of working out a compromise that would both restrict slavery in the territories and genuinely reassure Southern Whigs that the peculiar institution would be absolutely respected where it already existed.[47]

Choate was in a difficult position. He was a Webster man, who yet managed to remain on good terms with the Lawrence faction; moreover, when it came to presidential politics he had a very strong sense of "availability." He was among the Massachusetts delegates to the Philadelphia convention and supported Webster there, but once Taylor was chosen he supported the nomination with considerable enthusiasm. Indeed, it seems likely that he went to Philadelphia assuming that Taylor would win and accepting that as a necessary tactical move if the Whigs were to have any chance in 1848. Sumner recalled that Lawrence told him, some ten days before the convention, that Choate was for Taylor: *"I have not seen him*—but he is for Taylor." At any rate, as soon as Choate returned from Philadelphia he appeared at a Whig ratification meeting in Faneuil Hall to urge all Whigs to support the decision of the "mighty mass of Whigs throughout the Union."[48]

Choate campaigned extensively and effectively for Taylor, assuring his fellow Whigs that the general would never use the veto power to prevent a Whig Congress from keeping California free. The Democratic candidate, Cass, he denounced as consumed with a "desperate, insane passion for territorial conquest and foreign war," but his bitterest shafts were reserved for the young Whigs like Sumner and Charles Francis Adams, who, through the "desperate and profligate device of geographical parties," were destroying the basic assumption which made the political system work. A reference in a campaign speech at Salem to Edward Everett who "could be a philosopher, a scholar, and a progressionist, without being a renegade," was widely taken as a slap at Summer; in another speech at Worcester he referred, amid "repeated cheers," to John Quincy Adams as the "Last Adams."[49]

To the Taylor Club of Salem he announced what would be the burden of his political speeches for the next decade: whatever the future would bring—and he hoped it would bring no new territory, no fundamental shift in the location of national power —but whatever it brought,

> we . . . stand by the shipping articles and the ship the whole voyage round. . . . We go for the Union to the last beat of the pulse and the last drop of blood. We know and feel that there—there—in that endeared name —beneath that charmed Flag—among those old glorious graves, in that ample and that secure renown,—that there *we have garnered up our hearts—there we must either live, or bear no life.* With our sisters of the Republic, less or more, we would live and we would die,—"one hope, one lot, one life, one glory."

To the Free-Soilers, many of them formerly Webster Whigs, Choate's enthusiasm for Taylor was just one more example of his general lack of principle. "The Taylor party will sacrifice the Wilmot Proviso in Congress," commented the *Boston Daily Republican,* just exactly as they did in the Convention at Philadelphia, if it is necessary to their success. With Rufus Choate, politics, like law, constitutes an exercise of the faculties of reasoning and imagination solely. To get a murderer acquitted upon a plea of somnambulism, or to get a president made by a process which will betray liberty with a kiss, is simply a trial of refined skill: it is nothing else. . . . Mr. Choate's argument at Salem in behalf of General Taylor, like his argument in behalf of Tirrell, told well at the time; but who knows right from wrong will ever be able to look back upon either, and praise the moral nature of the maker?[50]

The entry of the Free Soil party into the election, did not, as Choate had warned, give the election to Cass—indeed it enabled the Whigs to take New York from the Democrats and to win the election. Choate was elated: "Is not this sweet?" he exclaimed to a friend. "Is it not sweet? The whole country seems to me a garden to-night, from Maine to New Orleans." But the bitterness of the past few months could not be washed away, on either the personal or the political level. Choate patched up his relations with Sumner somewhat—but the old intimacy was never resumed. And the conscience Whigs had severed their connection with the cotton Whigs for good. Abbott Lawrence was inclined to welcome the departure of troublesome dissidents, but, like the other traditional Whig leaders, he was finding it increasingly hard to cope with the new political realities. "It is very difficult to maintain one's influence and position," he wrote rather querously to John Davis, "in a community where there are so many ultraisms and so much of the *one idea*. All these *ists* and *isms* are antinational—I cannot therefore sympathize with any of the *cliques* whose views of government do not extend all over the union." In an attempt to cope with the rise of anti-slavery, the Whig leaders would increasingly find themselves falling back on "one idea" themselves—the Union.[51]

As they watched other institutions of national unity and stability fail around them, Whigs turned increasingly for salvation to the one institution whose power and strength seemed to be growing —the law. "The Whig party," said a Webster Whig in 1848, "is, and always has been, the party in favor of the supremacy of Law and the maintenance of Order—in short, the party pledged to uphold constitutional and legal government." It had also been the party of the American system, a party with a coherent plan for systematic national economic development. By the late forties, however, though Choate might still cling to the idea of the "great and glorious city," it was clear that anything resembling much positive content in Whig policies would be disastrous at the polls and divisive to the party itself. The Whig convention that nominated Taylor produced no platform—as the *Atlas* said defensively, "the Whig platform is the constitution; that is broad enough for us." As the possibility of uniting on any purposeful plan for the future development of the nation faded before the seemingly insoluble problem of slavery, all that was left to hold both the party and the nation together was a common adherence to the rules, rules flexible enough to allow men to pursue their own separate paths, adjust differences when those paths met, and prevent them from realizing how little they had in common.[52]

Whigs developed an essentially dualistic attitude towards the law. On one level, as they encountered law in their daily lives as businessmen or professional lawyers, they regarded it instrumentally: the courts were the day-to-day arena in which the adjustments necessary to the development of a dynamic economy were being worked out. But overlaying this pragmatic attitude there developed an increasing tendency towards a mystical reverence for the law, not as an instrument of policy, but as an overarching guarantee of that order and unity that seemed increasingly precarious. In his address to the law school at Cambridge—an address that contains perhaps the most complete statement of his conservatism—Choate quoted for his audience "the striking platonisms of Coleridge" on the law:

> "No space contains it, time promises no control over it
> . . . the more I think of it, the more do I find it to possess
> a reality out of myself, and to be a phantom of my own
> imagination;—that all but the most abandoned men ac-
> knowledge its authority, and that the whole strength and
> majesty of my country are pledged to support it; and yet
> that *for me* its power is the same with that of my own
> permanent self, and that all the choice which is permitted
> to me consists in having it for my guardian angel or my

avenging fiend. This is the spirit of Law. . . . This is the
true necessity which compels man into the social state,
now and always by a still beginning, never ceasing, force
of moral cohesion."[53]

In the metaphor of a somewhat outmoded cosmology—which
conservatives were fond of using—it was law that kept the spheres
in their places; it bound them together in one system, yet it also
stood between them and prevented them from falling together
into a mass. In the world of men, too, law bound men together
into one system, yet stood between them to guarantee each one
his own property and rights and prevent them from devouring
each other.[54]

For the Whigs, "justice" meant securing "every man his own
exactly and uniformly." Accomplish this, Choate told the lawyers,
and "absolutism itself is found tolerable." Fail to accomplish it,
and "liberty—slavery, are but dreary and transient things." He
referred them to Aristotle's conclusion that injustice was the
"grand and comprehensive cause of the downfall of democracies."[55] This view of justice as an essential component of the
state was a major element of classical political thought. Yet, for
Aristotle, the prime ligament of the state was not justice, but
friendship—"the bonds which unite men engaged in shared activi-
ties"—an ideal that may only be possible in small, homogeneous
and aristocratic societies. In a large, heterogeneous democracy,
the analogue of "friendship" was "fraternity," a notion which
implied the dissolution of all boundaries, the levelling of all dis-
tinctions, especially the distinction of property. The Whigs preferred justice and the law.[56]

Whigs perceived the law essentially as a principle of restraint:
it had the same role in society as self-control had in the individual.
Whig political philosophy was built upon a theory of human nature that saw man as a creature of ravenous and destructive passions, always a potential savage under the civilized exterior, who
must constantly hold in check his baser impulses. Yet the energy
and the passion were as necessary to the masculine character of the
individual or the nation (how else could the wilderness be subdued?) as the iron self-discipline that reined them in—it was the
tension between the two that produced the admirable character.
The prime example was George Washington as described by Jared

Sparks: "his temperament was ardent, his passions strong, and amidst the multiplied scenes of temptation and excitement through which he passed, it was his constant effort and ultimate triumph to check the one and subdue the other."[57]

In the political sphere, the Whigs increasingly came to view "self-government" as analogous to individual self-discipline, and they came to regard the constitution not so much as the instrument through which the people delegated some of their sovereign power for specific purposes, but as the way in which they had objectified the republican virtue of self-restraint. "As he who ruleth his own spirit is greater than he who taketh a city," said a contributor to the *American Review*, "so was the adoption of the Federal Constitution a greater event than the renowned declaration of rights, or the great victory which terminated the contest." To Choate, the various American constitutions represented a voluntary renunciation by the people of certain possibilities of action; they were an embodied superego "whereby the people, exercising an act of sublime self-restraint, have intended to put it out of their own power forever, to be passionate, tumultuous, unwise, unjust."[58] Without such bonds of restraint, the terrible energy of the people would be released, not to build, but to destroy. "Keep the constitution and the constitution will keep you," he had warned the Senate in opposing the annexation of Texas. "Break into it in search of secret curiosities which you cannot find there, and there is no longer security—no longer anything between you and us, and the unappeasable, unchained spirit of the age."[59]

The American constitutions were in theory creations of the people and alterable by them. Thus submission to their restraint was compatible with freedom. On the other hand, if they were to perform their principal function as iron bands of restraint, then it was better that people should come to think of them not as instruments of their will, but as something outside and independent of themselves. What was true of constitutions was true of the law in general. There was a growing tendency in the nineteenth century for men to think of law as a product of political organization, a natural offspring of the national life, as Lieber called it, "the expression of the *will of human Society*." Yet Whigs like Choate were anxious that this notion should not be too practically and vulgarly construed. "It is one of the distemperatures to which an unreasoning liberty may grow," he warned in his law school speech,

> to regard *law* as no more nor less than just the will—the actual and present will—of the actual majority of the nation. [But in that case] how can it gain a moment's hold on the reverential sentiments of the heart, and the profounder convictions of the judgment? How can it impress a filial awe; how can it conciliate a filial love; how can it sustain a sentiment of veneration; how can it command a rational and animated defence. . . . Oppose now to this, the loftier philosophy which we have learned. In the language of our system, the law is not the transient and arbitrary creation of the major will, nor of any will. It is not the offspring of will at all. It is the absolute justice of the State, enlightened by the perfect reason of the State.[60]

It was this kind of mystification that, along with its technicalities, had enraged those radical opponents of the common law who had dreamed of a purely American law, owing nothing to feudal Europe, reduced to simple, rational codes, easily comprehensible by the average man. Choate took no very prominent part in the struggle over codification that raged in the 1830s and, as Perry Miller has shown, encapsulated much of the ethos of Jacksonian democracy. Choate's overall estimate, however, of what the law should be and do placed him on the side of the defenders of the common law against the codifiers. By the mid-forties, the battle had essentially been won. The treatises of Kent and Story and texts like Greenleaf's *Evidence* helped to establish the common law as a rational "science" rather than a mere jumble of inherited and obsolete rulings. By their wide circulation, these works helped to spread a considerable degree of uniformity in legal development in the different states. Perhaps most important of all, as the massive volumes of reports rolled off the presses, a great body of precedent, adapted to specific American cases, and authoritatively explained, was being built up to solidly entrench the common law within the profession and the society.[61]

The common law did indeed, as its votaries never tired of maintaining, have many advantages—principally that while preserving a core of defense of individual rights, it could move more flexibly than any code to deal with new developments. To the conservative, however, it had an even more fundamental appeal: because it was constructed in so piecemeal a fashion, it could be perceived as organic, as growing rather than made; because the many decisions that made it up were from so many different sources, it took on an impersonal, almost inevitable quality. With its origins lost in remote antiquity, slowly adapting itself to the demands of the future, the common law seemed naturally adapted to the national community as described by Burke. "Is there not something in the study and administrative enjoyment of an elaborate, rational, and ancient jurisprudence," Choate asked the law school audience,

> which tends to raise the law itself, in the professional and in the general idea, almost up to the nature of an independent, superior reason, in one sense out of the people, in one sense above them,—out of and above, and independent of, and collateral to, the people of any given day? Invisible, omnipresent, a real yet impalpable existence, it seems more a spirit, an abstraction,—the whispered yet authoritative voice of all the past and all the good,—than like the transient contrivance of altogether such as ourselves. We come to think of it, not so much as a set of provisions and rules which we can unmake, amend, and annul, as of a guide whom it is wiser to follow, an authority whom it is better to obey, a wisdom which it is not unbecoming to revere, a power—a superior—whose service is perfect freedom. Thus at last the spirit of the law descends into the great heart of the people for healing and for conservation.[62]

The authority of law, conceived in this fashion, derived not from any identifiable sovereign will, but from the authority of the great stream of civilization itself. Choate thought of the law, as it had become naturalized in the United States, as an inheritance not merely from England, but from all the civilized ages of the past, "one mighty and continuous stream of experience and reason, accumulated, ancestral, widening and deepening and washing itself clearer as it runs on, the grand agent of civilization, the builder of a thousand cities, the guardian angel of a hundred generations." The law was the most important thread in that great social fabric in which men must be taught to feel themselves enmeshed from birth to death, as impersonal and inevitable as the law of gravity. To resist, perhaps even to question, law, was not merely to disobey legitimate authority, it was to put oneself outside the community.[63]

A bonus of such a noble vision of the law, of course, was that some of the nobility could be expected to rub off on its practitioners. Deference was hard to come by in Jacksonian America and lawyers could not expect much of it; the battle for respect was still being waged in the 1840s as in the heyday of the agitation to codify the law in the 1830s. Nor was the day-to-day business of the office and the courts usually such as to keep the average lawyer continually aware of the exalted nature of his calling. In the privacy of his office Choate, too, could be thrown into despondency by the daily grind. "To be a good lawyer is no more than to be a good carpenter," he complained once to a student, "it's a knack, simply moving a machine."[64]

In speaking to the fledgling lawyers at Cambridge, however, it was necessary to take a broader view and keep up morale. If they remembered that they were not merely earning a living but bound to a calling, it would enable them to soar above all the barbs flung at them by a jealous populace. It would raise the profession from

> a dexterous art and a subtle and flexible science,—from a cunning logic, a gilded rhetoric, and an ambitious learning, wearing the purple robe of the sophists, and letting itself to hire,—to the dignity of almost a department of government,—an instrumentality of the State for the well-being and conservation of the State.

In the circumstances of America, well being and conservation amounted to the same thing. Conservatism was not merely the natural tendency of the legal profession, it was their highest duty. Lest any of his young audience should be seduced by the dying reverberations of codification into a desire to make a name by tinkering with the majestic edifice of the law, he reminded them that "to keep the city is only not less difficult and glorious than to build it." The ambitious legal reformer, Lord Brougham, had adopted the maxim of Augustus—that he had found Rome brick and left it marble. "Yes," said Choate, "but he found Rome free, and left her a slave. He found her a Republic, and left her an empire! . . . We find our city of marble, and we will leave it marble. . . . To that office, to that praise, let even the claims of your profession be subordinated. *Pro clientibus saepe; pro lege, pro republica semper.*"[65]

"Let reverence for the laws," said the young Abraham Lincoln in 1838, "become the *political religion* of the nation." This gave the legal profession as a whole a priestly function as guardian of the mysteries, but it gave an especially vital role to the judiciary. The judge assumed a particularly luminous role in Whig philosophy; he appeared to be the last repository in American society of a "paternal" authority, derived not from the people but from the more fundamental authority of the law he served and his own expertise in it.[66] This seemingly anomalous position provided a constant opportunity for friction, and the legal profession was always vehement to deny that, as their opponents charged, judges *made* the law. "The phrase, *'Judge-made law,'*" declared Professor Greenleaf sternly, "belongs only to the ignorant and unreflecting . . . [the judge] has merely ascertained and declared the sense of the community." But he was quick to add that this "sense of the community" was not what was expressed "through executive functionaries" or "vociferated in the popular clamor of the day." It was the permanent sense of the community embedded in the law.[67] The judge, through his learning, was able to tease out the intimations of directions latent within the body of the law and apply them to new circumstances. Sometimes this could result in breathtaking coups—as in *Marbury* v. *Madison* in which Chief Justice Marshall had divined judicial review as contained dormant within the logic of the constitution. To Choate this decision was the cornerstone of a conservative interpretation of the constitution.

> That the framers of the Constitution intended this should be so, is certain; but to have asserted it against the Congress and the Executive,—to have vindicated it by that easy yet adamantine demonstration than which the reasonings of the mathematics show nothing surer—to have inscribed this vast truth of conservatism on the public mind, so that no demagogue, not in the last stage of intoxication, denies it,—this is an achievement of states-

manship of which a thousand years may not exhaust or reveal all the good.[68]

The power of this decision, as Choate described it, lay in two things: its assertion of the independence of the judge against the elected representatives of the people, and its convincing demonstration of his authority, which compelled the public mind. Conservatives were always anxious that judges should be men of learning and high character since this was part of their intrinsic rather than delegated authority. Indeed, Whigs seemed to have hoped that through the growing power of the judiciary the leadership of the "best men" might be reintroduced into American democracy. Classical republicanism rested on the idea that the people would defer to natural excellence; from the Whig point of view, this had not been the case in the political sphere. The courts might be the last refuge of a natural aristocracy—if they could be preserved inviolate from popular control.[69]

Preserving the courts from politics was becoming harder to do; as pressure for codification lessened, Democratic pressure to make judges more responsive to the people grew. Many people were not convinced that the judiciary was, as the Whigs always claimed, "above" politics, and, by the late forties, a growing movement in the states to make their judiciaries elective for short terms was increasingly successful.[70] The Whigs rallied to the defense with the determination of those who feel they are defending a last bastion. "Shall we have Kents and Spencers, Storys and Marshalls *elected?*" demanded a contributor to the *American Review,* after the new constitution of New York had provided for judges of the state supreme court to be elected for eight-year terms. Not only would the people not choose the best qualified, but the "best and ablest" men would not put themselves up for election and subject themselves to the sordid calumnies of American politics. This "extraordinary innovation in the greatest department of the State," commented an editorial note, was "fraught with danger to the very foundations of Social Order."[71]

Even when the elective principle was not yet triumphant and judges served for life, there were still ways both of harassing and pressuring the judiciary. in 1843, the Democratic legislature of Massachusetts reduced the salaries of supreme court judges and also removed the adjutant general by legislative address, because he had lent arms to the government of Rhode Island during the Dorr rebellion. As a way of removing an unpopular official, the legislative address was easier and less cumbersome than impeachment. Twice Choate defended judges who were attacked in this way.[72]

The first case, in 1849, concerned a justice of the peace of Worcestershire County, James Carter, who had been excessively zealous in his administration of the liquor laws; a number of people in his district petitioned the legislature for his removal. The second case, seven years later, involved a judge of the Supreme Court of Maine, Woodbury Davis, apparently a political appointee of an outgoing Whig governor, who had refused to accept the dismissal of the incumbent sheriff and the appointment of a new one by the incoming Democratic governor. The Democratic legislature resolved to remove him by address; the judge imported an impressive team of legal talent from Boston, led by Choate, for his defense.[73] In both cases Choate asserted that what was at stake was the separation of powers that ensured that the American polity should be "a Government of laws, and not of men." The great principle of the American constitution was the independence of the judiciary and the greatest threat to this independence was the "morbid development of the power of the Legislature." The security of individual rights depended upon an impartial bench that "owns no master but the law, and no duty but justice." The independent judge, though he might block the transient will of temporary majorities, was the ultimate defense of "American liberty"—"whose essence, whose end, whose boast, whose fruit is, security."[74]

Choate won the case for Judge Carter and lost the case for Judge Davis. His greatest effort on behalf of an independent judiciary, however, was in the Massachusetts Constitutional Convention of 1853. The system of representation in the state, with the growth and shift of population, had become inequitable, but since Whigs almost always managed to carry the state, they were not much disposed to tinker with it. The convention was the work of the coalition between Democrats and Free-Soilers that had been formed in 1850 to defeat the Whig candidate for governor, Robert Winthrop. The coalition got control of the legislature, elected a Democrat, George S. Boutwell, as governor and passed a bill calling for a referendum on the desirability of a convention to remodel the constitution. This was voted down in the election of 1851, but narrowly approved in 1852, though the Whigs managed to regain control of the state. The margin in favor of a convention came largely from the rural counties and the subsequent convention would resolve itself more nearly into a contest between country and city than between Left and Right.[75]

The Whigs had been opposed to the whole notion of constitutional revision. Sinister designs were afoot, warned the Whig State Convention in 1851; the coalition merely wanted to consolidate their hold on the government and their alliance "on the basis of share and share alike in the public plunder." Once a convention had been approved by the people, however, they determined to make the best of it—a reform from the present system of election by majority to election by plurality, for example, would obviously work to their advantage as the strongest party in the state. The *Atlas,* now edited by the future Republican leader, William Schouler, implored the Whigs to realize that "the tendency of the age, and of our institutions is towards giving increased power to the people" and that "true conservatism lies not in blindly and madly opposing that which is inevitable." These sentiments were echoed by Edward Everett, who wrote to the president of the Young Men's Whig Club:

> It is a matter of great importance to choose members of the Convention who are *reasonably* conservative; by which I mean not men prejudiced against all change; but men uninfected with the radical and disorganizing notions of the 'Coalitionists.' I would rather have sound constitutional democrats in the Convention than men of the latter class; indeed I would be glad at any rate to have *sound constitutional* men irrespective of party.[76]

Although they won the state election of 1852, however, the Whigs suffered a disastrous defeat in the election of delegates to the convention. This was due partly to the fact that the rural areas were more over-represented than usual because even the smallest towns sent delegates; partly to the defeat of a ten-hour-day law in the Whig legislature, which lost them some of the working-class vote; partly to a tactical blunder. The Democrats and Free-Soilers had long championed the secret ballot and the Whigs opposed it. The coalition legislature of 1851 enacted it, and, while their Whig successors did not dare abolish it entirely, they made the use of sealed envelopes for the ballot "optional." This new law was rammed through only five days before the elections for the convention and seemed a blatant attempt to enable Whig manufacturers to intimidate their workers at the polls. The result was that out of 422 delegates only 146 were Whigs.[77]

A large number of farmers were elected, especially from the western part of the state, but most of these took little part in the deliberations. Boston sent a powerful, solidly Whig delegation, made up almost equally of lawyers, merchants and other professional men. Choate, who was then attorney general, was its most prominent member. Boston had closed its ranks against the Free-Soilers, but Sumner and Richard Henry Dana got themselves elected by more sympathetic small western towns. Once the convention began, it was clear that much festering discontent had been released and that more than the electoral system would be reformed. The judiciary, the militia, Harvard, the question of general incorporation laws, were all thrown into the arena.[78]

The convention began with a debate on the secret ballot issue, on the question of whether a vacated seat should be filled according to the question originally put to the people on the holding of a convention, stipulating the secret ballot, or according to the law of March 1853 making it optional. Choate's first speech of the convention championed the constitutional supremacy of an act of the legislature over any supposed referendum by the people and reminded the delegates that they were not a revolutionary body, but assembled "according to the will of the people, but a will expressed in strict and precise form of law." In the course of this speech he asked the convention to spare the ancient language of the constitution, "those historical phrases of the old glorious school of liberty . . . in their very rust"—an unfortunate phrase that gave the reformers the opportunity to opt for the "ever new, bright, perennial."[79]

At least on the question of representation, however, the party divisions would not be as ideologically neat as these phrases suggest. The question was a politically complicated one: on paper the rural areas were already over-represented—Worcester County, for example, sent the same number of representatives to the legislature as Boston, though Boston had twelve thousand more inhabitants. Still, representation was tied to some extent to population, and, as the rural population continued to decline, an increasing number of small towns would lose the right to send annual delegates. The Whig strength lay in the urban and industrial areas which they managed to control through the general ticket system of voting. Boston always sent a solid block of Whig members to the legislature, even though Democrats and Free-Soilers might poll thirty to forty percent of the popular vote in the city. The main Democratic and Free-Soil strength lay in the rural and especially western areas of the state. Thus the coalition desire to break the hold of the Whigs in the state coalesced with growing rural discontent and suspicion of the industrial cities, especially Boston. In the convention, then, the coalition championed a rearrangement of the representation system that was, in terms of population, even more inequitable than the existing one. Every town, even the smallest, would be able to send at least one representative to the legislature, and no city should have more than thirty—thus cutting Boston's representation by one-third. The Whigs, on the other hand, proposed a new district system with representation proportioned to population.[80]

The exigencies of politics thus found the Democrats and Free-Soilers taking a firm Burkean stand on "the old principle of the right of corporate representation for the towns," while Rufus Choate, as chief spokesman for the Whig position, rose to champion rational justice and the "rights of man." It was, he maintained, purely a dispute "between artificial privilege and natural justice . . . between town lines and human beings." Under the coalition proposal, a little more than one-quarter of the inhabitants of the state would send more representatives to the legislature than all the rest. The coalition proposal would sacrifice the "rights of men" to "the accidents of place." "Is it all at once found that accident; that the past—and not reason, conscience, and free will —can alone determine the form of the Constitution?" He assured the delegates that Boston was not Paris and there was no danger of "consolidation." In any case, it was absurd to talk of separate "interests" that had to be protected and balanced against each other. Massachusetts had the good fortune to possess a homogeneous population, not widely dispersed, "every man within a day's ride of every other," and with a total harmony of interests. And this fortunate homogeneity and harmony enabled Massachusetts to "raise this word or this thing equality, from an idea in the mind,

a phrase in the Bill of Rights, into realized government." Necessity, it was true, sometimes enforced inequities, but the

> one great aim of true reform, and a real progress, is
> peaceably and gradually to remove the artificial inequali-
> ties which history had produced; to cause the law to tend
> ever towards the perfectly humane, and the perfectly
> just; and to bring civil and political rights nearer and
> nearer to the rights of nature.

Choate's definition of reform was akin to what another conservative Whig, Abraham Lincoln, would see as the central meaning of
the Declaration of Independence and thus directly applicable to
what ought to be the nation's attitude towards slavery. To Choate
it appears to have been merely a useful argument in the context
of the present debate, without resonance to the deeper issues of
the age.[81]

Many eyebrows must have been raised as, at the height of his
speech, Choate paused to rebuke Burke and spare a word of praise
for Tom Paine. Listening to Democrat eloquence on representation by towns, he said, reminded him of Burke on the fall of Marie
Antoinette and the end of the age of chivalry. It made men weep,
but when they "began to discern that all this eloquence, and music
. . . turned back the golden wheels of the car of reform, and shut
the gates of mercy on the masses of mankind; when they found
in the happy phrase of Paine, that 'he pitied the plumage and
forgot the dying bird,'—the spell was broken forever." The irony
of the whole situation was not lost on the participants. "I rise, Sir,"
said the Democrat, George Boutwell, in reply to Choate, "as a
Conservative—an unusual character for me. My friend, the
learned gentleman from Boston, has taken his seat a Progressive
—he will pardon me—a still more unusual character for him."
The position of both parties was determined largely through political expediency, but the Whigs had the advantage. Their argument was entirely compatible with "enlightened conservatism,"
whereas there was little to be said for the coalition position except
that it would enable them to "dish the Whigs."[82]

The other major issue of the convention proved to be the
independence of the judiciary. George F. Hoar said that he and
several other Free-Soilers had only agreed to constitutional revision on the stipulation that the judiciary should not be touched,

and judicial tenure had not been part of the propaganda campaign for the convention. In the convention itself, the committee on the judiciary included Choate and Marcus Morton, a Democrat, but also a former justice of the state supreme court. The committee recommended no change in the appointment or tenure of judges. But it found itself facing a groundswell of "Jacksonian" discontent with the undemocratic nature and unaccountability of the courts. The Democrat Benjamin Hallett acknowledged that judges were independent of "the people" but wondered if they could really be considered independent of "the political and social influences that surround them—these cliques, these clubs, those circles, that are drawn around them as men and politicians before they are judges, and under the influence of which they go upon the bench." Two amendments came from the floor—to have judges elected rather than appointed and to make their term of office ten years rather than life. Some Free-Soilers joined the demand to make the bench more responsive to popular feeling because of their disgust at the way in which the Massachusetts judiciary had upheld the Fugitive Slave Law. For others, however, their Whiggish devotion to the independent judge outweighed their outrage at particular decisions. They rallied to support the Whig opposition on this point. Richard Henry Dana, who otherwise worked with the coalition, gave one of the great speeches of the convention in favor of retaining the appointment and life tenure of judges.[83]

Choate made one of his most impressive speeches in defense of the old judicial tenure. "It was," noted Dana in his journal, "one of the great efforts of his life, such a speech as a man may be happy to have lived to hear." Joseph H. Choate, who as a boy heard him deliver the speech, remarks on how much plainer and unadorned it was than most of his speeches, designed to reach beyond the delegates in the convention to "the fishermen of Essex, the manufacturers of Worcester and Hampden, and the farmers of Berkshire" and convince by the weight of its argument and the depth of his feeling. "As he retired from the old Hall of the House of Representatives, leaning heavily upon the arm of Henry Wilson, all crumpled, dishevelled and exhausted, I said to myself that some virtue had gone out of him. . . ."[84]

The essence of the question, said Choate, was what kind of appointment and tenure would be likely to secure the best possible judiciary. And then he drew an eloquent, and formidable, portrait of the ideal judge. In the first place, he must be a man of prodigious learning:

> He is to know, not merely the law which you make, and the legislature makes, not constitutional and statute law alone, but that other ampler, that boundless jurisprudence, the common law, which the successive generations of the State have silently built up; that old code of freedom which we brought with us in the Mayflower and Arbella, but which in the progress of centuries we have ameliorated and enriched, and adapted wisely to the necessities of a busy, prosperous, and wealthy community,—that he must know. And where to find it? In volumes which you must count by hundreds, by thousands; filling libraries; exacting long labors,—the labors of a life-time, abstracted from business, from politics.

Secondly, he must be a man of rigid probity and independent spirit.

> If a law is passed by a unanimous legislature, clamored for by the general voice of the public, and a cause is before him on it, in which the whole community is on one side and an individual nameless or odious on the other, and he believes it to be against the Constitution, he must so declare it,—or there is no judge.

And lastly, he should inspire love and awe.

> I would have something of the venerable and illustrious attach to his character and function, in the judgment and feelings of the commonwealth . . . that he be a man towards whom the love and trust and affectionate admiration of the people should flow.

He finished the portrait by quoting the testament to the good judge from the Book of Job: "The young men saw me, and hid themselves; and the aged arose and stood up. The princes refrained talking, and laid their hand upon their mouth." The people could not have the intimate and detailed knowledge to select a man capable of becoming such a judge, any more than they would know how to choose "a professor of the higher mathematics or of intellectual philosophy." Even if appointed by the governor with the expert advice of the profession as at present, a limited tenure that made reappointment dependent on party favor destroyed his independence of politics. Only appointment for life could make Choate's ideal portrait a practical possibility.[85]

He concluded with a new interpretation of the essential "balance" of the American system of government. To maintain, as the advocates of an elective judiciary did, that appointment for life was anti-republican and inconsistent with liberty, ignored the fact that the American system was basically dualistic. There were two sides to the American—or at least the Massachusetts—character. On the one hand, "they have nothing timorous in them, as touching the largest liberty," but "there is another side to their character; and that is the old Anglo-Saxon instinct of property; the rational, and the creditable desire to be secure in life, in reputation, in the earnings of daily labor, in the little all which makes up the treasures, and the dear charities of the humblest home." Correspondingly, "our political system . . . aims to accomplish a twofold object, to wit: liberty and security. To accomplish this twofold object we have established a twofold set of institutions and instrumentalities." The essential balance of the constitution then lay not in the division between the different branches of government, but between the entire "political" system—including mass meetings, the polls, the press, and free speech—on the one hand, and the law and the courts on the other. It was a balance between power and restraint, between will and discipline.[86]

The eloquence of Choate and Dana defeated the Democratic proposals, and Dana noted in his diary "the judiciary question was considered as settled. . . . The rejoicings and congratulations of the Boston members and the conservative men generally know no bounds." The rejoicing was short lived. The Democratic press rebuked the pusillanimity of the convention, and six days later the proposal to limit the tenure of judges (though not to elect them) was revived. This time it passed. Choate endeavored to get this provision at least presented to the people separately rather than incorporated into the new constitution, but to no avail.[87] In the event, however, it did not matter, for the new constitution was soundly defeated by the people in the November elections. Schouler credited Choate's speech on the judiciary, "more than any other utterance in the whole convention," with carrying "the people against the submitted changes." Whether or not this is so, the attempt to tamper with the judicial system does seem to have been one of the most important factors in the popular rejection, together with the patently inequitable system of representation proposed. The Whig party threw all its energies into getting the constitution defeated, and they were joined by some Democrats, like Marcus Morton, who disapproved of what the convention had come up with, and some lapsed Whig Free-Soilers, like John G. Palfrey and Charles Francis Adams. The final vote was essentially sectional—all the coastal counties opposed the proposed constitution; the western counties were in favor. Though major constitutional change had been rejected, individual propositions of the 1853 proposal—such as election by plurality, popular election of county officials including district attorneys, and the secret ballot —were adopted in the next few years. Massachusetts was, however, one of the few states to retain her appointed and life-tenured judiciary.[88]

Though the convention had come to nothing, some personal reputations had been won and lost. Of Choate, Dana noted in his journal:

> Choate has held his own. What more could he do? He has shown himself the brilliant, rich, philosophical orator, the scholar, and the kindly, adroit and interesting man. He has not commanded respect as a man of deep convictions, earnest purpose, and reliable judgment. But he is felt to be the greatest rhetorical genius of the day.[89]

Partly as a result of the fiasco, the Whigs won the next state election, though it was the last time they were to carry Massachusetts. Nonetheless, the defeat of the new constitution seems to indicate that the Whig idea of the judiciary as the guardian of the law and the constitution, even against the people themselves, had taken a strong hold—at least in Massachusetts. The legal profession, while it might not be loved, and while it had not become quite a new clergy, or even a clerisy, had managed to attach itself, as necessary interpreters, to the "organic law" of society—the constitution. Moreover, they had succeeded to a remarkable degree in attaching the idea of that "organic law" to the idea of restraint. Indeed, in a newspaper attack on the proposed constitution, George Ticknor Curtis put forward the notion of restraint as peculiarly American.

The object of this constitution, or permanent law, was to set bounds to the action of the majority, by restraining their legislative power within certain limits; and the Judiciary was established, as the umpire, to determine when those limits are transcended. As the idea of limiting the power of a self-governing people was a purely novel and American idea; so, too, the particular limitation resorted to was wholly new and peculiar to ourselves.

Increasingly in the years before the Civil War, Americans were coming to see their existence as a society as depending upon the bounds and restraints provided by law. One result of this was a tendency to resolve problems of politics into questions of law, and thus to take them out of the realm of discussion and adjustment into the realm of authority and obedience. Another was the tendency to equate order with positive law. The constitution was the "organic law," declared Charles Francis Adams. "By *organic* law I mean that rule by which the society, of which we are all members, is kept together, and without which we should all fly apart." Thus anything less than total fidelity to the seamless web of law portended not merely temporary disorder but the collapse of society itself.[90]

FIVE

SLAVERY AND THE UNION

"$\mathcal{W}$E SAIL AMID ten thousand shoals," Choate had written to James Marsh in 1837, "and beyond them all is that vast lee-shore, the slavery question, on which we are at last to go to pieces."[1] By 1850, that lee shore was looming ever nearer and more dangerous and for the remainder of his life Choate's political activity was devoted to preventing the frail vessel of the Union from breaking up upon it. The Compromise of 1850, avoiding any congressional pronouncement on slavery in the territories recently acquired from Mexico and giving the South the moral concession of a tough fugitive slave law, was the last major effort of the old-line conservative Whigs to repair relations between the sections. Clay's proposal and Webster's famous Seventh of March speech in defense of it were offered against a backdrop of growing Southern anger and threats of secession which made the imminent breakup of the Union seem entirely possible. Nonetheless, however much the conservative Whigs of Massachusetts, and particularly its business community, desired to preserve the Union, the abandonment of the Wilmot Proviso, and particularly the new Fugitive Slave Law, were hard pills to swallow.[2]

Webster's speech, which even-handedly distributed the blame for the crisis between the North and the South, and supported the proposed fugitive slave law, not only infuriated abolitionists and Free-Soilers but also dismayed many staunch Webster Whigs. "If he could have said a few things differently . . ." lamented Winthrop. Edward Everett confided to him that he did not think Massachusetts would ever accept the fugitive slave provisions—he himself would not "perform the duty which it devolves 'on all good citizens.' I admit the theoretical right of the South to an efficient extradition law, but it is a right that *cannot be enforced.* "³ Yet conservative Whigs swallowed their misgivings and rallied in support of Webster, and eight hundred prominent Bostonians, Choate among them, signed a public letter thanking him for pointing out the right path in an "apparent conflict of duties." Everett, who did not sign the letter, told Winthrop that he had been at a dinner in which "everyone present, and they were Webster's fastest friends (the Curtises, Choate, Judge Warren and Ticknor), argued that he had committed himself very unfortunately on that point [the fugitive slave law], and yet every one, except Frank Gray and myself, had signed the letter expressing entire concurrence in the doctrines of the speech."⁴

The reservations of men like Choate stemmed not so much from opposition to Webster's fundamental position as from a realization of the touchy nature of Massachusetts public opinion on the slavery issue. The task now was to rally that opinion to the belief that what had been at stake was the Union and that Clay and Webster had saved it. While the increasingly Free-Soil *Atlas* denounced the Seventh of March speech, the major Whig newspapers, the *Advertiser* and the *Courier,* fell into line behind it. Prominent lawyers, including the two professors of the Harvard Law School, and leading clergymen, including Choate's minister, Nehemiah Adams, spoke publicly in defense of the Compromise. Opinion veered more sharply in Webster's favor when, on the sudden death of President Taylor, he entered Fillmore's cabinet as secretary of state. Nonetheless, the demoralization was sufficient for the Whigs to lose control of Massachusetts in the November elections to the coalition of Free-Soilers and Democrats. The state of the party, like the state of the Union, made a rallying of public opinion to accept the Compromise imperative. Choate was away in Europe while the measures passed through Congress, but he was back in time to give the closing address at a great bipartisan "Union meeting" held in Faneuil Hall at the end of November.⁵

The meeting was in response to a notice posted in the "Merchants' Reading Room" and in the newspapers, addressed to those citizens who "reverence the Constitution of the United States; who wish to discountenance a spirit of disobedience to the laws of the land . . . who would regard with disfavor all further popular

agitation of subjects which endanger the peace and harmony of
the Union, and who deem the preservation of the Union the
paramount duty of every citizen." Five thousand men signed the
call and a huge audience turned out to hear Benjamin R. Curtis
denounce Theodore Parker and other anti-slavery men who had
advocated resisting the Fugitive Slave Law. "We have come
here," he said,

> not to consider particular measures of government, but
> to assert that we *have* a Government; not to determine
> whether this or that law be wise or just, but to declare
> that there *is* law . . . not to consult whether this or that
> course of policy is beneficial to our country, but to say
> that we yet *have* a country, and intend to keep it safe.[6]

These remarks not only set the tone of the meeting but reflected
what would be the essential Whig strategy from now on: to shift
the whole debate from the problem of slavery and its extension
to a basic question of law and order and national unity.

As a contemporary critic noted, slavery to Choate was "a
question like the Tariff or the United States Bank, only more
difficult and dangerous"—more dangerous because, unlike those
other political questions, slavery divided the nation on sectional
rather than party lines. Far more than the Democrats, the Whig
party had always had great difficulty in maintaining party unity
whenever slavery-related issues became politically prominent.[7]
The policy of the Whig leadership had always been to keep slavery
as far as possible out of the political arena; it was, as Jeremiah
Mason acutely said, "a subject . . . entirely unmanageable for any
practical purpose." The original Whig reaction to radical abolitionism, as Henry Adams pointed out, had been to nip it in the
bud before it could disrupt the fragile bonds of unity in party and
nation: "silence them; break up the meetings; put Mr. Garrison
in jail for safekeeping; *keep them quiet!*"[8] But, once surfaced, the
problem could not be suppressed and the Whigs had had to manage it as best they could, tacking before the wind, alternately, of
Northern indignation and Southern reaction. The policy urged by
Webster and Choate and other conservative Whigs in 1850 was
essentially a return to that earlier primitive reaction of "keep them
quiet." The only hope, they felt, for the continuance of the Union
and a return to "normal" politics was for the North not only to

accept loyally the provisions of the Compromise but to agree to suppress any further agitation or even discussion of the tender subject. Every well-disposed citizen, said Choate, should not only determine to accept "the whole body of measures of the compromise," but he should also, "according to his measure, and in his place, in his party, in his social, or his literary, or his religious circle, in whatever may be his sphere of influence, set himself to suppress the further political agitation of this whole subject."[9]

Choate concluded the meeting by solemnly warning his audience that however much some men might ridicule "union-saving," the Union *was* in extreme danger. More than most governments it was a highly artificial and therefore fragile structure; all the things—"identity of interest; closeness of kindred, contiguity of place; old habit; the ten thousand opportunities of daily intercourse"—that in a state like Massachusetts operated to preserve the state were missing from the national union. "I have sometimes thought," he said,

> that the States in our system may be compared to the primordial particles of matter, indivisible, indestructible, impenetrable, whose natural condition is to repel each other, or at least, to exist, in their own independent identity,—while the Union is an artificial aggregation of such particles; a sort of *forced state*, as some have said, of life, a complex structure made with hands, which gravity, attrition, time, rain, dew, frost, not less than tempest and earthquake, cooperate to waste away, and which the anger of a fool—or the laughter of a fool—may bring down in an hour; a system of bodies advancing slowly through a *resisting medium*, operating at all times to retard, and at any moment liable to arrest its motion; a beautiful, yet fragile creation, which a breath can unmake, as a breath has made it.[10]

The Union was a creation of "the reason and the will" and it could not survive either the perversion of that reason or the faltering of that will. Four years earlier he had developed for the law students at Harvard the Coleridgean theory that the health of the state depended essentially on the Idea of it reposing in the minds of its citizens, that the nation was a production, an exponent of a national mind. But in the United States, he now reminded his audience, such a national mind had hardly had time to develop. Ultimately, attitudes might become habits of mind, responses instinctive, but meanwhile public opinion must be painstakingly nursed along the proper lines and protected from temptations, for "the grand incorporation" could only be accomplished by "carefully cultivated and acquired habits and states of feeling; by an enlightened discernment of great interests . . . by a voluntary determination to love, honor, and cherish," by tolerance and the determination to emphasize common interests and traditions and kindly ignore "the offensive particulars in which we differ." It was only by "a prolonged and voluntary educational process, that the fine and strong spirit of NATIONALITY" might be made "to penetrate and animate the scarcely congruous mass."[11]

The fundamental importance of maintaining proper public opinion meant that the principal enemies of the Union were those Northern "disorganizers" who insisted on regarding slavery as a moral issue and on keeping it in the forefront of public attention. If this was philanthropy, said Choate, it was a philanthropy "whose means are bad faith, abusive speech, ferocity of temper, and resistance to law; and whose fruit, if it ripens to fruit, will be woes unnumbered to bond and free."[12] He was to return again and again to an attack on this misguided philanthropy which, by its obsession with one issue, was driving the sections further and further apart. In July 1851, he was asked to give the oration at the first anniversary of the Story Association of the Dane Law School. As Everett noted disapprovingly, he "took no notice of Judge Story, the Association or the Law School" but launched into an attack on the Free-Soilers and all agitation over slavery. "I am sorry you are coming," he said to Richard Henry Dana as they shook hands on the platform before the ceremonies began, "I shall have to offend you." Since this was supposed to be a non-political occasion, and since some of the distinguished men present were Free-Soilers, Dana was probably not alone in thinking the speech "improper and inappropriate."[13] Choate, however, was too genuinely agitated over what he felt were real and too-little-appreciated dangers to the nation, to care much about decorum.

The speech was in many ways a coda, colored by the specific circumstances of the times, to his address of 1846. To the general duty of serving and upholding the state, the legal profession must now consider it their especial duty to uphold the Compromise of

1850, in all its provisions. The lawyer, above all others, should not succumb to the linked charms of sentiment and absolutes. "It is so easy to be allured by a glittering abstraction; it is so easy to take the Declaration of Independence and deduce from it the doctrine of universal emancipation; to sketch in marked colors the dark details of the life of the slave." Certain classes of people easily fell into this trap—the young, "men of letters, poets, the clergy, women." But the lawyer had to possess the masculine quality of political realism, for "to exercise this conservative influence, to beget a distrust of individual and unenlightened judgment, on matters of such vast import and extent, and to foster a religious reverence for the laws, is the *new duty* which the times demand of the legal profession." The extent to which most of the legal profession, and especially the judiciary, did in fact uphold the Fugitive Slave Law of 1850, not solely on strictly legal grounds, but on grounds of public policy as necessary to the peace and preservation of the Union, shows how far they had come to accept Choate's prescription for them as not merely practitioners of the law, but servants of the state.[14]

Choate saw the present crisis as essentially a clash between virtue, in its classical masculine sense as those qualities which sustain a republic, and virtue in its more modern, "feminine" sense of strict adherence to certain moral and religious principles. Philanthropy had grown at the expense of patriotism and "passionate morality" was making war on "the virtue which sustains the Union." Like his philosophical mentors, Burke and Coleridge, indeed like all conservatives, he profoundly distrusted what he liked to think of as the application of "abstract" reason to practical affairs, the taking of any principle, political or religious, to its logical conclusion. Behind the ideologue stood the guillotine and such purism always ended in blood.[15] However idealistic their intentions, only disaster could stem from those reformers who insisted on "taking the Lord's Prayer and the Declaration of Independence, and fraudulently and scandalously undertaking to deduce from them the dogma of instantaneous and universal emancipation."[16] Modern man had to remember that he lived in several different spheres at once and that the qualities required of him as a Christian, for example, were not always applicable to his role as a citizen, where he must be guided, not by love and compassion, but by the secular virtues of duty, prudence, good faith, patriotism.

The frequent inability to differentiate between these separate spheres was what made the individual conscience such an untrustworthy guide to political action. "The capital defect of the day," he told the Story Association,

> is, not that conscience is too much worshipped, but that it is not properly limited. Men think that by the mere feeling within them of a sense of right, they can test great subjects to which the philosophy of ages leads the way, and can try a grand complex polity, embracing a multitude of interests and conflicting claims and duties. But these ethical politics do not train the citizen *ab extra* to be enlightened on these subjects.

Brought up, like most New Englanders of his generation, on the Scottish school of philosophy, he could hardly deny the existence of an innate moral sense, but he felt that, like intelligence, it was not of much use without education. Before the duty of following their conscience, men had the duty of "having a conscience which can know and discern the qualities of things and thus judge fairly." The conscience must learn from "History; from Politics; from the Study of Life." "Morality should go to school. It should consult the builders of Empire and learn the arts imperial by which it is preserved, ere it ventures to pronounce on the construction and laws of nations and commonwealths."[17]

Only the "instructed conscience" was a safe guide to practical conduct in the world of politics, and for this instruction the teaching of lawyers was a better guide than the preaching of the clergy. Choate was profoundly irritated by any attempt of the churches to expand their proper sphere and meddle with the affairs of the polity. The New England clergy, he told Parker, could see only one side of the slavery question. "A comparison of duties or a yielding of an impracticable good, for the far grander good of a nationality pregnant with happiness to generations—they seem unable to apprehend." While religion belonged to man in a universal sense and directed his relationship with eternity, the law belonged to man as citizen in a particular place and time. Because the law was the result of the experienced deliberations of statesmen and judges, it was in many ways itself the embodiment of the "instructed conscience." The wise man would realize the inadequacy of his own inner voice by the side of this majestic authority.[18]

Sympathy, to Choate, was a personal emotion that should not be allowed to sway the decisions of public life. When the Hungarian revolutionary, Louis Kossuth, toured the United States in 1851 in a personally triumphant, but politically unsuccessful, bid for aid, Choate, like most American conservatives, sympathized with the plight of Hungary but was adamant that America should remain strictly uninvolved in European affairs. He wrote to Charles Sumner, now in the Senate, congratulating him on a speech taking that position,

> steering skillfully between *coldshoulderism and inhospitality* on the one side, and the splendid folly and wickedness of co-operation on the other. Cover the Magyar with flowers—lave him with perfumes, serenade him with eloquence—and let him go home alone . . . if he will not live here. Such is all that is permitted to wise States—aspiring to "true grandeur."[19]

After Kossuth's departure, Choate gave a Phi Beta Kappa address at the University of Vermont which summarized his conception of the proper position of the United States vis-à-vis European upheavals. Parallels with the proper attitude of Northerners toward the agitation over slavery were clear throughout the address.

Americans had thrilled to the eloquence of Kossuth's appeal, but they should reflect that it had been an appeal "not to the interests, not to the reason, not to the prudence, not to the justice, not to the instructed conscience of America and England; but to the mere emotion of sympathy for a single family of man oppressed by another." It had been an appeal for pity. Although the sympathies of individuals should always be on the side of the oppressed, for *nations,* sympathy must be strictly subordinated to national interest. As to what the national interest was, that was a question for "wise statesmanship," for the "Science of Practical Politics" to decide. What was the duty of America to the oppressed of the world? Essentially, self-preservation and self-cultivation as a shining example of a republic, displaying

> the *largest measure of liberty* which the civil life of man admits, combined with the least alloy of constraint and force with which civil life can consist, embodied in law

and order—announcing itself to the recognition of the world in the form of a rising state, already in the first class of eminence and consideration.[20]

In the practical affairs of life, men were not faced with duty, but with *duties,* sometimes conflicting. Choate had learned from Cicero, his master among the classical writers, as Burke and Coleridge were among the moderns, that the man who would act wisely in the world must learn that there was a hierarchy of duties and virtues and that the most compelling were those that contributed to the maintenance of human society.[21] The preservation and progressive enhancement of the nation must always be considered the highest of all good things because the nation state was the framework that made the moral life possible. He loved to echo the dictum of Cicero that the building of states was the most acceptable of human acts to God.[22] And if that end was commanded as the instrumentality by which "millions of men, through many generations and ages, will come one after another to the great gift of social being," then, were not "the means of insuring that end commanded also?"

> And if so, are not the traits, the deeds, the care, the valor, the spirit of nationality, the obedience to the collective will and reason as expressed through the prescribed organic form; . . . are they not highest in the scale of things commanded? Must not "being" in the antithesis of Hooker, go before even "well being?"[23]

In forming the federal Union, the founding fathers had entered into the "most sacred and awful and tender of all the relations,—the relation of country." They had done so because they had learned from the history of ancient Greece and of "the beautiful and miserable Italian republics of the Middle Age" that they had no alternative but "to become dearest friends or bitterest enemies." The preservation by later generations of this great instrumentality for peace and progress might demand the sacrifice of lesser goods and lesser duties—in particular it required the determination not to indulge one's sympathy for the slave to the extent where it endangered the continuance of this "marriage of more than two, for more than a fleeting natural life." Once philanthropy violated the express and implied pledges of the constitution, aroused the anger and disgust of a whole section by attacking the character of slaveholders, then philanthropy must be "arrested and rebuked by a 'higher law.' In this competition of affections, Country,—'omnes omnium charitates complectens,' the expression, the sum total of all things most dearly loved, surely hold the first place."[24]

As his use of the phrase "higher law" suggests, Choate was determined to fight moral fire with moral fire. He recognized that by 1850 the agitation against slavery, and particularly against the Fugitive Slave Law, had touched the moral imagination of a large section of the North. It was not sufficient to offer as a counter-argument the prudential reasons for obeying the law, or the practical economic benefits of the federal union. Men must be converted to patriotism, as they had been converted to anti-slavery, through an appeal to the moral sense. If assent to the Compromise measures and to the spirit behind them was to be real and lasting, then it must be based on a principled, even joyful, choice of the greater over the lesser good. Men must be disabused of the modern heresy that saw patriotism as merely the primitive forerunner of universal benevolence and love of humanity. Only patriotism, experienced as a total emotional, imaginative and moral conviction of the transcendent worth of the nation, patriotism perceived as "moral virtue," could ever hope to heal the breach between North and South and relegate slavery to the limbo of untouchable and undiscussable things.[25]

Against the background of the first major violation of the Fugitive Slave Law—the snatching of the ex-slave Shadrach from a Boston courtroom—Choate delivered an address on George Washington in which he tried to demonstrate his conception of what an effective patriotism must be.

> To form and uphold a State, it is not enough that our judgments believe it to be useful; the better part of our affections must feel it to be lovely. It is not enough that our arithmetic can compute its value, and find it high; our hearts must hold it priceless, above all things rich or rare. . . . It is not enough that a man thinks he can be an unexceptionable citizen, in the main, unless a very unsatisfactory law passes. He must admit, into his bosom, the specific and mighty emotion of patriotism. He must

love his country, his whole country, as the place of his birth or adoption, and the sphere of his largest duties; as the playground of his childhood, the land where his fathers sleep, the sepulchre of the valiant and and wise, of his own blood and race departed; he must love it for the long labors that reclaimed and adorned its natural and its moral scenery; for the great traits and great virtues of which it has been the theatre; for the institution and amelioration and progress that enrich it; for the part it has played for the succor of the nations. A sympathy indestructible must draw him to it. It must be of power to touch his imagination. All the passions which inspire and animate in the hour of conflict must wake at her awful voice.[26]

Thus possessed, the fortunate patriot would be hardly aware that he was faced with a conflict of moral choices; he would know with total emotional certainty where his duty lay.

Certainly Choate's own devotion to the Union was so all-consuming that it is doubtful if he felt great pangs of conscience in accepting the Compromise of 1850 and the Fugitive Slave Law. There is no reason to doubt his sincerity when, in his campaign speeches of 1848, he had referred to slavery as a great evil, or when, in defending the rendition of fugitives, he mourned "that there is a slave who needs to run, or a master who desires to pursue." He appreciated quite well some of the psychic costs of slavery. "I have never yet, however," he told Parker, "seen the good argument that slavery wasn't better for the blacks than freedom, as regards merely their *sensations*—the gratification of their merely sensual wants. But slavery makes their whole moral and intellectual character a *wreck;* and if they are women, they are damned."[27]

Yet he could also refer glibly and facetiously to the states of the upper South breeding and selling "the little black rascals."[28] It is clear that he was not personally touched by the existence of slavery. Perhaps his Hellenism made slavery as an institution more acceptable to him; temperamentally, certainly, he was more stirred by the heroic fighter than the passive victim. Perhaps that lack of a sense of "absolute right," which a college classmate had noted, prevented him from responding to the events of the 1850s, as an increasing number of his fellow conservatives did, with moral outrage.[29] He refused, for example, to address a Faneuil Hall meeting called to express the indignation of Boston at the physical attack on Sumner in the Senate by Preston Brooks of South Carolina in retaliation against the Massachusetts Senator's speech on Kansas, and is reported to have asked "if blows on the head with a gutta percha stick would hurt a man much?" "Brooks' act of scoundrelism in beating Charles Sumner was his own act, not the act of the South," he told Parker. "It is *small* to make it a southern act."[30] All in all, he does not seem to have found it a difficult matter to settle his conscience on the plight of the slave. When, in the 1856 campaign, he deserted the Whigs for the Democrats, a friend asked him what had become of his Whig anti-slavery opinions. "I have settled that matter," he replied,

I am bound to seek the greatest amount of moral good for the human race. I am to take things as I find them, and work according to my best judgment for the greatest good of the greatest number, and I do not believe it is the greatest good to the *slave* or the *free* that four million of slaves should be turned loose in all their ignorance, poverty, and degradation to trust for a home and a living.

As long as the indispensable framework of the Union was maintained, the "slow and sure reformer—Time" could be safely relied upon to resolve the problem of the black man in America.[31]

On October 24, 1852, Daniel Webster died. Whether or not they agreed with his later policies, all his contemporaries seem to have felt that one of the great lights of American politics had gone out. None felt the loss more keenly than Choate, whose political career and political ideas had been tied intimately to Webster's. Though he would stand up to Webster fearlessly if they met on opposite sides in the courtroom, in politics he "seemed to submit to the control of a master mind." Choate needed heroes and he found in Webster a personality that could wear the mantle of greatness and be a "national man" more convincingly, he came to realize, than he ever could. The seventeen years difference in their ages enabled Choate to offer a filial deference and admiration to the older man. Whenever Webster dropped into his office, a student recalled, Choate "would almost hover around him as an innocent, admiring, full-hearted girl." He found in Webster that personal force which he knew he lacked, and he agreed willingly to be subdued by it. He seemed to regard Webster, recalled one friend, "as a great mysterious power, or as a fundamental law, from which we need not attempt to escape or appeal."[32]

There were those who felt that Webster's influence over him had been detrimental. "When Webster desired to raise money," declared Edwin Whipple, "he sometimes got Choate to endorse his note; when Webster ventured on a daring political move, he got Choate to endorse his policy; and the result was that in either case the endorsement entailed on Choate pecuniary embarrassment or popular obloquy." "Your father," said Mrs. Choate more simply to her daughter, "has suffered a great deal from Mr. Webster." But Choate had chosen to be a disciple, rather than a leader, and he had chosen a man whose political philosophy and ideals of nationality fitted his own developing notions about America. Once he had chosen this identification, he maintained it without jealousy or regret; his self-abnegation before the greater man, constituting, as one acute observer put it, a kind of "artistic absorption" in Webster's career.[33]

He had been an enthusiastic campaigner in Webster's last bid to become the Whig presidential candidate in 1852. The campaign did not get off to a promising start. Choate and other Webster Whigs had organized a reception for Webster in Boston in April 1851, at which Choate was to welcome him as the savior of the Union. At the last moment—but two days after another escaped slave, Thomas Sims, had been returned to slavery under the provisions of the new law—the Whig aldermen of Boston had refused the group the use of Faneuil Hall. Webster was furious and his friends stunned. Choate wrote advising him to compose a dignified note reminding Massachusetts of his services to the state and to the nation, and added: "To tell the truth, considering . . . the indignation it will excite—the impression it will everywhere make—that you have indeed sacrificed your state for the nation—I am glad they have done it."[34]

He was probably right that the incident would redound to Webster's advantage. There was widespread indignation in the city and the common council disavowed their aldermen's action. Nonetheless, Webster was now convinced that little could be expected from the regular Whig leadership in Massachusetts—

the impetus for his nomination would have to come from independent "Webster men." Accordingly, Choate, Everett, George T. Curtis and several others formed themselves into a "central committee" and began circulating petitions on behalf of the nomination.

The Whig state convention in September, however, failed to produce any popular upsurge in Webster's favor and his supporters were reduced to organizing their own separate convention to put his name in nomination.[35] When the convention met in late November 1851, Choate was the keynote speaker. His message was the one that Webster himself had been expounding across the country in the previous months—that the only real issue before the country in the coming election was the preservation of the Union. Webster was the one man who had saved it on March 7, 1850 and the only candidate who could be trusted to pull it through the still perilous days ahead. He presented Webster— "my master, my friend, my more than guide, and philosopher and friend"—as a man who had chosen the stern path of duty, over the opportunity for easy popularity: "Who knew better than he that day how easy it would have been for a ten thousandth tithe of those gigantic abilities to have organized a free-soil party, and a free state sectionalism, and put himself at the head of it and made his fortune by that act? (Sensation.)" In that "conflict of great duties" he had chosen "the largest to be performed first." Such a man was obviously "the pilot for the wind and storm."[36]

Considerable excitement was generated at the convention, but Choate and the other Websterites, while enthusiasts, were not particularly efficient organizers. They blanketed the country with copies of Webster's speeches but failed to build up working organizations in strategic places. The result was that when the national Whig convention met in Baltimore in June 1852, Webster had hardly any strength outside the Northeast and it was clear that the contest was between President Fillmore, the candidate of the South, and General Winfield Scott, the candidate of those Northern Whigs who disapproved of the Compromise of 1850. Webster received twenty-nine votes on the first ballot, and never, in the fifty-three ballots it took to nominate Scott, got more than thirty-two. Choate was the most prominent member of the Massachusetts delegation, and like all the Websterites, entered the convention with ebullient overconfidence. The Webster men, "Choate included," reported a Fillmore supporter tartly, were "like a parcel of school boys waiting for the sky to fall, that they might catch larks."[37]

The initial proceedings went well, however, with the production of a party platform completely endorsing the Compromise measures of 1850. The chairman of the committee on resolutions was George Ashmun, an ardent Webster man. Henry Wilson, relying on the testimony of Alexander Stephens, states that both Webster and Choate had seen the resolutions in advance—Choate had called on Webster in Washington en route to Baltimore. The eighth resolution of the platform committed the Whig party to acceptance of the Fugitive Slave Law and the other compromise provisions as "a final settlement, in principle and substance, of the dangerous and exciting questions which they embrace," to the suppression of any further agitation, and to the maintenance of "this system as essential to the nationality of the Whig party and the integrity of the Union." At Choate's prompting, Webster personally underlined the phrase "in principle and substance" in his copy. When the resolutions were read in the hot, crowded hall, swarming with men on the floor and women in the galleries, there were immediate calls for Choate to speak and as he rose "the thousand fans ceased to flutter; and all was silent as death."[38]

Amidst frequent interruptions of cheering, Choate defended both the morality and the necessity of the Compromise, and the integrity of the man with which it was identified.

I thank God for the civil courage, which at the hazard of all things dearest in life, dared to pass and defend them, and "has taken no step backward." I rejoice that the healthy morality of the country, with an instructed conscience, void of offence toward God and man, has accepted them. Extremists denounce all compromises, ever. Alas! do they remember that such is the condition of humanity that the noblest politics are but a compromise—an approximation—a type—a shadow of good things—the buying of great blessings at great prices? Do they forget that the Union is a compromise; the Constitution—social life,—that the harmony of the universe is but the music of compromise, by which the antagonisms of the infinite Nature are composed and reconciled?

If the two great national parties could only agree to exclude slavery as a political issue they might do much "to embody and fix an important agreement of the national mind" and whatever the results of the coming election, it would at least be "one great jubilee of Union." There was also the practical party consideration, he reminded the delegates, that the Democratic convention had already endorsed the Compromise. If the Whigs did not make a commitment "as comprehensive and as unequivocally as they have, we shall be absorbed, scattered!—absorbed by the whirlpool,—scattered by the whirlwind of the sentiment of nationality which they have had the sagacity to discern and hide under." He concluded by attacking the Scott contingent for their equivocal position on the Compromise—against it in the Northern states, but hinting at eventual support in the South. "How much better to send up the Union flag at once to each masthead, blazing with 'Liberty and Union, now and for ever, one and inseparable,' and go down even so!"[39]

The enthusiasm from the audience that greeted this speech was too much for the Scott supporters, and Botts of Virginia rose to accuse Choate of using the debate on the resolutions to electioneer for Webster. A bland Choate disclaimed any intention of canvassing for his friend, but added: "Ah, Sir, what a reputation that must be,—what a patriotism that must be,—what a long and brilliant series of public services that must be, when you cannot mention a measure of utility like this but every eye spontaneously turns to, and every voice spontaneously utters, that great name of DANIEL WEBSTER!" There was laughter and cheers from the floor, and bouquets from the gallery were thrown at his feet. The day had been a considerable personal triumph for Choate. So much so indeed that some of the Southern delegates offered to put his name in nomination for the presidency—or at least the vice presidency. This was beyond the scope of Choate's ambitions, although he did receive a write-in vote on one of the ballots.[40]

His eloquence had made an impression, but it did nothing to enhance Webster's chances. The Massachusetts delegation gave a private dinner for the Southern Fillmore supporters to persuade them to come over to Webster. Choate, who had retired to bed with one of his sick headaches, was persuaded to come and add his voice to the pressure on the Southerners. He spoke for about fifteen minutes and with such effect that his audience, according to Brown, "sprang from their seats, jumped upon the chairs and benches, broke their glasses, and acted like wild men." But again, it made no difference. The Southerners offered a bargain: they would throw their support to Webster if his supporters could marshall forty Northern votes, if not, the Webster men should agree to support Fillmore. The forty votes were not forthcoming; the Websterites refused to unite with the Fillmore delegates in order to defeat Scott. The result was that the party emerged from the convention with a platform endorsing the compromise but a candidate who had little acceptability among Southern Whigs.[41]

As both Choate and Webster knew, the Baltimore convention marked the end of any presidential hopes for Webster. On his way back to Boston, Choate detoured to Washington to take tea with the Websters. It was a meal, he said, that reminded him "of the first meal after the return from the grave, when the full force of the bereavement seems to be realized. It was too deep an emotion for utterance." Some disgruntled Webster supporters, led by George T. Curtis, refused to accept the Baltimore decision and tried to drum up support for a separate Webster ticket. But Choate, for all his devotion to his mentor, was too much of a political realist to follow this route. He refused to do any campaigning for Scott, but he also held aloof from the movement to present Webster as an independent candidate. He was a Webster Whig, but first and foremost he was a Whig.[42] Webster's death freed him to make his position quite clear. When the president of the Young Men's Whig Club of Boston asked him to declare himself, he replied that he had always considered himself bound by the results of the Baltimore convention—though in view of his relations with Webster he had not thought it "decorous or right" to take any active part in Scott's campaign. There was no doubt that the interests of the country would be better served by a Whig administration than a Democratic one and the policy Webster had followed in domestic and foreign affairs was more likely to be continued by Scott than by Franklin Pierce. "It is quite needless to say, then, that I shall vote for the regularly nominated Whig ticket of electors."[43]

Choate's last service to Webster was to pronounce his eulogy, first before a meeting of the Suffolk Bar and then more formally before a convocation of faculty, students and alumni of Dartmouth College. He received this invitation soon after Webster's death, but the meeting was not scheduled until the end of the following July so that he had almost a year to work on the speech. He no doubt brooded over the subject during the following months, but the actual writing, as usual with him, was done at the last minute. He told a friend that he feared the occasion would be a failure, because although he had been given so long to write it, the eulogy had turned out to be "one of the most hurried things he had ever done." He delivered it late in the afternoon in the college chapel, packed to capacity, with thousands crowded outside, first in heat, then in rain. He spoke for a hundred and forty minutes, reported the *Boston Courier* and it seemed "like so many seconds." He spoke without gesture and without reference to his notes.[44]

Choate knew that this speech was the greatest opportunity of his career as an orator. It is weighty and dignified, full of his long, rolling, cumulative sentences. Parker called it the best example of his "academic style," and perhaps for that reason it reads less well to a modern sensibility and seems less lively and memorable than some of his more ephemeral pieces, written when he was less overawed by the occasion. But the oration was more than a demonstration of Choate's own prowess, more than a celebration of his friend and leader, it was a vindication not only of a man but of a policy and an ideal of statesmanship.[45]

The first part of the eulogy was devoted to a resumé of Webster's career, interwoven through his actions or his words, it seemed, with most of the great moments of the history of a rising and expanding America: "What American landscape will you look on; what subject of American interest will you study; what source of hope or of anxiety, as an American, will you acknowledge that it does not recall him?"[46] The conclusion, and most telling part of the oration, was a reply to those who had seen Webster, after the Seventh of March speech, as a fallen angel who had "sinned against his own conscience." In particular it was a reply to the obituary sermon of Theodore Parker who had mourned him as a lost leader, a failed hero.[47]

In vindication Choate returned to the ideas he had expressed in his Story Association speech two years earlier—that the duties of citizenship, and particularly of statesmanship, required not merely conscience but an instructed conscience that could decide *"according to the real qualities of things."* When what was at stake was the duty of preserving or destroying the order of things in which we are born; the duty of executing or violating one of the provisions of organic law which the country, having a wide and clear view before and after, had deemed a needful instrumental means for the preservation of that order; . . . then it is not enough to relegate the citizen, or the public man, to a higher law, and an interior illumination, and leave him there. . . . To fit her to be the mistress of civil life . . . [the conscience] must come out for a space from the interior round of emotions, and subjective states and contemplations, and introspection, 'cloistered, unexercised, unbreathed'—and . . . survey the objective realities of the State; ponder thoughtfully on the complications, and impediments, and antagonisms which make the noblest politics but an aspiring, an approximation, a compromise, a type, a shadow of good to come . . . and there learn civil duty *secundum subjectam materiam.* [48]

Webster had chosen to devote his great powers and talents to the *vita activa,* to the upholding of "a recent, delicate, and complex political system," to dedication to "the concrete of things." It had been charged, by "those who come from the reveries of a cloistered speculation to judge a practical life" that he had added nothing to "universal law, and first principles; and philosophical ideas." But why should this be thought to diminish him? To Choate, to direct the affairs of men and nations was to live the heroic life, and heroes faced choices of a grandeur and portentousness from which their cloistered critics were protected. Parker remarks that what Choate's oration attempted to convey was not only "the mere usefulness, but the essential splendor" of Webster's career. And indeed, the driving impulse behind the oration was to raise the public estimate of the political life. A statesman like Webster had to consider expediency, but he was not a creature of it; rather he was an heroic figure who touched more nearly than any intellectual the essential tragedy of the human condition: that in the world of action, man must choose, and not between good and evil, but between evils. Compromise was not merely prudential; in affairs of state it had about it a tragic grandeur and the pathos attendant on things "bought at great price."

It was not enough that Compromise be seen as the essential law of the universe, it must also be perceived as an act of public virtue and moral courage.[49]

The conservative Whigs of Massachusetts had rallied to the Compromise of 1850 because they had thought it would prove a final settlement of the major difficulty between the sections and they might comfortably return to the pursuit of prosperity, harmonious business relations with the South, and "normal" politics. And indeed, by 1853, as the memory of the rendition of the slave Sims back to slavery faded amidst general prosperity, it did seem as though Compromise had fulfilled its function. But, in January 1854, this complacency was shattered when Stephen Douglass of Illinois introduced the Kansas-Nebraska bill in the Senate. This casual repeal of the Missouri Compromise—which Northern Whigs of all varieties had considered sacrosanct—reopened the whole question of the expansion of slavery. It also seemed a piece of calculated aggression on the part of the South. The cotton Whigs who had labored so hard to meet Southerners half-way, to safeguard both their interests and their sensibilities, felt betrayed. In late February 1854, they held a great protest meeting in Faneuil Hall, addressed by the most soundly conservative of the party: Abbott Lawrence, Robert Winthrop, George Hillard, George Ticknor—"the 1850 men," as Richard Henry Dana called them. "All men agree that the audience were far ahead of the speakers," he reported. "All attempts to get up applause for the measures and men of 1850 failed, and even Webster's great name fell dead, while every sentiment hostile to the Compromise Measures of 1850, and everything of the Free-Soil character went off with rapturous applause."[50]

Choate was not present at the meeting. He wrote to Everett, now in the Senate, that he had been too sick and too busy to go. This was probably more than a diplomatic illness; his health had been troublesome since the previous fall, he had been overworking, and he was desperately anxious about his youngest daughter, who was suffering from some kind of nervous illness. Dana, who called on him the following month at his house, where he had been confined for a few days, found him in low spirits. Choate said that he had worked too hard that winter, "harder than I ever did before." And added: "I have to do it to drown sorrow . . . as some men take to drink or gaming." Dana commented, "This is, no doubt, true. The insanity of his favorite daughter put him into such a state that he seemed to have no alternative than incessant absorbing labor, or despair."[51]

Yet, while Choate did not approve of the Kansas-Nebraska bill, he was not as outraged by it as Abbott Lawrence. To Everett, who wrote to him from the Senate asking advice on what line to take, he replied somewhat equivocally and vaguely:

> As far as I can possibly discern, the whole *free world* of the United States seems likely to demand the observance of the Missouri Compromise. I must say, that I think that a speech and a course adhering to that great adjustment, and reconciling that with the compromises of 1850, will be claimed here, and I should be amazed and grieved, if this could do harm anywhere. Yet for myself, I should consult the *spirit* of the proceeding of 1850 and execute that, whithersoever it led. But I cannot yet see how that should demand such a measure as this of Mr. Douglas.

Everett was hoping for the next Whig nomination for the presidency, and delicately Choate warned him not to say anything rash: "We feel the deepest solicitude that you should not be drawn into a position which can impair your large prospects, and . . . we hope you may defeat the further extension of slavery on grounds and by reasonings that will not lose you one American heart of judgment anywhere."[52]

Everett's careful speech in the debate—opposing the bill, defending the compromise of 1850, deploring the existence of slavery, disclaiming any intention to attack the peculiar institutions of Southerners or any feeling of unkindness towards them, and closing with faith in the power of Providence to bring good out of evil—met with Choate's complete approval. Indeed, it was no doubt pretty much what he would have said himself. The situation in Massachusetts was stable, he assured his friend. The Faneuil Hall meeting had not stirred up any undesirable reaction: "There seems no danger of anything violent, sectional, of or belonging to the organizations of *isms*. There is even no bitterness towards the South—but hatred and contempt towards all free state men who favor the bill and who seek to profit by the agitation in any way."[53]

Choate underestimated the impact of the Kansas-Nebraska bill on conservative Northern opinion. How dramatic the shift had been was revealed in the reaction to the capture in Boston of another fugitive slave, Anthony Burns. In the case of Thomas Sims, three years earlier, conservative Boston had rallied to the forces of law and order and, whatever their personal repugnance, had determined that the provisions of the Fugitive Slave Law should be faithfully followed. Choate had played a minor role in that incident. A group of abolitionist lawyers, led by Samuel Sewell and Richard Dana tried to get Sims out of the hands of the United States marshal, by getting a criminal warrant issued against him for having stabbed the police officer who arrested him. They were foiled by the conservative Democrat commissioner, Benjamin Hallett, who issued a federal warrant on the same charge. Sumner and Dana applied to the United States circuit court for a writ of habeas corpus on the grounds that Hallett's warrant was fraudulent. The marshal hastily sent for Benjamin R. Curtis and Rufus Choate to come and defend the legality of Hallett's warrant. As young lawyers, twenty years earlier, they had both appeared in the case of the slave child Med, Curtis on behalf of the owner, Choate on behalf of the slave. Now they collaborated in defense of procedures that would return Sims to slavery.[54]

By the time Burns was arrested, on May 26, 1854, the reaction of sound men to the return of fugitive slaves had altered materially. "Men who would not speak to me in 1850–51 and who were enrolling themselves as special policemen in the Sims affair," Dana noted in his journal, "stop me in the street and talk treason. This is all owing to the Nebraska bill. . . . The Webster delusion is passing off." The Cotton Whigs were anxious, however, that any effort on behalf of Burns should be directed by safe conservatives. Amos A. Lawrence approached Dana, on behalf of "a number of active 1850 men" and offered to put up the retainer if he would employ an "eminent Whig counsel." Dana accordingly approached Choate, but Choate was more consistent than Lawrence and declined. It had been, Dana noted, "an amusing interview."

> I asked him to make one effort in favor of freedom, and told him that the 1850 delusion was dispelled, and all men were coming round, the Board of Brokers and Board of Aldermen were talking treason, and that he must come and act. He said he should be glad to make

an effort on our side, but that he had given written
opinions ag. us, in the Sims case, on every point, and that
he could not go ag. them.

'You corrupted your mind in 1850.'

'Yes. *Filed* my mind.'

'I wish you would *file it in Court,* for our benefit.'[55]

When he did act in an offshoot of the Burns case, it was on
the side of law and order. Expecting trouble when Burns was
returned to the South, the mayor of Boston called out the militia
and put the city under virtual martial law. In scuffles with the
troops, several citizens were hurt and one of them brought an
action against the mayor and the militia commander for assault.
Choate, Hillard, and Hallett acted for the defense, claiming that,
in the heated circumstances of the time, the authorities had acted
within their rights to maintain peace and order. Choate, in particular, played upon the idea that there had been a real atmosphere
of violence created by the anti-slavery agitators; there had, after
all, been an abortive attempt to forcibly rescue Burns from the
Court House: "That meeting in Faneuil Hall! They counseled *no
violence.* Oh no—no violence! The dial *spoke* not, but it made most
manifest signs, and pointed to the stroke of *murder;*—three *hours*
afterwards, Batchelder was killed! Oh no—no violence! no violence!" The plaintiff's counsel objected strongly to this kind of
innuendo, but Choate won the case.[56]

In early 1855 Choate suffered a slight accident to his knee,
which became inflamed, and an operation had to be performed to
remove an abscess. He was confined to his house for four months
and, while he was in no particular danger during the illness, it
appears to have had a profound effect upon him. The experience
of taking the ether before the operation haunted him with its
intimations of mortality. He told Parker that the experience had
been "very pleasant till the moment came of utterly surrendering
consciousness; then death itself could not have been more awful
to him, and he struggled in himself as for life." Parker thought
that he came out of the illness subdued and slower. He no longer
had the ebullient capacity to carry on several lines of thought at
once. He would now say: "Let us finish one thing at a time; we
are now upon this point. When we finish this, we will go to that."
In his public speaking "he no longer tore a passion to tatters," and

composed his orations to be read rather than heard. They were delivered now in a "comparatively low voice," often with "rather the tone of poetic soliloquy than of direct and pointed exhortation. Indeed, often he became quite inaudible." He seemed "haunted and overawed by the shadow of his past deeds of splendor, and with little more to hope for save to keep his career from shrinking under the comparison." He had had, in conventional terms, a successful career, but it had been a success of the middle range that had missed greatness. Speaking once of Edward Everett he remarked that Everett had been "the most promising young man in America. And yet he has hardly succeeded." But then he added: "still . . . when one considers what it is truly to succeed, why should he not be called successful?"—a rueful assessment of his own life as much as his friend's.[57]

As Choate recuperated from his illness, there was little in the American political scene to relieve his depression. Observing the continuing decline of the Whig party, upheavals in Kansas, the emergence of the frankly sectional Republican party, and Massachusetts given over to a Know-Nothing legislature, he could only write bitterly to a friend abroad:

> Your estate is gracious that keeps you out of hearing of our politics. Anything more low—obscene—feculent— the manifold oceanic heavings of history have not cast up. We shall come to the worship of onions—cats—and things vermiculate. . . . If any wiser saw or instance, ancient or modern, occurred to me to express the enormous impossible inanity of American things, I should utter it.[58]

He found some consolation in his children and his books; spending the day at the house of his married daughter just outside Boston, "alone in a little library in a garden, held, as it were, to the very breast of June," he reflected: "these are the places and the moments for that discourse in which is so much more of our happiness than in actualities of duty, or even in hope."[59] He also seemed more dependent on the friendship of others, more open to intimacy. In spite of their differences on slavery, he remained on very cordial terms with Richard Henry Dana, who appears to have been particularly susceptible to the Choate spell. "I never talk with Choate without something worth remembering and very agreeable to hear being said," he noted in his journal. "You do not know what a hold he had on me," he lamented on the older man's death, "or rather what a *necessity of life* he had become to me. When I have seen anything peculiar in the development of human nature, of social or political systems, I have thought, 'I will tell that to Choate'—and then, Is he indeed dead?" Choate also became much more intimate with Edward Everett, who called on him frequently to bring him books and news when he was laid up with his injured knee. They had known each other for more than thirty years, but Everett had never been in Choate's house until the previous fall, when Choate was slightly ill and, at the prompting of a mutual friend, Everett had called on him. Everett was touched to find an engraving of himself on one side of the fireplace, with a bust of Cicero before it.[60]

The state of politics was "so hopelessly discouraging," Choate remarked to Parker, that a man might "be pardoned for entirely abandoning it for the present, and giving neither aid, advice or anything else to his country." But, as his health improved, he found that he could not keep clear of politics. One result of the Southern Whig support for the Kansas-Nebraska bill had been the collapse of the Whigs as a national party. Many Northern Whigs were moving into the ranks of the new Republican party, which had sprung up in opposition to Douglas' bill out of a fusion of Free-Soilers and dissidents from the other parties. Others were attracted by the meteoric rise of the American party or Know-Nothings, organized around nativist and anti-Catholic feeling against immigrants, but also managing to incorporate a rag-bag of temperance, anti-slavery, and reformist inclinations.[61] Choate, like some other conservative Whigs, found the Americans a lesser evil than the Republicans. His dislike of Catholicism gave him a certain sympathy with the anti-popery aspects of the new party and he could see in the appeal to "Americanism" and hostility to foreign elements a way of diverting national attention away from the divisive issue of slavery. He even advised Parker, "as a matter of policy," to join "these Know-Nothings," since they had "an immense fulcrum of power. Every laboring man of America who sees a foreigner ill-clad and conditioned, standing in the fields of labor, and underselling him in his labor, will have a native American ticket in his pocket."[62]

Choate himself, however, still remained loyal to what remained of orthodox Whiggery in Massachusetts. Webster, when dying, is said to have told Choate "You have a great futute before you if you go with the party and direct them." To rally the Whigs as a national party of the Union, the constitution, and law and order, would probably have been beyond anyone's capabilities by 1855. It was certainly beyond Choate's. As a sympathetic friend commented, he "could go with the party—he could even go against it; but the instinct of leadership was weak in him; to control the party was work to which he was not fitted."[63] He could perform one last act of piety for the Whigs, however, and speak in the campaign for the state elections in 1855. He was elected a delegate to the Massachusetts Whig convention in October 1855 and, though he could not attend, he sent a public letter of encouragement, urging the Whigs not to disband the party. He discounted the possibility of fusion with the Know-Nothings, and concentrated his attack on the new Republican party. His objections to the Republicans were on the same grounds as those against the Free-Soilers—they had no policy outside of opposition to the extension of slavery, and they were unequivocally a "geographical" party. He concluded with a Madisonian assessment of the role of party in America. Parties had helped rather than hindered "the slow and difficult growth of a consummated nationality." However sharp the conflicts, they had been ideological not sectional; "there were no Alleghenies nor Mississippi rivers in our politics. Such was the felicity of our condition, that the very dissensions which rent small republics in twain, welded and compacted the vast fabric of our own." Those men who would create a "geographical" party forgot how far party politics created public opinion. Sectional politics would teach the American public to think of themselves as belonging not to one nation, but to two separate and opposed entities.

> All party organization tends towards faction. This is its evil. But it is inseparable from free governments. To choose his political connection aright is the most delicate and difficult duty of the citizen. We have made our choice, and we abide by it. *We join ourselves to no party that does not carry the flag and keep step to the music of the Union.*

The last sentence caught the public imagination and passed into the general repertoire of opposition to the Republicans.[64]

At the end of the month he spoke at a Faneuil Hall meeting in support of the Whig slate in the state elections, and the entire speech was an expansion of his earlier letter. The duty of the Whigs was to stop the Republicans, for they were the kind of organization with which the system was not equipped to cope. In a striking figure, he compared the Union to

> a stupendous fabric of architecture; a castle; a capitol; suppose the capitol at Washington. It is a fortress at once, and a temple. The great central dome swells to heaven. It rests grandly on its hill by its own weight kept steadfast, and seemingly immovable; Titan hands might have built it; it may stand to see the age of a nation pass by. But one imperfection there is; a seam in the marble; a flaw in the iron; a break scarcely visible, yet a real vertical fissure, parting by an imperceptible opening from top to foundation the whole in two. The builder saw it, and guarded against it as well as he might; those who followed, to repair, with pious and skilful hands, tried by underpinning, by lateral support, by buttress and buttress alternately, to hold the disjointed sides in contact. Practically, it was becoming less formidable; the moss was beginning to conceal it even.

Now the Republicans were proposing to knock out all the supports and build up on either side of the fissure competing camps of hate. "The basis of the organization is reciprocal sectional hate." Blinded by this hatred, the Republicans would teach all Americans to look back upon their national history as constituting nothing but the continued aggressions of the slave power, all "mere and sheer negro-breeding and negro-selling."[65]

The Know-Nothings swept the state in 1855, as they had the year before; Choate's consolation for the defeat of the Whigs was the equally poor showing of the Republicans. "Although the details and instruments are less satisfactory than could have been wished," he commented, "the election is a real victory of intense American feeling. . . . I think it leaves only two great parties, both national to the cannon's mouth, in the field."[66] He repeated to Parker that the Know-Nothing party was "the one for every young man to join who has any hopes," but in the national election of 1856, in which the Whigs could not manage to field a candidate of their own, he chose to vote, not like many other old-line Whigs, for the American candidate, Fillmore, but for the Democrat, James Buchanan. This was a considered decision after much agonizing and against the background of escalating violence in Kansas and in Washington, and he intended to make it public. "Silence in such a sad state of things as environs us now," he told Parker, "is profoundly ignominious." The opportunity came when the Whigs of Maine asked him to come and speak.[67]

He declined the invitation, but sent a long letter, setting forth his opinion of Whig duty in "the present crisis." The first duty of any good Whig, indeed now their only duty, was to stop the Republicans. Men deceived themselves if they thought the Union would survive a Republican victory. It might be true that the Republicans did not threaten any legitimate Southern interest; it might be true that the Southern states needed the Union as much as the Northern states did. But

> in appreciating the influences which may disturb a political system, and especially one like ours, do you make no allowance for passions, for pride, for infirmity, for the burning sense of even imaginary wrong? Do you assume that all men, or all masses of men in all sections, uniformly obey reason; and uniformly wisely see and calmly seek their true interests? Where on earth is such a fool's Paradise as that to be found?

If the Republicans won the coming election, they would win entirely on Northern votes.

> To the fifteen States of the South that government will appear an alien government. . . . It will represent to their eye a vast region of States organized upon anti-slavery, flushed by triumph, cheered onward by the voices of the pulpit, tribune, and press; its mission to inaugurate freedom and put down the oligarchy; its constitution the glittering and sounding generalities of natural right which make up the Declaration of Independence. And then and thus is the beginning of the end.[68]

This geographic party that would do so much harm, was after all, entirely unnecessary. Nature would keep slavery out of the territories of Utah, New Mexico, Washington and Minnesota.

Only in Kansas was there a possibility of its spread, and, if the federal government would only do its duty and keep the peace there, Kansas would of its own accord opt for freedom. Since no true Unionist Whig could vote Republican, the choice, he concluded, lay between the Democrats and the American party. For himself, since he could not entirely approve of either the creed or the methods of the Know-Nothings, and since he felt that the contest would be essentially between the Democrats and the Republicans, he intended to vote for Buchanan, who seemed "to represent that sentiment of nationality, tolerant, warm, and comprehensive,—without which, without increase of which, America is no longer America."[69]

The letter fell like a bombshell in Whig circles.[70] "What must you have felt," Francis Lieber, now a Frémont supporter, wrote sympathetically to George Hillard,

at perusing Choate's letter? I don't recollect anything that has grieved me so much for years. It reads almost like eloquent drunkenness. What was he about? If a man like Choate had been silent it would have been intelligible, but to speak, to speak at this juncture for one part (not party) alone and that hostile to his past, and, above all, to come out for a candidate with such a platform as Buchanan's, and to praise Buchanan's political life—this, by Choate, passes my understanding. There are but two ways of explaining it; either he wants something, which is so paltry that it cannot be entertained for a moment; or he so hates Sumner and the set now *in* in Massachusetts, that his passion pitched him over to the other side of the board. Choate was, and I dare say still is, a worshipper of Webster, and he probably thinks Sumner a vile, inexcusable enemy to the Great Man. Still I cannot understand how he lost all self-control, unless there were physical reasons, some nervous excitement. If I were conversing with you, I would state some curious things I have observed. I am very, very sorry.[71]

Hillard could only explain Choate's action as due to a doctrinaire vein of "French-ism running through his Yankee structure." Feeling that the Republicans were wrong he had jumped to the opposite extreme. "Webster was always to him what the long pole is to the rope dancer: a steadying element."[72]

Many people were not so unwilling as Lieber to entertain the thought that Choate "wanted something." Rumors were rife that he had struck a bargain with Buchanan that he would be given the attorney-generalship of the U.S., or the first vacancy on the Supreme Court, or that he had turned against Fillmore because he had *not* received any offer of an office from him. He received a number of anonymous letters denouncing his stand, and also a number of public ones, attacking his "timid conservatism."[73]

In view of the recent sacking of Lawrence, Kansas, by pro-slavery forces, not to mention the attack on Sumner in the Senate, Choate's delicacy towards Southern opinion seemed sheer servility. "Your allusions to Kansas are so equivocal," said one correspondent, "that one hardly knows whether you condemn the propagandists of slavery, or only censure them for too much exhilaration of spirits." "How much more, Mr. Choate," demanded another, "would you have Freemen bear . . . in the name of liberty I ask, what will satisfy your timid and humble soul? We have drawn our line of demarcation: 36/30. Where is yours? *Anywhere* or *nowhere?*" Choate was typical, declared a choleric Maine Republican of "the cold, selfish, unfeeling, enfeebled, trembling, old Aristocrats" who had ruined the once-glorious Whig party. More temperately, Josiah Quincy declared that the Maine letter betrayed the characteristic fault of the legal mind—the tendency to approach every question not as a "search after truth," but as "a trial of skill."[74]

Apart from his apparent complacency over the fate of Kansas, Choate's major blunder in the letter had been his contemptuous reference to "the glittering and sounding generalities of natural right which make up the Declaration of Independence." It had always been the aim of Choate and other conservative Whigs to reduce the Declaration to the status of an historical document— "that passionate and eloquent manifesto of a revolutionary war," as Choate called it, hardly to be considered out of its specific time and place—and to put the concrete legalities of the constitution at the center of American consciousness. The storm of protest that greeted his cavalier dismissal, however, showed how seriously a great many Americans took the Declaration, not as a past relic, but as a living text. "Glittering generalities!" exploded Emerson, "they are blazing ubiquities!"[75] Though Choate attached great importance to the role of public opinion in the modern world, the unfortunate remark was a measure of his own insensitivity to popular idealism. It certainly furnished a good deal of ammunition to the growing Republican forces. The words of the Declaration might be "sneered at as 'glittering generalities' by the nerveless conservative, who 'has ever opposed every useful reform, and wailed over every rotten institution as it fell,' " maintained Henry Wilson on the Fourth of July, "but they live in the throbbing hearts of the toiling millions." They are the "definitions and axioms of free society," declared Abraham Lincoln, "the electric cord . . . that links the hearts of patriotic and liberty-loving men together," the moral principle that constituted the most vital bond tying men to the nation.[76]

After the publication of the Maine letter, Choate was deluged with requests to make campaign speeches. But he had not joined the Democratic party, and the personal abuse he had suffered and the estrangement from old political colleagues made him unwilling to plunge into the rough and tumble of a political campaign. He decided to make only one speech—before a bi-partisan Union meeting at Lowell just before the election. He was given a rousing welcome and proceeded to deliver one of his best and most trenchant political addresses. He allowed himself a brief complaint at the way his motives had been misconstrued, at "that discriminating injustice and insolence of dictation which claims freedom of thought and purity of motive for itself, and allows them to others and denies them to me," but the heart of the speech was a shrewd challenge to the Republicans to state their intentions plainly. "Tell us exactly what you really propose to do about slavery, without phrases." To rest one's political platform on the Declaration of Independence was rather like resting it on the Bible and should produce the same raised eyebrows among men who expected politics to have some minimal content. There was no evidence that the triumph of the Republicans would make any difference to the existence or extension of slavery, and meanwhile their style of political propaganda was undermining national unity and degrading the tone of public life. The effects of the new party in the North had only been to make political discussion "intolerant, immoral, abusive and insolent to those who differ" and its polarizing tactics had placed moderate men and national men, North and South, in a false position, by presenting to them the alternative of treason to the whole or treason to the section,— thus putting moderate counsels to shame and destroying the influence which might help to restore the good temper and generous affection of the parts and the whole.[77]

Moreover, though it was founded on resistance to "the slave power," in fact the party could hardly be said to be of much practical good to the blacks. "It excites hatred of the master, but no prudent, nor reasonable, nor useful love of the slave." To stimulate animosity between North and South could only "retard the training for freedom and postpone the day of its gradual and peaceful attainment. If ye so hate the master, or so fear him, or so contend with him, that ye rivet the fetters of the slave or lengthen the term of his slavery, what reward have ye or has he?"[78]

He explained his own decision to vote for James Buchanan in the coming election: for all its faults, the Democratic party "had burned ever with that great master-passion this hour demands— a youthful, vehement, exultant, and progressive nationality." There is no reason why this explanation should not be taken at its face value. Lieber's hypothesis that Choate's actions could only be explained by a brooding resentment of Charles Sumner seems farfetched and contrary to all the contemporary accounts of Choate's character. He had always appreciated the "American feeling" of the Democrats, though he had been repelled by the expansionist jingoism that was sometimes evoked by that feeling.[79] But now the cruder elements of nationalism perhaps served better than the more refined as a barrier to disunion. The hope that anti-slavery might be drowned and forgotten in a sea of Americanism was what had drawn him towards the Know-Nothings. "The 'American' sentiment and Slavery are really the only questions absorbing to the people, unless a war arises," he had told Parker the year before. "The American sentiment must be powerful, practically, for it takes hold of the grosser and most vulgar sensibilities and ideas."[80] In this shape it was a potentially dangerous emotion, but, as he had conceded to William Evarts, "he who knows he can govern him and put him to canonical service may lawfully raise the devil himself." Though restraint might be needed in the future,

today we need it all, we need it all!—the hopes—the boasts—the pride—the universal tolerance—the gay and festive defiance of foreign dictation—the flag—the music—all the emotions—all the traits—all the energies, that have won their victories of war, and their miracles of national advancement,—the country needs them all now to win a victory of peace. That done, I will pass again, happy and content, into that minority of conservatism in which I have passed my life.[81]

In conclusion, he asked his audience to bear patiently the taunts of being "Union-Savers," for suppose that by

some vote openly and courageously given, some sincere conviction plainly expressed, we could do something to earn the reality of the praise which they give us in jest, —something for the safety, something for the peace, of this holy and beautiful house of our fathers,—something were it ever so little,—would not this be compensation for the laughter of fools; aye! for alienated friendships, averted faces, and the serpent tooth of slander—a thing worth dying for, and even worth having lived for?[82]

It was a moving speech, but it almost ended in tragedy. The meeting was held on the second floor of an old building and the room was crammed to overflowing with some four or five thousand people. Halfway through Choate's speech there was an ominous cracking sound and the floor seemed to shift. Benjamin Butler, who was on the platform, went to investigate and found that the floor was at the point of giving way. A thunderous round of applause might be fatal. Butler returned and whispered to Choate "If I can't get this crowd out quietly, we shall all be in hell in five minutes." He told the crowd to leave quietly, and he and Choate remained on the platform while they filed out. "Did you think," murmured Choate to his erstwhile Democratic enemy, as he and Butler at length emerged from the building, "that both of us would go to the *same* place?"[83]

Choate finished his speech from a hastily built platform outside his hotel, and all ended happily. When Buchanan won the election, Choate probably felt that the collapse of the Union had been averted in the same nick-of-time fashion. Yet he also could not deny feeling a sense of impending doom. "There is a certain gloomy and dangerous sense in which I am 'gratified,' " he wrote to Everett,

> But 'renown and grace'—where are they? . . . I entreat you to give him [Buchanan] and all conservative men an idea of a patriotic administration. Kansas must be free— suâ sponte and the nation kept quiet and honest—yet with a certain sense of growth—nor unmindful of opportunities of glory.[84]

Moreover, an analysis of the election results indicated that the Republican party had done very well, sweeping New England and carrying all but five of the free states. The American party, on the other hand, had been substantially annihilated, which meant that the election of 1860 would be a face-off between the Republicans and a Democratic party less and less able to make a showing in the North. That summer, Choate had predicted to his son-in-law that there would be civil war between North and South within ten years. "If the Democrats . . . have prudence and good temper, they can tide the trouble over for a while, . . . but I fear they will not show such moderation and prudence."[85]

The year 1857 was thoroughly depressing. The Dred Scott decision, which had the effect of "nationalizing" slavery, prompted dissenting opinions from two eminently conservative justices, John McLean of Ohio, and Benjamin R. Curtis of Massachusetts, and alienated moderates in general. Turmoil continued in Kansas and, in the summer, a financial panic hit the North that left an aftermath of depression and widespread unemployment. The depression threw into sharper relief a fact that had been apparent for some time. The great Northern cities, particularly Boston and New York, contained slums of the European kind, filled with a seemingly permanent class of the poverty stricken, breeding-grounds of vice, disease and crime. The United States, it seemed, no longer was the "Happy Land," exempt from the great blight that marred the civilization of the Old World. "The perishing classes appeal as loudly to our conscience," wrote a despairing contributor to the North American Review, "and the dangerous classes to our fear, as if we too had a thousand years history behind us."[86] As it became harder to think of America as "Utopia sobered, realized, to be fitted according to an idea," America as fact, as a nation,—"Being before well-being"—became increasingly important. Union was a rock to cling to.

Choate had no further ambitions for public life. Though he could have had some office after the election of Buchanan, he refused to accept anything. His decision to vote for the Democrats had been a disinterested one and he wanted it to appear so. He took no part in the state elections of 1858. "Mr. Choate," reported the Republican *New York Tribune,* "by particular desire of his party, by a resolute, praiseworthy, and almost incomprehensible effort, refrained from making any speeches during the campaign." In the last two years of his life Choate spoke in public only on non-partisan occasions and on topics designed to remind his countrymen of the hallowed memory of the founding fathers, of Webster, of the transcendent claims of nationality and the almost holy status of the Union.[87]

He found a certain comfort in looking away from the ill will and uncertainties of the present to the triumphs and tragedies of the past, stripped by history of the messy ignominies and sordidness of present politics. In February 1857, he gave a curious address before the Mechanic Apprentices Library Association on "The Eloquence of Revolutionary Periods." The bulk of the talk was devoted to an appreciation of Demosthenes and Cicero as last-ditch defenders of free states on the verge of destruction by military despots. Taking a brief detour through Grattan as the orator of the struggle for Irish independence ("with a view to the repetition of the address before the Charitable Irish Society," according to Everett), the address culminated in a portrayal of John Adams as the great orator of the American Revolution.[88]

In discussing Cicero, Choate offered a moving objection to the new notion of history as a "long, fatal flow . . . of development and necessity" in which each new state was necessary and therefore right. In this view, Cicero, protesting the overthrow of the Roman Republic, "mistook the time; and died contending vainly and ungracefully with destiny." But, demanded Choate, "is *success* all at once to stand for the test of the excellency of dignity and the excellency of honor?" When a philosophy can see "no grandeur in the struggle of free-will with circumstance, and of virtue and conscience with force, and feel no sympathy with the resistance which patriotism desperately attempts against treason, I reject and hoot it incredulously."[89]

This little aside shows how much Choate still was, in fact, a man of the Enlightenment, who regarded history more as a series of examples of virtue, than as the steamroller of fate. The lecture as a whole also showed how much Choate's imagination was stirred by the historical contemplation of "interesting times." The orator born to take part in revolution had the luck to be part of the "epic and the tragic matter of the story of nations," to deal with "large, elementary, gorgeous ideas," to persuade to the "highest and most heroic" actions, to be an actor in "the sublimest crisis of the State—of man." The crisis through which he felt his own generation to be living, however, did not appear to him as "sublime."[90] He ended the address with a paean to Webster depicting him as a great man who, in a sense, had missed the highest greatness because he had missed the Revolution and had been born in a "quiet, civil age." "Assisted by that unequalled organ of speech, the Greek language of Demosthenes, might he not have rolled an equal thunder, and darted an equal flame?"

Horace Greeley's *New York Tribune* answered Choate's rhetorical question by pointing out that Webster's public life *had* been lived in times of destiny, when the United States was struggling with the problem of whether it was to be "a nation of freemen or a nation of oligarchs." "Why should we suppose," the *Tribune* demanded, that Webster

"would have rolled an equal thunder and flashed an equal flame" with Demosthenes over the threathened liberties of fifty thousand Greeks, when he rolled no thunder and flashed no flame over the threatened liberties of thirteen millions of Americans? Would he "have breathed virtue into decaying Greece" when he had very little to breathe into our decaying Democracy?[91]

Conservatives can hardly be expected to appreciate equally the revolutions of the present and those of the past—not only because of their distaste for unrest but also because they fail to see any vital resemblance. "It was well said of Webster," remarked Wendell Phillips, "that he knows well the Hancock and Adams of 1776, but he does not know the Hancocks and Adamses of to-day." No better than Webster was Choate able to see a Phillips or a Theodore Parker as a latter-day Hancock or Adams, any more than it would have occurred to him to find in the new styles of oratory that men like Phillips were forging—terse, pithy, colloquial, elliptical, personal, often vicious—examples to be included in "the eloquence of revolutionary periods."[92]

Choate was now at the height of his fame at the Bar and loaded down with legal business. In 1858, he gave only two public speeches, both of them designed to stimulate patriotic attachment to the Union as a way of "rising above" the factionalism of the hour. The first was the concluding lecture in a series sponsored by the Mercantile Library Society, on "Jefferson, Burr and Hamilton." In it he suggested that the statesmen who had steered the Revolution and then the constitution to success should serve as examples to their less Olympian descendants.

> They were men, unlike some of the lesser lights who have since filled their seats, who were not crazy for liberty, nor demented for slavery; they were men who never thought to set the North against the South, the East against the West, and still less to stir the strife for personal ends—men to whom a Topeka and a Lecompton question would be but a small ripple in the surface of the unfathomable deep of their patriotism.[93]

He paid the obligatory tribute to Washington—"he was our FATHER . . . our whole country was the object of his solicitude"— and gave a more wary endorsement of Jefferson, but Hamilton was his hero. Hamilton, who laid the foundations for judicial review in the 88th Federalist; who envisaged the United States as a great industrial nation; who, above all, "sooner than every one," had realized that what America needed was "not a league, but a government" and so had transformed the meeting to revise the Articles of Confederation into a true constitutional convention. "I dwell," he added,

> on that time from 1780 to 1789 because that was our age of civil greatness. Then, first, we grew to be *one*. In that time our nation was born. That which went before made us independent. Our better liberty, our law, our order, our union, our credit, our commerce, our rank among the nations, our page in the great history we owe to this.

Independence was the work of the *higher passions*. The Constitution was the *slow product of wisdom*. [94]

The extent, however, to which America could indeed be said to be *one* was, he knew, dubious. In an address, given on the Fourth of July before the Young Men's Democratic Club, on "American Nationality—its Nature—some of its Conditions, and some of its Ethics," Choate summarized the results of twenty years of his thinking about the cultivation of national consciousness in America and the conflicting pulls of patriotism and philanthropy. In accepting the invitation to speak, he had insisted that this be a strictly non-partisan occasion, but in fact he could not resist taking pot-shots at what had become his favorite target: that philanthropy —"so it calls itself,—pedantry, arrogance, folly, cruelty, impiousness, I call it, fit enough for a pulpit, totally unfit for a people; fit enough for a preacher, totally unfit for a statesman."[95] Civic virtue on the other hand, "masculine and intelligent," would recognize that true philanthropy must be subsumed in patriotism, for the "true useful human life" was "the national life."

> Beneath that order, that government, that law, that power, reform is easy and reform is safe—reform of the man, reform of the nation. . . . Under that wing . . . there is . . . room, motive, capacity for labor, for culture, for preparation; for the preaching of the gospel of peace to all, for elevating by slow, sure, and quiet gradations down to its depths, down to its chains, society itself.

Seen in this light, men could cheerfully say "we are philanthropists in proportion as we are unionists." This "American philanthropy," while "safe" and "circumscribed," also had its glorious visions, but they were visions of justice achieved through harmony, not discord: "we hear the chain breaking, but there is no blood on it, none of his whom it bound, none of his who put it on him; we hear the swelling chorus of the free, but master and slave unite in that chorus, and there is no discordant shriek above the harmony." The agency in all this, of course, was time.[96]

If time alone could be trusted to solve the problem of slavery, it could not be relied upon to produce a strong spirit of nationality. Because the United States was a federal nation, with the states "sovereignties, *quasi*, but sovereignties still," the American served "two masters." Moreover, it was within the "inviolate borders" of the states that the day-to-day interests of most men lay; it was the law and the police of the state that protected property and persons; the schools of the state that molded the young, the charities of the state that cared for the unfortunate, "their image, their opinions, their literature, their morality are around us ever, a presence, a monument, an atmosphere." And so the state easily acquired the loyalty that arises naturally out of local and domestic ties, memories of childhood and "the sense of home and security and of property under law." The problem was how to "direct this spontaneous sentiment of hearts to the Union."[97]

America, Choate had always realized, was in a sense a "grand abstraction"; as a nation it was "to an extraordinary degree, not a growth, but a production;—it has origin in the will and the reason, and . . . the will and the reason must keep it alive, or it can bear no life." All men are born into some kind of society, but the organization of human societies into the nation-state was not a necessary response to the exigencies of human existence. It was, rather, a conscious decision based on the realization that only within the wider sphere of the nation could men achieve their highest and most diverse potential; it was the way in which men, rearing their heads above the unself-conscious life of the traditional community, created for themselves a formal structure, with limits defined but large enough, in which they could work out a more ambitious and more conscious existence.[98]

Choate often used the language of organism, but his keen awareness of the fragility of the American nation and of the nation's dependence on the continuing "will and reason" of the people to sustain it, separated his nationalism, in tone at least, from some of the more extreme doctrines of unconditional loyalty to a leviathan state that emerged during the Civil War—and were intimated even before then. There is nothing in Choate, for example, corresponding to the chilling words of Henry Clay in 1850:"What is an individual man? An atom . . . a mere speck . . . a drop of water . . . a grain of sand. . . . Shall a being so small, so petty, so fleeting, so evanescent, oppose himself to the onward march of a great nation, to subsist for ages and ages to come?" It did not matter "if, in the march of this nation to greatness and power, we should be buried beneath the wheels that propel it onward." Choate, however, always conceived of the nation as the house in which the individual attained his fullest human stature, not the juggernaut which reduced him to a speck of dust.[99]

Choate never denied nor wished to deny the reality of the states, and he never explicitly denied the right of secession. In the "theories of some schools" he remarked non-committally, the states had the right to secede from the compact they had made, and the right to "call out their young men and their old men under the pains of death to defy the sword point of the federal arm." He once remarked to Parker that the great danger in the American system was that "a State, *qua* a State, in its sovereign capacity, shall declare war and take the field. Whenever a State, *qua* a State, shall come out against the national government, we can't do anything; for that which ordinarily would be *treason,* is, as it were, saved from being so by the flag of the State." His anxiety to conciliate Southern opinion was due to his conviction that the presence of the South in the Union must be voluntary, not coerced. While he feared the creation of a middle term between the state and the Union—the section—he believed that local loyalties to the state were quite capable of being bound up in larger loyalty to the nation. The alacrity with which the North responded to the call to defend the Union in 1861 seems to indicate that he was right.[100]

The Northern willingness to fight to preserve the Union indicates also how deeply the idea of the Union had penetrated men's consciousness. A vote for the Republican party did not, as Choate imagined, imply an indifference to the Union, merely an unwillingness to let the South dictate the terms on which it should be maintained. By the time of the Civil War, the Union, as Paul C. Nagel has shown, had become a complex symbol, embracing a wide range of meanings, "encompassing Security, Progress, Destiny, the Glorious Past, and a Divine or Natural Order." Phillip Paludan has recently suggested, however, that, more than anything else, Northerners had come to associate the Union with the maintenance of "law and order" and particularly with the everyday experience of self-government and the building of institutions. It was precisely this instinctive connection between Union and order, and disunion and anarchy, that the conservative orators had done so much to foster.[101]

Webster habitually associated the Union with the order of the universe, and Choate, in this address of 1858, used the same kind of metaphor with striking effect. "Every day, still," he reminded his audience,

> we are in committee of the whole on the question of the Constitution or no Constitution. I have heard that if the same Omnipotence which formed the universe at first should suspend its care for a day, primeval chaos were come again. Dare we risk such a speculation in politics and act on it? Consider how new is this America of yours! . . . What enables us then to withhold for a moment the sustaining hand?[102]

Like Jonathan Edwards' image of the sinner over the fire, the image of the universe suspended over chaos was terrifying. The citizen was asked to believe that primeval chaos was equally near in the political realm. It was his anxious responsibility to keep it at bay.

This kind of imagery invited mockery. "Mr. Choate," commented Henry Wilson, "was unfortunately always penetrated with the idea that the Universe was flying to pieces." Richard Dana produced a very good parody of a Choate speech at a public meeting "to preserve the Law of Gravitation."

> Choate: Why, let but the last, lingering, lifeless leaf of a decayed December foliage fall from its parent trunk against the law of Gravitation, and there were a discord through the universe not to be healed until the sea shall give up its dead! (Tremendous applause) In the new Heaven and new earth of the Apocalyptic vision, there may be a new law of Gravitation, or no Gravitation at all; but I respectfully suggest a doubt, a query, whether we had best begin the experiment in the Eighth District quite yet. (Laughter and cheering)[103]

Nevertheless, by the time of the attack on Fort Sumter, it had become almost a commonplace that peaceable partition of the nation was impossible; that, but for the Union, America would be ravaged by the internecine warfare that had destroyed the Greek and Italian republics; that warfare between states would somehow lead to a breakdown of law and order within the states; that there could be no intermediate term between Union and anarchy. As a symbol, the Union subsumed all those salutary restraints, internal and external, which were, conservatives insisted, responsible for the distinctive American contribution to the world: ordered liberty.[104]

Choate's speech on behalf of the Union and American nationality turned out to be his last major public address. The marks of failing health were noticeable while he spoke, and at times he was almost inaudible. But he seemed to rally during that winter and his future biographer, Samuel Gilman Brown, who saw him once or twice in court, was struck by his vigor and "exuberance of spirits." He spoke briefly at a gathering of old Websterites to celebrate the seventy-seventh anniversary of the great man's birthday. He was confident, he said, that eventually Americans would recognize and appreciate Webster's "civil courage" and realize that "common sense, good temper, good nature, and not the pedantry of logical abstraction, and the clamor of intemperate sectional partisanships, are the true guides of life."[105] The address was essentially a resumé of his funeral oration, but he made a great impression on the audience by his "gaunt, sunken" appearance, his glittering eyes, and his slow, stately declamation of the peroration, punctuated by "sublime" pauses. Hillard called the speech "something more than brilliant," and added: "Choate has two real, vital ideas; one is the Union, the sense of nationality; and the other is admiration, idolatry of Webster. Whenever he pulls out one of these stops he talks earnestly and from conviction, but at all other times he is only the most brilliant of advocates."[106]

Two months later, Choate spoke at another semi-private gathering, the celebration by the congregation of the Essex Street Church of the settlement of their minister, Nehemiah Adams. The meeting was intended as a vote of confidence, for Adams had received a good deal of censure for a book he had written on slavery, entitled *A South Side View of Slavery*. The book was of the genre in which the innocent is enlightened by experience: Adams, after signing the petition of the New England clergy against the extension of slavery into Kansas and Nebraska, had gone South on a visit with all the usual New England prejudices. Actual contact with the realities of the system, however, had convinced him that God allowed slavery as a "school" for the African, and in the final chapter, entitled "Cheerful Views," he had decided that all could be safely left in the hands of a benevolent deity. Adams had also endorsed the Compromise of 1850, but apart from these two brief excursions on the side of conservatism, he kept aloof from any kind of political commitment or comment upon events of the day. This, to Choate, seems to have been his prime virtue.[107]

The speech, considering the occasion, was a curious one. It summarized very clearly, and bluntly, his conception of religion as a strictly compartmentalized element of social order which must never be allowed to transcend its sphere and give direction to either the political or the intellectual life. Although the *Origin of Species* had not yet come out, controversy over theories of evolution and their compatibility with religion had been raging since the publication of Robert Chambers' *Vestiges of the Natural History of Creation,* in 1844. After a fairly perfunctory tribute to Adams' character, Choate launched into a passionate defense of freedom of scholarly inquiry as something quite outside the legitimate sphere of religious authority. "Do we not all of us hold," he demanded,

> that outside of this special, authoritative, written revelation, . . . there is another system still, a mental and moral nature, which we may with great propriety expose, and which we may very wisely and fitly study and enjoy? . . . What is there in all this to prevent us from trying to open, if we can open, the clasped volume of that elder, if it may be that obscurer Scripture? . . . What is there to hinder us, if we dare to do it, from going down with chemists and physiologists to the very chambers of existence, and trying thence to trace, if we may, the faint lines by which matter rose to vitality, and vitality welled up first to animals, and then to man? What is there to prevent us from trying to trace the footsteps of God in history, . . . from trying to explore the spirit of Plato? . . . Because you believe the Old Testament, as well as the New, cannot you read a classic in the last and best edition, if you know how to read it?

"We have attached ourselves to this congregation," he concluded, because it had appeared not incompatible with "the largest and most generous mental culture, and the widest philanthropy, that are necessary in order to complete the moral and mental development and accomplishment of man."[108]

In fact, Choate seems to have chosen this particular church

because, combined with the traditional forms of orthodoxy, it knew its own, rather humble, place. The modesty of this particular pulpit had extended to the world of politics, too, and Choate gave hearty thanks that, retiring from the "heated" world of politics on the Sabbath, "never in an introductory prayer, never in a hymn . . . never by any illustration in any sermon, by any train of association, right or wrong, was I carried back into the world that I had left." No minister had the right to use the authoritative eminence of the pulpit to make pronouncements on matters in which he was not qualified.

> He will have learned from his Bible that the race of man is of kindred blood,—all of it; and he will have learned from his Bible, or from Nature, that all men stand on an equality of right and responsibility and duty before God. But how far these glorious generalities are modified and controlled by civil society of any description, which is also the work of God; how far these rays of light, as Burke beautifully expresses it, come to be refracted when they go into such a medium as this; how far history shapes all systems . . . does he know aught of this?

He should stick to religion: "for that exactly we prize, and for that exactly we pay him." This blunt statement produced as many ripples as his earlier pronouncement on the Declaration of Independence and gave rise to a new party cry: "the Gospel according to Choate."[109]

The following day, March 29, he made his last argument before a full Bench, in *Fitchburg Railroad* vs. *Gage,* a case involving a practice that was to become highly controversial after the Civil War, the levying of differential freight rates. In April he appeared in a case at Salem, but was too ill to finish it. This was his last appearance in court and he never went to his office again. He was not in pain, but he was suffering from increasing weakness and attacks of nausea. It was discovered after his death that he had been suffering from Bright's disease, but, at the time, his doctors could not arrive at a diagnosis. That frequent resort of nineteenth-century medicine, foreign travel, seemed to offer some hope; he decided to spend the summer in England. But at the last moment he changed his mind and went instead to stay a month with his daughter, Helen Bell, in the Dorchester suburbs. There he spent the time reading, or being read to, or listening to music, or driving into town for books or to the shore to sit and watch the ocean. Except for weakness and lassitude he seemed content. " 'What can a person do,' he once said after looking long at a beautiful landscape, 'life is not long enough—.' "[110]

Eventually, he made up his mind to leave for England. He wrote notes to a few friends, made up a list of books to take with him (the Bible, the Psalms, the *Iliad,* the *Georgics,* Bacon, Shakespeare, Milton, Coleridge, Macaulay . . .), and made a last trip to Boston. Coming down the courthouse steps, he ran into Joseph Willard, the clerk of the superior court, who wished him a pleasant voyage, and asked if he would be in Boston in the fall. "He put his arm around my neck in the most affectionate manner," recalled Willard, "and patting me softly, said, "Mr. Willard, I expect to be about here a hundred years.' "[111] He sailed from Boston, accompanied by his son, on June 29, but by the time the ship reached Halifax on the following evening, the ship's doctor had decided he was too ill to continue and should be put ashore. The ship docked at midnight; George Hillard, who was also on board on his way to England, helped Rufus Jr. find a carriage and then accompanied them both to a boarding house to which they had been directed. The place not only turned out to be further from the docks than they had thought, but they arrived to find it completely full. Hillard had to return to the ship, leaving Choate upon a sofa, "pale and exhausted, but patient and uncomplaining, his luggage in the street at the door, and his son at that midnight hour wandering about the streets of Halifax, seeking a temporary shelter for a dying father." The son eventually found a pleasant third-floor room overlooking the harbor and had his father transferred to it. For the next twelve days Choate remained there, attended by the surgeon of the flag-ship of the British fleet, and watching from his bed the ships below him in the harbor. "If a schooner or sloop goes by," he told his son as he dozed off, "don't disturb me, but if there is a square-rigged vessel, wake me up." He remained cheerful and mentally alert and seemingly convinced that he would recover, but on the evening of the July 12 he said suddenly that he felt faint and lapsed into a coma. He died early the following morning.[112]

The news of his death brought tributes from Bar associations and the press in many parts of the country and, in Boston, from not only the Suffolk Bar but also the many organizations with which he had been associated or to whom he had lectured. On July 22, a public meeting of mourning was held in Faneuil Hall, hung with black and white crepe and with windows darkened for the occasion, at which Edward Everett gave the principal eulogy. During the meeting the ship bearing Choate's body arrived from Canada. The following day, after a funeral service in the Essex Street Church, the body was taken in procession through the streets of Boston and Cambridge to the tolling of bells and the booming of minute guns, to be buried in the family plot at Mount Auburn.[113]

Choate was remembered for a long time in New England, but he was remembered for what he was and what he had said rather than for what he had done. His extraordinary personality with its intimations of hidden depths and of unfulfilled promise, his rather weird charm, his deft phrases, such as "an instinct for the jugular," which quickly merged into the general stock of language—all held the imagination of those who had known him and intrigued those who had not.[114] Yet Choate's thought, too, is worth consideration by the student of the American past. He was by no means a systematic thinker, but then conservatism is not a systematic philosophy. Indeed, it might be said that in so far as thinking becomes systematic it ceases to be conservative. What Choate did was articulate, with considerable felicity, a body of ideas and attitudes to which a fairly sizable number of post-revolutionary ante-bellum Americans subscribed.

He spoke for men who, even if they would not meet the ideological criteria of someone like Russell Kirk, nevertheless thought of themselves, and were thought of by their opponents, as conservatives. Unlike many Southern conservatives (who have somehow seemed more "genuine" to latter-day men of the Right in search of spiritual grandfathers), these men did not yearn sentimentally for a tradition that they really did not have, but attached themselves squarely to one they did. They read Burke, but they also read the *Federalist Papers,* and did not think them incompatible. They traced their political ancestry to the Puritans and linked themselves to a tradition that was solidly Protestant, republican, commercial, burgher. They, of course, shared a good many of the assumptions of their political opponents—otherwise they could hardly have engaged so vigorously in the political, economic and

intellectual worlds that they had in common. Nonetheless, ante-
bellum Whiggery offers a valuable counterpoint especially to the
romantic anarchism and perfectionism that, to later commentators, has seemed the most essentially "American" aspect of these
years.[115]

There is much that is both attractive and wise in Choate's
conservativism. He was an advocate of a moderate, conciliatory
and "good-tempered" foreign policy, opposing interference with
the affairs of other nations and cautious on the subject of expansion. He propounded a nationalism that was highly emotional but
that managed to steer clear of "spread-eaglism" and also, though
he was tempted by it, of nativism. Though the idea of a homogeneous population appealed to him, ultimately his nationalism was
not a matter of blood but of imagination, and this psychic identification was as available to the adopted as to the native son. He saw
government, not as a necessary evil to be pared away as much as
possible, but as an agency to meet at least certain human wants and
thus obligated to stimulate both the economy and the national
"mind." At the same time, he knew that politics as an activity is
a matter of compromise and adjustment and that prudence is the
greatest of political virtues. When he praised "common sense,"
"good temper," and "good nature," it was because he saw these,
like Burke before him, as *political* virtues which enabled men of
different interests to live together with a minimum of coercion.[116]

Choate was a self-conscious conservative who did not think
that man could usefully be contemplated outside of the social or
political order. Man was a naturally political creature who built
institutions as a way of self-molding. The state as the greatest of
his constructions was not a prison but the most complete expression of his creativity. Freedom, to be human, must be achieved
within the patterns of form and meaning that men laid over the
amorphousness of nature to domesticate it, and so was associated
not with simplicity, but complexity. A multi-layer governmental
structure, a complex system of law, an increasingly differentiated
economy and a diverse and proliferating intellectual life all contributed to men's freedom and their development. The image he
offered of America as a "holy and beautiful city" was, in spite of
that "holy," not a millennial vision but an affirmation that America
must be a consciously constructed civilization, a purification rather
than a departure from the long tradition of Western civilization.

Within this "city" the mind would flourish—and so would the economy. Choate had a healthy respect for the material base of life and an unabashed delight in material progress. In that more innocent economy he could see both the sonnet and the steamboat as manifestations of the same creative energy, and he did not separate the world of intellect and sensibility from the mundane—but equally adventurous—worlds of commerce and enterprise and politics. Since all arose out of a fundamental national culture, they would all tend to flourish or decay at the same time. Choate's "city" encompassed a considerable diversity of occupations, styles of life, and opinions, but this was not incompatible with community, as long as men realized that they were united, not in a fraternal order, which depended on like-mindedness, but in a political one, by their role as citizens and by their common devotion to the overarching structure of the state as the delimiting space within which there was peace, security, justice and stimulus to achievement.

This political philosophy stems from a long Western tradition and has considerable adaptability and capacity for growth. But politics is the realm of action, and the test of any set of political ideas and attitudes is how well they help men cope with the most prominent political problems of their time. "Slavery," as the *New York Tribune* pointed out in an obituary, "is the surest touch-stone of political character at the present time, and the test was fatal to Mr. Choate"—and to the leadership of the Whig party. "The leaders of the Northern Whigs," wrote a contributor to the *Nation,* "were, above all others, the men whose duty it was to control and guide the anti-slavery movement, yet all they did was to try to put it aside and forget it and pretend that it had no right to exist."[117] The basic hazard of the conservative temperament is that its fear of chaos and instinctive desire for harmony will make it incapable of assimilating or directing any movement for change. Choate's reaction of sheer panic, when he confronted the threat of disunion in the 1850s, indicates that he ignored some of the better parts of his own philosophy. He insisted that "will and reason" must uphold the Union, but did not offer "will and reason" as means of dealing with the problem of slavery. In opposing the annexation of Texas, he himself had realized how irresistible the public's aversion to slavery was becoming. Does the annexationist, he had demanded then, reflect how vast a change the sentiments of civilization have undergone on that whole subject since eighteen hundred and twenty? . . . Can he not read the gathering signs of the times? . . . Does he not see and feel that in that interval, a public opinion has been generated, has been organized, wholly new, aggressive, intolerant of the sight, intolerant of the cry of man in chains? Does he not see and feel with what electrical force and speed it strikes from one quarter of the globe to another, and is spreading to enfold the whole civilized world like an atmosphere?[118]

Yet only a few years later, he could disregard his own diagnosis and imagine that this new "atmosphere" could be obliterated, that this new consciousness could be suppressed.

What Choate and men like him failed to realize, a mistake fatal in a conservative, was that the growing anti-slavery sentiment was not, except on its more vocal fringes, particularly radical—indeed, most of the men who moved into the ranks of the Free Soil, and then the Republican, party were as conservative as Choate himself on other issues, and in basic outlook. Moreover, anti-slavery was not the inflated product of "outside agitators"; it had its roots deep in authentic American traditions. America does have tradition, asserted James Russell Lowell, "men are yet alive who felt the first thrill of that fateful Declaration." Wendell Phillips too could claim the Puritans as ancestors—not for respectability but for the repudiation of authority and institutions before the claims of righteousness. The Cotton Whigs, who had eliminated anger from their churches, were merely repelled by the note of Old Testament righteous wrath in so much anti-slavery propaganda.[119] They felt, no doubt rightly, that it was incompatible with a stable and civilized society. But the anger was genuine and came from some deep well-spring of New England life. What the great majority of the Northern public wanted, as Lincoln saw, was not immediate abolition, but to be able "to rest in the belief" that slavery was "in the course of ultimate extinction." And this belief had to rest on some real evidence, not pious assurances that time would solve the problem. All Choate could offer at the end was "being before well-being." But this was surely to mistake the nature of that national identity with which he was so concerned.

The idea of America had always had some moral content, some vital ideological component. Choate's image of the "city" as that moral content offered greater possibilities for a humane civilization than Manifest Destiny and greater complexity and completeness than anti-slavery. But this image could not exist without anti-slavery. Increasingly, men could not feel their country "to be lovely" by sheer act of will, as Choate seemed to advocate, in light of the, by now ineradicable, awareness of the unlovely facts. "Are we satisfied that America should have no other excuse for independent national existence than a superior facility of money-making?" demanded the journalist, George W. Curtis. "Does the production of twelve hundred million pounds of cotton fulfill the destiny of this continent in the order of Providence?"[120] It was because so many other conservative men also felt that America was indeed a nation and that the nation must enoble its citizens that they felt increasingly besmirched by the existence of slavery and by the growth of a pro-slavery body of opinion.

Yet, if Choate failed to understand why the slavery issue could not be repressed, on a deeper level he shared and articulated the existential fear of a large number of his countrymen, inevitable in a new, vast, and still amorphous society, that the boundaries and limits and restraints of life were too weak, that the order which enabled identity to be formed was shifting, and that therefore "being," as a firm grasp on the sense of self, was in danger. To be an "American" was an outline of identity into which the unsure personality could be fitted, providing both consciousness of self and community with others. If one wishes to understand why the Union had to be maintained at all costs, including the cost of war, Choate may be as useful a guide as Lincoln. For some, the Union may have come to symbolize the hope for democracy in the world, but it had also become a symbol of identity, a barrier to chaos, almost a synonym for "being."

NOTES

NOTE ON THE CITATION OF SOURCES

With the collaboration of the Choate family, Professor Samuel Gilman Brown of Dartmouth University produced *The Works of Rufus Choate with a Memoir of his Life* (Boston, 1862), in two volumes. Extracts from some of Choate's speeches not published in full were included in the Memoir. In 1870 he brought out the memoir of the life separately, *The Life of Rufus Choate* (Boston, 1870), with some slight additions and amendments. Whenever I have had occasion to refer to the biographical study I have used this second, separate edition of the *Life*. When I have quoted from the published speeches I have cited the earlier, *Works of Rufus Choate*.

CHAPTER ONE. FINDING A CAREER

1. Choate received forty-seven out of the fifty-one votes necessary to be elected to the Hall of Fame. See Louis Albert Banks, *The Story of the Hall of Fame* (New York, 1902), pp. 369–372; Frank W. Grinnell, "The Judicial System and the Bar (1820–1861)," in *Commonwealth History of Massachusetts,* ed. Albert Bushnell Hart, IV (New York, 1966; 1st pub., 1930), 60; Claude M. Fuess, *Rufus Choate: The Wizard of the Law* (New York, 1928), p. 278.

2. Clinton Rossiter, *Conservatism in America: The Thankless Persuasion* (rev. ed.; New York, 1962), p. 126; Louis Hartz, *The Liberal Tradition in America: An Interpretation of American Political Thought Since the Revolution* (New York, 1955), p. 97. A modern study by a political scientist that assesses Choate's conservatism within the outline laid down by Clinton Rossiter is David Bradstreet Walker, "Rufus Choate, An American Whig," (Ph.D. diss., Brown University, 1956).

3. Review of Samuel Brown, *The Works of Rufus Choate,* in *The Atlantic Monthly,* (Jan. 1863), p. 141.

4. Samuel Gilman Brown, *The Life of Rufus Choate* (Boston, 1870), pp. 1–2. The family were supposed to be of Huguenot descent, coming to England via Germany and Holland (*Boston Sunday Herald,* Nov. 18, 1894). Probably the most prominent member of the family until Rufus Choate himself was Colonel John Choate, who was a judge and member of the governor's council in the

1760s and who also built the Choate bridge, "the oldest stone arch bridge in the U.S.," over the Ipswich river (*The Boston Globe*, July 14, 1965, p. 16; and John D. Cogswell, *Memoir of Rufus Choate* [Cambridge, Mass., 1884], pp. 383–384). Rufus's grandfather, William Choate, had been a sea captain at twenty-five (Fuess, *Rufus Choate*, ch. 1).

5. Joseph H. Choate, *An Address Delivered at the Unveiling of the Statue of Rufus Choate in the Court House in Boston, October 15, 1895,* (Boston, 1895), p. 8.

6. Brown, *Life*, pp. 3, 7–8; Fuess, *Rufus Choate*, pp. 14–15; Edwin P. Whipple, "College Life of Rufus Choate," in *Some Noted Princes, Authors and Statesmen of Our Time*, ed. James Parton (Norwich, Conn., 1885), pp. 277–283. David Choate, MS Reminiscences, in Samuel Gilman Brown MSS, Houghton Library, Harvard University, Cambridge, Mass.

7. Brown, *Life*, pp. 4–5; Nehemiah Adams, D.D. *A Sabbath Discourse on the Death of the Hon. Rufus Choate Together with the Address at His Funeral* (Boston, 1859), p. 48; Richard Henry Dana, Jr., entry for March 27, 1854, *Journal*, ed. Robert F. Lucid (3 vols.; Cambridge, Mass., 1968), II, 621.

8. Brown, *Life*, pp. 6–11; Fuess, *Rufus Choate*, p. 26; David Choate, MS Reminiscences, Brown MSS.

9. "The revered school . . . has dwindled to 13 or 14 scholars, and no more likely to come," Rufus wrote home in his last few weeks at Hampton. By July he was determined to decamp too. "I want some time for relaxation and delivery from 'purgatory' previous to 'besetting' Dart. C" (Rufus to David Choate, June 17 and July 20, 1815, Rufus Choate MSS, Dartmouth College Archives, Hanover, N.H.).

10. Herbert Darling Foster, "Webster and Choate in College: Dartmouth under the Curriculum of 1796–1819," *Dartmouth Alumni Magazine* (April 1927), pp. 509–519; (May 1927), pp. 605–616; Richard Hofstadter, *Academic Freedom in the Age of the College* (New York 1955), p. 219.

11. Foster, "Webster and Choate in College," pp. 512–514. In Choate's day, 43 percent of the graduates went into the ministry, 33 percent into the law, 12 percent into teaching, and 9 percent into medicine *(ibid)*. For the dissatisfaction of students like George Perkins Marsh, see David Lowenthal, *George Perkins Marsh: Versatile Vermonter* (New York, 1958), pp. 23–24. Choate, on the other hand, seemed to have had no complaints. "The instruction we enjoy is most excellent," he wrote to David. "President Brown hears us in Horace and Prof. Shurtleff in Algebra and it is our own fault if we do not make suitable advances" (Nov. 5, 1816, Choate MSS, Dartmouth).

12. Rufus Choate to his son Rufus, March 6, 1852, in Brown, *Life*, p. 247; Rufus to David Choate, June 16, 1816, Choate MSS, Dartmouth; rpt. in Edward C. Latham, "Days of Controversy, 1816–1819," *Dartmouth Alumni Magazine* (June 1962), p. 10.

13. Maurice G. Baxter, *Daniel Webster and the Supreme Court* (Amherst, 1966), pp. 65–78; William Gwyer North, "The Political Background of the Dartmouth College Case," *New England Quarterly*, XVIII (June 1945), 181–203; Rufus to David Choate, March 12, 1817, Choate MSS, Dartmouth; rpt. in Latham, "Days of Controversy," p. 12.

14. John King Lord, *A History of Dartmouth College, 1815–1909* (Concord, N.H., 1913), pp. 131–137.

15. Rufus to David Choate, Nov. 8, 1817, Choate MSS, Dartmouth; rpt. in Latham, "Days of Controversy," pp. 12–13.

16. Lowenthal, *George Perkins Marsh*, pp. 24–25. The group also included John Wheeler and Joseph Torrey, both of whom became presidents of the University of Vermont after James Marsh (John J. Duffy, "Introduction," *Coleridge's American Disciples: The Selected Correspondence of James Marsh* [Amherst, 1973], pp. 8–13). This select group seems to have stimulated the whole student body. It "gave an impulse to the study and love of classical literature unknown before or since in that college. Friendly emulation and student pride led to daily canvassing of books published, authors read and works studied" ("Reminiscences of Nathan Crosby," in Joseph Neilson, *Memories of Rufus Choate, with Some Consideration of His Studies, Methods and Opinions, and of His Style as a Speaker and Writer* [Boston, 1884], p. 346).

17. Rev. Charles White to Samuel Gilman Brown, Jan. 23, 1860, Brown MSS; Washington to Rufus Choate, Nov. 4, 1820, Choate MSS, Dartmouth. James Marsh taught himself German, French, Hebrew and Italian while he was at Dartmouth, and Choate taught himself French. (Duffy, *Coleridge's American Disciples*, p. 11; Rufus to David Choate, Nov. 5, 1816, Choate MSS, Dartmouth). Choate visited Mme. de Staël's chateau at Coppet while on a visit to Europe in 1850 and said of her: "She helped to shape my mind, and to store and charm it. My love for her began in college, growing as I came nearer to the hour when such tongues must cease, and such knowledge vanish away" (Diary of Rufus Choate, Aug. 18, 1850, in Brown, *Life*, p. 226). For the impact of the Schlegels and Madame de Staël on American critical thought, see William Charvat, *The Origins of American Critical Thought, 1810–35* (New York, 1961; 1st pub., 1935), pp. 60–68.

18. Choate to James Marsh, Aug. 11, 1821, Brown MSS; rpt., with some omissions, in Brown, *Life*, pp. 24–25.

19. For burgeoning cultural nationalism and the importance of the literary nationalism of Europe, especially Germany, see Benjamin T. Spencer, *The Quest for Nationality: An American Literary Campaign* (Syracuse, 1957), ch. 3, esp. pp. 90–95. Choate, as president of the Social Friends (one of the two literary societies), delivered to the incoming freshmen a full oration instead of the customary short formal speech ("Reminiscences of George W. Nesmith," in Neilson, *Memories*, p. 264).

20. Brown, *Life*, pp. 18–20; John D. Willard to Brown, Jan. 30, 1860, Brown MSS; Dr. Boyden to Brown, Dec. 26, 1859, *ibid.;* White to Brown, Jan. 23, 1860, *ibid.;* G. P. Marsh, quoted in Caroline Crane Marsh, *Life and Letters of George Perkins Marsh* (New York, 1888), p. 16.

21. Rev. J. M. Masters to Brown, May 7, 1862, Brown MSS; White to Brown, Jan. 23, 1860, *ibid.;* Joseph Torrey, comp., *The Remains of the Rev. James Marsh* (Port Washington, N.Y., 1971; 1st pub., 1843), p. 27; General Henry K. Oliver, "Memoir of Choate in College," clipping from *Salem Gazette,* n.d., Rufus Choate MSS, Essex Institute, Salem, Mass.; E. C. Tracy, a classmate, and later editor of the *Vermont Chronicle,* in Brown, *Life*, p. 13. For the vogue of Byron in America, see William Ellery Leonard, *Byron and Byronism in America* (New York, 1965), esp. ch. 2. James Marsh, while condemning Byron's morality still felt that reading him "gives me new hope,

and I seem in reality to live a being more intense" (Torrey, *Remains,* p. 25).

22. Rufus to David Choate, Nov. 8, 1817, Choate MSS, Dartmouth.

23. "Reminiscences of Nathan Crosby," p. 347.

24. Boyden to Brown, Dec. 26, 1859, Brown MSS.

25. Rufus to David Choate, Nov. 8, 1817, Choate MSS, Dartmouth. He added: "By professions, I mean those of law and physic (for I do not think it quite right to talk of Divinity as a mere trade,) . . . and as I have no thought of entering except as such I should choose to omit it in the account."

26. Rufus to David Choate, March 25, 1819, Choate MSS, Dartmouth; Latham, "Days of Controversy," p. 32; R. Kent Newmyer, "Daniel Webster as Tocqueville's Lawyer: The Dartmouth College Case Again," *The American Journal of Legal History,* II (1967), 127–147; Lewis S. Feuer, "James Marsh and the Conservative Transcendentalist Philosophy," *New England Quarterly,* XXXI (March 1958), 3–31.

27. White to Brown, Jan. 23, 1860, Brown MSS.

28. Willard to Brown, Jan. 30, 1860, Brown MSS.

29. White to Brown, Jan. 23, 1860, Brown MSS.

30. Torrey, *Remains,* pp. 17–21; Feuer, "James Marsh," p. 8; Duffy, *Coleridge's American Disciples,* pp. 14–15.

31. David to Rufus Choate, Dec. 20, 1816, Choate MSS, Dartmouth; Thomas Sewall to Choate, May 7, 1816, Choate MSS, Dartmouth; Sewall to Choate, March 18, 1820, Brown MSS. For the important role of the religious crisis in adolescent life of the time, see Joseph Kett, *Rites of Passage* (New York, 1971), ch. 3, and Kett, "Growing up in Rural New England, 1800–40," in *Anonymous Americans,* ed. Tamara K. Hareven (Englewood Cliffs, N.J., 1971), pp. 1–16. Choate's attitude towards a clerical career is expressed in a letter to James Marsh the year after leaving Dartmouth. "Now for all the world, I would not submit myself to the labor of in the first place securely grounding myself in a set, any set, of theological doctrines, and then of holding fast to them as to be able to expose and defend them and erect on them the proper superstructure of moral and religious exhortation" (Aug. 11, 1821, copy in Brown MSS; the rest of the letter is in Brown, *Life,* pp. 24–25).

32. George Bush to Rufus Choate, Brown MSS. The first page is mutilated and the date and much else illegible, but it was probably written mid-1822. It is perhaps significant that Choate, who kept so little of his correspondence, should have kept this. It was not until some ten years later that the correspondence was resumed.

33. Brown, *Life,* p. 21; Fuess, *Rufus Choate,* pp. 36–37; Herbert Darling Foster, "The Ripley-Olcott-Leeds House," *Dartmouth Alumni Magazine* (April 1925), pp. 464–465. Choate's appearance is described in "Recollections of a Nomad," *Church's Bazaar,* n.d., pt. 6 [June 26, 1852], p. 165. Choate referred to his eye trouble and headaches in letters to David, Dec. 16, March, June 16, 1816 (Latham, "Days of Controversy," pp. 10–12). His valedictory speech, "The Fine Arts as Affecting the Republican Character," is printed in *The Dartmouth,* VII (Oct. 1872), pp. 115–117.

34. Fuess, *Rufus Choate,* pp. 41–42.

35. Arthur E. Sutherland, *The Law at Harvard: A History of Ideas and Men, 1817–1967* (Cambridge, Mass., 1967), pp. 53–73; Rufus to David Choate, Oct.

2, 1820, Choate MSS, Dartmouth; Brown, *Life,* p. 379.

36. Brown, *Life,* p. 23; Fuess, *Rufus Choate,* pp. 44–47; William Wirt to ?, July 22, 1822, rpt. in *The American Journal of Legal History,* II (1958), 256–258.

37. William Wirt to H. W. Miller, Dec. 20, 1833, in John V. Kennedy, *Memoirs of the Life of William Wirt* (Philadelphia, 1849), II, 419.

38. Fuess, *Rufus Choate,* p. 46; Edward G. Parker, *Reminiscences of Rufus Choate, The Great American Advocate* (New York, 1860), pp. 31, 256.

39. Choate to James Marsh, Aug. 11, 1821, Brown MSS, and in Brown, *Life,* pp. 24–25. Wirt was impressed with what little he saw of the young Choate and told Sewall his only deficiencies were a too close application to his books and a disinclination for company (Sewall to Mills Olcott, April 10, 1822, Choate MSS, Dartmouth).

40. Brown, *Life,* pp. 25–27.

41. Hugh S. Legaré, Aug. 24, 1816, in Richard Beale Davis, "The Early American Lawyer and the Profession of Letters," *Huntington Library Quarterly,* XII, no. 2 (Feb. 1949), 191–205, 198 (quotation).

42. Choate to James Marsh, Aug. 11, 1821, Brown MSS.

43. Choate to James Marsh, Nov. 28, 1823, Brown MSS.

44. Choate to James Marsh, Nov. 14, 1829, in Brown, *Life,* pp. 42–43. For the difficulties Marsh met in publishing the *Aids* and his efforts to get favorable reviews to offset orthodox disapproval, see John J. Duffy, "Problems in Publishing Coleridge: James Marsh's First American Edition of *Aids to Reflection,*" *New England Quarterly,* XLIII (June 1970), 193–208.

45. Choate to Marsh, Nov. 28, 1823, Brown MSS.

46. *Ibid.* This part of the letter is reprinted in Brown, *Life,* p. 28.

47. Brown, *Life,* pp. 29, 459.

48. Brown, *Life,* pp. 460–461. The other children were: Catherine, b. 1826, d. 1830; an infant who died at birth, 1828; Caroline, b. 1837, d. 1840 (Cogswell, *Memoir,* p. 434).

49. Fitch Poole, "Early Recollections of Rufus Choate" (1859), *The Historical Collections of the Danvers Historical Society,* XV (1927), 26–30.

50. John W. Black, "Rufus Choate," in *A History and Critique of American Public Address,* ed. William Norwood Brigance (New York, 1943), I, 435–436.

51. Samuel Eliot Morison, *The Maritime History of Massachusetts, 1783–1860* (Cambridge, Mass., 1921), ch. 14.

52. Fuess, *Rufus Choate,* p. 61; Boyden to Brown, Jan. 18, 1860, Brown MSS. The business venture was a scheme to establish a great lumber enterprise and mills at the headwaters of the Mississippi and float timber downstream to the growing towns which needed lumber. The scheme collapsed partly due to natural misfortunes and partly to the disinclination of the three lawyers to pay much attention to business outside their profession. The affair is recounted in Robert S. Rantoul, *Personal Recollections* (Cambridge, Mass., 1916), pp. 25–26.

53. Poole, "Early Recollections," p. 30.

54. Edwin P. Whipple, *Some Recollections of Rufus Choate* (New York, 1879), pp. 10–12.

55. Irving Browne, *Short Studies of Great Lawyers* (Albany, N.Y., 1878), pp. 358–359. "A new sort of thunder and lightening" is from an account of an early case by Asahel Huntington. While Choate was still at Danvers he appeared in

court at Salem in defense of two young men of the numerous and locally influential Crowninshield clan, charged with assaulting the wife of the owner of a dance hall in the small black colony settled at the head of the Salem and Boston Turnpike. He did not win the case, but in the course of the three-day trial he won a reputation. Huntington recalled "such words, such epithets, such involutions, such close and powerful logic all the while, such grace and dignity, such profusion, and waste even, of everything beautiful and lovely. No, not waste, he never wasted a word." The public crowded into and outside the courtroom to hear the new phenomenon (Asahel Huntington to Brown, June 1859, Brown MSS; the letter is partially reprinted in Brown, *Life,* pp. 32–3. ; the *Salem Gazette,* Nov. 18, 1825, described the case in a little more detail and assessed his argument as one of "great ingenuity").

56. Whipple, *Some Recollections,* p. 70; Browne, *Short Studies,* p. 364. In the summer of 1830 he acted as one of the junior counsels to Daniel Webster in a much publicized murder case (Brown, *Life,* pp. 38–39).

57. Browne, *Short Studies,* p. 360.

58. Whipple, *Some Recollections,* p. 35; John T. Morse, "The Bench and Bar," in *The Memorial History of Boston,* ed. Justin Winsor (Boston, 1881), IV, 602.

59. The concept of the "formative period" is Roscoe Pound's in *The Formative Era of American Law* (Boston, 1938). See also Perry Miller, *The Life of the Mind in America: From the Revolution to the Civil War* (New York, 1965), p. 109.

60. The number of lawyers grew dramatically in this period: there were 200 trained lawyers in Massachusetts in 1800, a ratio of 1 to every 2,872 of the population, by 1840 there were 640, a ratio of 1 to 1,153. By the 1830s the lawyers of Massachusetts were a well-established elite class. At a time when a college education was a very rare attainment, over two-thirds of Massachusetts lawyers had a degree. Most recruits to the profession were the sons of professional men or merchants and, by the 1840s, increasingly the sons of lawyers (Choate's farming background was already rather rare by 1820). They also tended overwhelmingly to marry daughters of other lawyers, doctors or ministers (Gerald W. Gawalt, "Sources of Anti-lawyer Sentiment in Massachusetts, 1740–1840," *The American Journal of Legal History,* XIV [1970], 283–307). For the widespread hostility to law and lawyers, see Arthur M. Schlesinger, Jr., *The Age of Jackson* (Boston, 1945), 322–333; Miller, *Life of the Mind,* pp. 99–109; Anton-Hermann Chroust, *The Rise of the Legal Profession in America* (Norman, Okla., 1965), II, 154–172.

61. Gawalt, "Sources," pp. 296, 304.

62. Alexis de Tocqueville, *Democracy in America* (New York, 1945; 1st pub., 1835), Vol. I, ch. 16. For the shift in power in this period from juries to judges, see William E. Nelson, *Americanization of the Common Law: The Impact of Legal Change on Massachusetts Society, 1760–1830* (Cambridge, Mass., 1975), pp. 165–174.

63. For Robinson, see Schlesinger, *Age of Jackson,* pp. 167–168.

64. Frederick Robinson, *A Letter to the Honorable Rufus Choate, Containing a Brief Exposure of Law Craft, and Some of the Encroachments upon the Rights and Liberties of the People* (Boston, 1831), p. 4.

65. Robinson, *A Letter,* pp. 12, 16.

66. "Address of Chancellor Kent before the Law Association of New York

City, October 21, 1836," *American Jurist,* XVI (Jan. 1837), 472.

67. *Ibid.*

68. Miller, *Life of the Mind,* pp. 99–155, esp. pp. 109–116, 139–142.

69. Choate to ?, May 5, 1846, in Parker, *Reminiscences,* pp. 307–308. That knowledge of the classical languages was essential in order to maintain the professions as authentically learned and a career for gentlemen was a widespread attitude on both sides of the Atlantic. The President of the Royal College of Physicians of London told a Commons select committee that he preferred to admit men from Oxford and Cambridge, who would have received a good classical but not medical education, because he thought a knowledge of Greek, Latin and mathematics "absolutely necessary with reference to the dignity and respectability of the profession" (W. J. Reader, *Professional Men: The Rise of the Professional Classes in 19th Century England* [London, 1966], p. 17).

70. Chroust, *Rise of the Legal Profession,* pp. 154–172. See also Matthew A. Crenson, *The Federal Machine* (Baltimore, 1975), for the growing inability of social institutions such as the Bar and the business community to regulate the conduct of their members.

71. Maxwell Bloomfield, "Lawyers and Public Criticism: Challenge and Response in Nineteenth-Century America," *The American Journal of Legal History,* XV (1971), 269–277, 269 (quotation).

72. Tocqueville, *Democracy,* I, 283–284.

73. Maxwell Bloomfield, "Law vs. Politics: The Self-Image of the American Bar (1830–60)," *The American Journal of Legal History,* XII, (1966), 306–323. See also Bloomfield, *American Lawyers in a Changing Society, 1776–1876* (Cambridge, Mass., 1976), ch. 5, for the efforts of legal spokesmen to create a suitable "image" for the lawyer in a democratic society.

74. Choate to George Bush, Aug. 21, 1833, in *Memoirs and Reminiscences of the Late Professor George Bush,* ed. Woodbury M. Fernald (Boston, 1860), pp. 322–323 (italics mine); "Rufus Choate," *Monthly Law Reporter,* XXV (1863), 266–267, quoted in Bloomfield, "Law vs. Politics," p. 318.

75. "Address of Chancellor Kent." This is not to say that the legal profession ceased to be a stepping stone to politics. Quite the contrary, between 1830 and 1860 the proportion of lawyers in the House of Representatives rose to well over 60 percent, but there was also a strong alternative ideological pull away from politics. For the occupational backgrounds of representatives, see Allan G. Bogue et al., "Members of the House of Representatives and the Process of Modernization," *Journal of American History,* LXIII (Sept. 1976), 275–302.

76. Bloomfield, "Law vs. Politics," pp. 314–318.

77. Newmyer, "Daniel Webster," pp. 145–146.

78. Fuess, *Rufus Choate,* pp. 66–69; Caleb Cushing's Journal for Feb. 5, 1829 is quoted in Claude M. Fuess, *The Life of Caleb Cushing* (2 vols.; New York, 1923), I, 88.

79. Fuess, *Rufus Choate,* pp. 65–71. A meeting to support Choate's candidacy resolved that the mere holding of office for a number of years did not "constitute a right to it" (*Salem Register,* Oct. 28, 1830). The career of the Crowninshields is discussed in Paul Goodman, *The Democratic Republicans of Massachusetts: Politics in a Young Republic* (Cambridge, Mass., 1964), pp. 108–118.

80. The story of the maneuverings at the nominating convention is in the *Salem Register,* Oct. 21, 25, 28 and Nov. 1, 1830; Choate to James Marsh, Nov. 14, 1830, James Marsh MSS, University of Vermont Library, Burlington, Vt. Most of the letter is reprinted in Brown, *Life,* p. 47.

81. Boyden to Brown, Jan. 8, 1860, Brown MSS; *Salem Register,* Oct. 28, 1830; a Mr. Wellington to Brown, Oct. 11, 1860, Brown MSS.

82. See the letter from "a Farmer," *Salem Register,* Oct. 25, 1830; Poole, "Early Recollections," p. 29. The final vote was 1,750 for Choate on the National Republican ticket, 767 for Crowninshield running as an independent, 352 for the Jacksonian, and 85 for another independent (Wellington to Brown, Oct. 11, 1860, Brown MSS). Election broadsides emphasized that Choate was an "Essex farmer's son" fighting a rich and powerful family (Choate MSS, Essex Institute, Salem, Mass.).

83. Choate to Marsh, Nov. 14, 1830, Marsh MSS.

84. Brown, *Life,* p. 46.

85. Rufus to David Choate, Dec. 11, 1831, Choate MSS, Dartmouth; Choate to George Bush, Feb. 12 and Jan. 21, 1832, in Brown, *Life,* pp. 52–53; William Carey Richards, *Great in Goodness: A Memoir of George N. Briggs, Governor of the Commonwealth of Massachusetts from 1844 to 1851* (Boston, 1866), p. 110.

86. Choate to Bush, Jan. 21, 1832, in Brown, *Life,* pp. 52–53. In November 1830 Choate had written to James Marsh saying that he would like to resume correspondence with Bush (Choate to Marsh, Nov. 14, 1830, Marsh MSS).

87. Rufus to David Choate, Dec. 11, 1831, Choate MSS, Dartmouth.

88. Choate kept in close contact with the friends who had worked for his election, particularly Jonathan Shove, the banker, who was also involved in supplying domestic wool to the woolen factories of New England. He asked them for advice on tariff questions involving the wool business: "Tell me why the duty on *coarse* wool—not grown here should not be reduced. . . . Be so good as to furnish me with the requisite information by answering these questions" (Choate to Jonathan Shove, Dec. 30, 1831, Choate MSS, Essex Institute, rpt. in "Rufus Choate Letters," *Essex Institute Historical Collections,* LXIX [1933], 85). In turn he kept them posted on likely developments. "I advise you to make your present arrangements on the calculation of a great shock to wool and woolens," he wrote to Shove in the midst of the debates on the tariff (Choate to Shove, June 3 [1832], *ibid.*).

89. *Salem Register,* Oct. 21, 1830.

90. *Salem Observer,* April 21, 1832.

91. Choate's speech on revolutionary pensions, arguing that they should be given as just compensation, not charity, and without a "means test" is in Joseph Gales and William Winston Seaton, *Register of Debates,* LXXXII (April 9, 1832), 2,447–2,458.

92. Choate's speech was printed in pamphlet form: *Speech of Mr. Choate of Massachusetts on the Bill to Alter and Amend the Several Acts Imposing Duties on Imports, House of Representatives, U.S., June 13, 1832* (Washington, D.C., 1832), p. 16.

93. Brown, *Life,* pp. 49–50; Choate to Jonathan Shove, June 15, 1832, Choate MSS, Essex Institute, and in "Rufus Choate Letters," pp. 82–83.

94. Rufus to David Choate, June 3, [1832], Choate MSS, Dartmouth;

Choate to Edward Everett, Nov. 10, 1832, in Brown, *Life*, pp. 54–55.

95. Choate to Jonathan Shove, Dec. 25, [1832], "Rufus Choate Letters," pp. 83–85.

96. *Ibid.*, p. 84; Gales and Seaton, *Register of Debates*, XCI (Jan. 15, 1833), 1,064–1,078, 1,077 (quotation).

97. Choate to Leverett Saltonstall, Jan. 19 [1833], Leverett Saltonstall MSS, Massachusetts Historical Society, Boston, Mass.

98. Choate to George Bush, Jan. 29, 1833, in Fernald, *Memoirs and Reminiscences*, pp. 321–322; also in Brown, *Life*, pp. 56–57, but not complete. Choate evidently set aside particular days for his correspondence and dealt with much of it at once, using many of the same phrases. His letter to Saltonstall of the same date in Saltonstall MSS is in parts almost identical.

99. Wellington to Brown, Oct. 11, 1860, Brown MSS.

100. Brown, *Life*, p. 58. Choate's speech was made on March 28, 1834, and was reprinted as a pamphlet, *Speech of Mr. Choate on the Question of the Removal of the Deposits* (Washington, D.C., 1834). Webster by now had also adopted this tactic: "the very man, of all others, who has the deepest interest in a sound currency, and who suffers most by mischievous legislation in money matters, is the man who earns his daily bread by daily toil" (Webster in the Senate, Jan. 31, 1834, rpt. in *The Works of Daniel Webster* [Boston, 1890; 1st pub., 1851], III, 506–551, 534 [quotation]).

101. Choate to David A. White, April 5, 1834, Choate MSS, Dartmouth.

102. Choate to John Davis, Feb. 9, 1834, John Davis MSS, American Antiquarian Society, Worcester, Mass.

103. Choate to Warwick Palfray, Jr., Jan. 31, 1834, "Rufus Choate Letters," pp. 86–87. Both Lynn Marshall, in "The Strange Stillbirth of the Whig Party," *American Historical Review*, LXXII (Jan. 1967), 445–468, and Ronald P. Formisano, in "Political Character, Antipartyism and the Second Party System," *American Quarterly*, XXI (Winter 1969), 683–709, find a reluctance among Whigs to accept the inevitability and legitimacy of tightly organized voter-oriented parties, as opposed to loose alliances of gentlemen elected as natural leaders of their localities. This does not seem to have been true of younger Whigs like Choate and Cushing, however. For Webster's brief rapprochement with Jackson, see Richard N. Current, *Daniel Webster and the Rise of National Conservatism* (Boston, 1955), pp. 79–81; E. Malcolm Carroll, *Origins of the Whig Party: A Dissertation* (Durham, N.C., 1925), pp. 78–96; Sidney Nathans, *Daniel Webster and Jacksonian Democracy* (Baltimore, 1973), pp. 48–66; Irving H. Bartlett, *Daniel Webster* (New York, 1978), pp. 135–142.

104. Choate to Daniel Webster, Aug. 12, 1833, *The Letters of Daniel Webster*, ed. C. H. Van Tyne, (New York, 1968; 1st pub., 1902), pp. 184–185.

105. Choate to Mills Olcott, Jan. 1, 1832, Choate MSS, Dartmouth.

106. Choate to Webster, Aug. 12, 1833, *Letters of Daniel Webster.*

107. Edward Everett to Thomas W. Ward, Feb. 18, 1834, Thomas W. Ward MSS, Massachusetts Historical Society, Boston, Mass. At least for the purpose of money raising, Everett was quite prepared to describe the current party battles as "nothing less than a war of *numbers* against *property*" and to ask what would have happened if Webster, a poor farmer's son, had used his power on the side of "the levellers." For the *Atlas* affair, see Fuess, *Life of Caleb Cushing*, I, 146–

148, and Donald E. Emerson, *Richard Hildreth* (Baltimore, 1946), p. 51. For the campaign to squash alternatives to Webster as the national Whig candidate, see Choate to Edward Everett, Jan. 11, 1835, Edward Everett MSS, Massachusetts Historical Society, Boston, Mass.; Nathans, *Daniel Webster*, pp. 90–98; Carroll, *Origins*, pp. 118–148.

108. Choate to John Davis, Feb. 9, 1834, Davis MSS.

109. Daniel Webster to John Davis, Aug. 14, 1834, Choate to Davis, Aug. 23, 1834, Caleb Cushing to Davis, Aug. 28, 1834, Davis MSS; Fuess, *Life of Caleb Cushing*, pp. 87–88; Arthur B. Darling, *Political Changes in Massachusetts, 1824–48: A Study of Liberal Movements in Politics* (New York, 1925), pp. 114–119; Nathans, *Daniel Webster*, pp. 83–89.

110. Charles Francis Adams, ed., *Memoirs of John Quincy Adams* (New York, 1970; 1st pub., 1874–1877), IX, 115, diary entry for March 28, 1834; Choate to Briggs, Nov. 10, 1832, Choate MSS, Dartmouth.

111. Brown, *Life*, p. 200; Edward L. Pierce, *Memoir and Letters of Charles Sumner* (Boston, 1878), I, 126, 147; Parker, *Reminiscences*, pp. 91–92.

112. See the letter signed by Warren Dutton, Edward Everett, Abott Lawrence, Franklin Dexter, and Rufus Choate, Aug. 20, 1834, to John Woods of Hamilton, Ohio, editor of the *Hamilton Intelligencer*, in John Perry Pritchett, " 'Friends' of the Constitution, 1836," *New England Quarterly*, IX (Dec. 1936), 679–683. Pritchett states that if Webster won, Everett would go to the Senate in his place and Choate would become Whig candidate for governor of Massachusetts, but this is clearly an error. Everett was Webster's choice as governor and did become governor in 1835; John Davis was Webster's choice as his replacement in the Senate. See Webster to Jeremiah Mason, Jan. 10, 1835, in George Ticknor Curtis, *Life of Daniel Webster* (New York, 1870), I, 504–505; Choate to Edward Everett, Jan. 11 and Jan. 21, 1835, Everett MSS.

113. Choate to Edward Everett, April 27, 1835, Everett, MSS.

114. Sidney Nathans, "Daniel Webster: Massachusetts Man," *New England Quarterly*, XXXIX (1966), 161–181, esp. 162–163. For the young Webster Whigs' attempts to make Webster palatable to the "war-loving and hot west," see Choate to Everett, Jan. 16, 1835, Everett MSS.

115. Choate to James Marsh, March 12, 1837, copy in Brown MSS.

116. *Ibid.*

117. Rev. Masters to Brown, May 7, 1862, Brown MSS.

118. Judge Wilde to Caleb Cushing, in Fuess, *Life of Caleb Cushing*, I, 189. The phrases are Wilde's, but he added: "Mr. Choate spoke in flattering terms of your speech; but he agrees with me entirely in the sentiments above expressed."

119. The case, Commonwealth v. Aves, is reported in 35 Mass. (18 *Pick.*) 193 (1836), and the arguments of counsel and the decision were also printed in pamphlet form, *Case of the Slave-Child, Med: Report of the Arguments of Counsel, and of the Opinion of the Court in the Case of Commonwealth v. Aves; Tried and Determined in the Supreme Judicial Court of Massachusetts* (Boston, 1836). The quotations from Choate's arguments are from p. 30 of that pamphlet. Curiously, there is no mention of this case in Brown's *Life*.

120. Leonard W. Levy, *The Law of the Commonwealth and Chief Justice Shaw* (Cambridge, Mass., 1957), pp. 62–71. The decision did not affect the position

of fugitive slaves since Med was not a runaway, but had been brought into the state by the wife of her owner. For the ambiguities of the case, see Robert M. Cover, *Justice Accused: Antislavery and the Judicial Process* (New Haven, 1975), p. 94; Lydia M. Child to Rev. Convers Francis, Sept. 4, 1836, *Letters of Lydia Maria Child* (Boston, 1883), p. 21. A footnote adds: "The expectations thus excited that Mr. Choate would become an opponent of slavery were doomed to disappointment; during the latter years of his life he was utterly hostile to the antislavery movement."

121. A. P. Putnam, D.D., in Neilson, *Memories*, p. 252; Brown, *Life*, p. 61. Charles Sumner to Francis Lieber, Feb. 21, 1842, in Pierce, *Memoir and Letters*, II, 201–202.

122. Thomas Carlyle, "The Stump Orator" (1850), in *Latter-Day Pamphlets* (London, 1872), p. 157. For the Greek conception of speech as at the heart of politics, see Hannah Arendt, *The Human Condition* (Chicago, 1958), pp. 24–27, and *passim*.

123. Brown, *Life*, pp. 59–62; Edward G. Parker, *The Golden Age of American Oratory* (Boston, 1857). Theodore Parker thought that however meretricious many public speeches were, it was the oratory of the day, rather than its literature, which truly captured the "American spirit" (Henry Steele Commager, ed., *Theodore Parker: An Anthology* [Boston, 1960], p. 180). For the importance of oratory in ante-bellum America, see Russel B. Nye, *Society and Culture in America, 1830–1860* (New York, 1974), pp. 136–146; Daniel Boorstin, *The Americans: The National Experience* (New York, 1965), pp. 302–325; Barnet Baskerville, "Principal Themes of Nineteenth Century Critics of Oratory," *Speech Monographs*, XIX (March 1952), 11–38. Bower Aly and Grafton P. Tanquary give a long list of the various "occasions for speaking" in ante-bellum America in "The Early National Period, 1788–1860," in *A History and Criticism of American Public Address*, ed. William Norwood Brigance (New York, 1960), I, 73–89.

124. Claude M. Fuess, *The Life of Daniel Webster* (2 vols.; Hamden, Conn., 1963; 1st pub., 1930), I, 297; Parker, *Reminiscences*, p. 490; Ticknor is quoted in Fuess, *Life of Daniel Webster*, I, 287.

125. Ota Thomas, "The Teaching of Rhetoric in the United States During the Classical Period of Education," in *History and Criticism*, ed. Brigance, I, 193–209; Baskerville, "Principal Themes," pp. 27–38; Choate, Journal, June 23, [1844], in Brown, *Life*, pp. 119–120.

126. Goodrich's lectures are reproduced in Warren Guthrie, "The Development of Rhetorical Theory in America, 1635–1850," *Speech Monographs*, XIV (1947), 5 (quotation); Ralph Waldo Emerson, "Eloquence" (1867), in *The Complete Works of Ralph Waldo Emerson* (New York, 1968; 1st pub., 1904), VIII, 111–133, 114–115 (quotation). See also the earlier essay on the subject (1847), in Vol. VII, in which he described the power of speech as *humanizing* personal ascendancy. For Emerson's love of eloquence, see also F. O. Matthiessen, *American Renaissance* (London, 1941), pp. 14–24.

127. *The Odyssey*, bk. 8, ll. 166–175; Choate's translation is in his Journal for Aug. 24, 1844, in Brown, *Life*, p. 123.

128. Nye, *Society and Culture*, p. 143; Parker, *Reminiscences*, p. 269; William Wetmore Story, "Reminiscences of Choate," Brown MSS; "Reminiscences of Rufus Choate," autograph notes of Rev. S. D. Phelps, about an election meeting

in 1840, in the *Springfield Republican*, [April 23], 1940, clipping in Rufus Choate MSS, Dartmouth College Archives, Hanover, N.H.; Wendell Phillips, Speech before the Massachusetts Anti-slavery Society, Jan. 30, 1852, in *Speeches, Lectures and Letters* (Boston, 1863), p. 61; Ralph Waldo Emerson, *Journals and Miscellaneous Notebooks*, (1841–1843), ed. William H. Gilman and J. E. Parsons (Cambridge, Mass., 1970), VIII, 359.

129. Neilson, *Memories*, pp. 97, 379; Parker, *Reminiscences*, pp. 122–123; Choate, Journal, May 13, June 24, 1843, in Brown, *Life*, pp. 92–93, 99. On either side of the mantel in his study Choate kept a bust of Demosthenes and of Cicero.

130. Neilson, *Memories*, p. 101; William Mathews, *Oratory and Orators* (Chicago, 1879), p. 377. Choate liked to use words from technical fields like medicine that were still somewhat esoteric in general use. He was credited with having first used the word "sporadic" in an American law court. *Boston Daily Advertiser*, Feb. 23, 1858. (The O.E.D. cites as the first non-medical or scientific use of "sporadic," Horace Bushnell in *Christian Nurture* in 1847.)

131. Mathews, *Oratory*, p. 367; Whipple, *Some Recollections*, pp. 93–97. It used to be said of his long string of adjectives that he "drove a substantive and six" (Mathews, *Oratory*, p. 377).

132. Rev. Joseph Tracy, in Brown, *Life*, pp. 426–427. Coleridge, who also used parentheses a great deal, defended the habit on the gounds that "they are the *drama* of reason and present the thought growing, instead of mere *Hortus siccus*" (quoted in John Colmer, *Coleridge: Critic of Society* [Oxford, 1959], p. 120).

133. Choate, "The Power of a State Developed by Mental Culture," (1844), in Brown, *The Works of Rufus Choate, with a Memoir of His Life* (2 vols.; Boston, 1862), I, 394–413, 395 (quotation).

134. Edmund Burke, *A Philosophical Enquiry into . . . the Sublime and Beautiful*, in *Writings and Speeches* (Boston, 1901), I, 133; Parker, *Reminiscences*, p. 261. John H. Schaar, "Legitimacy in the Modern State," in *Power and Community: Dissenting Essays in Political Science*, ed. Philip Green and Sanford Levinson (New York, 1969), pp. 314–315.

135. Choate, Journal, Aug. 24, 1844, in Brown, *Life*, p. 124. For the importance of the "commonplace" in classical rhetorical theory, see Walter J. Ong, S.J., *Rhetoric, Romance, and Technology: Studies in the Interaction of Expression and Culture* (Ithaca, N. Y., 1971), pp. 36–38. Sometimes Choate's quotations were too uncommon for his audience. Once in a court speech he quoted from *Ivanhoe* "throw over our spices and robe the roaring ocean with our silks" without explicit attribution and the *Boston Courier* wrote it up as a specimen of Choate's genius (Mrs. W. S. Robinson, ed., *"Warrington" Pen Portraits: A Collection of Personal and Political Reminiscences, from 1848 to 1876, from the Writings of W. S. Robinson* [Boston, 1877], p. 461).

136. Richard M. Weaver, *The Ethics of Rhetoric* (Chicago, 1953), ch. 7.

137. Parker, *Reminiscences*, p. 60.

138. Parker, *Golden Age* p. 88; Boorstin, *Americans*, p. 390. The Boston lady is quoted in Josiah Quincy, *Figures of the Past* (Boston, 1883), p. 309; Archibald MacLeish, *The Power of the Spoken Word: Address before the Annual Meeting of the American Academy of Arts and Letters and the National Institute of Arts and Letters, 1944* (n. pub., 1944), p. 11.

139. Clifford Geertz, "Ideology as a Cultural System," in *Ideology and Discontent,* ed. David E. Apter (New York, 1964), p. 65. For a distinction between popular opinion and the opinion of a "public," defined as a community "by virtue of possessing common ends, purposes, and rules of procedure," see Robert Nisbet, "Public Opinion Versus Popular Opinion," *The Public Interest,* no. 41 (Fall 1975), pp. 166–192.

140. Clement Hugh Hill, "Memoir of Hon. Rufus Choate," *Massachusetts Historical Society Proceedings,* XI (1896–1897), 126.

141. The strengths and weaknesses of the Boston patricians are interestingly explored in Martin Green, *The Problem of Boston: Some Readings in Cultural History* (London, 1966). A succinct account of gentry values and culture can be found in Paul Goodman, "Ethics and Enterprise: The Values of a Boston Elite, 1800–1860," *American Quarterly,* XVIII (Fall 1966), 437–451. The most sensitive discussion is in David B. Tyack, *George Ticknor and the Boston Brahmins* (Cambridge, Mass., 1967), pp. 173–183. See also Edward Everett Hale, *A New England Boyhood* (Boston, 1893); Henry Adams, *The Education of Henry Adams* (New York, 1931; 1st pub., 1918), pp. 29–35; Henry Adams, "Life, Letters and Journals of George Ticknor," *North American Review,* CXXIII (1876), 210–215. The word "disorganizers" is from a letter of George Ticknor defending the right of Boston elite society to discipline its rebels (Ticknor to George S. Hillard, July 17, 1848, in George S. Hillard et al., eds., *Life, Letters and Journals of George Ticknor* [Boston, 1876], XI, 235). The phrase about "the abyss" is from Alan Tate's meditation on that other ante-bellum "civilization"—Virginia (Alan Tate, *The Fathers* [London, 1960; 1st pub., 1938], p. 186).

142. Adams, "Life, Letters and Journals," p. 213.

143. Parker, *Reminiscences,* p. 85; Brown, *Life,* p. 454. For the importance of the Athenaeum, see Ronald Story, "Class and Culture in Boston: The Athenaeum, 1807–1860," *American Quarterly,* XXVII (May 1975), 178–199. The average annual receipts of Choate's office from 1849–1859 were about $18,000, a solid though not spectacular income (Brown, *Life,* p. 405).

144. The description of Winthrop Place is from Walter Muir Whitehill, *Boston: A Topographical History* (Cambridge, Mass., 1963), p. 114. For the role of Harvard in the life of the Boston elite, see Ronald Story, "Harvard and the Boston Brahmins: A Study in Institutional and Class Development, 1800–1865," *Journal of Social History,* VIII (Spring 1975), 94–121. Choate does not, for example, appear to have known Hawthorne, although they had a mutual friend in George Hillard.

145. Hill, "Memoir," p. 130. For Adams, see Justin Winsor, ed., *Memorial History of Boston* (Boston, 1881), III, 410; also Nehemiah Adams, *The Reasonableness of Future, Endless Punishment* (Boston, 1958). Helen's quip is quoted in Paulina Cony Drown, *Mrs. Bell* (Boston, 1931), p. 84.

146. Robinson, *"Warrington" Pen-Portraits,* p. 459; Parker, *Reminiscences,* p. 85.

147. Choate to James Marsh, Nov. 14, 1830, Marsh MSS; [Isaac Taylor], *The Natural History of Enthusiasm* (London, 1834), p. 264.

148. In an address at the Essex Street Church Choate explained why men are drawn into churches: "custom, decorum, self-respect, general seriousness, and general appreciation of the personal and domestic uses of public worship,

a general appreciation that this life is introductory only, and these days of ours are only period of preparation, as well as consciousness and work, would have carried us, of course, to some congregation" (Rufus Choate, "Address" [March 28, 1858], *Memorial Volume by the Essex Street Church and Society, Boston, to Commemorate the 25th Anniversary of the Installation of Their Pastor Nehemiah Adams, D.D.* [Boston, 1860], pp. 22–40; part of this address is in Brown, *Life,* pp. 336–341).

149. Choate to George Bush, Jan. 7, 1844, in Brown, *Life,* p. 102; Theophilus Parsons, *Address Commemorative of Rufus Choate* (Boston, 1859), p. 36; Brown, *Life,* p. 455. For Choate's determination to keep religion entirely compartmentalized, see Choate, "Address" (March 28, 1858).

CHAPTER TWO. AN AMERICAN CONSERVATISM

1. Samuel Gilman Brown, *The Life of Rufus Choate* (Boston, 1870), pp. 60–64; *Essex Register,* May 25, 1840.

2. Brown, *Life,* pp. 453–454; "Reminiscences of Rufus Choate," autograph notes of Rev. S. D. Phelps about an election meeting in 1840, in the *Springfield Republican* [April 23], 1940, clipping in Rufus Choate MSS, Dartmouth College Archives, Hanover, N.H.; Edward G. Parker, *Reminiscences of Rufus Choate, the Great American Advocate* (New York, 1860), pp. 89–90.

3. Claude M. Fuess, *Rufus Choate: The Wizard of the Law* (New York, 1928), pp. 97–98; David Bradstreet Walker, "Rufus Choate, An American Whig," Ph.D. diss., Brown University, 1956, p. 33; Clement Hugh Hill, "Memoir of Hon. Rufus Choate," *Massachusetts Historical Society Proceedings,* XI (1896–1897), 131; Theophilus Parsons to Samuel G. Brown, Jan. 1860, Samuel Gilman Brown MSS, Houghton Library, Harvard University, Cambridge, Mass.; John Clifford to Robert Winthrop, Jan. 30, 1841, Robert C. Winthrop MSS, Massachusetts Historical Society, Boston, Mass., Vol. XXXIII.

4. John Greenleaf Whittier to Caleb Cushing, Feb. 8, 1841, in Claude M. Fuess, *The Life of Caleb Cushing* (2 vols.; New York, 1923), I, 285. The "revolutionary" nature of the 1840 election lay not only in what Philip Hone called a "change of dynasty" but in the fact that the popular vote increased by more than 54 percent over 1836 (Robert Gray Gunderson, *The Log Cabin Campaign* [Lexington, Ky., 1957], p. 256). Choate never appears to have had the slightest qualms about the Whig tactics in this election. Since the Whigs won, he regarded the election as a triumph of democratic good sense. When Melbourne's Whig administration in England was replaced by that of Peel, he wrote to Sumner: "But mark you how much more *peacefully, purely, intellectually,* did this roaring democracy of ours change its whole government and whole policy, last fall, than England has done it now" (Choate to Sumner, [Sept. 1841], Charles Sumner MSS, Houghton Library, Harvard University, Cambridge, Mass.; Brown, *Life,* p. 81).

5. *Boston Courier,* Feb. 16, 1841; Charles Francis Adams, Diary, Feb. 24, 1841, Charles Francis Adams MS Diary, Massachusetts Historical Society, Boston, Mass.; Winthrop to John Clifford, Feb. 10, 1841, Winthrop MSS.

6. Choate's eulogy of Harrison is in the *Boston Advertiser,* April 22, 1841.

7. Sir Charles Lyell, *A Second Visit to the United States of North America*

(London, 1849), I, 265; Choate to Charles Sumner, Feb. 19, 1842 and June 21 1841, Sumner MSS. The letter of Feb. 19 is also in Brown, *Life,* p. 87. Glyndon G. Van Deusen, *The Jacksonian Era, 1828–1848* (New York, 1959), pp. 167–169, notes the decline of congressional "manners and morals" in the 1840s.

8. George Perkins Marsh to Brown, Dec. 24, 1859, Brown MSS. What remains of the correspondence between Lieber and Choate is in the Francis Lieber MSS, Huntington Library, San Marino, Calif.

9. Choate to Sumner, Jan. 24, 1842, in Brown, *Life,* p. 87; Choate to Lieber, Jan. 29, 1842, Dec. 18, 1841, Jan. 14, 1842, Lieber to Sumner, Feb. 1842, Lieber MSS. Lieber sent Choate a very detailed exposition of international law on the question of search, Dec. 25, 1841, which Choate then passed on to Webster (Choate to Lieber, Jan. 1, 1842, Lieber MSS). Choate, for his part, importuned Webster on Lieber's behalf without much success (Choate to Lieber, June 2 [or 20], 1842, Lieber MSS). For Lieber's career, see Frank Friedel, *Francis Lieber: Nineteenth-Century Liberal* (Baton Rouge, 1947).

10. Walker, "Rufus Choate," p. 109; U.S., Congress, Senate, *Journal,* 27th Cong., 1st sess., June 3, 1841, p. 20. The McLeod Case not only created great tension between the U.S. and Britain but also raised the touchy question of the judicial independence of individual states. McLeod, a Canadian, was arrested in New York in 1840 for the murder of an American citizen three years earlier during the *Caroline* affair. The British government demanded his release on the grounds that he had been acting under the instructions of his government during an act of war. Webster, who feared that the conviction of McLeod would lead to war with England, negotiated with Governor Seward of New York for his release; Seward refused to consider it. Webster wrote to the British minister in Washington demanding satisfaction for the *Caroline* burning, but essentially conceding the British position on McLeod himself. In the Senate Choate defended his handling of the whole affair against Democratic attacks on the grounds that both international law and common humanity demanded immunity for the individual acting on the instructions of his government and that individual states should not be allowed to drag a whole nation into war (Claude M. Fuess, *The Life of Daniel Webster* [2 vols; Hamden, Conn., 1963; 1st pub., 1930], II, 100–104).

11. Gunderson, *Log Cabin Campaign,* pp. 12–19; Joel H. Silbey, *The Shrine of Party: Congressional Voting Behavior, 1841–1852* (Pittsburg, 1967), pp. 49–50.

12. George Rawlings Poage, *Henry Clay and the Whig Party* (Gloucester, Mass., 1965; 1st pub., 1936), pp. 34–48; Sydney Nathans, *Daniel Webster and Jacksonian Democracy* (Baltimore, 1973), pp. 164–168.

13. Choate to John Davis, May 29 and June 27, 1841, John Davis MSS, American Antiquarian Society, Worcester, Mass., Vol. I, no. 71, no. 74.

14. Glyndon G. Van Deusen, *The Life of Henry Clay* (Boston, 1937), pp. 247–248.

15. Choate's speech is in U.S., Congress, Senate, *Congressional Globe,* 27th Cong., 1st sess., July 2, 1841, *Appendix,* X, 355–357, and partially reproduced in Brown, *Life,* pp. 71–77.

16. The Clay-Choate clash is reported in the *Congressional Globe,* 27 Cong., 1 sess., July 2, 1841, X, 140. The *New York Herald* is quoted in Poage, *Henry Clay,* p. 56, n. 11.

17. Hugh McCulloch, *Men and Measures of Half a Century* (New York, 1900), p. 200. The impact of the clash can be seen in the pains which Choate's biographer took to mitigate it (Brown, *Life*, pp. 78–79). As late as 1889 another admirer undertook to defend him, John Prince in the *Salem Gazette*, March 12, 1889. This was a reply to Eben F. Stone, "An Address Delivered before the Essex Bar on the Opening of the New Court House" (Salem, Feb. 2, 1889), *Essex Institute Historical Collections*, XXVI (1889), 1–50, in which Stone had commented on Choate's "lack of force" and "moral passion," which he attributed partly to his incapacity for hate (p. 18).

18. Webster kept in close touch with the Massachusetts senators; see, for example, his letter of August 25, 1841, to Choate and Bates urging the desirability of postponing the bank bill until the following session (Daniel Webster MSS, Library of Congress, Washington, D.C.).

19. Charles Francis Adams, ed., *Memoirs of John Quincy Adams* (New York, 1970; 1st pub., 1874–1877), II, 28 (diary entry for Nov. 5, 1841); Choate to Theophilus Parsons, Sept. 13, 1841, Rufus Choate MSS, Boston Public Library; Choate to Vincent Browne, July 11, 1841, Rufus Choate MSS, Essex Institute, Salem, Mass.; Choate to John Davis, Aug. 14, 1841, Davis MSS, Vol. I, no. 106.

20. Mangum's speech on an administration bill for a "Board of Exchequer" as a compromise substitute for a national bank is in *Congressional Globe*, 27 Cong., 2 sess., Dec. 30, 1841, XI, 75–77, 76 (quotation); Choate to Parsons, [Jan. 1842], Choate MSS, Boston Public Library; Choate to Lieber, Dec. 18, 1841, Lieber MSS. While most younger Whigs by the 1840s were prepared to accept the fact of mass suffrage, the Whigs still resisted the idea that it was a natural right. The Massachusetts Whigs in 1840, for example, objected to the Democratic proposal to remove the poll-tax qualification for voting in the state on the grounds that this would break down "all distinction between the virtuous and the vicious." A share in government was a privilege to which society admitted a man when he had demonstrated that he contributed to the wants of society (*Answer of the Whig Members of the Legislature of Massachusetts, Constituting a Majority of Both Branches, . . . to the Address of his Excellency Marcus Morton, Delivered in the Convention of the Two Houses, January 22, 1840* [Boston, 1840], p. 28).

21. Winthrop to Clifford, June 20, 1841, Winthrop MSS; Clifford to Winthrop, Aug. 18, 1841, *ibid.*

22. Choate to Parsons, Sept. 13, 1841, Choate MSS, Boston Public Library; Choate to Sumner [Sept., 1841], in Brown, *Life*, p. 81. Winthrop echoed his feeling: "if anti-slaveholders cannot be supported in office—slaveholders cannot" (Winthrop to Clifford, Aug. 7, 1841, Winthrop MSS). Fifteen years later, when Buchanan was running for the presidency, a senator who had been present at the debate wrote to Choate recalling the "cogency and splendor" of his argument and Buchanan's "vindictive and savage" hostility. Choate sent the letter on to Everett with a covering note pointing out "how *awful* is *History*" since "I am afraid I am to vote for Buchanan" (Choate to Everett, June 11, 1856, Edward Everett MSS, Massachusetts Historical Society, Boston, Mass).

23. M. E. Cruickshank, "Recollections of Rufus Choate," MS reminiscences of a woman who as a girl had lived with Choate's brother-in-law and had been assigned the task of bringing Choate tea and bathing his forehead when he returned prostrated from speaking in the Senate (Rufus Choate MSS, Library of

Congress, Washington, D.C.; Choate to Sumner, [February (?) 1844], in Brown, *Life,* p. 103; Choate to Parsons, [February (?) 1844], Choate MSS, Boston).

24. Choate to Sumner, Feb. 17, 1844, Sumner MSS. An earlier part of this letter is in Brown, *Life,* pp. 103–104.

25. Cruickshank, "Recollections," p. 2; Choate to John Davis, July 25, 1841, Davis MSS, Vol. I, no. 77; address of Edward Everett at a public meeting of mourning for Choate, July 22, 1859, in Brown, *Life,* pp. 380–381.

26. George Perkins Marsh to Brown, Dec. 24, 1859, Brown MSS.

27. Winthrop to Clifford, Aug. 15, 1844, Winthrop MSS.

28. Choate in the Senate, *Congressional Globe,* 27 Cong., 3 sess., Feb. 3., 1843, *Appendix,* XII, 222–229, 229 (quotation). For Webster's diplomacy, see Robert F. Dalzell, Jr., *Daniel Webster and the Trial of American Nationalism, 1843–1852* (Boston, 1973), pp. 35–45; Fuess, *Life of Daniel Webster,* II, 102–116. For the Maine boundary and the Ashburton treaty, see Charles M. Wiltse, "Daniel Webster and the British Experience," *Massachusetts Historical Society Proceedings,* LXXXV (1973), 58–77; Frederick Merk and Lois B. Merk, *Fruits of Propaganda in the Tyler Administration* (Cambridge, Mass., 1971), pp. 39–91; and Howard Jones, *To the Webster-Ashburton Treaty* (Chapel Hill, N.C., 1977).

29. Henry Adams, *The Education of Henry Adams* (New York, 1931; 1st pub., 1918), p. 33. For the network of trading and financial relations linking England and the Merchant community of the Northern States, see William Brock, "The Image of England and American Nationalism," *Journal of American Studies,* V (Dec. 1971), 225–245. Sir Charles Lyell, attending a Whig meeting in Faneuil Hall in 1845, heard Webster rebuke the blustering tone of the Democrats in regard to Oregon and commented: "I was amused to hear frequent references made to the recent debate in the British House of Commons, the exact words of Sir Robert Peel and others being quoted and commented upon, just as if the discussion had been simply adjourned from Westminster to Boston" (Lyell, *A Second Visit,* I, 141).

30. John Higham, *From Boundlessness to Consolidation* (Ann Arbor, 1969), pp. 8–12; *An Appeal to the Whig National Convention, in favor of the Nomination of Daniel Webster to the Presidency,* by "A Whig from the Start" (John Calvin Adams) (New York, 1848), p. 11.

31. "Will There Be War with Mexico?" *The American Review (The American Whig Review),* II (Sept. 1845), 227; see also Major L. Wilson, *Space, Time and Freedom: The Quest for Nationality and the Irrepressible Conflict, 1815–61* (Westport, Conn., 1974), pp. 114–119.

32. Choate in the Senate, May 10, 1842, in Samuel Gilman Brown, *The Works of Rufus Choate, with a Memoir of His Life* (2 vols.; Boston, 1862), II, 24–71, 70 (quotation).

33. William H. Goetzmann, *When the Eagle Screamed: The Romantic Horizon In American Diplomacy, 1800–1860* (New York, 1966), pp. 43–46; Choate in the Senate, Feb. 3, 1843, in Brown, *Works,* II, 223; Choate in the Senate, March 21, 1844, in Brown, *Works,* II, 171–172, 145. See also his speech of Feb. 22, 1844 in *Congressional Globe,* 28 Cong., 1 sess., XIII, 307–308. The Whigs were successful in getting the resolution to terminate the treaty of joint occupation of Oregon defeated—leaving the boundaries to be settled by the Polk administration.

34. Dalzell, *Daniel Webster,* pp. 51–58; Goetzmann, *When the Eagle Screamed,*

pp. 32–37. The growing restlessness of some of the younger anti-slavery men within the Whig party is described in Thomas H. O'Connor, *Lords of the Loom: The Cotton Whigs and the Coming of the Civil War* (New York, 1968), pp. 58–65; Kinley J. Brauer, *Cotton Versus Conscience: Massachusetts Whig Politics and Southwestern Expansion, 1843–1848* (Lexington, Ky., 1967), pp. 30–113, *passim;* and David Donald, *Charles Sumner and The Coming of the Civil War* (New York, 1960), ch. 6.

35. Lawrence's determination to prevent the abolitionists from capitalizing on the Texas question is described in Charles F. Adams' diary, March 20, 1844, quoted in Martin B. Duberman, *Charles Francis Adams, 1807–1886* (Cambridge, Mass., 1961), p. 89.

36. In May of 1842 Benjamin Rich and J. Ingersol Bowditch sent Choate a petition signed by eighty-one eminently respectable New Englanders, including several owners of merchant vessels, protesting the imprisonment of colored seamen in Southern ports, and asked him to present it to the Senate. The covering letter pointed out that the signers were all "men who have a real and deep interest in all that concerns the commerce of the country" and added "we hope that no fancied connection of this subject with any others" would prevent its receiving prompt attention from Congress (J. Ingersol Bowditch to Choate, n.d. [May, 1842]). Choate replied that he would immediately present the petition although he did fear "the 'fancied connection' to which you refer—which seems to make fools of many otherwise rational and estimable persons of the South" (Choate to Benjamin Rich and I. J. Bowditch, n.d. [May 12, 1842]). When Choate did not present the petition, however, the two men wrote on August 4 and again on September 6 asking what had happened. Choate replied that in view of the staunch opposition of Senator Berrien, the chairman of the Committee on the Judiciary, and "the exceeding importance of conducting our great measure of revenue through as harmoniously as possible" he had thought it best to postpone the petition until "a moment of less engagement and less excitement." He suggested that another session, or the Congress "to be elected under the *new Census,"* would probably be a better bet for a favorable reaction (Choate to Bowditch and Rich, Sept. 9, 1842). In November the two men asked him to return the petition (Rich and Bowditch to Choate, Nov. 9 and Nov. 21, 1842; this correspondence is in the Massachusetts Historical Society and is described in *Massachusetts Historical Society Proceedings,* XIX [1905], 406–408).

37. *Congressional Globe,* 27 Cong., 3 sess., Jan. 23, 1843, XII, 186; Robert C. Winthrop, Jr., *A Memoir of Robert C. Winthrop* (Boston, 1897), p. 32.

38. As a result of a fugitive slave case the Massachusetts legislature adopted a series of resolutions, among them a demand that the federal constitution be amended restricting representation to "free persons" alone, as a way of separating the constitution from any connection with slavery. John Quincy Adams presented these resolutions to the House and defended them vigorously; in the Senate they were presented by Bates. The Senate refused to even print the resolutions and Bates did not press the point. Choate said nothing (Brauer, *Cotton Versus Conscience,* p. 63; Henry Wilson, *History of the Rise and Fall of the Slave Power in America* [3 vols; New York, 1969; 1st pub., 1872], pp. 477–487, pp. 485–486 [quotations]; see also, Duberman, *Charles Francis Adams,* pp. 80–86).

39. Choate, "Speech before the Young Men's Whig Club of Boston, August

19, 1844" in Brown, *Works*, II, 267–283, 274 (quotation). Choate also spoke against the admission of Florida to the Union with provisions in her constitution forbidding the abolition of slavery or the discharge of colored seamen in her ports—on the grounds that these clauses were probably contrary to the federal constitution (*Congressional Globe*, 28 Cong., 2 sess., March 1, 1845, XIV, 379; *Niles National Register*, LXVIII (March 29, 1845), 57–63).

40. Choate, "Speech before the Young Men's Whig Club," p. 275.

41. Choate, campaign speech at Lynn, Sept. 4, 1844, *Salem Register*, Sept. 5, 1844. He expressed similar sentiments at meetings at Worcester and Roxbury in the same month. See *Boston Semi-Weekly Advertiser*, Sept. 7, and Sept. 14, 1844.

42. Choate "Speech Before Young Men's Whig Club," pp. 263, 280.

43. Brown, *Life*, p. 136; Brauer, *Cotton Versus Conscience*, p. 126. Choate's speech is partially reported in *Congressional Globe*, 28 Cong., 2 sess., Feb. 18, 1845, XIV, 303–304. For all its length, Choate's speech received very little attention in the Whig press (Brauer, *Cotton Versus Conscience*, p. 108; Choate to Parsons, n.d., [early 1845], Choate MSS, Boston Public Library; Choate to George P. Marsh, Aug. 30, 1845, George Perkins Marsh MSS, University of Vermont Library, Burlington, Vt.). The resolution, amended to allow possible annexation through negotiations, passed the Senate by a majority of two (Brown, *Life*, p. 138). With the true conservative's ability to assimilate the *fait accompli*, by 1850 Choate, whose imagination was always captured by military adventure and who was a great admirer of General Taylor, had become less opposed to territorial expansion: New England, he told Parker, was somewhat "anti-progressive" against the acquisition of territory. "She should catch that great gale of impulse, enthusiasm and enterprise, which is ever agitating and giving tone to *America*" (Parker, *Reminiscences*, pp. 237–238).

44. Louis Hartz, *The Liberal Tradition in America: An Interpretation of American Political Thought Since The Revolution* (New York, 1955); Lee Benson, *The Concept of Jacksonian Democracy: New York as a Test Case* (Princeton, 1961); Glyndon G. Van Deusen, "Some Aspects of Whig Thought and Theory in the Jacksonian Period," *American Historical Review*, LXIII (Jan. 1958), 305–322; and Edward Pessen, *Jacksonian America: Society, Personality and Politics* (Homewood, Ill., 1969), all support the view of a fundamental consensus between the parties. Wilson, *Space, Time and Freedom*, ch. 1, and Herbert Ershkowitz and William G. Shade, "Consensus or Conflict?: Political Behavior in the State Legislatures During the Jacksonian Era," *Journal of American History*, LVIII (Dec. 1971), 591–621, both demonstrate the real difference in ideology and political behavior between the parties.

45. Samuel P. Huntington, "Conservatism as an Ideology," *American Political Science Review*, LI (1957), 454–473. Huntington points out that Russel Kirk, the high priest of the New Conservatives of the 1950s, seems motivated more by a sentimental nostalgia than a vigorous commitment to existing institutions (pp. 471–473). As Clinton Rossiter remarked, "American conservatism must be judged by American standards, the standards of a country that has been big, diverse, rich, new, successful, and non-feudal, a country in which Liberalism has been the common faith and middle-class democracy the common practice" (*Conservatism in America: The Thankless Persuasion* [2nd ed., New York, 1962], p. 127).

46. In an article on the new "New Conservatives" of the 1970s, including Nathan Glazer, S. M. Lipset, Daniel Bell, Daniel P. Moynihan et al., Sheldon Wolin remarks that they appear to "have been traumatized by the Sixties." None of these men are reactionary, mystical, or necessarily Burkean, or religious, or believers in natural law; in the 1950s they were liberals. But the 1960s revealed a whole range of possibilities and dangers to the left, of which they had hardly been aware; an attack on institutions that they cherished, like the university, and an abandonment of accepted codes of political behavior; the universe seemed suddenly to have shifted. While analogies between past and present are always dangerous, it seems to me that their situation is very similar to the Whigs of the 1830s and 1840s, who were equally "traumatized liberals" (Sheldon S. Wolin, "The New Conservatives," *New York Review of Books*, XXIII [Feb. 5, 1976], pp. 6–11).

47. For a generally sympathetic appraisal and description of Whig thought, see Wilson, *Space, Time and Freedom*, esp. pp. 53–66, where he describes the American system as the " 'thesis' for the period from the War of 1812 to the Nullification Crisis." See also Wilson, "The Concept of Time and Political Dialogue in the United States, 1828–48," *American Quarterly*, XIX (Winter 1967), 619–644. Van Deusen, "Some Aspects of Whig Thought," finds the Whigs "dynamic and forward-looking, envisioning progress for all classes of society" (p. 318). A more recent discussion of Whig ideas and practice, however, Rush Welter, *The Mind of America, 1820–60* (New York, 1975), emphasizes the expedient nature of Whig thought. See especially, pp. 105–128 and 190–218. Clay's speech, Dec. 26–30, 1833, is quoted in Arthur M. Schlesinger, Jr., *The Age of Jackson* (Boston, 1945), p. 107. For the importance of the concept of "deference" in Anglo-American republican theory of the eighteenth century, see J. G. A. Pocock, "The Classical Theory of Deference," *American Historical Review*, LXXXI (June 1976), pp. 516–523. For its decline in American politics, see Ronald P. Formisano, "Deferential-Participant Politics: The Early Republic's Political Culture, 1789–1840," *American Political Science Review*, LXVIII (June 1974), 473–487.

48. Choate to Charles Sumner, n.d., [1843–1844], Brown, *Life*, p. 105. The phrase "Tom Painefied" has been left out of the printed version but appears in the MS letter that is in the Sumner MSS. Choate told Parker that, while he was in college, he read a book attacking Burke and was so angry he covered the margin with notes "such as 'd -d rascal,' etc." (Parker, *Reminiscences*, p. 255). He advised another student to learn Cicero and Burke by heart: "both superlatively great—the latter the greatest, living in a later age, belonging to the modern mind and genius . . . both knew everything" (Choate to Richard S. Storrs, Jr., Jan. 2, 1841, in Brown, *Life*, p. 33).

49. Choate, campaign speech at Salem, Sept. 28, 1848, *Salem Register*, Oct. 2, 1848. For an interesting interpretation of the difference in conceptions of American nationality and destiny between Democrats and Whigs—the Democrats thinking in spatial and non-temporal terms of extending the area of freedom, the Whigs with a view of the Union as a corporate enterprise dedicated to progressive development and improvement through time, requiring a homogeneous population and compact territory—see Wilson, *Space, Time and Freedom*, pp. 107–119; "Manifest Destiny and Free Soil: The Triumph of Negative Liber-

alism in the 1840's," *The Historian,* XXXI (Nov. 1968), 36–57; and "The Concept of Time and the Political Dialogue in the United States, 1828–1848," *American Quarterly,* IX (Winter 1967), 619–644.

50. The old ex-Federalist lawyer, Jeremiah Mason, for example, thought that as the American economy developed, the U.S. must eventually arrive at the same degree of separation of wealth and poverty as England, and that such a deep gap would not be compatible with American institutions in a system of universal suffrage. He was glad that it would be some time before the wealth of the U.S. approached that of England (George S. Hillard, ed., *Memoirs of Jeremiah Mason,* [Boston, 1917], p. 350). The "condition of England" question continued to haunt conservative Americans. See, for example, Charles Eliot Norton to John Stuart Mill in 1868: "the vast number of the people of England who barely support existence, who have no opening or hope of improvement in the present condition of society, and have nothing to lose if nothing to gain by change in the established order, is a fact that weighs heavily on one who comes from a hopeful country" ("Letters of John Stuart Mill, 1865–1870," *Proceedings of the Massachusetts Historical Society,* L [Oct. 1916], 15, n. 1). For misgivings about the effects of industrialization among early industrialists see, for example, Nathan Appleton quoted in Charles L. Sandford, *The Quest for Paradise: Europe and the American Moral Imagination* (Urbana, Ill. 1961), p. 77.

51. Henry A. Miles, "Lowell, As It Was, and As It Is," (1845), in *Lowell: An Early American Industrial Community,* prep. L. S. Bryant and J. B. Rae. (Cambridge, Mass., 1950), p. 31; Pessen, *Jacksonian America,* pp. 118–121; Oscar Handlin, *Boston's Immigrants* (rev. ed.; New York, 1968), pp. 72–87.

52. For the condition of labor see Norman Ware, *The Industrial Worker, 1840–1860* (Chicago, 1964; 1st pub., 1924), pp. 106–124; Roland Berthoff, *An Unsettled People: Social Order and Disorder in American History.* (New York, 1971), ch. 12.

53. Welter, *Mind of America,* pp. 122–128; Oscar and Mary Handlin, *Commonwealth: A Study of the Role of Government in the American Economy, Massachusetts, 1774–1861* (New York, 1947), ch. 10; Elliott R. Barkan, "The Emergence of a Whig Persuasion: Conservatism, Democratism, and the New York State Whigs," *New York History,* LII (Oct. 1971), 367–395.

54. Hamilton Andrews Hill, *Memoir of Abbott Lawrence* (Boston, 1883), p. 43; Massachusetts House, Document No. 50 (1845), in *Lowell,* pp. 253–263, 263 (quotation).

55. Eric Foner, *Free Soil, Free Labor, Free Men: The Ideology of the Republican Party before the Civil War* (New York, 1970), pp. 20–21. A writer in the *American Whig Review* in 1851 found the "evils resulting from the competition among laborers for the same employment," revealed in "such books as 'London Labor and the London Poor', 'Alton Locke' etc.," to be the "pit-fall of modern civilization." This *"gulf"* could only be avoided through protection ("Unity of the Whigs: Their Principles and Measures," *American Whig Review,* XIV [Sept. 1851], 183). By the mid forties the tariff was essentially all that remained of the American system; the Whigs had failed to get a national bank, Clay had bought Western votes for distribution by giving up his opposition to preemption (and thus to uncontrolled settlement in the West), and finally distribution itself was sacrificed in order to get the moderately protective tariff of 1842 through Con-

gress (Wilson, *Space, Time and Freedom*, p. 36; Van Deusen, *Jacksonian Era*, pp. 160–161). The growing material emphasis of the Whig party was in tune with the movement of the culture as a whole in which, according to Michael Kammen, by the 1840s " 'Peace & Plenty' had supplanted 'Liberty' as the dominant watchword" (Michael Kammen, *A Season of Youth: The American Revolution and the Historical Immagination* [New York, 1978], p. 102).

56. Schlesinger, *Age of Jackson*, p. 270; Foner, *Free Soil*, p. 15; Rufus Choate, "Dedication of the Peabody Institute, 1854," in Brown, *Works*, I, 470; *The Writings and Speeches of Daniel Webster*, X (Boston, 1903), 92. For the metaphysical quality of work, see Jerome H. Buckley, *The Triumph of Time: A Study of the Victorian Concepts of Time, History, Progress, and Decadence* (Cambridge, Mass., 1966), pp. 124–125.

57. Welter, *Mind of America*, pp. 122–128, 141–150; Foner, *Free Soil*, ch. 1; Melvyn Dubofsky, "Daniel Webster and the Whig Theory of Economic Growth, 1828–1848," *The New England Quarterly*, XLII (Dec. 1969), 551–572. Thurlow Weed is quoted in Sydney Nathans, *Daniel Webster and Jacksonian Democracy* (Baltimore, 1973), p. 144, n. 46; Lincoln is quoted in Foner, *Free Soil*, p. 14.

58. Thus the corporation became a great democratic institution in which the man of small means participated on equal terms with the rich; technology a means of binding the union closer together; the factory a salutary form of social discipline and the whole a tremendous boost for the only "real" kind of equality—equality of opportunity. On the corporation, see *Answer of the Whig Members*, p. 15, and Welter, *Mind of America*, p. 118. Railroads as "iron bands" of union became a commonplace of the time (Merle Curti, *The Roots of American Loyalty* [New York, 1946], pp. 115–118). By 1851 the *American Whig Review* was repudiating the idea that factories were inherently "demoralizing and mobocratic." On the contrary, men who were idle before were now given regular employment. "Yesterday they were without the restraint which rational control imposes, today they are under its influences" ("Nature and Effects of a Protective Tariff," *American Whig Review*, XIV [July 1851], 85).

59. Martin Green, *The Problem of Boston: Some Readings in Cultural History* (London, 1966), pp. 190–191; Leo Marx, *The Machine in the Garden: Technology and the Pastoral Idea in America* (New York, 1967; 1st pub., 1964), pp. 169–190. Emerson on the Whigs is to be found in his *Journals and Miscellaneous Notebooks*, ed. William H. Gilman and J. E. Parsons (Cambridge, Mass., 1970), VIII, 58–87 *passim*, 152.

60. Parker, *Reminiscences*, p. 237; Joseph Neilson, *Memories of Rufus Choate, with Some Consideration of His Studies, Methods and Opinions, and of His Style as a Speaker and Writer* (Boston, 1884), p. 167.

61. Choate in the Senate, April 12, 1844, in Brown, *Works*, II, 177; Nehemiah Adams, D.D., *A Sabbath Discourse on the Death of the Hon. Rufus Choate, Together with the Address at His Funeral* (Boston, 1859), pp. 48–49.

62. Choate, speech at Concord, July 4, 1844, in *Niles' National Register* (July 20, 1844), p. 326; speech in the Senate, April 15, 1844, in Brown, *Works*, II, 239–240. For Lincoln's delight in economic development and individual enterprise, see G. S. Boritt, *Lincoln and the Economics of the American Dream* (Memphis, 1978).

63. Choate, "The Power of a State Developed by Mental Culture," (1844) in Brown, *Works*, I, 394–413, 407 (quotation).

64. *Ibid.*, p. 408. Of the two necessary elements of all national greatness, "permanence and progression," Choate told the Senate, echoing Coleridge, who supplied the phrase, agriculture supplied the first and industry the second. Their interests were not really opposed; they were the "opposing yet not discordant powers, from whose reciprocal struggle is drawn out the harmony of the universe. The country is the home of rest. The town is the theatre of change. . . . You have provided well for permanence. Be not afraid of the agents of intelligent progress" (Choate in the Senate, April 15, 1844, in Brown, *Works*, II, 216–217). For Coleridge's ideas on the necessary balance between permanence and progression, see David P. Calleo, *Coleridge and the Idea of the Modern State* (New Haven, 1966), pp. 92–94.

65. Choate in the Senate, April 15, 1844, in Brown, *Works*, II, 213–214. Although his constituents might grumble that he did not speak enough, he did in fact deliver several long and effective speeches on the subject of protection, first in support of the moderately protective tariff of 1842, and again, in 1844, in defense of that tariff against the proposal of McDuffie of South Carolina to return to the provisions of the compromise tariff of 1833 (Choate in the Senate, March 14, 1842, in Brown, *Works*, II, 72–124; *Congressional Globe*, 27 Cong., 2 sess., August 27, 1842, XI, 953; April 12 and 15, 1844, in Brown, *Works*, II, 173–247; *Congressional Globe*, 28 Cong., 1 sess., May 31, 1844, *Appendix*, part 2, XIII, 753–757). He also spoke in favor of another bill much desired by the business community, the bankruptcy bill of 1842 (*Congressional Globe*, 27 Cong., 2 sess., Jan. 27, 1842, *Appendix*, XI, 105–106).

66. Adams, *A Sabbath Discourse*, p. 46 (see also Choate in the Senate, March 14, 1842, in Brown, *Works*, II, 90–91); Alexander Hamilton, "Report on Manufactures," *The Works of Alexander Hamilton*, ed. Henry Cabot Lodge (New York, 1971; 1st pub., 1904), IV, 70–198, esp. 87–95.

67. Choate in the Senate, April 12 and 15, 1844, in Brown, *Works*, II, 173–247, 214, 216 (quotations). The attempt to reconcile commercial activity with the disinterestedness necessary to republican virtue can be seen for example in Nathan Appleton's memoir of Abbott Lawrence. He admitted that the motive of the merchant is always individual gain, but added "there is no occupation which has a tendency to liberalize the mind more than that of the merchant" (Nathan Appleton, *Memoir of the Hon. Abbott Lawrence* [Boston, 1856], pp. 4–5).

68. Choate in the Senate, April 12 and 15, 1844, in Brown, *Works*, II, 215. A note appended to this speech in Brown, p. 245, explains that this passage was based upon a note by M'Culloch to Adam Smith's *Wealth of Nations* (Edinburgh ed., 1828), pp. 211–212.

69. Handlin, *Boston's Immigrants*, pp. 56–57; Justin Winsor, ed., *The Memorial History of Boston* (Boston, 1881), IV, 95–103; Choate to Lieber, Dec. 10, 1841, Lieber MSS (characteristically, Choate did nothing to follow up this interesting suggestion); "Political Responsibilities," *The American Whig Review*, XIV (Nov. 1851), 363; Edmund Burke, *Reflections on the Revolution in France* (1790) (Everyman's Library ed.; London, 1910), p. 82.

70. For example, the authors of *I'll Take My Stand* (New York, 1930).

71. See George Perkins Marsh, *The Goths in New England* (Middlebury, Vt.,

1843); for the racial character given to republican liberty by New England historians like Prescott and Motley, see David Levin, *History as Romantic Art* (New York, 1959), ch. 4.

72. Choate, "The Age of the Pilgrims the Heroic Period of Our History" (Dec. 1843), in Brown, *Works*, I, 371–393, 380, 379 (quotations). For the influence of Greek ideas on Calvin's political philosophy, especially on the necessity of leadership by the "best" men, see John T. McNeill, "John Calvin on Civil Government" in *Calvinism and the Political Order*, ed. George L. Hunt (Philadelphia, 1965), pp. 37–38; and for the importance of the tradition of classical political freedom and Renaissance "civic humanism" to a Puritan like Milton, see Hugh Trevor-Roper, "The Elitist Politics of Milton," *Times Literary Supplement*, (June 1973), pp. 601–603. Brown comments that the phrases "a state without a king" and "a church without a bishop" were "at once caught up and spread through the land. They became the burden of popular songs and led to a noteworthy discussion of the principles of church government between two eminent divines,—an Episcopalian and a Presbyterian—of New York" (Brown, *Life*, p. 101). Wendell Phillips used the phrase, without quotation marks, as late as 1881 (Wendell Phillips, "The Scholar in a Republic" [June 30, 1881], in *Representative Phi Beta Kappa Orations*, ed. Clark S. Northrup, William C. Lane and John C. Schwab [Boston, 1915], p. 195).

73. Rufus Choate, "The Age of the Pilgrims," Brown, *Works*, I, 381.

74. J. G. A. Pocock, *The Machiavellian Moment: Florentine Political Thought and the Atlantic Republican Tradition* (Princeton, N.J., 1975), esp. pt. 3.

75. Gordon Wood, *The Creation of the American Republic, 1776–1787* (Chapel Hill, N.C., 1969), pp. 610–615; Pocock, *Machiavellian Moment*, pp. 513–527.

76. Horace Bushnell, "The Founders, Great in their Unconsciousness" (1849), in *New England Society Orations*, ed. C. and E. W. Brainerd (2 vols.; New York, 1901), I, 97.

77. For the continuation of a "republican" philosophy into the nineteenth century, see Wilson Smith, *Professors and Public Ethics: Studies of Northern Moral Philosophers before the Civil War* (Ithaca, N. Y. 1956), pp. 78–79. Webster designated virtue by that particularly nineteenth-century word "character" (Dalzell, *Daniel Webster*, pp. 14–16). As Pocock demonstrated, the philosophy of "virtue" was not a unitary one. The Democrats developed one aspect of the tradition—finding in Jackson and the frontiersman exemplars of a dynamic will and natural energy superior to law and institutions and needing only continuous westward expansion to preserve the republic in liberty and vigor. This kind of *virtù*, however, was anathema to the Whigs—for whom popular virtue meant restraint, deference, reverence (Pocock, *Machiavellian Moment*, pp. 534–545).

78. For the problem of reconciling "economic man" with republican virtue, and reliance on the freehold possession of land as an "objective" guarantee of virtue, see Pocock, *Machiavellian Moment*, pp. 383–505; also Pocock, "Virtue and Commerce in the 18th Century," *The Journal of Interdisciplinary History*, III (Summer 1972), 119–134, esp. 132–133. The phrase "flushed majority . . ." is from an election campaign speech of 1848, *Speeches of Rufus Choate and R. C. Winthrop at the Whig State Convention, and the Last Letter of Captain Allison* (n.p., 1848), p. 4. Variations on the phrase crop up in several of his speeches.

79. Ralph Waldo Emerson, "Historic Notes of Life and Letters in New

England," in *The Portable Emerson,* ed. Mark Van Doren (New York, 1946), pp. 514–515; Robert A. Nisbet, *The Sociological Tradition* (London, 1967), pp. 21–55. American conservatives did not have an idealized middle ages to look back upon, but they did have the New England town of the early nineteenth century, a community where there were no great extremes of wealth and poverty, and the gradations of status, because unchallenged, were quite compatible with general good will (see the nostalgic accounts in George F. Hoar, *Autobiography of Seventy Years* [2 vols.; New York, 1903], I, 40–41, and in Harriet Beecher Stowe, *Old Town Folks* [Cambridge, Mass., 1966; 1st pub., 1869], ch. 5).

80. In this latter effort they were part of "one of the great enterprises of the 19th century" (Donald Fleming, *John William Draper and the Religion of Science* [Philadelphia, 1950], p. 89).

81. John Stuart Mill, "Coleridge," *London and Westminster Review* (March, 1840), rpt. in *Dissertations and Discussions* (2 vols.; New York, 1973; 1st pub., 1859), I, 393–474, esp. 414–416, 422–425, 425 (quotation). The way had already been prepared for the ideas of the German school, however, by the wide currency in the United States of the Scottish philosophers, whose social thought also emphasized development, the naturalness of civilization, and the primacy of emotion (Douglas Sloan, *The Scottish Enlightenment and the American College Ideal* [New York, 1971], p. 173).

82. Mill, "Coleridge," pp. 416–419. There were a large number of magazine articles on Burke in the first third of the nineteenth century in the United States. See Milton Bruce Byrd, "The American Vogue of Edmund Burke among Liberals 1765–1830" (Ph.D. diss., University of Wisconsin, 1953), p. 318. There were also almost a hundred articles on German historians in American magazines before 1846; Herder's philosophy of history was available in English by 1800 (George H. Callcott, *History in the United States, 1800–60: Its Practice and Purpose* [Baltimore, 1970], pp. 9–10). George Bancroft wrote a major review of Herder's *Ideas for a Philosophy of History* (1784), in *The North American Review,* XX (Jan. 1825), 138–147. For the influence of German historical ideas in the United States before the Civil War, see Richard A. Firda, "German Philosophy of History and Literature in the *North American Review,* 1815–60," *Journal of the History of Ideas,* XXXIII (Jan.-March 1971), 133–142. In the importance they gave to proper feeling, the Whigs attributed to it the same potent, if vague, instrumentality as Harriet Beecher Stowe. "What can any individual do [about slavery]?" she asked in *Uncle Tom's Cabin.* "There is one thing that every individual can do,—they can see to it that *they feel right* . . . the man or woman who *feels* strongly, healthily, and justly on the great interests of humanity, is a constant benefactor to the human race. See, then, to your sympathies in this matter!" (Harriet Beecher Stowe, *Uncle Tom's Cabin* [Boston, 1851], p. 495.)

83. The weakening of traditional forms of social control and the anti-institutional feeling of the ante-bellum period are discussed by George M. Fredrickson, *The Inner Civil War: Northern Intellectuals and the Crisis of the Union* (New York, 1965), pp. 7–22, and by Berthoff, *An Unsettled People,* chs. 13–15.

84. The rallying to institutions is described in Fredrickson, *Inner Civil War,* pp. 23–28. See also Allen Guttmann, *The Conservative Tradition in America* (New York, 1967), p. 155; and C. S. Henry, "The Position and Duties of the Educated Men of the Country" (1840), in his *Considerations on Some of the Elements and*

Conditions of Social Welfare and Human Progress (New York, 1861), pp. 63–108, 93–94 (quotation).

85. George S. Hillard, *An Oration Pronounced before the Inhabitants of Boston, July 4th, 1835* (Boston, 1835), pp. 21–22. The belief that only "reverence" could stave off anarchy was quite widespread—for example, the lawyer Albert Pike, a native New Englander, languishing in Arkansas, wrote in desperation to Caleb Cushing that the U.S. was about to be overtaken by anarchy. He proposed a nation-wide, non-party, "Conservative Republican Society" to work for good government and sent Cushing a manifesto for the movement beginning "We are thoroughly convinced that no political system, grounded on pure self-interest, with no inherent veneration for that which is old, venerable, time-honored, wise and virtuous, can long flourish or even subsist" (Pike to Cushing, March 2, 1843, Caleb Cushing MSS, Library of Congress, Washington, D.C.; Rufus Choate, "The Position and Functions of the American Bar, as an Element of Conservatism in the State: An Address Delivered before the Law School in Cambridge, July 3, 1845," in Brown, *Works*, I, 414–438, 423, 417 [quotations]).

86. H. D. Thoreau, "Civil Disobedience" (1849), in *The Writings of Henry David Thoreau* (New York, 1968; 1st pub., 1906), IV, 368. For the image of the garden, see Henry Nash Smith, *Virgin Land: The American West as Symbol and Myth* (Cambridge, Mass., 1950), and Marx, *Machine in the Garden*, pp. 141–144. For the conservative use of architectural imagery, see Guttmann, *Conservative Tradition*, pp. 49–68. Burke often used architectural images—in his "Letter to a Noble Lord" (1795), for example, he compared the monarchy to the Keep of Windsor of Castle (*Selected Writings of Edmund Burke*, ed. W. J. Bate [New York, 1960], p. 516; see also Walter D. Love, "Edmund Burke's Idea of the Body Corporate: A Study in Imagery," *The Review of Politics*, XXVII [April 1965], 184–197). The most famous American example of this kind of image of course is Lincoln's "A House divided against itself shall not stand" (1858) (St. Mark, ch. 3, 25), in *Collected Works*, ed. Roy P. Basler (New Brunswick, N.J., 1953), II, 461.

87. Choate, "Position and Functions," pp. 417–418. The overtones in this quotation are very strong—cf. Burke, *Reflections on the Revolution in France*, pp. 91–94.

88. *The American Review: A Whig Journal (The American Whig Review)*, II (Nov. 1845), 536; James T. Boulton, *The Language of Politics in the Age of Wilkes and Burke* (London, 1963), pp. 57, 98; Clifford Geertz, "Ideology as a Cultural System," in *Ideology and Discontent*, ed. David E. Apter (New York, 1964), pp. 218–220; Michael Walzer, "On the Role of Symbolism in Political Thought," *Political Science Quarterly*, LXXXII (1967), 191–204, esp. 194–195.

89. Michael Oakeshott, "On Being Conservative," in his *Rationalism in Politics* (New York, 1962), pp. 168–169. Choate, "Position and Functions," pp. 425, 431; Choate, "Valedictory," *The Dartmouth*, VII (Oct. 1872), 315–317, 316 (quotation). F. M. Barnard describes Herder's concern for the "humanization" of the masses—*Bildung*—as "not specifically intellectual, but rather an interactive social process in which men influence each other within a specific social setting and in which they receive from and add to their distinctive historical and communal heritage. This interactive and reciprocal building of new societal and political goals within a socio-cultural continuum represents for Herder the

true purpose of human association, the creative, continuous development of man" (F. M. Barnard, *J. G. Herder on Social and Political Culture* [Cambridge, 1969], p. 12). There was a copy of Herder's *Spirit of Hebrew Poetry* in Choate's library.

90. Choate, "Position and Functions," p. 422.

91. Francis Lieber to Charles Sumner, Aug. 24, 1837, quoted in Merle Curti, "Francis Lieber and Nationalism," *Probing Our Past* (Gloucester, Mass., 1962; 1st pub., 1955), p. 132. For a discussion of nationalism as primarily a matter of psychological identification, see Hans Kohn, *The Idea of Nationalism: A Study in Its Origin and Background* (New York, 1944), pp. 10–20; and David M. Potter, "The Historian's Use of Nationalism and Vice Versa," *American Historical Review,* LXVII (July 1962), 924–950.

92. Choate had read Edwards in college and remained an admirer. For Edwards' identification of the will with "the affections of the heart," see Norman S. Fiering, "Will and Intellect in the New England Mind," *William and Mary Quarterly,* XXIX (Oct. 1972), 515–558. Nathaniel Hawthorne, "English Note Books," *The Complete Works of Nathaniel Hawthorne,* Introduction and Notes by George Parsons Lathrop (Cambridge, Mass., 1883), VII, 478. One commentator notes that Choate's "peculiarly definite and individual conception of American nationality" made "our patriotism to a great extent the result of effort and will, instead of being the purely spontaneous sentiment of older lands" (William Everett, "Rufus Choate," *The New England Magazine* [Nov. 1896], p. 376).

93. Rufus Choate, "The Importance of Illustrating New-England History by a Series of Romances Like the Waverley Novels" (Salem, 1833), in Brown, *Works,* I, 319–346, 344 (quotation). For an interesting comparison of this address with George Bancroft's *History of the United States* as two sermons against mass egotism and selfishness, see Fred Somkin, *Unquiet Eagle: Memory and Desire in the Idea of American Freedom, 1815–1860* (Ithaca, N.Y., 1967), pp. 184–206. Choate's was of course only one voice among many calling for a distinctively "American" literature on American subjects (Hans Kohn, *American Nationalism* [New York, 1957], ch. 2, and Spencer, *Quest,* chs. 3 and 4). A statistical survey of American fiction during this period reveals that American writers took up Choate's challenge. Between 1830 and 1839 there were twenty-seven novels on the Revolutionary period. There were fifty-seven between 1840 and 1849, and nine in 1850; 10 percent of American fiction during the period was about the Revolution, 5 percent on the colonial period, together double the amount of fiction on the West or the frontier (Lyle H. Wright, "A Statistical Survey of American Fiction, 1774–1850," *Huntington Library Quarterly,* II (April 1939), 309–318. For the depiction of the Revolution in drama and the novel, see Kammen, *Season of Youth,* chs. 4 and 5.

94. [John O'Sullivan], "Editorial," *Democratic Review,* VI (Nov. 1939), 427. See also Paul C. Nagel, *This Sacred Trust: American Nationality, 1798–1898* (New York, 1975), pp. 105–109.

95. Hans Barth, *The Idea of Order: Contributions to a Philosophy of Politics,* trans. Ernest W. Hankamer and William M. Newell (Dordrecht, Holland, 1960), pp. 28, 44–46; David P. Calleo, *Coleridge,* pp. 56–57, 76–79; Choate, "Age of the Pilgrims," pp. 392–393. "Every incident of the doing and suffering of our fathers near that time" (of their landing), said a report of the Pilgrim Society,

"should be as fresh in our memories, as if it had occurred last week" (*Report* . . . *by a Committee of the Pilgrim Society*, [Boston, 1850], p. 4).

96. Alexis de Tocqueville, *Democracy in America* (2 vols; New York, 1945), II, bk. 2, ch. 2. For the Transcendentalist disassociation from the past, see R. Jackson Wilson, *In Quest of Community* (New York, 1968), ch. 1.

97. Francis Lieber, *Manual of Political Ethics, Designed Chiefly for the Use of Colleges and Students at Law* (Boston, 1838), II, 159; Choate, "Importance of Illustrating New-England History," p. 339.

98. Callcott, *History*, pp. vii–viii; Warren I. Susman, "History and the American Intellectual: Uses of a Usable Past," *American Quarterly*, XVI (1964), 243–263, esp. 253–254. For the primary intention of the New England antebellum historians to recreate the *experience* of the past and bring it vividly to life, see Levin, *History as Romantic Art*, ch. 1.

99. Henry Steele Commager, *The Search for a Usable Past and Other Essays in Historiography* (New York, 1967), p. 12; Spencer, *Quest*, pp. 92–93; Choate to Sarah Choate, July 9 [1854], in Brown, *Life*, p. 274; Job Durfee, "The Influence of Scientific Discovery and Invention on Social and Political Progress" (1843), in Northup, pp. 43–75, 75 (quotation). The *North American Review*, LXXII (April 1851), summed up much of the dissatisfaction with the "inhuman" sublime of the American landscape: "the scenery of a newly discovered country . . . however grand, however vast, however beautiful, has associated with it no *human* interest. . . . Nothing is so dear to us as close sympathy with our kind; desert places become populous, heaps of rubbish eloquent, when we know them to have been connected with great achievements, with human glory or suffering. The sympathy is more intense, the imagination more strongly impressed, the moral lessons more weighty, when there are visible and tangible memorials of the events" (p. 313). The difficulties in actually getting agreement and collecting money, however, were considerable, as the vicissitudes of the Bunker Hill Monument and the Washington Monument demonstrate (see Charles Warren, "Washington Centenial, 1832," *Massachusetts Historical Society Proceedings*, LXV [1932], 37–62, and Nathalia Wright, "The Monument That Jonathan Built," *American Quarterly*, V [Summer 1953], 166–174). It is perhaps evidence for Choate's faith in skilled urban workers as republican citizens that the Bunker Hill Association had to be rescued from its financial difficulties by the Massachusetts Charitable Mechanic Association and that from the beginning mechanics and carpenters contributed more than the business and professional classes (Wright, "Monument," p. 173).

100. Choate, "Importance of Illustrating New-England History," pp. 319, 320, 334, 331, 340; for the essentially conservative function of *vraisemblance* and the romance in general, see Perry Miller, "The Romance and the Novel," *Nature's Nation* (Cambridge, Mass., 1967), p. 248; and on Scott, see Georg Lukacs, *The Historical Novel* (London, 1969; 1st pub., 1962), pp. 29–69. Choate's own taste in scholarly history remained somewhat old fashioned. By the late 1850s he extended a cautious approval to Bancroft and said that Prescott gained on him, but he never cared for Macaulay: "All his History is a departure from the established rules of that sort of composition. He is far too *emphatic* and *certain* in his facts and conclusions for history. I like Gibbon better; there is more of an air of learning (in its technical sense) about him; not pamphlet and detail learn-

ing, such as Macaulay bristles with" (Parker, *Reminiscences,* pp. 287–288, 291). Historians were in fact moving towards providing the kind of "human interest" and revelation of daily life that Choate saw as the task of the romance. George Perkins Marsh thought that the historian must now broaden his scope to cover new sources: "It is only by a familiar knowledge of the everyday life of a people that we can acquire that sympathy of feeling which is an indispensable condition for the profitable or intelligent study of the history of any nation. To this end, we must know what have been the fortunes of the mass . . . we must see them at their daily occupations . . . invade the privacy of their firesides" (George Perkins Marsh, *The American Historical School* [Troy, N.Y., 1847], p. 10). Charles Francis Adams, in publishing the private papers of his grandparents, felt that he was contributing to "a new history of 'feeling' " (Earl N. Herbert, "Charles Francis Adams [1807–1886]: A Forgotten Family Man of Letters," *Journal of American Studies,* VI [Dec. 1972], 249–265, 262[quotation]).

101. Quoted in John D. Cogswell, *Memoir of Rufus Choate* (Cambridge, Mass., 1884), pp. 411–412. W. J. Bate speaks of the "tender protectiveness" of Burke's imagination as it turned to the "tragic past," and sees this tenderness as an essential part of the modern sensibility (Introduction to the *Selected Writings of Edmund Burke* p. 23). Fenimore Cooper had in some ways already begun to produce an American epic in the Leatherstocking series. The overt "message" of these works, the necessary advance of civilization into the wilderness, was one that suited Choate's own ideas. But as the public realized, the real hero of the series was Natty Bumpo, who was *not* a "civilizer" or builder, who traversed Nature leaving no trace behind. In the following years, Choate's fellow New Englander, Nathaniel Hawthorne, was to use the Puritan past for a series of romances. Like Choate, Hawthorne also regarded the early Puritans as giants who had left their mark on posterity—but he was far too ambivalent to have filled Choate's prescription. Whereas Choate found the essence of Puritan civilization in "the congregational church and the free school" ("Age of the Pilgrims," p. 385), Hawthorne picked on the prison (see *The Scarlet Letter,* in *Complete Works* V, 67, 76).

102. Burke, *Reflections,* p. 32; Choate, "Age of the Pilgrims," pp. 374, 392. For the development of a different myth of origins in the South, in a Cavalier rather than Puritan past, see Wesley Frank Craven, *The Legend of the Founding Fathers* (New York, 1965; 1st pub., 1956), pp. 130–133, and William R. Taylor, *Cavalier and Yankee* (New York, 1961), *passim.* For the cult of Washington, see William A. Bryan, *George Washington in American Literature* (New York, 1952). The Puritan feast of Thanksgiving spread from New England to other Northeastern states after 1817—but was regarded in the South with suspicion (Dixon Wecter, *The Hero in America: A Chronicle of Hero Worship* [New York, 1941], p. 44).

103. Jonathan Prescott Hall, "Discourse" (1847), in *New England Society Orations,* ed. C. and E. W. Brainerd, II, 11; George S. Cheever, "The Elements of National Greatness" (1842), *ibid.,* I, 293 (he was quoting Burke); George S. Hillard, "The Past and the Future" (1851), *ibid.,* II, 142; William Maxwell Evarts, "The Heritage of the Pilgrims" (1854) *ibid.,* II, 256.

104. Choate, "Age of the Pilgrims," pp. 374–375, 381–382.

105. Choate, "Thoughts on the New England Puritans" (1849). There is

no full report of this speech anywhere, but part of it is reproduced in Brown, *Life,* pp. 189–193, 190–191 (quotation). For the psychological problems of a post-revolutionary generation that had less opportunity for heroic self-assertion than their fathers, see George B. Forgie, *Patricide in the House Divided: A Psychological Portrait of Lincoln and His Age* (New York, 1979).

106. Choate, "Importance of Illustrating New-England History," p. 327. For the assimilation of the frontier west to conservative perceptions, see Welter, *Mind of America,* pp. 312–328.

107. [Charles Francis Adams], "Review of *An Historical Memoir of the Colony of New Plymouth,*" *North American Review,* L (April 1840), 336–357, 337 (quotation); George Bancroft, *History of the Colonization of the United States* (Boston, 1852; 1st pub., 1837), I, vii.

108. Quincy is quoted in Alexis de Tocqueville, *Journey to America,* ed. J. P. Mayer (London, 1959), p. 51; Jared Sparks, "Remarks on American History," in *The Boston Book* (Boston, 1837), p. 15; Edward Everett, *An Oration Delivered at Charlestown, on the 75th Anniversary of the Battle of Bunker Hill, June 17, 1850* (Boston, 1850), p. 38; Edwin P. Whipple, "Washington and the Principles of the Revolution" (1850), *Character and Characteristic Men* (Boston, 1866), p. 296.

109. Choate, "The Colonial Age of New England" (1834), in Brown, *Works,* I, 347–370, 350 (quotation); Choate, "Position and Functions," p. 420. For the increasingly common idea of the revolution as a "rite of passage," see Kammen, *Season of Youth,* ch. 6.

110. Marvin E. Gettleman, *The Dorr Rebellion: A Study in American Radicalism 1833–1849* (New York, 1973), pp. 72–79; Choate to Edward Everett, April 2, 1842, Everett MSS; "The Recent Contest in Rhode Island," *North American Review,* LVIII (April 1844), 371–435, 428–429, 422 (quotations). The position of the Rhode Island conservatives is well described by William M. Wiececk, " 'A Peculiar Conservatism' and the Dorr Rebellion: Constitutional Clash in Jacksonian America," *The American Journal of Legal History,* XXII (1978), 237–253. For the general conservative perception of the Rhode Island rebellion as a challenge to existing institutions, see George M. Dennison, *The Dorr War: Republicanism on Trial, 1831–1861* (Lexington, Ky., 1976), esp. chs. 5, 7 and epilogue; and "The Dorr War and the Triumph of Institutionalism," *Social Science Journal,* XV (April 1978), 39–58.

111. Gettleman, *Dorr Rebellion,* p. 82; "Recent Contest," p. 425; Edward G. Parker, *An Oration, July 4, 1856* (Boston, 1856), p. 19; Choate, "Colonial Age," p. 366; Lawrence is quoted in Hill, *Memoir,* p. 51. He was a member of the Massachusetts militia which was placed on the alert during the rebellion.

112. Choate, "Position and Functions," pp. 433, 421, 419.

113. Fredrickson, *Inner Civil War,* p. 135; George T. Curtis, *The True Uses of American Revolutionary History* (Boston, 1841), pp. 28–30; David B. Tyack, *George Ticknor and the Boston Brahmins* (Cambridge, Mass., 1967), pp. 199–201; Choate in *Brief Account of the Celebration of the 19th of April at Concord 1850* (n.p., n.d.), pp. 89–90. Walter LaFeber speculates on the transformation of the United States from a nation born in revolution to an anti-revolutionary society in his "American Historians and Revolutions," *Colloquium,* VIII (Spring 1970), pp. 1–6.

114. Whipple, "Washington," p. 322; Woodrow Wilson, "The Nature of

Democracy in the U.S." (1889), *The Papers of Woodrow Wilson,* ed. Arthur S. Link, et al. (Princeton, N.J., 1969), VI, 228, and quoted in LaFeber, "American Historians," p. 6.

CHAPTER THREE. THE SCHOLAR IN THE REPUBLIC

1. Choate, Journal, Dec. 9, 1844, in Samuel Gilman Brown, *The Life of Rufus Choate* (Boston, 1870), p. 128; Claude M. Fuess, *The Life of Daniel Webster* (2 vols.; Hamden, Conn., 1963; 1st pub., 1930), II, 140–141; Edward G. Parker, *Reminiscences of Rufus Choate* (New York, 1860), p. 283.

2. Choate, Journal, Dec. 9, 1844, in Brown, *Life,* p. 129;

3. Richard Henry Dana, Jr., before the Suffolk Bar after Choate's death, quoted in Brown, *Life,* p. 365. The incident of the Pliny quotation is recounted in Parker, *Reminiscences,* pp. 183–184. The quotation is from the twenty-third letter of the eighth book of the younger Pliny: *"Statim sapiunt, statim sciunt omnia; neminem verentur, imitantur neminem, atque ipsi sibi exempla sunt."* Choate to George Bush, Aug. 21, 1833, in Woodbury M. Fernald, *Memoirs and Reminiscences of the Late Professor George Bush* (Boston, 1860), p. 323.

4. Parker, *Reminiscences,* p. 80; reminiscences of his son-in-law and law partner, Joseph Bell, and of Edward Everett in Brown, *Life,* pp. 393, 380. For the large number of sizable private libraries in Boston, see Ronald Story, "Class and Culture in Boston: The Athenaeum, 1807–1860," *American Quarterly,* XXVII (May 1975), 178–199. Choate's library was small compared to those of Ticknor or Charles Francis Adams, but it cost about $40,000 and when less than half of its contents was sold on his death, fetched over $69,000 (*Catalogue of the Valuable Private Library of the Late Hon. Rufus Choate to be Sold at Auction* [Boston, 1859]).

5. Parker, *Reminiscences,* p. 264; Choate to Bush, Aug. 21, 1883, Fernald, *Memoirs;* Choate, Journal, n.d. [1844], in Brown, *Life,* p. 121.

6. Choate, note to a fragment of translation from Thucydides and Tacitus, in Brown, *The Works of Rufus Choate, with a Memoir of His Life* (2 vols.; Boston, 1862), II, 494; Journal, Sept. 29, 1844, n.d. [July-August], 1844, Dec. 15, 1844, Dec. 9, 1844, May 1843, in Brown, *Life,* pp. 125, 122–123, 129–30, 129, 91.

7. Parker, *Reminiscences,* p. 101; Dana, in Brown, *Life,* pp. 364–365.

8. Parker, *Reminiscences,* p. 120; Choate, Address at the Essex Street Church, March 28, 1859, in Brown, *Life,* p. 341: Choate, "Dedication of the Peabody Institute" (1854), in Brown, *Works,* I, 464–478, 476, 477 (quotations).

9. Parker, *Reminiscences,* pp. 83, 264; Choate to Bush, Feb. 12, 1832, in Brown, *Life,* p. 54.

10. Parker, *Reminiscences,* p. 239; Choate, Journal, Aug. 2, 1850, in Brown, *Life,* p. 219; Choate, Journal, Dec. 28, 1844, in Brown, *Life,* p. 131.

11. Choate, Journal, March 10, 1845, in Brown, *Life,* p. 134; Parker, *Reminiscences,* p. 73. Martin Green, *The Problem of Boston: Some Readings in Cultural History* (London, 1966), chs. 1–4, deals with Boston as a culture-sustaining city. He points out (p. 81) the number of young New Englanders who abandoned the law for literature in the early nineteenth century, including Ticknor, Prescott, Longfellow, Edward T. Channing, and Alexander and Edward Everett. It was still, however, necessary to stress that there was nothing dilettantish about writ-

ing: Ticknor, for example, in his *Life of William H. Prescott,* was anxious to show how laborious his historical work was, how much struggle and sacrifice to duty it entailed (David B. Tyack, *George Ticknor and the Boston Brahmins* [Cambridge, Mass., 1967], pp. 188–189).

12. Choate, Journal, n.d. [1845–50], in Brown, *Life,* pp. 195–196; Jerome H. Buckley, *The Triumph of Time: A Study of the Victorian Concepts of Time, History, Progress, and Decadence* (Cambridge, Mass., 1966), pp. 94–115, 124–125.

13. Choate, "Vacations—Private—Hints for Myself", and *"Vacations: By a Member of the Bar of Massachusetts, Advertisement,"* n.d. [1845], in Brown, *Life,* pp. 195–196, 198–199, 196, 199 (quotations).

14. Choate, "The Power of a State Developed by Mental Culture" (Nov. 18, 1844), in Brown, *Works,* I, 394–413, 405, 409–410 (quotations). For the Whig faith in education, see Rush Welter, *The Mind of America, 1820–60* (New York, 1975), pp. 276–285, and Michael B. Katz, *The Irony of Early School Reform* (Cambridge, Mass., 1968), pp. 1–112; see also Tyack, *George Ticknor,* pp. 204–212.

15. Rufus Choate, "Power of a State," in Brown, *Works,* I, 398, 248; Rufus Choate, "Address Delivered in South Danvers at the Dedication of the Peabody Institute, September 29, 1854," in Brown, *Works,* I, 464–478, 473, 474 (quotation).

16. Choate, "Address in South Danvers," p. 467; Francis Lieber, *Remarks on the Relation between Education and Crime* (Philadelphia, 1835), p. 18.

17. Choate, "Power of a State," p. 399; F. M. Barnard, *Herder's Social and Political Thought: From Enlightenment to Nationalism* (Oxford, 1965), pp. 121–122; David P. Calleo, *Coleridge and the Idea of the Modern State* (New Haven, 1966), p. 102; John Stuart Mill, "Coleridge" (1840), in *Dissertations and Discussions* (New York, 1973; 1st pub., 1859), I, 427–429.

18. For the rise and decline of the National Institute, see A. Hunter Dupree, *Science in the Federal Government* (New York, 1957), pp. 72–76; Madge E. Pickard, "Government and Science in the United States: Historical Backgrounds," *Journal of the History of Medicine and Allied Sciences,* I (April 1946), 254–289; Joel R. Poinsett, *Discourse on the Objects and Importance of the National Institute for the Promotion of Science* (Washington, D.C., 1841), p. 52; Sally G. Kohlstedt, *The Formation of the American Scientific Community* (Urbana, Ill., 1976), pp. 54–57.

19. *Third Bulletin of the Proceedings of the National Institute for the Promotion of Science* (Washington, D.C., Feb. 1842—Feb. 1845), p. 337. George P. Marsh drew up a report, in favor of extending aid to the Institute, that was presented by Choate in the Senate (see U.S., Congress, Senate, *Document 368,* 28th Cong., 1st sess., June 7, 1844; also David Lowenthal, *George Perkins Marsh: Versatile Vermonter* [New York, 1958], pp. 79–80). Many of the younger men of science were also skeptical about the usefulness of the Institute. One of Choate's colleagues on the "promotion" committee, Alexander Dallas Bache, who was to become one of the great entrepreneurs of American science, referred contemptuously to the membership as "pseudo-savants" (George Daniels, "The Process of Professionalization in American Science: The Emergent Period, 1820–60," *Isis,* LVIII [Summer 1967], 157).

20. The debate on the acceptance of the bequest in the 24th Congress is reprinted in William J. Rhees, *The Smithsonian Institution: Documents Relative to its*

Origin and History, 1835–1899 (Washington, D.C., 1901), I, 125–143; See also Dupree, *Science,* pp. 66–70.

21. Rhees, *Origins,* p. 225.

22. Asher Robbins, in the Senate, had proposed a national university like "the celebrated schools of Athens" (Jan. 10, 1839, in Rhees, *Origins,* pp. 163–171). Though the House gave little support to John Quincy Adams' "light-house of the skies," he not only turned the debate away from the idea of a traditional educational establishment but pointed out the distinction that, though blurred in the ensuing debates, was to become very important in the subsequent history of the Institution, between the diffusion and the increase of knowledge. He insisted that Smithson had intended to forward "the discovery of new truths or the invention of new instruments for the enlargement of human power," "progress in the march of the human mind" (Adams' speech in the House, March 5, 1840, in Rhees, *Origins,* pp. 184–206, 191, 193 [quotations]). For his strong personal involvement with the bequest, see *The Great Design: Two Lectures on the Smithsonian Bequest by John Quincy Adams,* ed. with an Introduction by Wilcomb E. Washburn (Washington, D.C., 1965). Bill S. 18, 28 Cong., 2 sess., Dec. 12, 1844, in Rhees, *Origins,* pp. 276–280.

23. Adams in the House, March 5, 1840, p. 196. Perry Miller discusses the widespread attitude towards astronomy as the most "sublime" of the sciences in *The Life of the Mind in America: From the Revolution to the Civil War* (New York, 1965), pp. 278–279. See also the memorials of Professor Walter R. Johnson, and Charles L. Fleischmann, 1838 and 1839, in Rhees, *Origins,* pp. 146–163; and "The Smithsonian Institute (sic)," *Southern Literary Messenger,* VI (Jan. 1840), 25–34.

24. Adams in the House, March 5, 1840, p. 195; "The Smithsonian Institute," p 26.

25. Edward Lurie, "Science in American Thought," *Journal of World History,* V (1965), 638–665. For the vogue of Bacon, see Arthur E. Ekirch, Jr., *The Idea of Progress in America, 1815–1860* (New York, 1951; 1st pub., 1944) pp. 106–131. For "Sublime Utility," see Miller, *Life,* pp. 287–308. "Things not words" was the proscription of the South Carolina chemist, Thomas Cooper (quoted in William J. Rhees, ed., *The Smithsonian Institution: Documents Relative to its Origins and History* [Washington, D.C., 1880], p. 838; see also William Darlington, M.D., "A Plea for a National Museum and Botanic Garden . . . December 3, 1841," in Rhees, *Documents,* pp. 903–908, 903, 907 [quotations]).

26. For envy of the facilities and social validation given to the European scholar see, for example, Joseph Henry to Alexander Dallas Bache, Sept. 6, 1846, in Wilcomb E. Washburn, "Joseph Henry's Conception of the Purpose of the Smithsonian Institution," in *A Cabinet of Curiosities: Five Episodes in the Evolution of American Museums,* ed. Walter Muir Whitehill (Charlottesville, Va., 1967), pp. 106–166; see also George Perkins Marsh, *Human Knowledge: A Discourse* (Boston, 1847), p. 3, and J. F. Jackson, "American Scholarship," *The Knickerbocker,* XXVIII (July 1846), 1–13, 13 (quotation).

27. Jesse H. Shera, *Foundations of the Public Library: The Origins of the Public Library Movement in New England 1629–1855* (Hamden, Conn., 1965; 1st pub., Chicago, 1949), pp. 208–211. Choate used the Gibbon example in his Senate speech (Horatio Hubbell to Hon. John Forsyth, Sept. 20, 1839, in Rhees,

Documents, p. 861; George Washington Greene, "Libraries," *North American Review,* XLV [July 1837], 116–149, 138 [quotation]). "A literary class is gradually forming itself into a distinct order," declared Greene, "but still dependent upon the other classes of society for its subsistence and its success, and destined to form for them a literature either superficial and ephemeral, or profound and durable, in exact proportion as its intellectual wants are neglected or supplied" *(ibid.).* Choate quoted extensively from this article in his speech in the Senate (in Brown, *Works,* II, 258–259).

28. Choate, Journal, Dec. 9, 1844, in Brown, *Life,* pp. 128–129; Choate in the Senate, Jan. 8, 1845, in Brown, *Works,* II, 248–264.

29. *Ibid.,* pp. 257, 260; Edmund Burke, *Reflections on the Revolution in France* (London, 1910; 1st pub., 1790), p. 93.

30. Choate in the Senate, Jan. 8, 1845, in Brown, *Works,* II, 256, 262.

31. *Ibid.,* pp. 253–254. The kind of lecture and foundation which Choate envisaged finds a modern example in Lionel Trilling's "Mind in the Modern World," delivered as the first annual Thomas Jefferson Lecture in the Humanities in Washington, D.C., April 1972. The lecture was "financed by the National Endowment for the Humanities 'to help bridge the gap between learning and public affairs' by enabling major thinkers to bring their 'wisdom, knowledge and experience to bear on contemporary concerns'" (*Times Literary Supplement* [Nov. 17, 1972], p. 1,385).

32. Charles B. Haddock, D.D., *The Patriot Scholar: An Oration Pronounced before the Phi Beta Kappa Society of Yale College* (New Haven, 1848), pp. 14, 15. Any random selection of academic addresses could provide copious evidences of this pervasive theme. Particularly useful are: Edward Everett, "The Circumstances Favorable to the Progress of Literature in America" (1824), in Joseph L. Blau, *American Philosophic Addresses, 1700–1900* (New York, 1946), pp. 60–93; Theophilus Parsons, *The Duties of Educated Men in a Republic* (Boston, 1835); Daniel Barnard, *An Address delivered before the Philoclean and Peithessophian Societies of Rutgers College* (New York, 1837); S. B. Ruggles, *The Duty of Columbia College to the Community . . .* (New York, 1857). The latter is a particularly bitter attack on what the writer saw as the sordid materialism of America and the need for great universities as a countervailing power. For a discussion of the moral duty of men of letters as seen by the New England intellectual "Establishment," see Daniel Walker Howe, *The Unitarian Conscience: Harvard Moral Philosophy, 1805–61* (Cambridge, Mass., 1970), pp. 174–204.

33. Coleridge worked out the idea of the "clerisy" and its institutional foundation in a National Church in *The Constitution of the Church and State According to the Idea of Each* (London, 1829), a copy of which appears in the Catalog of Choate's library. Coleridge defined the task of the clerisy as: "to preserve the stores and to guard the treasures of past civilization, and thus to bind the present with the past; to perfect and add to the same, and thus to connect the present with the future; but especially to diffuse through the whole community and to every native entitled to its laws and rights that quantity and quality of knowledge that was indispensable both for the understanding of those rights and for the performance of the duties correspondent" (p. 47). Auguste Comte developed similar ideas—giving to a "scientific priesthood" the vital political task of combatting the "intellectual anarchy" of the age (see Frank E. Manuel, *The Prophets*

of Paris [Cambridge, Mass., 1962], ch. 6; and Hans Barth, *The Idea of Order: Contributions to a Philosophy of Politics*, trans. Ernest W. Hankamer and William M. Newell [Dordrecht, Holland, 1960], pp. 115–120).

34. Choate in the Senate, in Brown, *Works*, II, 263–264.

35. "The Smithsonian Institution," *North American Review*, LXXIX (Oct. 1854), 441–464, 459 (quotation). Calhoun is quoted in Joseph Neilson, *Memories of Rufus Choate, with Some Consideration of His Studies, Methods and Opinions, and of His Style As a Speaker and Writer* (Boston, 1884), p. 260; Rhees, *Origins*, pp. 294, 305–312, 313, 315.

36. Rhees, *Origins*, pp. 319–322.

37. Owen's bill is in Rhees, *Origins*, pp. 321–331; his speech in its defense, pp. 334–349, 349, 343–344 (quotations). For Jacksonian attitudes towards "luxury," mental as well as physical, see John William Ward, *Andrew Jackson: Symbol for an Age* (New York, 1953), ch. 4; Major L. Wilson, "The Concept of Time and the Political Dialogue in the United States, 1828–48," *American Quarterly*, XIX (Winter 1967), 619–644, esp. 639–640.

38. *The New Englander*, IV (Oct. 1846), 605–607; Rhees, *Origins*, pp. 332–410, *passim;* Marsh in the House, April 23, 1846, in Rhees, *Origins*, pp. 371–387, 375 (quotation).

39. Marsh, in Rhees, *Origins*, pp. 383–384, 378–9. The definition of *Wissenschaft* is John Theodore Merz' in *A History of European Thought in the 19th Century* (4 vols.; London, 1904), I, 90, n. 1.

40. The final act is printed in Rhees, *Origins*, 429–434; the quotation from Thurman is in *ibid.*, p. 405. A copy of every book copyrighted in the U.S. was also to be deposited with the Institution.

41. Rhees, *Origins*, 436–438. "In decency," Marsh complained bitterly to a friend, "the Speaker should have put me upon the Board instead of persons whose plans had been decisively rejected" (Marsh to John R. Bartlett, Sept. 1, 1846, quoted in Washburn, "Introduction," *The Great Design*, ed. Washburn, p. 29). When Owen left Congress in December 1847, Marsh was appointed in his place by the new speaker, Robert Winthrop, and served until he became U.S. minister to Turkey in 1849 (Lowenthal, *George Perkins Marsh*, p. 86).

42. For Bache, see Nathan Reingold, "Alexander Dallas Bache: Science and Technology in the American Idiom," *Technology and Culture*, II (April 1970), 163–77, and Merle M. Odgers, *Alexander Dallas Bache: Scientist and Educator, 1806–1867* (Philadelphia, 1947). The phrase "bounty for research" is from an address by Bache, April 1844, quoted in Howard S. Miller, *Dollars for Research: Science and its Patrons in 19th Century America* (Seattle, 1970), p. 3.

43. Bernard Jaffe, *Men of Science in America* (New York, 1958), pp. 200–206; Henry, in a eulogy of Bache (1870), quoted in Odgers, *Alexander Dallas Bache*, p. 166.

44. For Jewett, see Joseph A. Borome, *Charles Coffin Jewett* (Chicago, 1951); Owen to Bache, Sept. 2, 1846, Alexander Dallas Bache Papers, Smithsonian Institution Archives, Washington, D.C.

45. Henry's program in its final form is in "Program of Organization of the Smithsonian Institution Adopted by the Board of Regents, Dec. 13, 1847," in *3rd Annual Report of the Board of Regents Presented to Congress, Feb. 19, 1849*, in *Reports etc. of the Smithsonian Institution . . .* (Washington, D.C. 1849), pp. 6–21.

The phrase "real working men of science" is from a letter from Henry to Bache, Aug. 9, 1838, quoted in Miller, *Dollars*, p. 9; Choate's report was later printed in the *Boston Daily Advertiser*, Jan. 29, 1855, and also quoted in *Report of the Hon. James Meacham* (Washington, D.C., 1854). See also Bache to Henry, Dec. 4, 1846, quoted in Wilcomb E. Washburn, "The Influence of the Smithsonian Institution on Intellectual Life in Mid-Nineteenth Century Washington," *Columbia Historical Society Records*, (1963–1965), pp. 96–121, 98 (quotation); for the compromise, see Washburn, "Joseph Henry's Conception," pp. 106–166.

46. Bache to Henry, June 29, 1847, quoted in Washburn, "Influence," p. 100; William J. Rhees, ed., *Smithsonian Institution: Journals of the Board of Regents* (Washington, D.C. 1880), Jan. 26, 1847, pp. 25–27.

47. Choate's library contained Agassiz' *Contributions to the National Institute*, A. Brown's *Philosophy of Physics* (1854), Whewell's *History of the Inductive Sciences* (1847), and seven volumes of the *Annual of Scientific Discovery*, ed. David A. Wells *(Catalogue)*. For his reactions to visiting Newton's rooms, see his Journal, Sept. 1, 1850, in Brown, *Life*, p. 229. Choate had considerable distaste for many of the objects of natural history. Caroline Marsh recounts a story of Choate retiring in horror from a small dinner party she gave, at which Spencer F. Baird, Marsh's protegé who became curator of the Smithsonian Museum, produced a live specimen of a rare snake for the pleasure of Agassiz, the guest of honor (Caroline Crane Marsh, comp., *Life and Letters of George Perkins Marsh*, [New York, 1886], I, 106). Henry's views on educated men as sustainers of civilization can be found in his *Thoughts on Education: The Introductory Discourse Delivered before the American Association for the Advancement of Education* (Washington, D.C., 1854). "Civilization itself may be considered as a condition of unstable equilibrium, which required constant effort to be sustained, and a still greater effort to be advanced. . . . A large number of highly educated men whose voice may be heard, and whose influence may be felt, is absolutely necessary to sustain the world in its present moral and intellectual development" (pp. 18, 19).

48. The ethical neutrality of science had stirred vague anxiety even among eighteenth-century enthusiasts for rational scientific methods. Goethe, for example, had feared that problems of being and meaning would be crowded out of mind by the success of the experimental sciences in dealing with the " 'How' of things" (Erich Heller, *The Disinherited Mind: Essays in Modern German Literature and Thought* [London, 1952], p. 16; the quotation from Coleridge is from the Preface to *Aids to Reflection*, quoted in William Walsh, *The Use of Imagination* [London, 1959], p. 61; see also, Matthew Arnold, "The Function of Criticism at the Present Time" in *Essays in Criticism: First Series* [London, 1898; 1st pub., 1865], p. 38). The phrase is anachronistic but seems to sum up what Choate had in mind (Choate, "Intervention of the New World in the Affairs of the Old;— the Duty, the Limitations and the Modes," Address at the Commencement of the University of Vermont, 1852). The bulk of this speech was on Kossuth. The fullest version seems to be in the *New York Daily Times*, Aug. 9, 1852; the manuscript does not appear to have survived and only a small portion, not the most interesting, is printed in Brown, *Life*, pp. 260–261. One might add too, that the sciences at this particular time did not resonate into the general culture, as the work of Newton had done in the educated world of the eighteenth century, or the theories of Darwin were to do in a few more years. While ante-bellum

Americans were fascinated by "science," it was the technology that offered the promise of transforming the world, rather than the theories that might explain it, that caught their fancy. Developments in electricity, for example, might provide the occasional metaphor for the poet, but the sciences were not producing the crucial twist of the mental kaleidoscope in which the pieces fall into a new "world view" (see Robert Oppenheimer, "The Growth of Science and the Structure of Culture," in *Science and the Modern Mind* ed. Gerald Holton, [Boston, 1958], pp. 63–73).

49. Choate, "Power of A State," pp. 401, 399, 411. For the attitude of the romantic poets towards the mind, see Basil Willey, *Nineteenth Century Studies: Coleridge to Matthew Arnold* (London, 1949), ch. 1; Arthur O. Lovejoy, "Coleridge and Kant's Two Worlds," in *Essays in the History of Ideas,* ed. Arthur O. Lovejoy (Baltimore, 1948); Trilling, "Mind in the Modern World," p. 1,382; Walsh, *Use of the Imagination,* p. 49. For Henry, see "Programme of Organization," p. 17. Many years later, in 1870, Henry, by now the venerable head of a distinguished institution, was questioned by a British parliamentary committee on the policy of the Smithsonian. He related that a number of papers on philosophy had been submitted for publication, "but the answer is, what are the evidences that they are true? and the rule adopted is to publish no unverified speculations." Thomas Huxley asked him whether, if one of Kant's *Critiques* had been submitted, he would have published it. The answer was no: "the indefiniteness of the subject" (*Journals of the Board of Regents,* p. 790). Henry's conception of science and verifiable knowledge did, however, leave room at the outer fringes for the social sciences: The first volume of the *Smithsonian Contributions to Knowledge* was the pioneering descriptive account by E. G. Squier and E. H. Davis of the Indian Mounds of the Mississippi valley (Washington, 1848).

50. It was the duty of the present management, Henry wrote in 1852, to "give the institution such an impulse in the proper direction that it cannot deviate from it without immediately arresting the attention of the enlightened public, both at home and abroad" (*Annual Report,* 1852, p. 225; *Journals of the Board of Regents,* pp. 28–30; Richard W. Leopold, *Robert Dale Owen: A Biography* [Cambridge, Mass., 1940], pp. 245–246; Lowenthal, *George Perkins Marsh,* p. 87).

51. Brown, *Life,* p. 200; Edward Everett to Henry Hallam, and to Sir Robert Peel, June 1850, Edward Everett MSS, Massachusetts Historical Society, Boston, Mass.; Webster to Choate, June 24, 1850, copy in Brown MSS.

52. Choate to Mrs. Choate, July 7 and 8, 1850, in Brown, *Life,* pp. 201–202; Choate, Journal, July 7, 1850, Brown MSS, and in Brown, *Life,* pp. 209–210; Choate to Edward Parker, July 1950, Parker, *Reminiscences,* p. 309; Journal, July 12, in Brown, *Life,* p. 211; Choate to Mrs. Choate, July 12, 1850, *ibid.,* p. 203.

53. Choate to Mrs. Choate, July 18, 1850, in Brown, *Life,* pp. 203–205; Journal, July 12, 1850 in Brown, *Life,* pp. 210–211; Choate to Parker [July 1850], in Parker, *Reminiscences,* pp. 310–311; the remark about Macaulay is in Parker, *Reminiscences,* p. 271, about Parliament, *ibid.,* p. 295.

54. Choate to Mrs. Choate, July 24, 1850, in Brown, *Life,* pp. 205–206; Journal, July 19, 20, 22, Aug. 2, 5, 7, 9, 18, 1850, in Brown, *Life,* pp. 211–219, 221–227, 215, 216–217, 219, 222–223, 224 (quotations).

55. Choate, Journal, Aug. 2, 1850, in Brown, *Life,* pp. 219–220. George Ticknor, who was widely travelled, also concluded that the advantages of living

in a moral republic outweighed the glories of the old world, since men "are more truly *men,* have wider views and a more active intelligence" (quoted in Tyack, *George Ticknor,* p. 168).

56. Choate, Journal, Sept. 1, 1850, in Brown, *Life,* pp. 229, 230.

57. Henry to Bache, March 30, 1847, in Washburn, "Joseph Henry's Conception," p. 119 (italics mine); Henry to Baird in William H. Dall, *Spencer Fullerton Baird: A Biography* (Philadelphia, 1915), pp. 208–209; *Smithsonian Institution, Annual Report* (1856), p. 43; Washburn, "Influence," pp. 107–109.

58. Charles Hodge to Henry, Dec. 5, 1846, in Washburn, "Joseph Henry's Conception," pp. 113–114; "Letters relative to the 'program of organization' of the Smithsonian Institution proposed by Professor Joseph Henry," in Rhees, *Documents,* pp. 961–994; Borome, *Jewett,* pp. 39, 43–63. Jewett organized a system of exchanges that by 1855 had given the Smithsonian the most extensive collection of the recent publications of learned societies in the United States. Jewett also took a prominent part in organizing the first convention of librarians in the world, in 1853 (Borome, *Jewett,* pp. 64–72).

59. "Report of the Assistant Secretary . . . for 1853," in Borome, *Jewett,* pp. 79–81; "Report of the Assistant Secretary . . . for 1848," in *Third Annual Report,* 49; Borome, *Jewett,* pp. 83–84. Jewett's account of the dispute between himself and Henry is in his testimony before the Congressional Committee, Feb. 9, 1855 (see the Journal of the Committee, in Joseph Henry Papers, Smithsonian Institution Archives, Washington, D.C.). Jewett complained that Henry "spoke of governing and disciplining the officers of the Institution as if we were unruly boys instead of men of education, associated together for high public purposes."

60. Choate to Jewett, Feb. 4, 1854, Rufus Choate MSS, Houghton Library, Harvard University, Cambridge, Mass. Most of this letter is printed in Brown, *Life,* p. 143. See also Choate to Caleb Cushing, Jan. 8, 1854, Cushing MSS; Borome, *Jewett,* p. 85.

61. Henry to Asa Gray, May 24, 1854, Asa Gray Papers, Harvard University, Cambridge, Mass. The special committee consisted of James A. Pearce, J. M. Mason, Richard Rush, John W. Maury, J. G. Totten, Bache and James Meacham. Their Report is in the *Journals of the Board of Regents,* May 20, 1854, pp. 101–112; Meacham's minority report was printed separately: *Report of Hon. James Meacham . . .* (Washington, D.C., 1854).

62. Jewett to George Livermore, June 15, 1954, in Borome, *Jewett,* pp. 83, 89, 90. See also the *Boston Post,* Feb. 7, 1855, which condemned Jewett for having waged a newspaper war against the Institution; and *Journals of the Board of Regents,* July 8, 1854, pp. 112–113. Choate complained to Jewett that he had not been notified of the upcoming meeting on July 8 until told by Jewett and that it was impossible for him to get to Washington on that date (Choate to Jewett, July 3, 1854, Choate MSS, Houghton).

63. *New York Tribune,* Dec. 26, 1854, Jan. 19, 1855. For similar expressions, see *New York Daily Times,* Oct. 4, 1852, Jan. 13, 1855; *Scientific American,* V (May 1850), 285. See also *Report of the Hon. James Meacham,* p. 59; Choate in the Senate, Jan. 8, 1845, in Brown, *Works,* I, 260; *Washington Evening Star,* May 24, 1854, quoted in Washburn, "Influence," p. 113.

64. *New York Daily Times,* Jan. 16, Jan. 19, 1855; *Journals of the Board of Regents,* Jan. 12, 1855, p. 115; Brown, *Life,* p. 144; Bache to Benjamin Pierce,

Jan. 20, 1855, Benjamin Pierce MSS, Houghton Library, Harvard University, Cambridge, Mass.

65. *Journals of the Board of Regents,* Jan. 12, 1855, p. 115; Choate to the Senate and House of Representatives, Jan. 13, 1855, in Brown, *Life,* pp. 144–146; and Rhees, *Origins,* pp. 511–512; Choate to Jewett, n.d., Choate MSS, Houghton.

66. Debate in Senate, Jan. 17, 1855, in Rhees, *Origins,* pp. 512–535.

67. Taney to Rush, Jan. 27, 1855, Benjamin Rush MSS, Princeton University Library, Princeton, N.J.; "The Smithsonian Institution," *North American Review* (Oct. 1854), pp. 1–24; "The Smithsonian Institution," *Christian Examiner* (Nov. 1854), pp. 385–395; "The Smithsonian Institution," *Putnam's Monthly,* IV (Aug. 1854), pp. 121–131. See also the *Boston Daily Advertiser,* Jan. 23, 25, 29, 1855; *Boston Atlas,* Jan. 27, 29, 30, 31, Feb. 9, Mar. 5, 6, 12, 1855. Benjamin A. Gould, under the pseudonym NPD, defended the regents and accused Jewett of incompetence in a series of articles in the *Boston Post* (Jan. 27, Feb. 5, 7, 13, 21, 22, 1855). These were later collected as a pamphlet, *The Smithsonian Institution* (Boston, 1855).

68. Letters from Benjamin Pierce and Louis Agassiz in support of Henry are quoted in the "Report of William H. Witte, . . . to the House," March 3, 1855, in Rhees, *Origins,* pp. 583–584. A memorial from the American Philosophical Society and a letter from the Academy of Natural Sciences are reprinted in the *National Intelligencer,* March 3, 1854; see also Choate to Upham, Feb. 2 and Feb. 9, 1855, Choate MSS, Houghton. Both letters are also in Brown, *Life,* pp. 146–149, but the last line of the latter is omitted after "morals." See also Washburn, "Joseph Henry's Conception," p. 128.

69. Upham's *Report* is in Rhees, *Origins,* pp. 557–574, 572–573 (quotation); Benjamin Pierce, *The Smithsonian Institution,* extracted from *American Journal of Science and Arts,* XX (2nd ser., July 1855), 17.

70. Benjamin Gould warned his fellow scientists in 1869 against siding with the current agitation against the classical curriculum in the colleges: "The Champions in this crusade occupy simply the utilitarian ground, and their alleged advocacy of science is in fact scarcely more than an advocacy of the useful arts. . . . The crusade is not in behalf of this or that form of intellectual progress; it is against such intellectual culture as has not some tangible end, capable of being represented in dollars, or finding expression in some form of physical well-being" (quoted in George H. Daniels, *Science in American Society: A Social History* [New York, 1971], p. 280).

George Ticknor, the elder statesman of New England letters, saw the natural sciences as the catalyst which would galvanize stagnant colleges into real universities. Writing to Sir Charles Lyell in 1859 about the situation at Harvard, he remarked: "I think the Lawrence Scientific School, with the Zoological and Paleontological Museum, may push through a true university and bring up the Greek, Latin, Mathematics, history, philosophy, etc., to the proper level. At least I hope so and mean to work for it" (Ticknor to Lyell, May 17, 1854 in *Life, Letters and Journals of George Ticknor* [Boston, 1876], II, 422).

71. *Boston Post,* Feb. 22, 1855; in the pamphlet form, pp. 29–30; Meacham

in the House, March 5, 1855, in Rhees, *Origins,* pp. 596, 597; Upham, *Report,* p. 562.

72. Borome, *Jewett,* p. 97; Washburn, "Influence," pp. 115–121. The museum, under the patient Baird, proved more resistent to the scorn of the pure scientist. Not only did Henry have to put up with it while alive, but when Baird succeeded him as secretary in 1878, the museum began to crowd out the support of original research (Washburn, "Joseph Henry's Conception," pp. 143–152); Choate to Jewett, Feb. 25, 1855, Choate MSS, Houghton.

73. Choate, MS Report to the Smithsonian Institution, n.d., Brown MSS.

CHAPTER FOUR. THE LAW AND THE STATE

1. Choate, Journal, Aug. 24, 1844, Sept. 29, 1844, in Samuel Gilman Brown, *The Life of Rufus Choate* (Boston, 1870), p. 124; Brown, *Life,* p. 406; Clement Hugh Hill, "Memoir of Hon. Rufus Choate," *Massachusetts Historical Society Proceedings,* 2nd ser., XI (Oct. 1896), 124–155.

2. Brown, *Life,* pp. 200, 406; Hill, "Memoir," p. 143. Until the partnership with Bell, apparently, the office had kept no books at all and Choate would merely make sudden raids upon his clients for unpaid fees when he happened to remember or when he was suddenly in need of money (Edward G. Parker, *Reminiscences of Rufus Choate,* [New York, 1860], pp. 94–95). Benjamin R. Curtis' professional receipts for 1857–1874 were about $650,000 (J. W. Hurst, *The Growth of American Law: The Law Makers* [Boston, 1950], p. 311).

3. Rev. J. M. Marsters to Brown, May 7, 1862, Samuel Gilman Brown MSS, Houghton Library, Harvard University, Cambridge, Mass.; Brown, *Life,* pp. 443–444; Parker, *Reminiscences,* p. 95.

4. Brown, *Life,* pp. 363–364, 408–415. "It is one of his peculiarities," wrote Edwin Whipple, ". . . that he combines a conservative intellect with a radical sensibility; and those irregular impulses of fancy and passion, which usually push men into the adopting of the reckless, desperate and destructive principles of legislation, he employs in the service of the calmest, most comprehensive, and most practical political wisdom, rooted deep in reason and experience. His fire *seems* to be that kind which sweeps in a devouring flame, to blast and desolate what is established and accredited; but it really is that fierce heat, which infuses energy and breathing life into maxims and principles, which are in danger of becoming ineffective, from their usual disconnection with the sensibility and imagination. He is a kind of Mirabeau-Peel," (Edwin P. Whipple, "Hon. Rufus Choate," *The American Review: A Whig Journal (The American Whig Review),* V [1847], 63–71, 66 [quotation]).

5. George Hillard to Francis Lieber, Sept. 1, 1856, Francis Lieber MSS, Huntington Library, San Marino, Calif.; Brown, note of conversation with W. Woodman, Brown MSS; Parker, *Reminiscences,* p. 301. Miriam's recollections are in Brown, *Life,* pp. 441–442, and Story's in a note to Brown, n.d. Brown MSS. An almost identical piece appears in Joseph Neilson, *Memories of Rufus Choate, with Some Consideration of His Studies, Methods and Opinions, and of His Style As a Speaker and Writer* (Boston, 1884), pp. 371–372. The rumor that he was an opium addict is discussed in Rev. J. M. Marsters to Brown, May 7, 1862, Brown MSS. Parker and Choate's minister, Nehemiah Adams, both vehemently denied

that he took opium (Parker, *Reminiscences,* pp. 74–75; Brown, *Life,* p. 455). He was very abstemious with liquor and seems to have relied on hot water and tea as stimulants (Parker, *Reminiscences,* p. 87).

6. Parker, *Reminiscences,* pp. 125–127, 91, 146; Edwin P. Whipple, *Some Recollections of Rufus Choate* (New York, 1879), p. 35; Richard Henry Dana, Jr., in Brown, *Life,* p. 362, and Justice Lord, in *ibid.,* pp. 399–400; Choate to Amory Holbrook, Dec. 6, 1840, Misc. MS Collection, Yale University Library, New Haven, Conn. To another student, Matthew Hale Carpenter, who was about to set up in Wisconsin, he not only gave money for the journey, but his guarantee of credit for $1,000 so that he might purchase an adequate law library before leaving (William Draper Lewis, ed., *Great American Lawyers,* III [S. Hackensack, N.J., 1971; 1st pub., 1909], 500–504).

7. Brown, *Life,* pp. 391–394, 447; Parker, *Reminiscences,* pp. 139–141; J. L. Thorndike to Brown, n.d., Brown MSS. His indifference to nature is from G. P. Marsh in Neilson, *Memories,* p. 377, and Marsh to Brown, Dec. 24, 1859, Brown MSS. He passed his distaste for the rural life on to at least one of his children: "Slap Nature's green face for me," said his daughter Helen to a friend venturing into the country (Paulina Cony Drown, *Mrs. Bell,* [Boston, 1931], p. 13).

8. Perry Miller, *The Life of the Mind in America: From the Revolution to the Civil War* (New York, 1965), pp. 135–137; see also the remarks of Caleb Cushing to the United States circuit court on the death of Choate: "Here . . . the system of legal practice requires of eminent counsel to be alike conversant with all the various branches of practice and of law, thus producing a more comprehensive state of mind, which is apparent, I think, in the greater tendency of generalization, and of the more eclectic quality of the legal mind in the United States [than in England]. Here jurisprudence is indeed preeminently a science, embracing all social interests, and rising from ordinary municipal questions to those of legislation and government, and preparing the erudite jurisprudent for the larger functions and duties of the statesmen" (unidentified newspaper clipping, Caleb Cushing MSS, Library of Congress, Washington, D.C.) Choate's cases included: murder, fraud, embezzlement, disputed wills, insurance claims, assault, slander, claims for damages, railroad petitions, boundary disputes, patent cases (Parker, *Reminiscences,* pp. 110, 194; Brown, *Life,* pp. 160–161, n. 1. Theophilus Parsons, *Address Commemorative of Rufus Choate,* [Boston, 1859], p. 21; Whipple, *Some Recollections,* p. 33).

9. This was the celebrated Dalton divorce case, 1857, involving manslaughter and charges of abortion as well as adultery. In his closing remarks Choate urged the jury to refuse the divorce so that a reconciliation might become possible. He won the case and the couple did later reconcile (Brown, *Life,* pp. 315–323; Parker, *Reminiscences,* pp. 477–478; Mrs. W. S. Robinson, ed., *"Warrington" Pen Portraits: A Collection of Personal and Political Reminiscences, from 1848 to 1876, from the Writings of W. S. Robinson* [Boston, 1877], pp. 457–460). Another celebrated divorce case in which he was involved was the Butler divorce in 1848–1849, in which he appeared as one of the counsel for Fanny Kemble. Her "Answer" to her husband's libel for divorce was drawn up largely by Choate and emphasized Butler's mental cruelty. Choate's impassioned speech on Kemble's behalf was apparently one of his most eloquent efforts—although the court

refused to accept the "Answer" in evidence (Dorothy Bobbé, *Fanny Kemble* [New York, 1931], pp. 240–242; Constance Wright, *Fanny Kemble and the Lovely Land* [New York, 1972], pp. 132–134; "Fanny Kemble's Answer," *New York Tribune*, Nov. 29, 30, Dec. 2, 1848).

10. Parker, *Reminiscences*, pp. 141–159 *passim*, p. 267; Whipple, *Some Recollections*, pp. 14–16.

11. Parker, *Reminiscences*, pp. 179, 186–188, 192, 324–325; George P. Marsh, in Neilson, *Memories*, p. 308; Irving Browne, *Short Studies of Great Lawyers* (Albany, N.Y., 1878), p. 373; Whipple, *Some Recollections*, pp. 48–50; Edward G. Parker, *The Golden Age of American Oratory* (Boston, 1858), p. 116; William Gardiner Hammond, *Remembrance of Amherst: An Undergraduate's Diary, 1846–48* (New York, 1946), p. 140. The students were given the day off so that they might go over to Northampton to hear Webster and Choate plead the Smith Will Case (1847) (*ibid.*, 137).

12. Choate, Journal, May 17, 1843, in Brown, *Life*, p. 94; Parker, *Reminiscences*, pp. 153–155; Edward B. Gillett, in Neilson, *Memories*, p. 337; George W. Minns, "Some Reminiscences of Rufus Choate," *The American Law Review*, XI (Oct. 1876), 1–23.

13. Charles G. Loring to Brown, Feb. 24, [1860], Brown MSS. In the Dalton divorce case, for example, he attempted to discredit one hostile witness by forcing her to admit that she had an illegitimate child (John W. Black, "Rufus Choate," in *A History and Criticism of American Public Address*, ed., William Norwood Brigance [New York, 1943], I, 434–458); Whipple, *Some Recollections*, p. 21.

14. Black, "Rufus Choate," pp. 451, 447–448; Parker, *Reminiscences*, pp. 177–178, 200.

15. Black, "Rufus Choate," pp. 448–453; Parker, *Reminiscences*, pp. 209–210. This incident horrified an English reviewer of Parker's book. To Parker it was evidence of Choate's luxuriant imagination—to the critic, of pure dishonesty ("An English Impression of Parker on Choate," rpt. from the *London Saturday Review* in *Boston Courier*, March 7, 1860).

16. There is no complete record of Choate's argument in the Tirrell trial. However, there was considerable coverage in the daily press—see particularly the *Boston Daily Advertiser* and *Boston Post*, March 26–30, 1846. An incomplete phonographic report of the trial was also printed as a pamphlet, *The Trial of Albert J. Tirrell . . .* (Boston, *Daily Mail*, Report, n.d.). Parts of Choate's argument are also in Brown's account of the trial (Brown, *Life*, pp. 160–170; see also Parker, *Reminiscences*, pp. 216–228; Hill, "Memoir," pp. 136–42).

17. *The Trial of Albert J. Tirrell*, pp. 28–31, 30 (quotation).

18. Parker, *Reminiscences*, p. 155; Hill, *"Memoir,"* pp. 138–142. It was the idea of somnambulism that seems especially to have infuriated many people, although the foreman of the jury declared afterwards that they had not been swayed by it. Apparently, the idea was suggested to Choate by Tirrell's relations, and Choate evidently found it sufficiently convincing to use it in Tirrell's second trial, this time for arson, in which he was also acquitted. The idea may not in fact be as outlandish as it appears: a Toronto psychiatrist, Alexander Bonkalo, believes that there is "a confused mental state between sleep and full consciousness during which normal people can sometimes commit acts of extreme violence"

and has collected a number of cases of homicide committed while the perpetrator was apparently asleep (Margie Casady, "The Sleepy Murderers," *Psychology Today* [Jan. 1976], pp. 79–83). Tirrell at any rate was impressed with the evidence of his own innocence. After his second acquittal he called on Choate and suggested that half the fee be returned since his lack of guilt was so obvious to two juries (Brown, *Life,* p. 170 n. 1).

19. Parker, *Reminiscences,* pp. 137, 216; Wendell Phillips, "Idols" (1859), in *Speeches, Lectures, and Letters,* (Boston, 1863), pp. 242–262, 254 (quotation). Many people felt that it was his experience with Tirrell that caused Choate to turn down the defense of Professor Webster in the murder of Dr. Parkman, although urged to take it. However, the reason appears to have been merely that Choate felt the only possible hope of success lay in a plea of manslaughter and Webster refused to consider this (George S. Boutwell, *The Lawyer, the Statesman and the Soldier,* [New York, 1887], pp. 11–12; Neilson, *Memories,* pp. 16–20). At Choate's death, in a eulogy before the Suffolk Bar, Benjamin R. Curtis found it necessary to issue a great defense of the duty of the advocate, in the Anglo-American system, to make as good a case for his client as he possibly can (quoted in Brown, *Life,* pp. 367–371).

20. Choate to Jeremiah Day, President of Yale, Aug. 22, 1844, Beinecke Library, Yale University, New Haven, Conn.; Chief Justice Shaw, in Brown, *Life,* pp. 182–188; Carl Brent Swisher, *Roger B. Taney: Jacksonian Jurist* (New York, 1935), p. 524.

21. Dr. Boyden to Brown, Jan. 18, 1860, Brown MSS; Nathan Crosby in Neilson, *Memories,* p. 349; Parker, *Reminiscences,* p. 299.

22. Brown, *Life,* p. 268; John D. Cogswell, *Memoir of Rufus Choate,* rpt. from the *Memorial Biographies of the New England Historic Genealogical Society* (Cambridge, Mass., 1884), pp. 428–429; J. L. Thorndike to Brown, n.d., Brown MSS.

23. The case before the Supreme Court was Thurlow v. Massachusetts, 46 U.S. (5 How.), 504 (1847); Claude M. Fuess, *Rufus Choate: The Wizard of the Law* (New York, 1928), pp. 161–162; Maurice G. Baxter, *Daniel Webster and the Supreme Court* (Amherst, 1966), pp. 213–217; for Fisher v. McGirr see 78 Mass. (1 Gray) 1 (1854) and Leonard W. Levy, *The Law of the Commonwealth and Chief Justice Shaw* (Cambridge, Mass., 1957), pp. 283–289. Choate's argument, *"Hon. Rufus Choate's Argument on the Constitutionality of the Massachusetts Anti-Liquor Law,"* was printed as an extra to the *Massachusetts Life Boat,* n.d., [Jan. 20, 1854]. A similar case involving the police power of the state and its relationship to the power of Congress to regulate commerce, was Norris v. City of Boston (1842). Choate, appearing for Norris, challenged a Massachusetts law, requiring captains landing alien passengers at Boston to pay $2.00 per head, as unconstitutional since it infringed the right of the federal government to regulate commerce (45 Mass. [4 Met.] 282 [1842]). He lost the case but it was appealed to the Supreme Court, where it was argued together with a similar case—the "passenger cases" (48 U.S. [7 Howard] 283 [1849]). Choate appeared with Webster, who led the attack, also concentrating on the commerce clause. The court by a bare majority overruled the Massachusetts decision and declared the passenger laws unconstitutional. The case aroused great interest since it had implications for the regulations of Southern states prohibiting free blacks from landing at Southern ports. One unfortunate effect of this decision was to make

it difficult for the states to regulate anything which might be construed as inter-
state commerce, and since the national government was reluctant to use its power
in this connection, this left a considerable gap (Baxter, *Daniel Webster*, pp.
218–226; Levy, *Law of the Commonwealth*, pp. 237–241; Fuess, *Rufus Choate*, pp.
162–163; Choate's arguments are not reported in either Metcalf or Howard).

24. Choate, Journal, June 24, 1843, June 23, 1844, n.d. (July-Aug. 1844),
in Brown, *Life*, pp. 97–98, 118–119, 121; Parker, *Reminiscences*, p. 265.

25. Roscoe Pound, *The Formative Era of American Law* (Boston, 1938), pp.
8, 81–82; Bernard Schwartz, *The Law in America* (New York, 1974), pp. 52–55;
James Willard Hurst, *Law and the Conditions of Freedom* (Madison, Wisc., 1956),
pp. 22–29; Miller, *Life of the Mind*, pp. 223–230; Levy, *Law of the Commonwealth*,
pp. 162–165. For the way in which the law served as a resource allocator and
operated to benefit dynamic and productive enterprise, particularly through the
granting of eminent domain to transportation and manufacturing corporations
and granting them a certain immunity to nuisance trespass and tort suits, see
Harry N. Scheiber, "Property Law, Expropriation, and Resource Allocation by
Government: The United States, 1789–1910," *Journal of Economic History*,
XXXIII (March 1973), pp. 232–251; also Scheiber, "The Road to Munn: Eminent domain and the Concept of Public Purpose in the State Courts," in *Law in
American History*, ed. D. Fleming and B. Bailyn (Boston, 1971), pp. 329–402,
esp. 364ff. Morton J. Horwitz argues persuasively that the legal system in ante-
bellum America operated to subsidize economic growth by shifting a dispropor-
tionate share of its costs onto the less economically dynamic segments of the
population (*The Transformation of American Law, 1780–1860* [Cambridge, Mass.,
1977], ch. 3).

26. Choate, *Abstract of the Arguments of the Hon. Rufus Choate and William D.
Northend, Esq., for the Petitioners, on the Petitions of Benjamin Goodridge, and 5,322
Other Legal Voters, for a Railroad from Danvers to Malden, before the Committee on
Railways and Canals, of the Massachusetts Legislature . . .* (Boston, 1847), p. 27;
Edward Chase Kirkland, *Men, Cities and Transportation: A Study in New England
History, 1820–1900* (Cambridge, Mass., 1948), I, 267–273, 284–285.

27. Boston & L. R. R. v. Salem & L. R. R., 68 Mass. (2 Gray) 1 (1854);
Levy, *Law of the Commonwealth*, pp. 124–126. In a somewhat similar case Choate
appeared before a legislative committee on behalf of the Essex Railroad and
asked that it be protected against the "fatal competition" of a parallel road
(*Application of the Salem and Lowell Railroad company for a parallel and competing
railroad from Salem to Danvers. . . . : Speech of Hon. Rufus Choate before the Joint
Legislative Railroad Committee, Boston, Feb. 28, 1851* [Boston, 1851], p. 10).

28. Kirkland, *Men, Cities, and Transportation*, p. 271; *Application of Robert
Codman and Others for a Railroad between South Dedham and Boston, Making a
Connection with the Norfolk County Road: Speech of Rufus Choate before a Legislative
Committee, Boston, March 26, 1850* (Boston, 1850), p. 34.

29. *Abstract of the Arguments of Hon. Rufus Choate and William D. Northend*
pp. 26, 28. The phrase "the middling man" is from *Argument for the Division of
Worcester County, on the Petition of O. L. Huntley and Others, before Legislative Committee, April 1854, by Hon. Rufus Choate* (Boston, 1854), p. 66. In spite of this
common-sense approach, however, Choate too, when in full cry before a jury,
was not above scare tactics on the dire consequences if the sanctity of contracts

was forgotten. On one occasion, speaking for a defendant corporation, he closed with the warning: "I know we're unpopular. . . . But let me say that when it shall come to pass that contracts can be set aside, in a court of law, because they're unpopular, our whole social organization will tumble to the ground. Only let me remind you, that the house you live in, Mr. Foreman, is yours and not mine, only by *contract.* The bed you sleep on, and you and you (looking at the successive jurymen) is yours and not mine, only—by contract; and when I say, it shall happen that contracts are legally evaded, there will be the real red republicanism in full riot among us—Red Republicanism! Yes, *scarlet red"* (Parker, *Reminiscences,* pp. 461–462).

30. *Abstract of the Arguments of the Hon. Rufus Choate and Charles Theo. Russell, Esq., for the Petitioners, on the Petition of David Pingree, and Over 3,000 Other Legal Voters, for a Railroad from Salem to Malden, before the Committee on Railways and Canals of the Massachusetts legislature . . . 1846* (Boston, 1846), p. 59. Choate seemed to fight cases involving productive enterprise, or the man who was making "two blades of grass grow where one grew before" (one of his favorite phrases), with particular enthusiasm. See, for example, *Day. v. Berkshire Woolen Co., U.S. Circuit Court, District of Mass., 1849.* A new dam built by Day for a new factory had been destroyed by employees of the woolen mill upstream on the grounds that it interfered with their operations. Choate urged the jury to remember that Day was a bold entrepreneur who was providing new opportunities for capital and labor—he represented *new* enterprise, that the old corporation was operating to block. There is a phonographic report of this trial inserted in the copy of E. S. Chesbrough and C. E. Durant, *Letters on Hydraulics* (New York, 1849), in the Boston Athenaeum. Choate's address to the jury is pp. 391–464.

31. There were fifty-seven patent cases before the Supreme Court between 1816 and 1835, 395 between 1836 and 1859 (Charles Warren, *A History of the American Bar* [New York, 1966], p. 457). For hostility to the "monopoly" of patents, see, for example, *New York Tribune,* Sept. 18, 1848, quoted in Carleton Mabee, *The American Leonardo: A Life of Samuel F. B. Morse* (New York, 1969; 1st pub., 1943), p. 308. This hostility can perhaps be seen in another patent case in which Choate was involved, Colt v. Massachusetts Arms Co., F. Cas. 161 (No. 3030) (C.C.D. Mass., 1851). Choate was counsel for the defendant, though he was ill for the trial, which was conducted by his junior. The jury found for Colt, but they awarded him damages of only $1.00 (Martin Rywell, *The Trial of Samuel Colt* [Harriman, Tenn., 1953], pp. 256, 327).

32. *Report of the Case of William W. Woodworth as Administrator etc. v. Rudolphus C. Edwards et al.* (Auburn, 1848), p. 187. Choate's first appearance before the Supreme Court had been in a patent case—which he lost (Prouty v. Draper, 41 U.S. [16 Pet.] 336 [1842]).

33. The cases involving the Morse telegraph patent in which Choate was involved were Smith v. Downing, 22 F. Cas. 511 (No. 13036) (C.C.D. Mass. 1850) and Smith v. Clark 22 F. Cas. 487 (No. 13027) (C.C.D. Mass. 1850), both argued in Boston in 1850 before the U.S. Circuit Court. There is a largely illegible MS brief for Smith v. Downing in Brown MSS, and a letter from William F. Channing, June 19, 1850, describing the past history of the discovery of electromagnetism and giving the priority to Royal E. House of Vermont. See also, Mabee, *American Leonardo,* pp. 307–317. The decisive Supreme Court case

vindicating Morse was O'Reilly v. Morse (56 U.S. 15 How.) 61 (1854).
34. 10 F. Cas. 678 (No. 5569) (C.C.D. N.J., 1852); Baxter, *Daniel Webster,* pp. 153–154; Ralph F. Wolf, *India Rubber Man: The Story of Charles Goodyear* (Caldwell, Idaho, 1939), pp. 179–202; Parker, *Reminiscences,* p. 273; Black, "Rufus Choate," p. 448; Miller, *Life of the Mind,* pp. 177–182. Miller remarks (p. 178) that Webster and Choate appearing on opposite sides indicates that "even at this date the self-advertised 'conservatives' could not entirely agree about patents." I imagine it means merely that Choate argued the case for which he was hired and held out for a jury trial because he thought it more likely he could win before a jury. Choate's speech is entirely lost: although remarked on in the press, it was not reported. There is, however, a printed brief (*Circuit Court of the U.S. Horace H. Day ads. Charles Goodyear. In Equity. Points for the Defendant* [New York, 1852]).

35. Commonwealth vs. the Farmers & Mechanics Bank, 38 Mass. (21 Pick.) 542 (1839), 546 (quotation); Levy, *Law of the Commonwealth,* pp. 242–244, 310.

36. 74 Mass. (8 Gray) 45 (1857); Parker, *Reminiscences,* p. 211.

37. Brown, *Life,* p. 421; Levy, *Law of the Commonwealth,* pp. 154–155.

38. Levy, *Law of the Commonwealth,* pp. 154–155, 166–182, 164–165. For a general discussion of the significance of the "rise of the negligence principle" in American law, see Horwitz, *Transformation,* pp. 85–99; and for Farwell v. Boston & W. R. R., see pp. 209–210.

39. *Argument for the Division of Worcester County, before a Legislative Committee, by Hon. Rufus Choate, in Senate Chamber, April 1856* (n.pub. , n.d.), p. 5. See also *Argument for the Division of Worcester County . . . April 1854.*

40. *Argument for the Division of Worcester County . . . 1856,* p. 6; *Reply to Mr. Choate's Argument, for the Division of Worcester County . . . by a Citizen of Worcester County* (Worcester, 1855), p. 23.

41. Donald G. Mathews, *Slavery and Methodism: A Chapter in American Morality, 1780–1845* (Princeton, N.J., 1965), pp. 247–282, 269 (quotation). The case, Bascom v. Lane is in 2 F. Cas. 994 (No. 1089) (C.C.D.N.Y. 1851). A complete stenographic report of the trial was also printed: *The Methodist Church Property Case . . . May 17–29, 1851,* by R. Sutton, Special and Congressional Reporter (Richmond and Louisville, 1851). See also Brown, *Life,* pp. 242–244.

42. Enoch L. Fancher, Choate's junior in the case, in Neilson, *Memories,* p. 257; Mathews, *Slavery,* p. 282; Choate, *The Methodist Church Property Case,* p. 231.

43. Choate, *The Methodist Church Property Case,* pp. 235, 257.

44. *Ibid.,* pp. 236–239, 268, 291; Parker, *Reminiscences,* pp. 201–202.

45. Fancher, in Neilson, *Memories,* p. 258; Parker, *Reminiscences,* pp. 201–202; Choate, Speech at Salem, Sept. 28, 1848, in *Salem Register,* Oct. 2, 1848.

46. Thomas H. O'Connor, *Lords of the Loom: The Cotton Whigs and the Coming of the Civil War* (New York, 1968), pp. 77–81; Kinley J. Brauer, *Cotton versus Conscience* (Lexington, Ky., 1967) pp. 229–245; Frank Otto Gatell, "Conscience and Judgment: The Bolt of the Massachusetts Conscience Whigs," *The Historian,* LXXI (Nov. 1958), 18–45; Henry Wilson, *History of the Rise and Fall of the Slave Power in America* (New York, 1969; 1st pub., 1872), II, 135–139.

47. *Atlas,* June 12, 1848; O'Connor, *Lords,* pp. 77–78. Lawrence, who had once told Edward Everett, "Mr. Everett, we shall live to see the banks of the Upper Mississippi connected by iron bands with State Street," after detailing his

property and investments to John Davis, explained "my interests are those of the whole country, and cannot be separated" (Lawrence to Davis, Feb. 3, 1849, John Davis MSS, American Antiquarian Society, Worcester, Mass.; Hamilton Andrews Hill, *Memoir of Abbott Lawrence* [Boston, 1883], p. 13).

48. Charles Sumner to Nathan Appleton, Aug. 31, 1848, Charles Sumner MSS, Boston Public Library; *Boston Courier,* June 17, 1848.

49. Choate, Speech at Salem, Sept. 28, 1848; Speech at Worcester, Sept., 1848, *Speeches of Rufus Choate and R. C. Winthrop, at the Whig State Convention . . .* (n.pub., n.d. [1848]), p. 2.

50. Choate, Speech to Taylor Club of Salem, Oct. 17, 1848, in Brown, *Life,* p. 181; "Warrington," *Boston Daily Republican,* Oct. 5, 1848, in Robinson, ed., *"Warrington" Pen Portraits,* pp. 185–186.

51. Brown, *Life,* p. 182. A letter from Choate to Sumner of 1851 congratulating him on a speech on Kossuth, begins "My Dear Sir," not "Dear Sumner" as in the past (Charles Sumner MSS, Houghton Library, Harvard University, Cambridge, Mass.); O'Connor, *Lords,* pp. 80–82. David Donald credits Sumner with a decisive role in steering the Massachusetts Free-Soilers into a coalition with Massachusetts Democrats rather than attempting a reconciliation with the Whigs (David Donald, *Charles Sumner and the Coming of the Civil War* (New York, 1961), pp. 178–182); Abbott Lawrence to John Davis, Feb. 3, 1849, Davis MSS.

52. *An Appeal to the Whig National Convention, in Favor of the Nomination of Daniel Webster to the Presidency,* By "A Whig from the Start" [John Calvin Adams] (New York, 1848); *Atlas,* July 10, 1848. For the increasing Whig reliance on constitutionalism, see Rush Welter, *The Mind of America, 1820–60* (New York, 1975), pp. 201–211.

53. Choate, "The Position and Functions of the American Bar, as an Element of Conservatism in the State" (1845), in Brown, *Works,* I, 414–438, 436–437 (quotation). The Coleridge quotation is from *The Friend*—with slight verbal changes by Choate. See Perry Miller, ed., *The Legal Mind in America from Independence to the Civil War* (New York, 1962), p. 272 n. 5.

54. See, for example, William Wirt on law-as-restraint as the essential principle of the physical and the moral worlds, quoted in Miller, *Life of the Mind,* p. 210. In an essay upon "the meaning of America," Robert Wiebe has suggested that the American preoccupation with constitutional forms and legal structure was the inevitable response to a society segmented into discrete compartments each pursuing its own interests and demanding security from intrusion. When the segments unavoidably met, they needed a simple set of commonly accepted rules and an arbiter—the law. "If the Constitution and Supreme Court guaranteed a common American game, an array of very specific laws provided the rules by which participants must play. The former would hold them together, the latter apart" (Robert Wiebe, *The Segmented Society* [New York, 1975], pp. 19–23, 146–154, 150 [quotation]).

55. Choate, "Position and Functions," p. 435.

56. Harry V. Jaffa, *The Conditions of Freedom: Essays in Political Philosophy* (Baltimore, 1975), pp. 108–109; Miller, *Life of the Mind,* pp. 226–230.

57. Miller, *Life of the Mind,* pp. 207–238; Sparks is quoted in Harvey Wish, *The American Historian* (New York, 1960), p. 48.

58. William A. Hackett, "Sketch of the Life and Character of John Jay," *American Review (American Whig Review)*, II (1845), 59; Choate, "Position and Functions," p. 420. The voluntary self-limitation of the people through constitutional forms became a very live issue during the Dorr war in Rhode Island. In a case arising from that affair, Luther v. Borden, argued before the Supreme Court in 1848, Benjamin Hallett for the Dorrite plaintiff said that what was at stake was "whether the theory of American free government for the States of this Union is available to the people in practice; in short, whether the basis of popular sovereignty is a living principle, or a theory." The people, he argued, should never relinquish their right to originate and amend their governments directly, for the moment that they merely accepted or rejected amendments framed by the legislature, they were no longer sovereign. "For this is the vital distinction between the American principle of free institutions, and the European principle of *legitimate* government" (*The Right of the People to Establish Forms of Government: Mr. Hallett's Argument in the Rhode Island Causes*. . . . [Boston, 1848], pp. 7, 47).

59. Choate in the Senate, Feb. 18, 1845, U.S., Congress, Senate, *Congressional Globe*, 28th Cong., 2nd sess., XIV, 304; Story, in his *Commentaries on the Constitution* pointed out that a constitution, though *originating* in consent, "becomes, when ratified, obligatory, as a fundamental ordinance or law" and ∤ derived its "obligatory force as a *law* and not as a compact" (in Elizabeth Kelley Bauer, *Commentaries on the Constitution, 1790–1860* [New York, 1952], pp. 281–282).

60. Professor Greenleaf opened his introductory lecture at the Cambridge Law School with this definition of law from Lieber's *Political Ethics* ("Notes of Professor Greenleaf's Introductory Lecture at the Present Term," *The Law Reporter*, I [Dec. 1838], pp. 217–223, 217 [quotation]; Roscoe Pound, *The Spirit of the Common Law* [Boston, 1921], p. 150; Choate, "Position and Functions," p. 430).

61. Miller, *Life of the Mind*, pp. 239–265; Daniel Boorstin, *The Americans: The National Experience* (New York, 1965), pp. 36–42; Roscoe Pound, *The Place of Judge Story in the Making of American Law* (Cambridge, 1914), pp. 39–50. The emphasis on law as a "science" discoverable by reason, as Morton Horwitz points out, legitimates the professional lawyer as an expert and removes from him any taint of political motivation (Morton J. Horwitz, "The Conservative Tradition in the Writing of American Legal History," *The American Journal of Legal History*, XVII [1973], pp. 275–294).

62. Choate, "Position and Functions," p. 436. Choate's language here, though extravagant, was by no means isolated in its mystical reverence for law. Compare, for example, Horace Bushnell in 1837: "Law is uttered by the National Life—not by some monarch, magistrate, or legislature, of to-day, or of any day, but by the state; by that organic force of which kings, magistrates, legislatures, of all times, have been but the hands, and feet, and living instruments" ("The True Wealth or Weal of Nations" [Yale, 1837], in *Representative Phi Beta Kappa Orations* ed. Clark S. Northup, William C. Lane and John C. Schwab [Boston, 1915], pp. 17–18). Whigs were fond of quoting Hooker on Law, whose "voice is the harmony of the world and whose seat is in the bosom of God" (see, for example, George Ticknor Curtis, *The True Uses of American Revolutionary*

History [Boston, 1841], p. 28); James T. Fields, in Neilson, *Memories,* p. 303.

63. Choate, "Position and Functions," p. 432. Choate was an admirer and student of the civil as well as the common law (R. S. Storrs in Neilson, *Memories,* p. 285). Although, according to Roscoe Pound (*The Spirit of the Common Law,* p. 154), the German historical school of jurisprudence had little influence in the United States till after 1870, certainly to see law as essentially growing out of historical experience seems to have been common in the 1840s. Even the federal constitution could be interpreted as an evolved, rather than made, structure. See, for example, the Review of the Madison Papers in *American Jurist* (Jan. 1842) by E. L. C., who maintained that the Constitution "was not an artificial structure invented by the genius of the patriot statesmen of the Convention," but a "representation of the political and moral condition of the people of the United States." Its history could not be found merely in the Journals of the Convention, "you might as well seek to trace every change which the majestic oak has undergone, since its embryo first appeared in the acorn" (p. 395).

64. Rev. J. M. Marsters to Brown, May 7, 1862, Brown MSS.

65. Choate, "Position and Functions," pp. 416, 437–438.

66. Abraham Lincoln, "Address before the Young Men's Lyceum of Springfield" (1838), *Collected Works,* ed. Roy P. Basler (9 vols; New Brunswick, N.J., 1953–1955) I, 108–115, 112 (quotation); for the importance of the idea of paternal authority in conservative thought, see Hanna Fenichel Pitkin, "The Roots of Conservatism: Michael Oakeshott and the Denial of Politics," in *The New Conservatives: A Critique from the Left,* ed. Lewis A. Coser and Irving Howe, (New York, 1974), pp. 243–288.

67. Greenleaf, "Introductory Lecture," pp. 217, 218. In fact, one of the most striking legal developments in the first half of the nineteenth century was the extent to which "common law judges regularly thought about the sort of far-reaching changes that would have been regarded earlier as entirely within the powers of the legislature" (Horwitz, *Transformation,* pp. 1–2). There had also been, in the early years of the century, a significant shift in the balance of power between judge and jury as the function of finding the law became the prerogative of the judge, who now instructed the jury (William Nelson, *The Americanization of the Common Law: The Impact of Legal Change on Massachusetts Society, 1760–1830* [Cambridge, Mass., 1975], pp. 86–88).

68. Choate, "Position and Functions," pp. 429–430. Michael Oakeshott describes political activity as "the amendment of existing arrangements by exploring and pursuing what is intimated in them." This might apply equally well to the activity of judges in the Anglo-American legal system (Michael Oakeshott, *Rationalism in Politics* [New York, 1962], pp. 123–124).

69. Carl J. Friedrich, *Tradition and Authority* (New York, 1972), pp. 80–81; Miller, *Life of the Mind,* pp. 233–238.

70. The judiciary was made elective in Georgia (1777), in Mississippi (1832), in New York (1845), in Wisconsin (1848), in California (1849), in Kentucky, Michigan, Missouri, Pennsylvania and Virginia (1850), in Indiana, Maryland and Ohio (1851), in Louisiana (1852), in Tennessee (1853), in Kansas (1855), and in Iowa, Minnesota and Oregon (1857) (Francis R. Aumann, *The Changing American Legal System: Some Selected Phases* [Columbus, 1940], p. 186); Welter, *Mind of America,* pp. 212–218. Judges were not, in fact, always politically

impartial: the judiciary of Rhode Island, for example, openly took sides against the Dorrites (John S. Schuchman, "The Political Background of the Political-Question Doctrine: The Judges and the Dorr War," *The American Journal of Legal History*, XVI [1972], 111–125).

71. "The New Constitution: Article VI—the Judiciary," *The American Review (The American Whig Review)*, IV (Nov. 1846), 520–531.

72. See the protests in *Review of the Proceedings*, pp. 24–31, and *The Law Reporter*, VII (July 1844), 113–114. The Dorr war considerably excited sympathies in Massachusetts, the Democrats supporting Dorr, the Whigs, the Charter government. Choate defended three members of the Rhode Island Militia indicted for forcibly kidnapping several supporters of Dorr, who had taken refuge in Massachusetts, and taking them back to imprisonment in Rhode Island. He contended that the violation of due process was justifiable as an act of necessity during a rebellion (Commonwealth v. Blodgett, *The Law Reporter*, VI [1843], 120–121; *Boston Daily Advertiser*, April 28, 1843).

73. *Proceedings of the Senate and House of Representatives, upon the Petition of George R. M. Withington and Others, Praying That James G. Carter Be Removed from his Office of Justice of the Peace. . . .* (Boston, 1849); *Boston Post*, April 5, 1849. Choate's speech for Carter is also partially reproduced in Parker, *Reminiscences*, pp. 394–411. Choate's "Argument on the removal of Judge Davis of Maine" is in Brown, *Works*, II, 342–386. The circumstances of the case are in Louis Clinton Hatch, *Maine: A History* (Somersworth, N.H., 1974; 1st pub., New York, 1919), pp. 391–396. Choate's junior counsel was Richard Henry Dana, Jr., who appears to have done most of the preparation for the case (Dana, entries for April 1856, *Journal*, ed. Robert F. Lucid [3 vols.; Cambridge, Mass., 1968], II, 687–688).

74. *Proceedings of the Senate and House*, pp. 7, 9; "Argument on the Removal of Judge Davis," in Brown, *Works*, II, 370, 354. In spite of Choate, the legislature went ahead with the address; Davis then appealed the case to the supreme court of Maine. Dana, in the *Monthly Law Reporter*, exhorted them: "Never to our recollection, since the grand American principle of constitutional authority over legislatures and executive magistrates sprang into being, has the judiciary of a State been charged with a more momentous duty" ("On the Removal of Judge Woodbury Davis," *Monthly Law Reporter*, XCI [June 1856], 61–83, 83 [quotation]). The court, however, decided that it had no jurisdiction (Hatch, *Maine*, p. 396).

75. Samuel Shapiro, "The Conservative Dilemma: The Massachusetts Constitutional Convention of 1853," *New England Quarterly*, XXXIII (June 1960), 207–224.

76. *Proceedings of the Whig State Convention, . . . September 10, 1851* (n.pub., n.d.), pp. 18–19. The Central Committee by 1853 was being cautiously favorable (see Jean Carol Kenney, "An Analysis of Political Alignments in Massachusetts as revealed in the Constitutional Convention of 1853" [M.A. thesis, Smith College, 1951], pp. 28–29). The *Atlas* is quoted in William G. Bean, "The Transformation of Parties in Massachusetts with Special Reference to the Antecedents of Republicanism from 1848 to 1862" (Ph.D. diss., Harvard University, 1922), p. 147; see also Edward Everett to Harvey Jewell, Feb. 5, 1853, Harvey Jewell MSS, Boston Athenaeum.

77. Shapiro, "Conservative Dilemma," pp. 210–211; Michel Brunet, "The

Secret Ballot Issue in Massachusetts Politics from 1851 to 1853," *New England Quarterly*, XXV (Sept. 1952), 354–362. Whigs always insisted that if the urban working class tended to vote the same way as their employers this was not because they were intimidated but because they had "the intelligence to perceive that the interests of all classes are in harmony." (*Answer of the Whig Members of the Legislature of Massachusetts . . . to the Address of his Excellency Marcus Morton . . . January 22, 1840* [Boston, 1840] p. 29). In the convention, however, it was alleged that the manager of the Boott mills had warned his workers they would be sacked if they voted the coalition ticket (Shapiro, "Conservative Dilemma," p. 211 n. 14).

78. Lists of the delegates with occupations are in Alexis Poole, *Statistical View of the Executive and Legislative Departments of the Government of Massachusetts 1853* (Boston, 1853), pp. 17–26. The complete debates in the Convention were published in three volumes: *Official Report of the Debates and Proceedings in the State Convention, Assembled May 4th, 1853. . . .* (Boston, 1853). Besides Shapiro and Kenney, cited above, the fullest accounts are Samuel Eliot Morison, *A Manual for the Constitutional Convention, 1917* (Boston, 1917), pp. 41–63; and James Schouler, "The Massachusetts Convention of 1853," *Massachusetts Historical Society Proceedings*, XVIII (Nov. 1903), 30–48.

79. *Official Report*, I, 116–121, 121, 120 (quotation); Ernest McKay, *Henry Wilson, Practical Radical: A Portrait of a Politician* (Port Washington, N.Y., 1971), p. 81.

80. Shapiro, "Conservative Dilemma," pp. 208–210, 212–214. Rural areas tended to regard political power as having been *stolen* from them by the "money power of State Street" and the "State Street cabal, called the 'Suffolk Whig Nominating Convention'" (*Inequality of the Old Constitution, Advantages of the New* [n.pub., n.d.] (1853)).

81. *Official Report*, I, 927; Choate's speech, pp. 876–891, 887, 881, 884, 882, 883 (quotations). Lincoln regarded the declaration that "all men are created equal" as setting up "a standard maxim for free society . . . constantly looked to, constantly labored for, and even though never perfectly attained, constantly approximated" ([1857], *Collected Works*, II, 406).

82. *Official Report*, I, 887, 891.

83. George F. Hoar, *Autobiography of Seventy Years* (New York, 1903), I, 172; Morison, *Manual for the Constitutional Convention*, pp. 54–55; *Official Report*, II, 828; Shapiro, "Conservative Dilemma," pp. 214–215. The *Sims* case (see Chapter 5) was frequently cited in the debate on the independence of the judiciary (Richard M. Cover, *Justice Accused: Antislavery and the Judicial Process* [New Haven, 1975], pp. 177–178).

84. Dana, entry for July 17, 1853, *Journal*, II, 557; Joseph H. Choate, *Address delivered at the Unveiling of the Statue of Rufus Choate in the Court House in Boston, October 15, 1898* (Boston, 1899), pp. 25–26.

85. Choate's speech on the judiciary is in *Official Report*, II, 799–810, and also in Brown, *Works*, II, 284–310. I have quoted from the latter (pp. 286, 287, 288, 299). For the importance to the self-image of the legal profession that it be, and be *seen* to be, learned, see Miller, *Life of the Mind*, pp. 134–143.

86. Choate, in Brown, *Works*, II, 310, 308.

87. Dana, entries for August 2, July 17, 1853, *Journal*, II, 558, 557; Mori-

son, *Manual for the Constitutional Convention,* pp. 60–65; Shapiro, "Conservative Dilemma," pp. 219–224; *Official Report,* III, 685–693;

88. Schouler, "Massachusetts Convention," p. 38; Morison, *Manual for the Constitutional Convention,* pp. 60–63; Hoar, *Autobiography,* pp. 175–178. Hoar points out that one of the effects of making sheriffs and district attorneys elective was that it made it difficult to enforce unpopular laws such as the liquor laws and the laws regulating the employment of children in factories. The final vote for and against the constitution, county by county, is in *Official Report,* III, Appendix, pp. 756–767. As Jean Carol Kenney points out, the fact that the vote for the Whig gubernatorial candidate exceeded the vote against the constitution in all the western counties indicates that some western Whigs crossed party lines and voted for the constitution (Kenney, "Analysis of Political Alignments," p. 90).

89. Dana, entry for August 2, 1853, *Journal,* II, 565.

90. (George Ticknor Curtis), "Letters of Phocion," *Boston Daily Advertiser* and *Courier,* Aug.–Nov. 1853, in *Discussions on the Constitution Proposed to the People of Massachusetts by the Convention of 1853* (Boston, 1854), p. 77; Charles Francis Adams, "Address to the Citizens of Quincy . . . November 5, 1853," in *ibid.* p. 237.

CHAPTER FIVE. SLAVERY AND THE UNION

1. Choate to James Marsh, March 12, 1837, copy in Samuel Gilman Brown MSS, Houghton Library, Harvard University, Cambridge, Mass.

2. Thomas H. O'Connor, *Lords of the Loom: The Cotton Whigs and the Coming of the Civil War* (New York, 1968), pp. 83–85; Martin Duberman, *Charles Francis Adams, 1807–1886* (Cambridge, Mass., 1961), pp. 166–167; David Donald, *Charles Sumner and the Coming of the Civil War* (New York, 1961), pp. 184–185.

3. Robert Winthrop to John Clifford, March 10, 1850, Robert C. Winthrop MSS, Massachusetts Historical Society, Boston, Mass, Vol. XXXV; Edward Everett to Winthrop, March 21, 1850, *ibid.*

4. Letter to Hon. Daniel Webster, April 2, 1850, signed by Choate and others, appeared in the *Boston Daily Advertiser* and is reprinted in Samuel J. May, *Some Recollections of Our Antislavery Conflict* (Boston, 1869), p. 407; see also Edward Everett to Winthrop, May 8, 1850, Winthrop MSS, Vol. XXXV.

5. Edward L. Pierce, *Memoir and Letters of Charles Sumner* (Boston, 1893), pp. 111, 206–207; David D. Van Tassel, "Gentlemen of Property and Standing: Compromise Sentiment in Boston in 1850," *New England Quarterly,* XXIII (Sept. 1950), 307–319; Robert F. Dalzell, Jr., *Daniel Webster and the Trial of American Nationalism, 1843–1852* (Boston, 1973), pp. 214–222.

6. Samuel Gilman Brown, *The Works of Rufus Choate with a Memoir of His Life* (2 vols.; Boston, 1862), II, 311; *Proceedings of the Constitutional Meeting at Faneuil Hall, November 26, 1850* (Boston, 1850), p. 7. The Democratic leader, B. F. Hallett, also spoke and denounced any resistance to law as treason *(ibid.).*

7. Clement Hugh Hill, "Memoir of the Honorable Rufus Choate," *Massachusetts Historical Society Proceedings,* XI (1896–1897), 124–155; Thomas B. Alexander, *Sectional Stress and Party Strength: A Computer Analysis of Roll-Call Voting Patterns in the United States House of Representatives, 1836–1860* (Nashville, Tenn., 1967), pp. 111–112.

8. Jeremiah Mason to George Ticknor, April 3, 1836, *Memoirs of Jeremiah*

Mason, ed. G. S. Hillard (Boston, 1917), p. 350; Henry Adams, Review of *Life, Letters, and Journals of George Ticknor, North American Review,* CXXIII (July 1876), 214.

9. Choate, Speech delivered at the Constitutional Meeting in Faneuil Hall, Nov. 26, 1850, in Brown, *Works,* II, 311–326, 319 (quotation).

10. *Ibid.,* pp. 314, 315. Free-Soilers and anti-slavery men in general tended to ridicule fears for the Union as a mere political smoke-screen. *The Boston Daily Chronotype* referred to Choate's speech as "a most delicious piece of acting in a deeply tragic vein. Mr. Choate demonstrated the Union to be so fragile that it is really a miracle it has not been disintegrated long ago. What a mercy that this secret has been discovered while there is some dough left" (Nov. 27, 1850).

11. Choate at the Constitutional Meeting.

12. *Ibid.,* p. 312.

13. Edward Everett, Journal, July 15, 1851, Edward Everett MSS, Massachusetts Historical Society, Boston, Mass. Everett added, however, "there is something indescribably fascinating in his manner and matter. I think I have never listened to a public speaker who carried away his audience so completely;" Richard Henry Dana, Jr., entry for July 15, 1851, *Journal,* ed. Robert F. Lucid (3 vols.; Cambridge, Mass., 1968), II, 438. The Free-Soil *Boston Commonwealth* denounced the celebration as "little else than a hunker pro-slavery speech-making occasion" (quoted in the *Daily Advertiser,* July 21, 1851).

14. Choate's speech to the Story Association is reported in detail, though not exactly verbatim, in the *Boston Daily Advertiser,* July 17, 1851, and the *Boston Post,* July 16, 1851. There is also a very short extract in Brown, *Life,* pp. 245–246. The first quotation here is taken from the account in the *Advertiser,* the second from the extract in Brown, *Life,* p. 246. For the political implications involved in judicial decisions on the Fugitive Slave Law, see Robert M. Cover, *Justice Accused: Antislavery and the Judicial Process* (New Haven, 1975), pp. 217–252. Chief Justice Shaw, for example, in upholding the constitutionality of the Fugitive Slave Law, made much of the supposed "fact" that the thirteen states would never have been able to forge a Union in the first place without some kind of provision for the return of runaway slaves. A fugitive slave law was a necessity of Union; thus the question of the constitutionality of the 1850 law was fused with the question of its political expediency (see Leonard W. Levy, "Sims' Case: The Fugitive Slave Law in Boston," *The Journal of Negro History,* XXXV [Jan. 1950], 39–74). Similarly, the Dred Scott decision, as David Potter has pointed out, was a result of the Supreme Court deliberately seeking "to face a major public question and to exercise an influence on public affairs rather than to retreat into narrow legalism" (David Potter, *The Impending Crisis, 1848–1861* [New York, 1976], p. 286).

15. Choate to the Story Association, *Boston Post,* July 16, 1851. Coleridge, in his philosophical battle with Rousseau, insisted that the state was not a church and that the affairs of men must be guided not by pure reason or pure morality but by the political wisdom acquired through the understanding (David P. Calleo, *Coleridge and the Idea of the Modern State* [New Haven, 1966], pp. 66–67, 130–131). For the conservative apprehension of the potential ruthlessness of reformers, see Daniel Aaron, "Conservatism, Old and New," *American Quarterly,* VI (Summer 1954), 99–109, esp. 107–109.

16. Choate, Speech at the Massachusetts Whig Convention to nominate

Daniel Webster as presidential candidate, Faneuil Hall, Nov. 25, 1851. This quotation is taken from the shorthand version of the speech appearing in the *Boston Courier*, Nov. 26, 1851. Wendell Phillips, who sat in the gallery during the meeting, remembered the phrase as the "infamous ethics, that from the Declaration of Independence and the Sermon on the Mount deduced the duty of immediate emancipation" (Wendell Phillips, "Speech on the Surrender of Sims, Jan. 20, 1852," in *Speeches, Lectures and Letters* [Boston, 1863], p. 60). Possibly either the reporter or the editor of the *Courier* thought "infamous ethics" too strong a phrase that should be edited out. Phillips said that the remark was met with silence from the audience, "though Rufus Choate uttered it to an assembly of Webster Whigs."

17. Choate to the Story Association, in Brown, *Life*, p. 245.

18. Choate to the Story Association, *Boston Daily Advertiser*, July 17, 1851; *Boston Post*, July 16, 1851; Edward G. Parker, *Reminiscences of Rufus Choate, The Great American Advocate* (New York, 1860), p. 278. Many conservative clergy were quick to disavow the radical promptings of conscience. At the Pilgrim Celebration of 1853, for example, the Rev. George W. Blagden, of Boston, was careful to make it clear that while the Pilgrims were honored for following their conscience, this was not "a perverted or misguided conscience. . . . They are not, therefore, to be classed for a moment, in our minds, with the modern social fanatics of our day" (*An Account of the Pilgrim Celebration at Plymouth, August 1, 1853* [Boston, 1853], pp. 105, 106). The problem of individual conscience versus the law was particularly acute in the New England of the 1850s, but as Hegel recognized, it was a latent problem for modern societies in general (see the discussion in Judith N. Shklar, *Freedom and Independence* [Cambridge, 1976], pp. 81–88).

19. Choate to Charles Sumner, Dec. 21, 1851, Charles Sumner MSS, Houghton Library, Harvard University, Cambridge, Mass. For an account of the reaction to Kossuth in the United States, see Norman A. Graebner, *Ideas and Diplomacy: Readings in the Intellectual Tradition of American Foreign Policy* (New York, 1964), pp. 264–268. Generally Democrats were more likely than Whigs to favor some kind of American intervention, though there was considerable vagueness as to what form this would take. In Massachusetts the coalition-dominated legislature brought in a report stating that the American Revolution had not been merely a local event and that the United States was now a great power and could not remain insulated from events in the rest of the world (*Kossuth in New England: A Full Account of the Hungarian Governor's Visit to Massachusetts, . . . with His Speeches and the Addresses That Were Made to Him, Carefully Revised and Corrected* [Boston, 1852], pp. 289–307). To conservative Whigs like Abbott Lawrence, Democratic enthusiasm for intervention in European affairs was just another facet of their general lust for expansion. "It is evident," he wrote to Webster, "that we have arrived at a point in our history when all our wisdom will be required to prevent the acquisition of Mexico (and perhaps of other territory), and the adoption of the new doctrine of intervention" (Lawrence to Webster, Jan. 15, 1852, Hamilton Andrews Hill, *Memoir of Abbott Lawrence* [Boston, 1884], p. 89).

20. Choate, "Intervention of the New World in the Affairs of the Old,—the Duty, the Limitations, and the Modes," Address at the University of Ver-

mont, Aug. 1852. There is a short extract from the address in Brown, *Life,* pp. 260–263, but the fullest account is in the *New York Daily Times,* Aug. 9, 1852.

21. Choate to the Story Association, *Boston Daily Advertiser,* July 17, 1851, *Boston Post,* July 16, 1851. Cicero discusses the conflict and hierarchy of duties in *De Officiis,* particularly Book One. See, for example, *Cicero on Moral Obligation,* trans. John Higginbotham (Berkeley, 1967), esp. pp. 93–96.

Cicero had a prodigious influence on Western thought from the Renaissance throughout the eighteenth century, both as a stylist and a political moralist. In the nineteenth century his reputation began to decline somewhat—largely due to disparagement by the German historian of ancient Rome, Theodor Mommsen, who regarded him as a "trimmer." Choate, however, remained passionately loyal to Cicero, whom he said he never read without being "encouraged and strengthened; his views of life are always healthy and cheerful and sound." Edward Parker remarked that Choate always spoke with particular affection of Cicero. "He said nothing made him fret more than the modern German attacks on Cicero as a pusillanimous trimmer. He said he wanted to set Cicero *right* before the world." In an 1857 lecture called "The Eloquence of Revolutionary Periods," Choate praised Cicero extravagantly. The *New York Tribune* (Feb. 25, 1857), in noting the lecture, disputed his estimate and raised the accusation that Cicero had opposed Caesar until he was firmly in power and then flattered him. Choate, according to Parker, "took the matter up, exactly as if a warm personal friend of his own had been assailed," and got Parker to write some articles in reply which were published the following month in the *Boston Traveller* (Parker, *Reminiscences,* pp. 290, 82, 494–495); for Cicero's influence and reputation, see Higginbotham, "Preface," *Cicero on Moral Obligation,* trans. Higginbotham, pp. 24–30.

22. This sentiment occurs in the "Dream of Scipio" in Book 4 of *De Republica.* In the translation of Michael Grant it reads: "For of all things that are done on earth nothing is more acceptable to the Supreme God, who rules the whole universe, than those gatherings and assemblages of men who are bound together by law, the communities which are known as states" (*Cicero on the Good Life,* trans. Michael Grant [Middlesex, Eng. 1971], p. 344). Choate paraphrased this idea several times in his speeches (see, for example, Choate at the Constitutional Meeting, Nov. 26, 1850, p. 323). In a speech on Washington in February 1851, he quoted it to his audience in Latin (Brown, *Life,* p. 235).

23. Choate, "Address on Washington," Feb. 1851, in Brown, *Life,* pp. 232–238, 235–236 (quotations). This address was given twice, in Charlestown and in Boston.

24. Choate at the Constitutional Meeting, Nov. 26, 1850, pp. 322, 323, 324.

25. Choate to the Story Association; Choate, "Address on Washington," pp. 233–234; Choate in Faneuil Hall, Nov. 25, 1851, *Boston Courier,* Nov. 26, 1851.

26. Choate, "Address on Washington," pp. 237–238. The echoes of Burke in this passage are very strong, particularly of the famous passage in *Reflections on the Revolution in France* in which he laments the demise of chivalry, concluding with "to make us love our country, our country ought to be lovely" ([Everyman's Library ed.; London, 1910], p. 75). For the rescue of Shadrach, see Stanley W. Campbell, *The Slave Catchers: Enforcement of the Fugitive Slave Law, 1850–1860*

(New York, 1972; 1st pub., 1968), pp. 148–151. The rescue created considerable furor both in Boston and in Washington. President Fillmore issued a proclamation requiring all citizens to support the law. Eight people were arrested and brought to trial for the rescue, but none were convicted.

27. Choate at the Constitutional Meeting, Nov. 26, 1850, p. 319; Parker, *Reminiscences,* pp. 291–292.

28. Choate to Theophilus Parsons, n.d. (Feb. 1842), Rufus Choate MSS, Boston Public Library.

29. See Chapter One, p. 14; Charles White to Brown, Jan. 23, 1860, Brown MSS.

30. Moncure Conway, "Rufus Choate," *The Dial,* I (Aug. 1860), 457–469, 462 (quotation). The whole article is a violent attack (Parker, *Reminiscences,* p. 292).

31. "Reminiscences of Nathan Crosby," in Joseph Neilson, *Memories of Rufus Choate* (Boston, 1884), p. 351; Choate in Faneuil Hall, Nov. 25, 1851, *Boston Courier,* Nov. 26, 1851.

32. Edwin P. Whipple, *Some Recollections of Rufus Choate* (New York, 1879), pp. 47, 51; Rev. H. Winslow to Brown, Nov. 5, 1860; Rev. J. M. Marsters to Brown, May 7, 1862; Dr. Boyden to Brown, Jan. 18, 1860, all three in Brown MSS.

33. Whipple, *Some Recollections,* p. 44; Paulina Cony Drown, *Mrs. Bell* (Boston, 1931), p. 6; Bertrand Walker, *Rufus Choate* (Indianapolis, n.d.), p. 12. Though this pamphlet is undated, it is obviously by someone who had known Choate, at least slightly.

34. Robert F. Dalzell, Jr., *Daniel Webster and the Trial of American Nationalism, 1843–1852* (Boston, 1973), pp. 229–231; Peter Harvey, *Reminiscences and Anecdotes of Daniel Webster* (Boston, 1878), pp. 181–193; Choate to Webster, April 16, 1851, Daniel Webster MSS, Library of Congress, Washington, D.C.

35. Dalzell, *Daniel Webster,* pp. 231–242.

36. Choate in Faneuil Hall, Nov. 25, 1851, *Boston Courier,* Nov. 26, 1851.

37. Dalzell, *Daniel Webster,* pp. 255–258; Claude M. Fuess, *The Life of Daniel Webster* (2 vols; Hamden, Conn., 1963; 1st pub., 1930), II, 287; Francis Granger to Fillmore, June 30, 1852, quoted in Dalzell, p. 259. By September, however, Choate was telling Parker that there had never been "the shadow of a chance" for Webster's nomination (Parker, *Reminiscences,* pp. 259–260).

38. Henry Wilson, *The Rise and Fall of the Slave Power in America* (New York, 1969; 1st pub., 1872), II, 368–369; the resolutions were published in the *Boston Daily Advertiser,* June 24, 1852; see also John Clark to Brown, March 8, 1860, Brown MSS.

39. Choate's speech is in Brown, *Life,* pp. 251–259, 252–253, 256, 254, 257 (quotations).

40. Brown, *Life,* p. 258; Clark to Brown, March 8, 1860, Brown MSS; Parker, *Reminiscences,* pp. 65–66; *Boston Daily Advertiser,* June 17, 1852.

41. Brown, *Life,* p. 260; Dalzell, *Daniel Webster,* pp. 269–277.

42. Harvey, *Reminiscences,* pp. 195–197; Dalzell, *Daniel Webster,* pp. 285–295. Rumors were rife as to what the old-line Webster supporters would do. *The Boston Daily Bee* assured its readers that "the Choates, Everetts, Stevensons

and Curtises" were still true to Webster; at a pro-Webster meeting in August a supporter declared that Choate had told him "he would not go for Scott, but would go for Webster" (*The Boston Daily Bee*, Aug. 6, Aug. 25, 1852). Choate, himself, however, said nothing publicly.

43. Choate to Harvey Jewell, Oct. 30, 1852, in Brown, *Life*, pp. 265–267, 266–267 (quotation). Everett sent him a letter expressing similar sentiments (Everett to Jewell, Oct. 29, 1852, Harvey Jewell MSS, Boston Athenaeum).

44. Parker, *Reminiscences*, p. 66; Brown, *Life*, p. 269; *Boston Courier*, July 29, 1853; Charles Caverno, *Reminiscences of the Eulogy of Rufus Choate on Daniel Webster* (Boston, 1914), p. 12.

45. Parker, *Reminiscences*, pp. 67–68. The oration caught widespread attention. Henry Raymond of the *New York Times* travelled to Hanover personally to report the occasion and the eulogy was printed as delivered on the first two pages of the *Times* for July 30, 1853. On this occasion Choate gave Raymond both his manuscript and a clerk to help him decipher it—and also looked over the final copy himself (John C. Sterling, *Daniel Webster and a Small College* [Hanover, N.H., 1965], pp. 22–24).

46. Choate, "Discourse Commemorative of Daniel Webster: Delivered before the Faculty, Students, and Alumni of Dartmouth College, July 27, 1853," in Brown, *Works*, I, 493–558, 547 (quotation). It was through this oration that the words "It is, Sir, as I have said, a small College. *And yet, there are those who love it—,*" became part of the Webster legend. This statement had not been included in the reports of Webster's argument in the Dartmouth College case. But when the news that Choate was going to give a eulogy of Webster was announced, Chauncey A. Goodrich, the professor of rhetoric at Yale, who had been present in the court, sent him a detailed letter of reminiscence, including this quotation (Sterling, *Daniel Webster*, pp. 13–14; see also the letter of thanks from Choate to Goodrich, Dec. 4, 1852, Rufus Choate MSS, Yale University Library, New Haven, Conn.).

47. Choate, "Discourse Commemorative of Daniel Webster," pp. 552–558; Theodore Parker, "Discourse Occasioned by the Death of Daniel Webster," in *The Collected Works of Theodore Parker*, ed. Frances P. Cobbe, (London, 1863), XII, 10–107.

48. Choate, "Discourse Commemorative of Daniel Webster," pp. 553–554.

49. *Ibid.*, p. 534; Parker, *Reminiscences*, p. 67. "These *book men,*" Choate once burst out to Parker, "who know nothing *about affairs*, about actually *governing* men, and how difficult it is to steer,—for them to sit in their studies, and judge Cicero and Webster! It's absurd" (*ibid.*, p. 296).

50. O'Connor, *Lords of the Loom*, pp. 93–100; William G. Bean, "Party Transformations in Massachusetts, with Special Reference to Antecedents of the Republican Party, 1848–1860" (Ph.D. diss., Harvard University, 1932), pp. 184–186; Dana, entry for Feb. 11, 1854, *Journal*, II, 618–619.

51. Choate to Everett, March 1, 1854, Everett MSS; Brown, *Life*, p. 271; Dana, entry for March 27, 1854, *Journal*, II, 621–622. The letters from Choate to his daughter Sarah (1831–1875), who spent the summers of 1853 and 1854 in the country, indicate something less complete than "insanity" (see Choate to

Sarah Choate, Aug. 1853, July 9, 1854, Sept. 1854, in Brown, *Life,* pp. 270–271, 274–275, 276–277).

52. Choate to Everett, Feb. 4, 1854, in Brown, *Life,* pp. 272–273.

53. Paul Revere Frothingham, *Edward Everett: Orator and Statesman.* (Cambridge, Mass., 1925), pp. 347–349; Choate to Everett, March 1, 1854, Everett MSS.

54. O'Connor, *Lords of the Loom,* pp. 96–97; Levy, "Sims' Case," pp. 39–74; Dana, entry for April 13, 1851, *Journal,* II, 421–423.

55. Dana, entry for May 26, 1854, *Journal,* II, 628. Lawrence said he was "willing to pay to have some one besides R. H. Dana who is a free-soiler" (note reporting Dana's lack of success, in margin of letter from F. E. Parker to Amos A. Lawrence, May 27, 1854, Amos A. Lawrence MSS, Massachusetts Historical Society, Boston, Mass). It is not clear exactly what the "written opinions" that Choate referred to were, since they do not appear to have survived. Presumably one was the defense of Hallett's writ, on which he collaborated with Curtis. He may also have given advice to the commissioner, George Ticknor Curtis, in preparing his decision on the case. In that decision Curtis cited an early case in which Choate had argued the losing side, Commonwealth v. Farmers & Mechanics Bank, in answer to one of the objections of the prisoner's counsel (*Trial of Thomas Sims . . . Arguments of Robert Rantoul, Jr., and Charles G. Loring with the Decision of George T. Curtis, Boston, April 7–11, 1851* [Boston, 1851], p. 44).

56. Charles Emery Stevens, *Anthony Burns: A History* (Williamstown, Mass., 1973; 1st pub., 1856), pp. 124–150. For the case, William H. Ela v. Jerome U. C. Smith et al., which dragged on for some time, see the *Boston Daily Advertiser,* Feb. 20, 23, 24, 25, 1858. The quotation is from Parker's reminiscences of the case (Parker, *Reminiscences,* p. 473).

57. Parker, *Reminiscences,* pp. 56–58; Thorndike to Brown, n.d., Brown MSS.

58. Choate to Charles Eames (the American Minister at Caracas), June 29, 1855, in Brown, *Life,* pp. 279–280.

59. Choate to Mrs. Charles Eames, June 29, 1855, in Brown, *Life,* pp. 280–281.

60. Brown, *Life,* p. 279; Dana, entry for Jan. 16, 1853, *Journal,* II, 530; Dana to Brown, Dec. 19, 1859, Brown MSS, and quoted in Brown, *Life,* p. 400; Everett to Mrs. Charles Eames, Nov. 22, 1854, Everett MSS.

61. Parker, *Reminiscences,* p. 282; O'Connor, *Lords of the Loom,* pp. 114–121. The Know-Nothings swept Massachusetts in 1854 and 1855 and declined pretty rapidly thereafter. Their spectacular rise was due to a mixture of causes—a reaction against the rapid increase in the number of foreign immigrants in the United States (Boston in 1855 had over 50,000 Irishmen out of a population of 310,000); disappointment at the defeat of the revised constitution of 1853, which was blamed on the Catholic vote; the feeling that the immigrants were hostile on the question of slavery. The Know-Nothings in Massachusetts were as much anti-slavery as nativist—one of their accomplishments in 1855 was the passing of a personal liberty law—and formed a kind of bridge over which many Whigs eventually found their way into the Republican party (Bean, "Party Transformations," p. 262; George H. Hayes, "A Know-Nothing Legislature," *Annual Report of the American Historical Association* [1896], pp.

177–187). For the importance of the Know-Nothings in the political realignments of the 1850s, see Michael F. Holt, *The Political Crisis of the 1850's* (New York, 1978), pp. 159–181.

62. Everett to Mrs. Charles Eames, Nov. 22, 1854, Everett MSS; Parker, *Reminiscences,* pp. 276–277.

63. "Reminiscences of Dr. Boyden," in Neilson, *Memories,* p. 311.

64. Choate to Peter Butler, Jr. and Bradley N. Cummings, secretaries of the Whig Convention at Worcester, Mass., Oct. 1, 1855, in Brown, *Life,* pp. 284–287. The importance of sharp party conflicts in containing sectional strife is part of the thesis of Holt's brilliant study of the politics of the 1850s. What caused the disintegration of the second party system, according to Holt, however, was not the irresponsibility of third and sectional parties, but the voter alienation produced by the growing consensus and lack of real conflict between the two major parties by the 1850s (Holt, *Political Crisis,* ch. 5).

65. Choate, Speech delivered in Faneuil Hall, Oct. 31, 1855, in Brown, *Works,* II, 327–341, 330, 336, 340 (quotations).

66. Choate to Rev. Chandler Robbins, Nov. 12, 1855, in Brown, *Life,* pp. 287–288.

67. Parker, *Reminiscences,* p. 292; Brown, *Life,* p. 300. Some men still hoped that they might persuade him to join the Republicans. William Evarts sent him a copy of a speech he had made at a great Republican meeting in New York, and Choate replied with more moderation than he usually displayed towards that party: "To say that I see my way clear to *act* with you were premature. Blessings are bought with a price. We may pay too high for good sentiments and desirable policy. I hate some of your associates and recognize no necessity at all for a Presidential campaign on a platform less broad than our whole *Area.* But if you, and enough such, see your way clear and safe, why, lead and work, and he who knows he can govern him and put him to canonical service may lawfully raise the devil himself—so say the schoolmen" (Choate to Evarts, n.d. [May 20, 1856], Brown, MSS).

68. Choate to E. W. Farley et al. of the Maine Whig State Central Committee, Aug. 9, 1856, in Brown, *Life,* pp. 301–307, 305, 306 (quotations).

69. *Ibid.,* p. 307.

70. The letter forced others to make public declarations of where they stood. "Choate's course threw suspicion on all Conservative men who were silent" (Robert C. Winthrop, Jr., *A Memoir of Robert C. Winthrop* [Boston, 1897], p. 187; Andrew W. Crandall, *The Early History of the Republican Party, 1854–56* [Boston, 1930], p. 241). The *Boston Daily Advertiser* regretted Choate's course: "We part from him with pain" (August 15, 1856). The *Courier,* on the other hand, reprinted the letter as a "flyer" and appended to it the words of Henry Clay in 1839, warning that abolitionism was the real danger to the Union (August 14, 1856). The letter was widely reprinted in the press throughout the country and copies distributed as pamphlets (Albert J. Beveridge, *Abraham Lincoln, 1809–1858,* II [Boston, 1928], 413).

71. Francis Lieber to George Hillard, Aug. 17, 1856, Francis Lieber MSS, Huntington Library, San Marino, Calif. The manuscript breaks off at this point.

72. George Hillard to Lieber, Sept. 1, 1856, Lieber MSS.

73. Brown, *Life,* p. 311; *Freedom versus Slavery: Letters from Henry B. Pearson,*

late of the Philadelphia Bar, to Hon. Rufus Choate . . . (Portland, Me., 1856), pp. 15–16; Charles Lowell, *Errors of Great Men and the Dotage of Old Fogies* (Ellsworth, Me., 1856), p. 9. Choate replied to one allegation that he had been disappointed by not receiving an office from President Fillmore. (See his letter denying any wish for public office, to John Carroll Walsh, Sept. 15, 1856, in Brown, *Life,* pp. 311–312).

74. William Giles Dix, *The Presidency: A Reply to the letter of Hon. Rufus Choate. . . .* (Boston, 1856), p. 25; Pearson, *Freedom versus Slavery,* p. 9; Lowell, *Errors of Great Men,* p. 10; Josiah Quincy, *Remarks on the Letter of the Hon. Rufus Choate . . . August 30, 1856* (n.pub., n.d.), p. 2.

75. Choate to Maine Whigs, p. 304; Hill, "Memoir," pp. 147–148. Emerson is quoted in Moncure D. Conway, *Emerson at Home and Abroad* (Boston, 1882), p. 310. The phrase "glittering generalities" was not new in 1856. A note in Bartlett's *Familiar Quotations* reveals that in 1849 a reporter, Franklin J. Dickman, reviewing a lecture Choate gave in Providence for a local newspaper, wrote: "We fear that the glittering generalities of the speaker have left an impression more delightful than permanent." The note concludes that Dickman must be given the credit for inventing the phrase, unless he was merely echoing something Choate himself had said in the lecture (which does not appear to have survived). Of course, the phrase may have already been in common use in 1849, but I have not come across it (*Familiar Quotations by John Bartlett* [13th rev. ed.; Boston, 1955], p. 490).

76. Henry Wilson, July 4, 1859, quoted in Rev. Elias Nason and Hon. Thomas Russell, *The Life and Public Services of Hon. Henry Wilson, late Vice-President of the United States* (Boston, 1876), p. 258; Abraham Lincoln to Henry L. Pierce and others, April 6, 1859, in *Collected Works of Abraham Lincoln,* ed. Roy P. Basler, (9 vols.; New Brunswick, N.J., 1953–1955), III, 375, and speech, July 10, 1858, *ibid.,* II, 500. See also Lincoln's speech on the Dred Scott decision (1857) in which he objected vigorously to Douglass' attempt to make the Declaration refer merely to the specific historical circumstances of a colonial revolt, making it "mere rubbish—old wadding left to rot on the battlefield after the victory is won" (*ibid.,* II, 408).

77. Brown, *Life,* p. 308; *Boston Courier,* Oct. 29, 1856; *Boston Daily Evening Transcript,* Nov. 1, 1856; Choate, "On the Political Topics Now Prominent before the Country," Oct. 28, 1856, in Brown, *Works,* II, 387–414, 392, 397, 410 (quotations).

78. Choate, "On the Political Topics," p. 411.

79. *Ibid.,* p. 412. Compare his speech at Worcester, in 1848, in which he had conceded that there were some good things about the Democrats—"I like their nationality and their spirit of union, after all" (*Speeches of Rufus Choate and R.C. Winthrop at the Whig State Convention* [n.pub., 1848]). Choate was not the only Whig who by the 1850s was beginning to feel that expansive nationalism might be a necessary antidote to internal discord. An article in the *American Whig Review* in 1851 claimed that all "empires" naturally absorb adjacent territory. When they cease to do this decline sets in and this decline is preceded by civil wars. "In the absence of a foreign policy the American Empire, like the Russian and the British, falls into hostile parties within its own boundaries, and its Union is endangered. Let the attention of the people and the Government be turned

upon territories adjoining, whose inhabitants look to it for protection against hostile and uncongenial powers: the spirit of internal discord will be stilled by the sense of nationality, and the enthusiasm of military and commercial enterprise" ("Civil Discord Duty-Free," *The American Whig Review*, XIII [Feb. 1851], 116–125, 117 [quotation]).

80. Parker, *Reminiscences*, p. 286.

81. Choate to Evarts, [May 20, 1856], Brown MSS; Choate, "On the Political Topics," p. 412.

82. *Ibid.*, p. 414.

83. Brown, *Life*, pp. 309–310; Claude M. Fuess, *Rufus Choate: The Wizard of the Law* (New York, 1928), pp. 214–215.

84. Choate to Everett, Nov. 17, 1856, Everett MSS. This letter also appears in Brown, *Life*, p. 323, but is misdated 1857. Everett knew Buchanan quite well and corresponded with him. He had apparently mentioned to Choate the idea of preparing a set of policy papers for the new president.

85. Allan Nevins, *Ordeal of the Union* (New York, 1947), II, pp. 512–514; Edward E. Pratt in Nielson, *Memories*, p. 201.

86. Louis Filler, *The Crusade Against Slavery: 1830–1860* (New York, 1960), pp. 252–254; O'Connor, *Lords of the Loom*, p. 125–126; Oscar Handlin, *Boston's Immigrants* (New York, 1968; 1st pub., 1941), ch. 4; *North American Review*, LXXIX (Oct. 1854), 409 (this was a review of an English book on juvenile delinquency).

87. Choate, Journal, Aug. 2, 1850, in Brown, *Life*, p. 220; Brown, *Life*, p. 311; the *New York Tribune* is quoted in Winthrop, *Memoir*, p. 208.

88. Choate, "The Eloquence of Revolutionary Periods," Feb. 19, 1857, in Brown, *Works*, I, 439–463; Edward Everett to Mrs. Charles Eames, Feb. 28, 1857, Everett MSS. Everett, who had heard the speech on the second occasion, added: "It left on my mind rather a sad impression, as Choate's addresses almost always do; for I think in Choate's countenance there is an expression of sadness, if possible beyond even mine; and he seldom if ever says anything at which Democritus himself could smile; whereas at times, you know, I venture on a joke, though commonly a pretty melancholy one." It is true that in public speaking Choate's wit was kept strictly for his "party political" speeches.

89. Choate, "Eloquence of Revolutionary Periods," pp. 456, 457.

90. *Ibid.*, pp. 442, 445, 444.

91. *Ibid.*, p. 462; *New York Tribune*, Feb. 25, 1857.

92. Wendell Phillips, "Public Opinion" (1852), in *Speeches, Lectures and Letters* (Boston, 1863), p. 53. Robert Winthrop called Wendell Phillips' oratory the "eloquence of abuse" (quoted in Irving H. Bartlett, *Wendell Phillips* [Boston, 1961], p. 196). The change in oratorical styles which was taking place in the fifties was pointed up in dramatic fashion, as Russel Nye points out, in 1863 at Gettysburg, when the classical oratory of Edward Everett was completely cast into the shade by the few terse words of Abraham Lincoln (Russel B. Nye, *Society and Culture in America, 1830–1860* [New York, 1974], pp. 145–146).

93. The manuscript of this lecture does not appear to have survived. There is no complete report anywhere, but Brown gives a large excerpt in *Life*, pp. 324–331. There is also a fairly extensive report in the *Boston Daily Journal*, March 12, 1858, which includes things not in Brown—the quotation is from this source.

94. *Boston Daily Journal,* March 12, 1858; Brown, *Life,* pp. 325, 326. In the 1850s, the name of Washington became a kind of talisman for conservatives who feared for the Union. The *North American Review* in 1857, urging that his birthday be made a national holiday, spoke of that "canonized name" as a "bond of union, a conciliatory memory, and a glorious watchword," before which "sectional animosity is awed into universal reverence" ("Holidays," *North American Review,* CLXXV [April 1857], p. 363). Edward Everett, in his tireless lecture tours to raise money for the preservation of Mount Vernon, never failed to remind his audience of Jefferson's words to Washington, "North and South will hang together while they have you to hang to" (Frothingham, *Edward Everett,* p. 379).

95. Brown, *Life,* p. 332; Choate, "American Nationality," July 5, 1858, in Brown, *Works,* II, 415–440, 432 (quotation).

96. *Ibid.,* pp. 434, 438–439.

97. *Ibid.,* pp. 420–421, 430–431.

98. *Ibid.,* pp. 432, 427. James Russell Lowell delivered a blistering attack on this address in the new *Atlantic Monthly.* One of the many points on which he challenged Choate was the idea that nationality must be kept alive by the reason and the will. "It must be a matter of instinct, or it is nothing." Moreover, sentimental appeals to the glories of a national past were futile in face of the great hordes of immigrants. "Shall we talk of the constancy of Puritan Pilgrims to the Romanist Irishman?" This, however, oversimplifies Choate's position: to him the relation of past and present was never a strictly organic one, the past had always to be appropriated by an act of the imagination. Thus, with a little education, the American past should be as available to the newcomer as to the native born (James R. Lowell, "The Pocket-Celebration of the Fourth," *Atlantic Monthly,* II [Aug. 1858], 374–382).

99. For the growth of organic theories of the state during and after the Civil War, see Merle Curti, *The Roots of American Loyalty* (New York, 1946), pp. 173–199, and George M. Frederickson, *The Inner Civil War: Northern Intellectuals and the Crisis of the Union* (New York, 1965), pp. 130–150. Clay is quoted in Paul C. Nagel, *This Sacred Trust: American Nationality, 1798–1898* (New York, 1971), p. 161.

100. Choate, "American Nationality," pp. 420–421; Parker, *Reminiscences,* p. 281.

101. Paul C. Nagel, *One Nation Indivisible: The Union in American Thought 1776–1861* (New York, 1964), p. 281 (quotation); Phillip S. Paludan, "The American Civil War Considered as a Crisis of Law and Order," *American Historical Review,* LXXVII (Oct. 1972), 1,012–1,034.

102. See for example, Webster's speech on the "Dignity and Importance of History" (1852), in which he spoke of the dissolution of the Union and the abolition of the law of gravity as bringing the same kind of total confusion (Daniel Webster, *The Writings and Speeches of Daniel Webster* [Boston, 1903], XIII, 463–497; Choate, "American Nationality," pp. 429–430).

103. Henry Wilson is quoted in Pearson, *Freedom versus Slavery, letters from Henry R. Pearson,* p. 15; Richard Henry Dana, Jr., "The Great Gravitation Meeting" (1851), *Speeches in Stirring Times* (Boston, 1910), pp. 172, 174.

104. Nagel, *One Nation,* pp. 258–273; Paludan, "American Civil War," pp.

1,017–1,019. The kind of fusion that was taking place of the idea of Union and the notion of social order, and of disunion with both civil and social war was summed up in an anonymous poem quoted in Congress in 1860: "Dissolve the Union! Be like France / When 'Terror' reared her bloody lance, / And man became destruction's child, / And woman in her passions wild, / Danced in the life-blood of her queen, / Before the dreadful guillotine" (quoted in Nagel, *One Nation,* p. 271). In 1861 President Lincoln defined secession as "the essence of anarchy" (*Collected Works,* IV, 268).

105. Brown, *Life,* pp. 332, 334–335; Choate, "Speech on the Birthday of Daniel Webster, January 21, 1859," in Brown, *Works,* II, 441–450, 448 (quotation).

106. Parker, *Reminiscences,* pp. 58–59; George Hillard to Lieber, Feb. 3, 1859, Lieber MSS.

107. "Reminiscences of E. D. Sanborn," in Neilson, *Memories,* pp. 329–330; Nehemiah Adams, D.D., *A South Side View of Slavery* (Boston, 1855), pp. 9–10, 208–209.

108. Choate's speech is printed in full in *Memorial Volume by the Essex Street Church and Society, Boston, to Commemorate the 25th Anniversary of the Installation of their Pastor, Nehemiah Adams, D.D., March 28, 1859* (Boston, 1860), pp. 22–40; this particular quotation also appears in an extract from the speech in Brown, *Life,* pp. 338–341. According to Dana, Choate was one of the first men in New England to read Sir William Hamilton, the philosopher who attempted to revitalize British philosophy by grafting aspects of Kantian idealism onto the indigenous stock of Scottish common sense. He is perhaps best remembered now for having led Thomas Huxley to agnosticism, but he was an important figure in the attempt to reconcile science and religion. His solution was to shut each up in such watertight epistomological boxes that they could hardly meet to contend. Hamilton's "Philosophy of the Unconditioned," which appeared in the *Edinburgh Review* in 1829, removed God to the realm of the "Unknowable," where He could not be touched by the vulgar prying of science. But it also made safe a whole world of the secularly and relatively "knowable" whose exploration could cheerfully be undertaken without worrying about theological consequences. For Choate's reading of Hamilton, see Dana, in Brown, *Life,* p. 366, and Rev. J. M. Marsters to Brown, May 7, 1862, Brown MSS. For Hamilton, see John Theodore Merz, *A History of European Thought in the Nineteenth Century* (New York, 1965; 1st pub., London, 1904–1912), III, 379–381, and Elizabeth Flower and Murray G. Murphey, *A History of Philosophy in America* (New York, 1977), I, 264–267. For the controversy over Chambers' *Vestiges,* see Edward J. Pfeifer, "United States," *The Comparative Reception of Darwinism,* ed. Thomas F. Glick (Austin, Texas, 1972), pp. 168–175.

109. Choate in *Memorial Volume,* pp. 32, 36, 35; "Reminiscences of Sanborn," p. 330.

110. Brown, *Life,* pp. 341–345, 351 n. 1; Fitchburg R.R. v. Gage is reported in 78 Mass. (12 Gray) 393 (1859). Choate had argued that common carriers were required to transport freight at uniform rates to any party. The court, however, decided that as long as the rate was "reasonable" it did not

matter if it was discriminatory (see Leonard W. Levy, "Chief Justice Shaw and the Formative Period of American Railroad Law," *Columbia Law Review,* LI [March 1951], 327–348).

111. Brown, *Life,* pp. 345–346; Joseph A. Willard, *Half a Century with Judges and Lawyers* (Boston, 1895), pp. 256–257.

112. Brown, *Life,* pp. 347–351.

113. *Ibid.,* pp. 351–352, 376–387; *Boston Courier,* July 23, 1859.

114. Choate said of John Quincy Adams that he had "an instinct for the jugular and the carotid artery, as unerring as that of any carnivorous animal" (Brown, *Life,* p. 417).

115. For conservative exemplars of the ante-bellum period, Russell Kirk offers Orestes Brownson and Nathaniel Hawthorne, but does not mention Daniel Webster (Russell Kirk, *The Conservative Mind* [Chicago, 1953]); for Emerson's vision of the "radically free" individual liberated from society, as typical of much ante-bellum thinking and experience, see R. Jackson Wilson, *In Quest of Community,* (New York, 1968), ch. 1.

116. Burke wished to preserve from the contagion of the French Revolution the "inbred integrity, piety, good nature, and good humour of the people of England." "Letter to a Noble Lord" (1795), *Selected Writings of Edmund Burke,* ed. W. J. Bate (New York, 1960), pp. 493–516, 512 (quotation).

117. *New York Daily Tribune,* July 29, 1859; Review of *Addresses and Orations of Rufus Choate, Nation,* XXVII (1878), pp. 287–288.

118. Choate, "Speech before the Young Men's Whig Club of Boston" (1844), in Brown, *Works,* II, 267–283, 276 (quotation).

119. James Russell Lowell, "Pseudo-Conservatism" (1850), *The Anti-Slavery Papers of James Russell Lowell,* II (New York, 1969; 1st pub., 1902), 197–203, 202 (quotation); Russel B. Nye, "History and Literature: Branches of the Same Tree," in *Essays on History and Literature,* ed. Robert H. Bremmer (Columbus, 1966), pp. 123–159; Gilbert Osofsky, "Wendell Phillips and the Quest for a New American National Identity," *Canadian Review of Studies in Nationalism,* I (Fall 1973), 15–46.

120. Abraham Lincoln, "Speech at Springfield, Ill., June 16, 1858," *Collected Works,* II, 461–489, 461 (quotation); George William Curtis, "Oration to the Graduating Class, Union College" (1857), in George William Curtis, *Orations and Addresses* (New York, 1894), I, 58.

BIBLIOGRAPHY

MANUSCRIPT COLLECTIONS

The most important collections of manuscripts by or relating to Choate are the Rufus Choate and the Samuel Gilman Brown collections in Houghton Library, Harvard University (the latter includes some of the material Brown collected for his *Life* of Choate); and the Choate collection in the Dartmouth College Archives, Hanover, N.H.

There are also small collections of letters and other relevant material in the following:

Choate, Rufus. MSS. Boston Public Library.
————. MSS. Essex Institute, Salem, Mass.
————. MSS. Library of Congress, Washington, D.C.
————. MSS. Yale University Library, New Haven, Conn.
Cushing, Caleb. MSS. Library of Congress, Washington, D.C.
Davis, John. MSS. American Antiquarian Society, Worcester, Mass.
Everett, Edward. MSS. Massachusetts Historical Society, Boston, Mass.
Lieber, Francis. MSS. Huntington Library, San Marino, Calif.
Marsh, George Perkins. MSS. University of Vermont Library, Burlington, Vt.
Saltonstall, Leverett. MSS. Massachusetts Historical Society, Boston, Mass.
Sumner, Charles. MSS. Boston Public Library.
————. MSS. Houghton Library, Harvard University, Cambridge, Mass.
Webster, Daniel. MSS. Library of Congress, Washington, D.C.

I have also found the following manuscript collections useful.
Adams, Charles Francis. MS Diary. Massachusetts Historical Society, Boston, Mass.
Lawrence, Amos A. MSS. Massachusetts Historical Society, Boston, Mass.
Winthrop, Robert C. MSS. Massachusetts Historical Society, Boston, Mass.

I have also used the microfilm of manuscripts assembled for the edition of the Papers of Joseph Henry now in progress, edited by Nathan Reingold.

PUBLIC DOCUMENTS

Congressional Globe
Journal of the United States Senate
Register of Debates in the Congress of the United States

NEWSPAPERS

Boston *Atlas*
Boston *Courier*
Boston *Daily Advertiser*
Boston *Semi-Weekly Advertiser*
Boston *Daily Bee*
Boston *Daily Chronotype*
Boston *Daily Evening Transcript*
Boston *Daily Journal*
Boston *Post*
Essex *Register*
New York *Daily Times*
New York *Tribune*
Salem *Gazette*
Salem *Observer*
Salem *Register*

LEGAL CASES

Bascom v. Lane, 2 F. Cas. 994 (No. 1089) (C.C.D.N.Y., 1851).
Boston & L.R.R. v. Salem & L.R.R., 68 Mass. (2 Gray) 1 (1854).
Case of the Slave-Child, Med., Report of the Arguments of Counsel, and of the Opinion of the Court in the Case of the Commonwealth v. Aves. Boston, 1836.
Commonwealth v. Aves, 35 Mass. (18 Pick.) 193 (1836).
Commonwealth v. Blodgett, *The Law Reporter,* 6 (1843), 120.
Commonwealth v. Farmers & Mechanics Bank, 38 Mass. (21 Pick.) 542 (1839).
Day v. Berkshire Woolen Co., U.S. Circuit Court, District of Mass., 1849. Phonographic Report.
Fisher v. McGirr, 67 Mass. (1 Gray) 1 (1854).
Fitchburg R.R. v. Gage, 78 Mass. (12 Gray) 393 (1859).
Goodyear v. Day, 10 F. Cas. 678 (No. 5569) (C.C.D.N.J., 1852).
The Methodist Church Property Case. Reported by R. Sutton. Richmond, 1851.
Norris v. City of Boston, 45 Mass. (4 Met.) 282 (1842).
O'Reilly v. Morse, 56 U.S. (15 How.) 61 (1854).
Prouty v. Draper, 41 U.S. (16 Pet.) 336 (1842).
Report of the Case of William W. Woodworth as Administrator etc. v. Rudolphus C. Edwards et al. Auburn, 1848.
Shaw v. Boston & W.R.R., 74 Mass. (8 Gray) 45 (1857).
Smith v. Clark, 22 F. Cas. 487 (No. 13027) (C.C.D. Mass., 1850).
Smith v. Downing, 22 F. Cas. 511 (No. 13036) (C.C.D. Mass., 1850).
Thurlow v. Massachusetts, 46 U.S. (5 How.) 504 (1847).

Trial of Thomas Sims . . . Arguments of Robert Rantoul, Jr., and Charles G. Loring with the Decision of George T. Curtis, Boston, April 7–11, 1851. Boston, 1851.
The Trial of Albert T. Tirrell. Boston *Daily Mail* Report, n.d. [1846].

PRINTED PRIMARY SOURCES

The most important printed sources for the life and ideas of Rufus Choate are the following:

Brown, Samuel Gilman. *The Life of Rufus Choate.* Boston, 1870. And *The Works of Rufus Choate, with a Memoir of His Life.* 2 vols. Boston, 1862. These were compiled with the assistance of the Choate family.

Neilson, Joseph. *Memories of Rufus Choate, with Some Consideration of His Studies, Methods and Opinions, and of His Style as a Speaker and Writer.* Boston, 1884. This includes a number of letters from friends and acquaintances.

Parker, Edward G. *Reminiscences of Rufus Choate, the Great American Advocate.* New York, 1860. Parker became a student in Choate's law office in 1845 and remained on quite intimate terms with him for the next fourteen years. The book contains, besides Parker's reminiscences, conversations between the two men that Parker put on paper immediately after they had occurred. It also includes some of Choate's legal arguments that do not appear in the *Works.* Some of Choate's acquaintances did not entirely approve of this book, largely because of the informality and "off the cuff" nature of some of the reported conversations. See Charles G. Loring to Brown, Feb. 24, 1861. Brown, MSS, Houghton. However, the book is probably as trustworthy as most reminiscences.

The following speeches and legal arguments by Choate do not appear in the *Works:*

Abstract of the Arguments of the Hon. Rufus Choate and Charles Theo. Russell, Esq., for the Petitioners, on the Petition of David Pingree, and Over 3,000 Other Legal Voters, for a Railroad from Salem to Malden, before the Committee on Railways and Canals of the Massachusetts Legislature . . . 1846. Boston, 1846.

Abstract of the Arguments of the Hon. Rufus Choate and William D. Northend, Esq., for the Petitioners, on the Petitions of Benjamin Goodridge, and 5,322 Other Legal Voters, for a Railroad from Danvers to Malden, before the Committee on Railways and Canals, of the Massachusetts Legislature. . . . Boston, 1847.

Application of Robert Codman and Others for a Railroad between South Dedham and Boston, Making a Connection with the Norfolk County Road: Speech of Rufus Choate before a Legislative Committee, Boston, March 26, 1850. Boston, 1850.

Application of the Salem and Lowell Railroad Company for a Parallel and Competing Railroad from Salem to Danvers . . . : Speech of Hon. Rufus Choate before the Joint Legislative RailRoad Committee, Boston, February 28, 1851. Boston, 1851.

Argument for the Division of Worcester County, on the Petition of O. L. Huntley and Others, before Legislative Committee, April 1854, by Hon. Rufus Choate. Boston, 1854.

Argument for the Division of Worcester County, before a Legislative Committee, by Hon. Rufus Choate, in Senate Chamber, April, 1856. N.p., n.d.

Catalogue of the Valuable Private Library of the Late Hon. Rufus Choate to be Sold at Auction. Boston, 1859.

Circuit Court of the U.S.: Horace H. Day vs. Charles Goodyear, in Equity, Points for the Defendant. . . . New York, 1852.

"The Fine Arts as Affecting the Republican Character," *The Dartmouth,* VII (1872), 135–137.

"Hon. Rufus Choate's Argument on the Constitutionality of the Massachusetts Anti-Liquor Law," *Massachusetts Life-Boat,* extra ed. [Jan. 20, 1854].

"Intervention of the New World in the Affairs of the Old—the Duty, the Limitations, and the Modes," *New York Daily Times,* Aug. 9, 1852.

"Rufus Choate Letters," *Essex Institute Historical Collections,* LXIX (1933), 82–88.

Speech of Mr. Choate of Massachusetts on the Bill to Alter and Amend the Several Acts Imposing Duties on Imports, House of Representatives, U.S., June 13, 1832. Washington, D.C. 1832.

Speech of Mr. Choate on the Question of the Removal of the Deposits. Washington, D.C., 1834.

Speech at Concord, July 4, 1844, *Niles' National Register,* July 20, 1844, p. 326.

Speech at Lynn, *Salem Register,* Sept. 5, 1844.

Speech at Salem, *Salem Register,* Oct. 2, 1848.

Speech at the Story Association, July 15, 1851, *Boston Daily Advertiser,* July 17, 1851, and *Boston Post,* July 16, 1851.

Speech at Whig Convention, November 25, 1851, *Boston Courier,* Nov. 26, 1851.

Speeches of Rufus Choate and R. C. Winthrop at the Whig State Convention, and the Last Letter of Captain Allison. N.p., 1848.

Speeches at Worcester and Roxbury, *Boston Semi-Weekly Advertiser,* Sept. 7, 14, 1844.

"Valedictory," *The Dartmouth,* VII (Oct. 1872), 315–317.

OTHER PRIMARY SOURCES

Adams, Charles Francis, ed. *Memoirs of John Quincy Adams.* Vol. IX. New York, 1970; 1st pub., 1874–1877.

Adams, Henry. "Life, Letters and Journals of George Ticknor," *North American Review,* CXXIII (1876), 210–215.

Adams, John Quincy. *The Great Design: Two Lectures on the Smithsonian Bequest,* ed. with an Introduction by Wilcomb E. Washburn. Washington, D.C., 1965.

Adams, Nehemiah, D.D. *A Sabbath Discourse on the Death of the Hon. Rufus Choate, Together with the Address at His Funeral.* Boston, 1859.

———. *A South Side View of Slavery.* Boston, 1855.

An Account of the Pilgrim Celebration at Plymouth, August 1, 1853. Boston, 1853.

An Appeal to the Whig National Convention, in Favor of the Nomination of Daniel Webster to the Presidency. By "A Whig from the Start" (John Calvin Adams). New York, 1848.

Answer of the Whig Members of the Legislature of Massachusetts, Constituting a Majority of Both Branches, to the Address of His Excellency Marcus Morton, Delivered in the Convention of the Two Houses, January 22, 1840. Boston, 1840.

Appleton, Nathan. *Memoir of the Hon. Abbott Lawrence.* Boston, 1856.

Boutwell, George S. *The Lawyer, the Statesman and the Soldier.* New York, 1887.

Brainerd, C. and E. W., eds. *New England Society Orations.* 2 vols. New York, 1901.
Brief Account of the Celebration of the 19th of April at Concord 1850. N.p., n.d.
Browne, Irving. *Short Studies of Great Lawyers.* Albany, N.Y., 1878.
Burke, Edmund. "Letter to a Noble Lord." In *Selected Writings of Edmund Burke,* ed. W. J. Bate. New York, 1960.
———. "A Philosophical Enquiry into . . . the Sublime and Beautiful." In *Writings and Speeches.* Vol. I. Boston, 1901.
———. *Reflections on the Revolution in France.* Everyman's Library ed. London, 1910.
C. E. L. Review of Madison Papers, *American Jurist,* XXI (Jan. 1842), pp. 394–415.
Caverno, Charles. *Reminiscences of the Eulogy of Rufus Choate on Daniel Webster.* Boston, 1914.
"Children of the Perishing and Dangerous Classes," *North American Review,* LXXIX (1854), 406–423.
Choate, Joseph H. *An Address Delivered at the Unveiling of the Statue of Rufus Choate in the Court House in Boston, October 15, 1895.* Boston, 1895.
"Civil Discord Duty-free," *The American Whig Review,* XIII (1851), 116–124.
Cogswell, John D. *Memoir of Rufus Choate.* Rpt. from the *Memorial Biographies of the New England Historic Genealogical Society.* Cambridge, Mass., 1884.
Coleridge, Samuel Taylor. *The Constitution of the Church and State According to the Idea of Each.* London, 1829.
Conway, Moncure. "Rufus Choate," *The Dial,* I (1860), 457–469.
Curtis, George Ticknor. *Life of Daniel Webster.* New York, 1870.
———. *The True Uses of American Revolutionary History.* An Oration Delivered before the Authorities of the City of Boston, on Monday, the Fifth of July, 1841. Boston, 1841.
Dana, Richard Henry, Jr. *Journal.* Ed. Robert F. Lucid. 3 vols. Cambridge, Mass., 1968.
———. "On the Removal of Judge Woodbury Davis," *Monthly Law Reporter,* XCI (June 1856), 61–83.
———. *Speeches in Stirring Times and Letters to a Son.* Boston, 1910.
Discussions on the Constitution Proposed to the People of Massachusetts by the Convention of 1853. Boston, 1854.
Dix, William Giles. *The Presidency: A Reply to the Letter of Hon. Rufus Choate.* Boston, 1856.
Emerson, Ralph Waldo. *Journals and Miscellaneous Notebooks.* Vol. VIII. Ed. William H. Gilman and J. E. Parsons. Cambridge, Mass., 1970.
———. "Eloquence" (1867). In *The Complete Works of Ralph Waldo Emerson,* VIII, 111–133. New York, 1968; 1st pub., 1904.
———. "Historic Notes of Life and Letters in New England." In *The Portable Emerson,* ed. Mark Van Doren, pp. 513–542. New York, 1946.
Everett, Edward. *An Oration Delivered at Charlestown on the 75th Anniversary of the Battle of Bunker Hill.* Boston, 1850.
Everett, William. "Rufus Choate," *The New England Magazine* (Nov. 1896), pp. 376–378.

Fernald, Woodbury M., ed. *Memoirs and Reminiscences of the Late Professor George Bush.* Boston, 1860.

[Gould, Benjamin A.] *The Smithsonian Institution.* Boston, 1855.

Greene, George Washington. "Libraries," *North American Review,* XLV (1837), 116–149.

Greenleaf, Simon. "Notes of Professor Greenleaf's Introductory Lecture at the Present Term," *The Law Reporter,* I (1838), 217–223.

Hackett, William A. "Sketch of the Life and Character of John Jay," *The American Review (The American Whig Review),* II (1845), 59.

Haddock, D. D. *The Patriot Scholar: An Oration Pronounced before the Phi Beta Kappa Society of Yale College.* New Haven, 1848.

Hale, Edward Everett. *A New England Boyhood.* Boston, 1893.

Harvey, Peter. *Reminiscences and Anecdotes of Daniel Webster.* Boston, 1878.

Henry, C. S. "The Position and Duties of the Educated Men of the Country" (1840), in his *Considerations on Some of the Elements and Conditions of Social Welfare and Human Progress.* New York, 1861.

Henry, Joseph. *Thoughts on Education: The Introductory Discourse Delivered before the American Association for the Advancement of Education.* Washington, D.C., 1854.

Hill, Clement Hugh. "Memoir of Hon. Rufus Choate," *Massachusetts Historical Society Proceedings,* XI (1896–1897), 123–155.

Hill, Hamilton Andrews. *Memoir of Abbott Lawrence.* Boston, 1884.

Hillard, George S. *An Oration Pronounced before the Inhabitants of Boston, July 4th, 1835.* Boston, 1835.

———. *Life, Letters and Journals of George Ticknor.* 2 vols. Boston, 1876.

———, ed. *Memoirs of Jeremiah Mason.* Boston, 1917.

Hoar, George F. *Autobiography of Seventy Years.* 2 vols. New York, 1903.

"Holidays," *North American Review,* LXXXIV (1857), 334–363.

Inequality of the Old Constitution, and Advantages of the New. N.p., n.d. [1853].

Jackson, J. F. "American Scholarship," *The Knickerbocker,* XXVIII (July 1846), 1–13.

Kent, James. "Address of Chancellor Kent before the Law Association of New York City, October 21, 1836," *American Jurist,* XVI (1837), 472.

Kossuth in New England: A Full Account of the Hungarian Governor's Visit to Massachusetts, with His Speeches, and the Addresses That Were Made to Him, Carefully Revised and Corrected. Boston, 1852.

Lieber, Francis. *Manual of Political Ethics, Designed Chiefly for the Use of Colleges and Students at Law.* Boston, 1838.

———. *Remarks on the Relation between Education and Crime.* Philadelphia, 1835.

Lincoln, Abraham. *Collected Works.* 9 vols. Ed. Roy P. Basler. New Brunswick, N.J., 1953–1955.

Lowell, Charles. *Errors of Great Men and the Dotage of Old Fogies.* Ellsworth, Maine, 1856.

Lowell, James Russell. *The Anti-Slavery Papers of James Russell Lowell.* New York, 1969; 1st pub., 1902.

———. "The Pocket Celebration of the Fourth," *The Atlantic Monthly,* II (1858), 374–382.

Lyell, Sir Charles. *A Second Visit to the United States of North America.* 2 vols. London, 1849.

McCulloch, Hugh. *Men and Measures of Half a Century.* New York, 1900.
Marsh, George Perkins. *The American Historical School.* Troy, N.Y., 1847.
––––––. *The Goths in New England.* Middlebury, Vt., 1843.
––––––. *Human Knowledge: A Discourse.* Boston, 1847.
Mathews, William. *Oratory and Orators.* Chicago, 1879.
May, Samuel J. *Some Recollections of Our Antislavery Conflict.* Boston, 1869.
Meacham, James. *Report on the Smithsonian Institution.* Washington, 1884.
Memorial Volume by the Essex Street Church and Society, Boston, to Commemorate the 25th Anniversary of the Installation of Their Pastor, Nehemiah Adams, D.D. Boston, 1860.
Mill, John Stuart. "Coleridge." In *Dissertations and Discussions.* 2 vols. New York, 1973; 1st pub., 1859.
Minns, George W. "Some Reminiscences of Rufus Choate," *The American Lawyer Review,* XI (Oct. 1876), 1–23.
National Institute for the Promotion of Science. *Third Bulletin of the Proceedings.* Washington, D.C., 1842–1845.
"Nature and Effects of a Protective Tariff," *The American Whig Review,* XIV (1851), 81–86.
"The New Constitution: Article VI—the Judiciary," *The American Review (The American Whig Review),* IV (Nov. 1846), 520–531.
Northup, Clark S., William C. Lane, and John C. Schwab, ed. *Representative Phi Beta Kappa Orations.* Boston, 1915.
Official Report of the Debates and Proceedings in the State Convention, Assembled May 4th, 1853. 3 vols. Boston, 1853.
O'Sullivan, John. "Editorial," *Democratic Review,* VI (1839), 427–428.
Parker, Edward G. *The Golden Age of American Oratory.* Boston 1857.
––––––. *An Oration, July 4, 1856.* Boston, 1856.
Parsons, Theophilus. *Address Commemorative of Rufus Choate.* Boston, 1859.
Pearson, Henry B. *Freedom Versus Slavery: Letters from Henry B. Pearson, Late of the Philadelphia Bar, to Hon. Rufus Choate . . .* Portland, Maine. 1856.
Phillips, Wendell. *Speeches, Lectures and Letters.* Boston, 1863.
Pierce, Benjamin. *The Smithsonian Institution.* Boston, 1855.
Pierce, Edward L. *Memoir and Letters of Charles Sumner.* 3 vols. Boston, 1878.
The Pilgrim Society. *Report by a Committee.* Boston, 1850.
Poinsett, Joel. *Discourse on the Objects and Importance of the National Institute for the Promotion of Science.* Washington, D.C., 1841.
"Political Responsibilities," *The American Whig Review,* XIV (1851), 359–367.
Poole, Fitch. "Early Recollections of Rufus Choate" (1859), *The Historical Collections of the Danvers Historical Society,* XV (1927), 26–30.
Proceedings of the Constitutional Meeting at Faneuil Hall, November 26, 1850. Boston, 1850.
Proceedings of the Senate and House of Representatives, upon the Petition of George H. M. Withington and Others, Praying That James G. Carter Be Removed from His Office of Justice of the Peace. . . . Boston, 1849.
Quincy, Josiah. *Figures of the Past.* Boston, 1883.
––––––. *Remarks on the Letter of the Hon. Rufus Choate to the Whig State Committee of Maine.* Boston, 1856.
"The Recent Contest in Rhode Island," *North American Review,* LVIII (1844), 371–435.

"Recollections of a Nomad," *Church's Bazaar*, n.s., pt. 6 (1852), p. 165.
Reply to Mr. Choate's Argument, for the Division of Worcester County . . . by a Citizen of Worcester County. Worcester, 1855.
Review of the Proceedings in the Massachusetts Legislature for 1843; with an Appeal to the People against the Violent Course of the Majority by the Whig Minority. Boston, 1843.
Rhees, William J., ed. *Smithsonian Institution: Journals of the Board of Regents.* Washington, D.C., 1880.
————, ed. *The Smithsonian Institution: Documents Relative to Its Origins and History.* Washington, D.C., 1880.
————, ed. *The Smithsonian Institution: Documents Relative to its Origin and History, 1835–1899.* Washington, D.C., 1901.
Richards, William Carey. *Great in Goodness: A Memoir of George N. Briggs.* Boston, 1866.
Robinson, Frederick. *A Letter to the Honorable Rufus Choate, Containing a Brief Exposure of Law Craft, and Some of the Encroachments upon the Rights and Liberties of the People.* Boston, 1831.
Robinson, Mrs. W. S., ed. *"Warrington" Pen Portraits: A Collection of Personal and Political Reminiscences, from 1848 to 1876, from the Writings of W. S. Robinson.* Boston, 1877.
Smithsonian Institution, Annual Reports.
"The Smithsonian Institution," *Christian Examiner*, Vol. LXXIV (1854).
"The Smithsonian Institution," *North American Review*, LXXIX (1854), 441–64.
"The Smithsonian Institution," *Putnam's Monthly*, Vol. IV (1854).
"The Smithsonian Institute," *Southern Literary Messenger*, VI (1840), 25–34.
Sparks, Jared. "Remarks on American History." In *The Boston Book*, ed. B. B. Thatcher. Boston, 1837.
Stone, Eben F. "An Address Delivered before the Essex Bar on the Opening of the New Court House," *Essex Historical Collections*, Vol. XXVI (1889).
[Taylor, Isaac]. *Natural History of Enthusiasm.* London, 1834.
Tocqueville, Alexis de. *Democracy in America.* 2 vols. New York, 1945; 1st pub., 1835.
————. *Journey to America.* Ed. J. P. Mayer. London, 1959.
Torrey, Joseph, comp. *The Remains of the Rev. James Marsh.* Port Washington, N.Y., 1971; 1st pub., 1843.
"Unity of the Whigs: Their Principles and Measures," *The American Whig Review*, XIV (1851), 179–186.
Webster, Daniel. *The Letters of Daniel Webster.* Ed. C. H. Van Tyne. New York, 1968; 1st pub., 1902.
————. *The Works of Daniel Webster.* 6 vols. Boston, 1890; 1st pub., 1851.
————. *The Writings and Speeches of Daniel Webster.* Vol. X. Boston, 1903.
"A Whig Orator," *Nation*, XXVII (1878), 287–288.
Whipple, Edwin P. *Character and Characteristic Men.* Boston, 1866.
————. *Some Recollections of Rufus Choate.* New York, 1879.
————. "College Life of Rufus Choate." In *Some Noted Princes, Authors, and Statesmen of Our Time*, ed. James Parton, pp. 277–283. Norwich, Conn., 1885.
————. "Hon. Rufus Choate," *The American Review: A Whig Journal (The American Whig Review)*, V (1847) 63–71.

Whitman, Walter. "Tear Down and Build Over Again," *The American Review: A Whig Journal (The American Whig Review)*, II (1845), 536–538.
"Will There Be War with Mexico?" *The American Review: A Whig Journal (The American Whig Review)*, II (1845), 221–229.
Williard, Joseph A. *Half A Century with Judges and Lawyers*. Boston, 1895.
Wilson, Henry. *History of the Rise and Fall of the Slave Power in America*. 3 vols. New York, 1969; 1st pub., 1872.
Winthrop, Robert C., Jr. *A Memoir of Robert C. Winthrop*. Boston, 1897.
Wirt, William. "Letter, July 22, 1822," *The American Journal of Legal History*, II (1958), 256–258.

SECONDARY SOURCES
Aaron, Daniel. "Conservatism, Old and New," *American Quarterly*, VI (1954), 99–109.
Alexander, Thomas B. *Sectional Stress and Party Strength: A Computer Analysis of Roll-Call Voting Patterns in the United States House of Representatives, 1836–1860*. Nashville, Tenn., 1967.
Arendt, Hannah. *The Human Condition*. Chicago, 1958.
Aumann, Francis R. *The Changing American Legal System: Some Selected Phases*. Columbus, 1940.
Barkan, Elliott R., "The Emergence of a Whig Persuasion: Conservatism, Democratism, and the New York State Whigs," *New York History*, LII (1971), 367–395.
Barnard, F. M., *J. G. Herder on Social and Political Culture*. Cambridge, 1969.
———. *Herder's Social and Political Thought: From Enlightenment To Nationalism*. Oxford, 1965.
Barth, Hans, *The Idea of Order: Contributions to a Philosophy of Politics*. Trans. Ernest W. Hankamer and William M. Newell. Dordrecht, Holland, 1960.
Baskerville, Barnet. "Principal Themes of Nineteenth Century Critics of Oratory," *Speech Monographs*, XIX (March 1952), 11–38.
Bauer, Elizabeth Kelley. *Commentaries on the Constitution, 1790–1860*. New York, 1952.
Baxter, Maurice G. *Daniel Webster and the Supreme Court*. Amherst, 1966.
Bean, William G. "The Transformation of Parties in Massachusetts, with Special Reference to the Antecedents of Republicanism from 1848 to 1862." Ph.D. diss., Harvard University, 1922.
Benson, Lee. *The Concept of Jacksonian Democracy: New York as a Test Case*. Princeton, 1961.
Berthoff, Rowland. *An Unsettled People: Social Order and Disorder in American History*. New York, 1971.
Bloomfield, Maxwell. *American Lawyers in a Changing Society, 1776–1876*. Cambridge, Mass., 1976.
———. "Law vs. Politics: The Self-Image of the American Bar (1830–60)," *The American Journal of Legal History*, XII (1966), 306–323.
———. "Lawyers and Public Criticism: Challenge and Response in Nineteenth-Century America," *The American Journal of Legal History*, XV (1971), 269–277.
Boorstin, Daniel. *The Americans: The National Experience*. New York, 1965.

Borome, Joseph A. *Charles Coffin Jewett.* Chicago, 1951

Boulton, James T. *The Language of Politics in the Age of Wilkes and Burke.* London, 1963.

Brauer, Kinley J. *Cotton Versus Conscience: Massachusetts Whig Politics and Southwestern Expansion, 1843–1848.* Lexington, Ky., 1967.

Brigance, William Norwood, ed. *A History and Criticism of American Public Address.* Vol. I. New York, 1943.

Brown, Norman D. *Daniel Webster and the Politics of Availability.* Athens, Ga., 1969.

Brunet, Michel. "The Secret Ballot Issue in Massachusetts Politics from 1851 to 1853," *New England Quarterly,* XXV (Sept. 1952), 354–362.

Buckley, Jerome H. *The Triumph of Time: A Study of the Victorian Concepts of Time, History, Progress, and Decadence.* Cambridge, Mass., 1966.

Callcott, George H. *History in the United States, 1800–60: Its Practice and Purpose.* Baltimore, 1970.

Calleo, David P. *Coleridge and the Idea of the Modern State.* New Haven, 1966.

Campbell, Stanley W. *The Slave Catchers: Enforcement of the Fugitive Slave Law, 1850–1860.* New York, 1972; 1st pub., 1968.

Carroll, E. Malcolm. *Origins of the Whig Party: A Dissertation.* Durham, N.C., 1925.

Chroust, Anton-Hermann. *The Rise of the Legal Profession in America.* Vol. II. Norman, Okla., 1965.

Colmer, John. *Coleridge: Critic of Society.* Oxford, 1959.

Commager, Henry Steele. *The Search for a Usable Past and Other Essays in Historiography.* New York, 1967.

Cover, Robert M. *Justice Accused: Antislavery and the Judicial Process.* New Haven, 1975.

Crandall, Andrew W. *The Early History of the Republican Party, 1854–56.* Boston, 1930.

Craven, Wesley Frank. *The Legend of the Founding Fathers.* New York, 1965; 1st pub., 1956.

Crenson, Matthew A. *The Federal Machine.* Baltimore, 1975.

Current, Richard N. *Daniel Webster and the Rise of National Conservatism.* Boston, 1955.

Curti, Merle. "Francis Lieber and Nationalism." In *Probing Our Past,* ed. Merle Curti. Gloucester, Mass., 1959; 1st pub., 1955.

———. *The Roots of American Loyalty.* New York, 1946.

Dalzell, Robert F., Jr. *Daniel Webster and the Trial of American Nationalism, 1843–1852.* Boston, 1973.

Daniels, George H. *Science in American Society: A Social History.* New York, 1971.

———. "The Process of Professionalization in American Science: The Emergent Period, 1820–60," *Isis,* LVIII (1967), 151–166.

Darling, Arthur B. *Political Changes in Massachusetts, 1824–48: A Study of Liberal Movements in Politics.* New York, 1925.

Davis, Richard Beale. "The Early American Lawyer and the Profession of Letters," *Huntington Library Quarterly,* XII (1949), 191–205.

Dennison, George M. *The Dorr War: Republicanism on Trial, 1831–1861.* Lexington, Ky., 1976.

Donald, David. *Charles Sumner and the Coming of the Civil War.* New York, 1960.

Drown, Paulina Cony. *Mrs. Bell.* Boston, 1931.

Duberman, Martin. *Charles Francis Adams, 1807–1886.* Cambridge, Mass., 1961.

Dubofsky, Melvyn. "Daniel Webster and the Whig Theory of Economic Growth, 1828–1848," *New England Quarterly,* XLII (1969), 551–572.

Duffy, John J. *Coleridge's American Disciples: The Selected Correspondence of James Marsh.* Amherst, 1973.

――――. "Problems in Publishing Coleridge: James Marsh's First American Edition of *Aids to Reflection,*" *New England Quarterly,* XLIII (1970), 193–208.

Dupree, A. Hunter. *Science in the Federal Government.* New York, 1957.

Ekirch, Arthur E., Jr. *The Idea of Progress in America, 1815–1860.* New York, 1951; 1st pub., 1944.

Feuer, Lewis S. "James Marsh and the Conservative Transcendentalist Philosophy," *New England Quarterly,* XXXI (March 1958), 3–31.

Fiering, Norman S. "Will and Intellect in the New England Mind," *William and Mary Quarterly,* XXIX (1972), 515–558.

Filler, Louis. *The Crusade against Slavery, 1830–1860.* New York, 1960.

Firda, Richard A. "German Philosophy of History and Literature in the *North American Review,* 1815–60," *Journal of the History of Ideas,* XXXIII (1971), 133–142.

Foner, Eric. *Free Soil, Free Labor, Free Men: The Ideology of the Republican Party before the Civil War.* New York, 1970.

Formisano, Ronald P., "Deferential-Participant Politics: The Early Republic's Political Culture, 1789–1840," *American Political Science Review,* LXVIII (June 1974), 473–487.

――――. "Political Character, Antipartyism and the Second Party System," *American Quarterly,* XXI (1969), 683–709.

Foster, Herbert Darling. "The Ripley-Olcott-Leeds House," *Dartmouth Alumni Magazine* (1925), pp. 464–465.

――――. "Webster and Choate in College: Dartmouth under the Curriculum of 1796–1819," *Dartmouth Alumni Magazine* (1927), pp. 509–519, 605–616.

Fredrickson, George M. *The Inner Civil War: Northern Intellectuals and the Crisis of the Union.* New York, 1965.

Friedel, Frank. *Francis Lieber: Nineteenth-Century Liberal.* Baton Rouge, 1947.

Friedrich, Carl J. *Tradition and Authority.* New York, 1972.

Frothingham, Paul Revere. *Edward Everett: Orator and Statesman.* Cambridge Mass., 1925.

Fuess, Claude M. *The Life of Caleb Cushing.* 2 vols. New York, 1923.

――――. *The Life of Daniel Webster.* 2 vols. Hamden, Conn., 1963; 1st pub., 1930.

――――. *Rufus Choate: The Wizard of the Law.* New York, 1928.

Gattell, Frank Otto. "Conscience and Judgment: The Bolt of the Massachusetts Conscience Whigs," *The Historian,* LXXI (Nov. 1958), 18–45.

Gawalt, Gerald W. "Sources of Anti-lawyer Sentiment in Massachusetts, 1740–1840," *The American Journal of Legal History,* XIV (1970), 283–307.

Geertz, Clifford. "Ideology as a Cultural System." In *Ideology and Discontent,* ed., David E. Apter, pp. 47–76, New York, 1964.

Gettleman, Marvin E. *The Dorr Rebellion: A Study in American Radicalism, 1833–1849.* New York, 1973.

Goetzmann, William H. *When the Eagle Screamed: The Romantic Horizon in American Diplomacy, 1800–1860*. New York, 1966.

Goodman, Paul. *The Democratic Republicans of Massachusetts: Politics in a Young Republic.* Cambridge, Mass., 1964.

———. "Ethics and Enterprise: The Values of a Boston Elite, 1800–1860," *American Quarterly,* XVIII (1966), 437–451.

Graebner, Norman A., ed. *Ideas and Diplomacy: Readings in the Intellectual Tradition of American Foreign Policy.* New York, 1964.

Green, Martin. *The Problem of Boston: Some Readings in Cultural History.* London, 1966.

Gunderson, Robert Gray. *The Log Cabin Campaign.* Lexington, Ky., 1957.

Guthrie, Warren. "The Development of Rhetorical Theory in America, 1635–1850," *Speech Monographs,* Vol. XIV (1947), pp. 38–54.

Guttmann, Allen. *The Conservative Tradition in America.* New York, 1967.

Handlin, Oscar. *Boston's Immigrants.* Rev. ed. New York, 1968.

———, and Mary Handlin. *Commonwealth: A Study of the Role of Government in the American Economy, Massachusetts, 1774–1861.* New York, 1947.

Hartz, Louis, *The Liberal Tradition in America: An Interpretation of American Political Thought Since the Revolution.* New York, 1955.

Higham, John. *From Boundlessness to Consolidation.* Ann Arbor, 1969.

Holt, Michael F. *The Political Crisis of the 1850's.* New York, 1978.

Horwitz, Morton J. *The Transformation of American Law, 1780–1860.* Cambridge, Mass., 1977.

———. "The Conservative Tradition in the Writing of American Legal History," *The American Journal of Legal History,* XVII (1973), 275–294.

———. "The Emergence of an Instrumental Conception in American Law, 1780–1820." In *Law in American History,* ed. Donald Fleming and Bernard Bailyn. Boston, 1971, pp. 287–326.

Huntington, Samuel P. "Conservatism as an Ideology," *American Political Science Review,* LI (1957), 454–473.

Hurst, James Willard. *Law and the Conditions of Freedom in the Nineteenth-Century United States.* Madison, Wis., 1956.

Jaffa, Harry V. *The Conditions of Freedom: Essays in Political Philosophy.* Baltimore, 1975.

Jameson, E. D. *The Choates in America, 1643–96.* Boston, 1896.

Kenney, Jean Carol. "An Analysis of Political Alignments in Massachusetts as Revealed in the Constitutional Convention of 1853." M.A. Thesis, Smith College, 1951.

Kirk, Russell. *The Conservative Mind.* Chicago, 1953.

Kirkland, Edward Chase. *Men, Cities and Transportation: A Study in New England History, 1820–1900.* Vol. I. Cambridge, Mass., 1948.

Kohlstedt, Sally G. *The Formation of the American Scientific Community.* Urbana, Ill., 1978.

Kohn, Hans. *American Nationalism.* New York, 1957.

———. *The Idea of Nationalism: A Study of Its Origin and Background.* New York, 1944.

LaFeber, Walter. "American Historians and Revolutions," *Colloquium,* VIII (Spring 1970), pp. 1–6.

Latham, Edward C. "Days of Controversy, 1816–1819," *Dartmouth Alumni Magazine* (1962), pp. 10–13, 32.

Leonard, William Ellery. *Byron and Byronism in America.* New York, 1965.

Leopold, Richard W. *Robert Dale Owen: A Biography.* Cambridge, Mass., 1940.

Levin, David. *History as Romantic Art.* New York, 1959.

Levy, Leonard W. *The Law of the Commonwealth and Chief Justice Shaw.* Cambridge, Mass., 1957.

———. "Chief Justice Shaw and the Formative Period of American Railroad Law," *Columbia Law Review,* LI (1951), 327–348.

———. "Sims' Case: The Fugitive Slave Law in Boston," *The Journal of Negro History,* XXXV (1959), 39–74.

Lewis, William Draper, ed. *Great American Lawyers.* Vol. III. South Hackensack, N. J., 1971; 1st ed., 1909.

Lord, John King. *A History of Dartmouth College, 1815–1909.* Concord, N.H., 1913.

Love, Walter D. "Edmund Burke's Idea of the Body Corporate: A Study in Imagery," *The Review of Politics,* XXVII (April 1965), 184–197.

Lovejoy, Arthur O. "Coleridge and Kant's Two Worlds." In his *Essays in the History of Ideas,* pp. 254–276. New York, 1960; 1st pub., 1948.

Lowell: An Early American Industrial Community. Prep. L. S. Bryant and J. B. Rae. Cambridge, Mass., 1950.

Lowenthal, David. *George Perkins Marsh: Versatile Vermonter.* New York, 1958.

Lukacs, Georg. *The Historical Novel.* London, 1969; 1st pub., 1962.

Lurie, Edward. "Science in American Thought," *Journal of World History,* V (1965), 638–665.

Mabee, Carleton. *The American Leonardo: A Life of Samuel F. B. Morse.* New York, 1969; 1st pub., 1943.

McKay, Ernest. *Henry Wilson, Practical Radical: A Portrait of a Politician.* Port Washington, N.Y., 1971.

MacLeish, Archibald. *The Power of the Spoken Word: Address before the Annual Meeting of the American Academy of Arts and Letters.* N. pub., 1944.

Marshall, Lynn. "The Strange Stillbirth of the Whig Party," *American Historical Review,* LXXII (1967), 445–468.

Marx, Leo. *The Machine in the Garden: Technology and the Pastoral Idea in America.* New York, 1967; 1st pub., 1964.

Mathews, Donald G. *Slavery and Methodism: A Chapter in American Morality, 1780–1845.* Princeton, N.J., 1965.

Merk, Frederick, and Lois B. Merk. *Fruits of Propaganda in the Tyler Administration.* Cambridge, Mass., 1971.

Merz, John Theodore. *A History of European Thought in the 19th Century.* 4 vols. London, 1904.

Miller, Howard S. *Dollars for Research: Science and its Patrons in 19th Century America.* Seattle, 1970.

Miller, Perry. *The Life of the Mind in America: From the Revolution to the Civil War.* New York, 1965.

———. *Nature's Nation.* Cambridge, Mass., 1967.

————,ed. *The Legal Mind in America: From Independence to the Civil War.* New York, 1962.

Morison, Samuel Eliot. *A Manual for the Constitutional Convention, 1917.* Boston, 1917.

Morse, John T. "The Bench and Bar." In *The Memorial History of Boston,* ed. Justin Winsor, IV, 571–606 Boston, 1881.

Nagel, Paul C. *One Nation Indivisible: The Union in American Thought, 1776–1861.* New York, 1964.

————. *This Sacred Trust: American Nationality, 1798–1898.* New York, 1971.

Nathans, Sydney. *Daniel Webster and Jacksonian Democracy.* Baltimore, 1973.

————. "Daniel Webster: Massachusetts Man," *New England Quarterly,* XXXIX (1966), 161–181.

Nelson, William. *The Americanization of the Common Law: The Impact of Legal Change on Massachusetts Society, 1760–1830.* Cambridge, Mass., 1975.

Newmyer, R. Kent. "Daniel Webster as Tocqueville's Lawyer: The Dartmouth College Case Again," *The American Journal of Legal History,* II (1967), 127–147.

Nisbet, Robert A. *The Sociological Tradition.* London, 1967.

————. "Public Opinion versus Popular Opinion," *The Public Interest,* no. 41 (1975), pp. 166–192.

North, William Gwyer. "The Political Background of the Dartmouth College Case," *New England Quarterly,* XVIII (1945), 181–203.

Nye, Russel B. *Society and Culture in America, 1830–1860.* New York, 1974.

————. "History and Literature: Branches of the Same Tree." In *Essays on History and Literature,* ed. Robert H. Bremner. Columbus, Ohio, 1966, pp. 123–159.

Oakeshott, Michael. *Rationalism in Politics.* New York, 1962.

O'Connor, Thomas H. *Lords of the Loom: The Cotton Whigs and the Coming of the Civil War.* New York, 1968.

Odgers, Merle M. *Alexander Dallas Bache: Scientist and Educator, 1806–1867.* Philadelphia, 1947.

Ong, Walter J., S.J. *Rhetoric, Romance, and Technology: Studies in the Interaction of Expression and Culture.* Ithaca, N.Y., 1971.

Paludan, Phillip S. "The American Civil War Considered as a Crisis of Law and Order," *The American Historical Review,* LXXVII (1972), 1,013–1,034.

Pessen, Edward. *Jacksonian America: Society, Personality and Politics.* Homewood, Ill., 1969.

Pickard, Madge E. "Government and Science in the United States: Historical Backgrounds," *Journal of the History of Medicine and Allied Sciences,* I (April 1946), 254–280, 446–481.

Poage, George Rawlings. *Henry Clay and the Whig Party.* Gloucester, Mass., 1965; 1st pub., 1936.

Pocock, J. G. A. *The Machiavellian Moment: Florentine Political Thought and the Atlantic Republican Tradition.* Princeton, N.J., 1975.

————. "The Classical Theory of Deference," *American Historical Review,* LXXXI (June 1976), 516–523.

————. "Virtue and Commerce in the 18th Century," *The Journal of Interdisciplinary History*, III (Summer 1972), 119–134.

Potter, David. *The Impending Crisis, 1848–1861*. New York, 1976.

————. "The Historian's Use of Nationalism and Vice Versa," *The American Historical Review*, LXVII (1962), 924–950.

Pritchett, John Perry. " 'Friends' of the Constitution, 1836," *New England Quarterly*, IX (1936), 679–683.

Pound, Roscoe. *The Formative Era of American Law*. Boston, 1938.

————. *The Place of Judge Story in the Making of American Law*, Cambridge, Mass., 1914.

————. *The Spirit of the Common Law*. Boston, 1921.

Rantoul, Robert S. *Personal Recollections*. Cambridge, Mass., 1916.

Reingold, Nathan. "Alexander Dallas Bache: Science and Technology in the American Idiom," *Technology and Culture*, II (1970), 163–177.

Rossiter, Clinton. *Conservatism in America: The Thankless Persuasion*. 2nd ed. New York, 1962.

Sandford, Charles L. *The Quest for Paradise: Europe and the American Moral Imagination*. Urbana, Ill., 1961.

Schaar, John H. "Legitimacy in the Modern State." In *Power and Community: Dissenting Essays in Political Science*, ed. Philip Green and Sanford Levinson, pp. 276–327. New York, 1970.

Scheiber, Harry N. "Property Law, Expropriation, and Resource Allocation by Government: The United States, 1789–1910," *Journal of Economic History*, XXXIII (March 1973), 232–251.

————. "The Road to Munn: Eminent Domain and the Concept of Public Purpose in the State Courts." In *Law in American History*, ed. Donald Fleming and Bernard Bailyn, pp. 329–402, Boston, 1971.

Schouler, James. "The Massachusetts Convention of 1853," *Massachusetts Historical Society Proceedings*, XVIII (Nov. 1903), 30–48.

Schlesinger, Arthur M., Jr. *The Age of Jackson*. Boston, 1945.

Schuchman, John S. "The Political Background of the Political-question Doctrine: The Judges and the Dorr War," *The American Journal of Legal History*, XVI (1972), 111–125.

Schwartz, Bernard. *The Law in America*. New York, 1974.

Shapiro, Samuel. "The Conservative Dilemma: The Massachusetts Constitutional Convention of 1853," *New England Quarterly*, XXXIII (June 1960), 207–224.

Shera, Jesse H. *Foundations of the Public Library: The Origins of the Public Library Movement in New England, 1629–1855*. Hamden, Conn., 1965; 1st pub., 1949.

Silbey, Joel H. *The Shrine of Party: Congressional Voting Behavior, 1841–1852*. Pittsburg, 1967.

Sloan, Douglas. *The Scottish Enlightenment and the American College Ideal*. New York, 1971.

Smith, Wilson. *Professors and Public Ethics: Studies of Northern Moral Philosophers before the Civil War*. Ithaca, N.Y., 1956.

Somkin, Fred. *Unquiet Eagle: Memory and Desire in the Idea of American Freedom, 1815–1860.* Ithaca, N.Y., 1967.

Spencer, Benjamin T. *The Quest for Nationality: An American Literary Campaign.* Syracuse, 1957.

Story, Ronald. "Class and Culture in Boston: The Athenaeum, 1807–1860," *American Quarterly,* XXVII (May 1975), 178–199.

———. "Harvard and the Boston Brahmins: A Study in Institutional and Class Development, 1800–1865," *Journal of Social History,* VIII (1975), 94–121.

Susman, Warren I. "History and the American Intellectual: Uses of a Usable Past," *American Quarterly,* XVI (1964), 243–263.

Sutherland, Arthur E. *The Law at Harvard: A History of Ideas and Men, 1817–1967.* Cambridge, Mass., 1967.

Swisher, Carl Brent. *Roger B. Taney: Jacksonian Jurist.* New York, 1935.

Tyack, David B. *George Ticknor and the Boston Brahmins.* Cambridge, Mass., 1967.

Van Deusen, Glyndon G. *The Jacksonian Era, 1828–1848.* New York, 1959.

———. *The Life of Henry Clay.* Boston, 1937.

———. "Some Aspects of Whig Thought and Theory in the Jacksonian Period," *American Historical Review,* LXIII (1958), 305–322.

Van Tassel, David D. "Gentlemen of Property and Standing: Compromise Sentiment in Boston in 1850," *New England Quarterly,* XXIII (Sept. 1950), 307–319.

Walker, Bertrand. *Rufus Choate.* Indianapolis, n.d.

Walker, David Bradstreet. "Rufus Choate, An American Whig," Ph.D. diss., Brown University, 1956.

———. "Rufus Choate: A Case Study in Old Whiggery," *Essex Institute Historical Collections,* XCIV (1958), 334–355.

Walzer, Michael. "On the Role of Symbolism in Political Thought," *Political Science Quarterly,* LXXXII (1967), 191–204.

Warren, Charles. *A History of the American Bar.* New York, 1966; 1st pub., 1911.

Ward, John William. *Andrew Jackson: Symbol for an Age.* New York, 1955.

Ware, Norman. *The Industrial Worker, 1840–1860.* Chicago, 1964; 1st pub., 1924.

Washburn, Wilcomb E. "The Influence of the Smithsonian Institution on Intellectual Life in Mid–Nineteenth Century Washington," *Columbia Historical Society Records* (1963–1965), pp. 96–121.

———. "Joseph Henry's Conception of the Purpose of the Smithsonian Institution." In *A Cabinet of Curiosities: Five Episodes in the Evolution of American Museums,* ed. Walter Muir Whitehill, pp. 106–166. Charlottesville, Va., 1967.

Wecter, Dixon. *The Hero in America: A Chronicle of Hero Worship.* New York, 1941.

Weaver, Richard M. *The Ethics of Rhetoric.* Chicago, 1953.

Welter, Rush. *The Mind of America, 1820–60.* New York, 1975.

Wiebe, Robert. *The Segmented Society.* New York, 1975.

Willey, Basil. *Nineteenth Century Studies: Coleridge to Mathew Arnold.* London, 1949.

Wilson, Major L. *Space, Time and Freedom: The Quest for Nationality and the Irrepressible Conflict, 1815–61.* Westport, Conn., 1974.

———. "The Concept of Time and the Political Dialogue in the United States, 1828–48," *American Quarterly,* XIX (Winter 1967), 619–644.

———. "Manifest Destiny and Free Soil: The Triumph of Negative Liberalism in the 1840s," *The Historian,* XXXI (1968), 36–57.

Wilson, R. Jackson. *In Quest of Community.* New York, 1968.

Wiltse, Charles M. "Daniel Webster and the British Experience," *Massachusetts Historical Society Proceedings,* LXXXV (1973), 58–77.

Wish, Harvey. *The American Historian.* New York, 1960.

Wolin, Sheldon S. "The New Conservatives," *New York Review of Books,* XXIII (Feb. 5, 1976), 6–11.

INDEX